Rick Steves'

VIENNA

SALZBURG

& TIROL

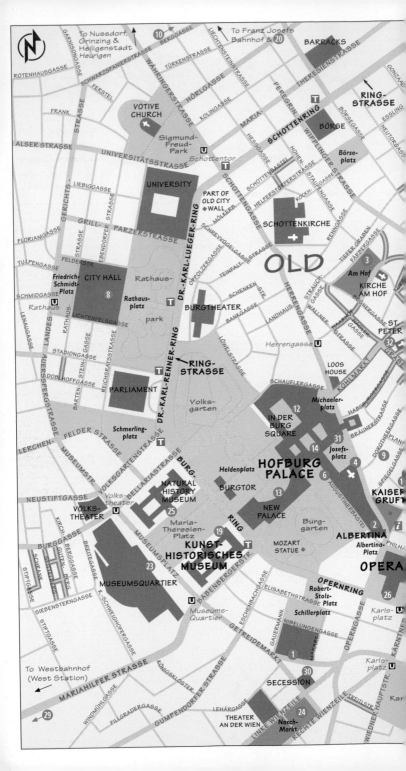

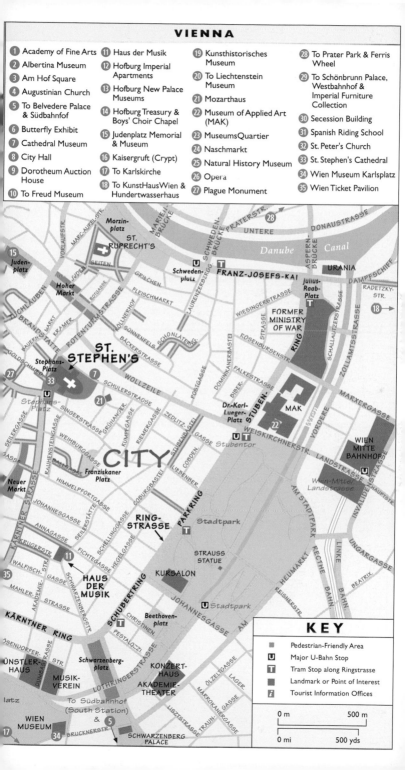

VIENNA

1. Academy of Fine Arts
2. Albertina Museum
3. Am Hof Square
4. Augustinian Church
5. To Belvedere Palace & Südbahnhof
6. Butterfly Exhibit
7. Cathedral Museum
8. City Hall
9. Dorotheum Auction House
10. To Freud Museum
11. Haus der Musik
12. Hofburg Imperial Apartments
13. Hofburg New Palace Museums
14. Hofburg Treasury & Boys' Choir Chapel
15. Judenplatz Memorial & Museum
16. Kaisergruft (Crypt)
17. To Karlskirche
18. To KunstHausWien & Hundertwasserhaus
19. Kunsthistorisches Museum
20. To Liechtenstein Museum
21. Mozarthaus
22. Museum of Applied Art (MAK)
23. MuseumsQuartier
24. Naschmarkt
25. Natural History Museum
26. Opera
27. Plague Monument
28. To Prater Park & Ferris Wheel
29. To Schönbrunn Palace, Westbahnhof & Imperial Furniture Collection
30. Secession Building
31. Spanish Riding School
32. St. Peter's Church
33. St. Stephen's Cathedral
34. Wien Museum Karlsplatz
35. Wien Ticket Pavilion

KEY

- Pedestrian-Friendly Area
- **U** Major U-Bahn Stop
- **T** Tram Stop along Ringstrasse
- Landmark or Point of Interest
- **i** Tourist Information Offices

0 m — 500 m
0 mi — 500 yds

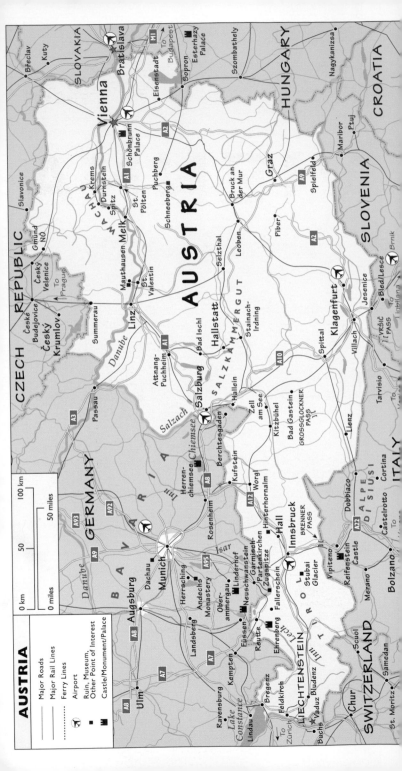

Rick Steves'

VIENNA

SALZBURG

& TIROL

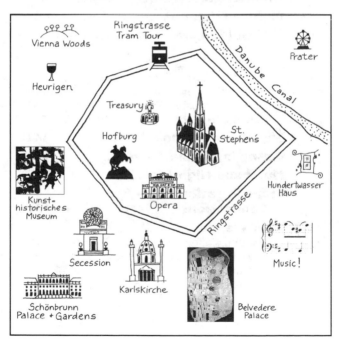

AVALON
TRAVEL

CONTENTS

INTRODUCTION

Austria offers alpine scenery, world-class museums, cobbled quaintness, and Wiener schnitzel. Unlike Germany, its industrious neighbor to the northwest, Austria is content to bask in its good living and opulent past as the former head of one of Europe's grandest empires. Austrians are relaxed, gregarious people who love the outdoors as much as a good cup of coffee in a café.

This book focuses on Vienna and all of its cultural offerings, as well as the Danube Valley, Salzburg, Hallstatt (the gem of the Salzkammergut Lake District), and the mountainous Tirol region. Because some sights just across the border are so scenic and interesting, this book also ducks into Germany (Bavarian sights) and even Slovakia (Bratislava).

I'll give you all the information and opinions necessary to wring the maximum value out of your limited time and money. If you plan three weeks or less in Austria and have a normal appetite for information, this book is all you need. If you're a travel-info fiend, this book sorts through all the superlatives and provides a handy rack upon which to hang your supplemental information.

Experiencing Europe's culture, people, and natural wonders economically and hassle-free has been my goal for three decades of traveling, tour guiding, and travel writing. With this new edition, I pass on to you the lessons I've learned.

The destinations covered are balanced to include a comfortable mix of cities and villages, mountaintop hikes and medieval castles, sleepy river cruises and sky-high gondola rides. While you'll find the predictable biggies (such as Mozart's house and the Vienna Opera), I've also mixed in a healthy dose of Back Door intimacy (thrilling mountain luges, a beer with monks, and a lakeside town reachable by boat). I've been selective, including only the most exciting sights. For example, there are dozens of quaint villages in Austria's Salzkammergut Lake District. I take you to only the most charming: Hallstatt.

The best is, of course, only my opinion. But after spending a third of my adult life exploring and researching Europe, I've developed a sixth sense for what travelers enjoy. The places featured in this book will make anyone want to slap-dance and yodel.

About This Book

Rick Steves' Vienna, Salzburg & Tirol is a tour guide in your pocket. It's organized by destinations—each a mini-vacation on its own, filled with exciting sights, homey and affordable places to stay, and memorable places to eat.

The book is organized this way:

Planning Your Time suggests a schedule with thoughts on how best to use your limited time.

Orientation includes tourist information, tips on public transportation, local tour options, helpful hints, and an easy-to-read map designed to make the text clear and your arrival smooth.

Sights, described in detail, are rated:

▲▲▲—Don't miss.

▲▲—Try hard to see.

▲—Worthwhile if you can make it.

No rating—Worth knowing about.

Self-Guided Walks take you through interesting neighborhoods, such as the old-town cores of Vienna and Salzburg.

Self-Guided Tours lead you through Vienna's major sights, including St. Stephen's Cathedral, the Hofburg Imperial Apartments and Treasury, and the Kunsthistorisches Museum. A breezy tram tour takes you around Vienna's Ringstrasse.

Sleeping describes my favorite hotels, from budget deals to splurges.

Eating serves up a range of options, from inexpensive pubs to fancier restaurants.

Transportation Connections outlines your options for traveling to destinations by train and bus. In car-friendly regions, I've included route tips for drivers.

The **Austrian History** chapter introduces you to some of the key people and events in this nation's complicated past, making your sightseeing that much more meaningful.

The **appendix** is a traveler's tool kit, with a handy packing checklist, recommended books and films, instructions on how to use the telephone, and useful phone numbers. You'll also find detailed information on driving and public transportation, as well as a climate chart, festival list, a hotel reservation form, and German survival phrases.

Study this book and put together the plan of your dreams. Then

	Map Legend			
⚡ Viewpoint	✈ Airport		Pedestrian Zone
➤ Entry Point	Ⓣ Taxi Stand	⚬⊞⊞⊞⊞⊞⊞⊞⚬	Funicular
ℹ Tourist Info	Ⓜ Metro Stop	------	Railway
WC Restroom	Ⓣ Tram Stop	⊢——⊣	Tram Line
⚑ Castle	Ⓑ Bus Stop	⫿⫿⫿⫿⫿⫿⫿⫿	Stairs
⛪ Church	⛴ Boat Stop	- - - - -	Trail
☪ Mosque	Ⓟ Parking	)▒▒▒▒(	Tunnel

Use this legend to help you navigate the maps in this book.

have a *wunderbar* trip! Traveling like a temporary local and taking advantage of the information here, you'll get the absolute most out of every mile, minute, and euro. As you visit places I know and love, I'm happy you'll be meeting some of my favorite Austrians.

PLANNING

Trip Costs

Five components make up your trip cost: airfare, surface transportation, room and board, sightseeing and entertainment, and shopping and miscellany.

Airfare: A basic round-trip flight from the US to Vienna should cost $1,000–1,800, depending on what city you fly from and when (cheaper in winter). Always consider saving time and money in Europe by flying "open jaw"—into one city and out of another—for instance, into Vienna and out of Munich.

Surface Transportation: For a two-week whirlwind trip of all my recommended destinations, allow $300 per person for public transportation (trains and buses) or $350 per person (based on two people sharing) for car rental, parking, gas, and insurance. Leasing is worth considering for trips of two and a half weeks or more. Car rental and leases are cheapest when reserved from the US. Train passes are normally sold only outside of Europe. You may save money by simply buying tickets as you go (see "Transportation," page 387, for details on renting cars and taking trains).

Room and Board: You can thrive in Austria on an average of $110 a day per person for room and board (less in small towns, more in big cities such as Vienna and Salzburg). A $110-a-day budget allows $10 for lunch, $25 for dinner, $5 for beer and *Eis* (ice cream), and $70 for lodging (based on two people splitting the cost of a $140 double room that includes breakfast). That's doable. Students and tightwads eat and sleep on $50 a day ($30 per hostel bed, $20 for meals and snacks).

Vienna, Salzburg & Tirol: Best Two-Week Trip by Train

Day	Plan	Sleep in
1	Fly into Vienna	Vienna
2	Vienna	Vienna
3	Vienna	Vienna
4	Vienna	Vienna (or head to Melk in evening if biking or cruising Danube on Day 5)
5	Danube Valley	Melk
6	To Salzburg via Mauthausen	Salzburg
7	Salzburg	Salzburg
8	Salzburg	Salzburg
9	To Hallstatt	Hallstatt
10	Hallstatt and Salzkammergut Lake District	Hallstatt
11	To Innsbruck	Hall or Innsbruck
12	Innsbruck; to Bavaria	Füssen or Reutte
13	Bavaria and castles	Füssen or Reutte
14	Fly out of Innsbruck or Munich (or train back to Vienna)	

With more time: Depending on your interests, you could easily spend several more days in Vienna (for museums, the music scene, going to cafés and wine gardens, day-tripping to Bratislava) and a couple more days in Salzburg (for the music scene, nearby sights, day-tripping to Berchtesgaden).

Sightseeing and Entertainment: In big cities, figure $9–15 per major sight (Vienna's Kunsthistorisches Museum-$14, Mozart's Residence in Salzburg-$9), $5 for minor ones, and $25–50 for bus tours and splurge experiences (such as concert tickets and alpine lifts). An overall average of $25 a day works for most. Don't skimp here. After all, this category is the driving force behind your trip—you came to sightsee, enjoy, and experience Austria.

Shopping and Miscellany: Figure $2 per stamped postcard, coffee, beer, and ice-cream cone. Shopping can vary in cost from nearly nothing to a small fortune. Good budget travelers find that this category has little to do with assembling a trip full of lifelong and wonderful memories.

When to Go

The "tourist season" runs roughly from May through September. Summer has its advantages: best weather, snow-free alpine trails, very long days (light until after 21:00), and the busiest schedule

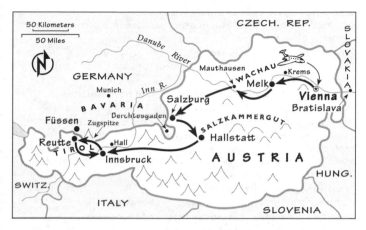

The countryside of southern Bavaria and western Tirol are great places to linger and explore (consider a day or two of car rental).

With a car: Pick up your car when you leave Vienna. After Melk (in the Danube Valley), drive to Hallstatt, with a stop at Mauthausen en route. After Hallstatt, head to Salzburg. From Salzburg, you can drive (via Berchtesgaden, if you're interested) through southern Bavaria en route to Füssen or Reutte. Then drive eastward through Tirol's Inn Valley to Innsbruck to drop off your car.

of tourist fun.

Travel during "shoulder season" (late April–June and Sept–early Oct) is easier and a bit less expensive. Shoulder-season travelers get minimal crowds, decent weather, the full range of sights and tourist fun spots, and the ability to grab a room almost whenever and wherever they like—often at a flexible price. Also, in fall, fun harvest and wine festivals enliven many towns and villages, while forests and vineyards display beautiful colors.

Winter travelers find concert seasons in full swing, with absolutely no tourist crowds, but some accommodations and sights are either closed or run on a limited schedule. Confirm your sightseeing plans locally, especially when traveling off-season. The weather can be cold and dreary, and nightfall draws the shades on sightseeing well before dinnertime. But dustings of snow turn Austrian towns and landscapes into a wonderland, and December offers the chance to wander through traditional Christmas markets.

You may find the climate chart in the appendix helpful.

Just the FAQs, Please

Whom do I call in case of emergency?
Dial 112 for police or medical emergencies in Austria (and in Germany as well).

What if my credit card is stolen?
Act immediately. See "Damage Control for Lost Cards," page 12, for instructions.

How do I make a phone call to, within, and from Austria?
For detailed dialing instructions, refer to page 380.

How can I get tourist information about my destination?
Austria has a network of local tourist information offices (listed in each chapter of this book), as well as a national tourist information office in the US (see page 375). Note that Tourist Information is abbreviated **TI** in this book.

What's the best way to pack?
Light. For a recommended packing list, see page 401.

Does Rick have other resources that could help me?
For info on Rick's guidebooks, public television series, free audiotours, public radio show, website, guided tours, travel bags, accessories, and railpasses, see page 376.

Are there any updates to this guidebook?
Check www.ricksteves.com/update for any changes to this book.

Can you recommend any good books or movies for my trip?
For suggestions, see page 378.

Sightseeing Priorities

Depending on the length of your trip, and taking geographic proximity into account, the following are my recommended priorities.

3 days:	Vienna
5 days:	Salzburg
7 days, add:	Hallstatt
10 days, add:	Danube Valley, Tirol, and Bavaria
14 days, add:	Innsbruck, Hall, and day trip to Bratislava
16 days, add:	More time in Vienna

(The itinerary and map on pages 4 and 5 includes everything on this list.)

Travel Smart

Your trip to Austria is like a complex play—easier to follow and to really appreciate on a second viewing. While no one does the same trip twice to gain that advantage, reading this book in its entirety before your trip accomplishes much the same thing.

Design an itinerary that enables you to visit the various sights at the best possible times. Note the days when sights are closed.

Do I need to speak some German?
Though most Austrians you'll encounter speak at least some English, it can be useful—and always polite—to learn and use basic German pleasantries. See the list of survival phrases (on page 402) and background information on the language barrier (page 382).

Do you have information on driving, train travel, and flights?
See "Transportation" on page 387.

How much do I tip?
Relatively little. For tips on tipping, see page 12.

Will I get a student or senior discount?
While discounts are not listed in this book, seniors (age 60 and over), students with International Student Identification Cards, teachers with proper identification, and youths under 18 often get discounts—but you have to ask. To get a teacher or student ID card, visit www.statravel.com or www.isic.org.

How can I get a VAT refund on major purchases?
See the details on page 13.

How do I calculate metric amounts?
Austria uses the metric system. A liter is about a quart, four to a gallon. A kilometer is six-tenths of a mile. I figure kilometers to miles by cutting them in half and adding back 10 percent of the original (120 km: 60 + 12 = 72 miles, 300 km: 150 + 30 = 180 miles). For more metric conversions, see page 398.

Saturday mornings are like weekday mornings, but by lunchtime, many shops close down through Sunday. Sundays have the same pros and cons as they do for travelers in the US (special events pop up, sights may have limited hours, shops and banks are closed, public transportation options are fewer, and there's no rush hour). Popular destinations are even more crowded on weekends.

Be sure to mix intense and relaxed periods in your itinerary. To maximize rootedness, minimize one-night stands. It's worth a long drive after dinner to be settled into a town for two nights. B&Bs are also more likely to give a good price to someone staying more than one night. Every trip (and every traveler) needs at least a few slack days. Pace yourself. Assume you will return.

Reread this book as you travel, and visit local tourist information offices. Upon arrival in a new town, lay the groundwork for a smooth departure; write down the schedule for the train or bus you'll take when you depart.

Plan ahead for laundry and picnics. Get online at Internet cafés or your hotel to research transportation connections, confirm events, check the weather, and get directions to your next hotel.

Major Holidays and Weekends

Popular places are even busier on weekends, and holidays can bring many businesses to a grinding halt. Plan ahead and reserve your accommodations and transportation well in advance. Mark these dates in red on your travel calendar: Easter weekend (April 2–4 in 2010), May 1, Christmas, December 26, and New Year's Day. Book ahead for any summer weekend and for the various music festivals in Vienna and Salzburg; check the list of festivals and holidays on page 397 in the appendix.

Buy a phone card and use it for reservations, reconfirmations, and double-checking hours.

Connect with the culture. Set up your own quest for the best Baroque building, Sacher torte, wine garden, or whatever. Enjoy the hospitality of the Austrian people. Slow down and be open to unexpected experiences. Ask questions—most locals are eager to point you in their idea of the right direction. Keep a notepad in your pocket for organizing your thoughts. Wear your money belt, and learn the local currency and how to estimate prices in dollars. Those who expect to travel smart, do.

PRACTICALITIES

Red Tape: You need a passport—but no visa or shots—to travel in Austria. Your passport must be valid for at least six months beyond the time you leave Europe. Pack a photocopy of your passport in your luggage in case the original is lost or stolen. If you're traveling beyond Austria, remember that, even as borders fade, when you change countries, you must still change telephone cards, postage stamps, and *Unterhosen*.

Time: In Austria—and in this book—you'll use the 24-hour clock. It's the same through 12:00 noon, then keep going: 13:00, 14:00, and so on. For anything over 12, subtract 12 and add p.m. (14:00 is 2:00 p.m.).

Austria, like most of continental Europe, is generally six/nine hours ahead of the East/West Coasts of the US. The exceptions are the beginning and end of Daylight Saving Time: Europe "springs forward" the last Sunday in March (two weeks after most of North America), and "falls back" the last Sunday in October (one week before North America). For a handy online time converter, try www.timeanddate.com/worldclock.

Business Hours: Most shops throughout Austria are open from about 9:00 until 18:00–20:00 on weekdays, but close earlier

Know Before You Go

Your trip is more likely to go smoothly if you plan ahead. Check this list of things to arrange while you're still at home.

Be sure that your **passport** is valid at least six months after your ticketed date of return to the US. If you need to get or renew a passport, it can take up to two months (for more on passports, see www.travel.state.gov).

Book your rooms well in advance if you'll be traveling during any major **holidays** (see "Major Holidays and Weekends," on the previous page). It's also smart to reserve rooms for your first night and during peak season.

Call your **debit- and credit-card companies** to let them know the countries you'll be visiting, so that they'll accept (and not deny) your international charges. Confirm your daily withdrawal limit; consider asking to have it raised so you can take out more cash at each ATM stop. Ask about international transaction fees.

If you're planning on **renting a car** in Austria, you're required to carry your US driver's license and an International Driving Permit (available at your local AAA office for $15 plus two passport photos; www.aaa.com).

I don't book ahead for events, but if you do, note that: In Vienna and Salzburg (especially during its festival), major **musical events** can be booked out for weeks—though there are plenty of live music options available without advance booking. And booking will guarantee you a seat to see the **Lipizzaner Stallions** (see page 51), **Vienna Boys' Choir** (page 167), and performances at the **Opera** (page 41), though again, I prefer cheap, on-the-spot experiences (such as same-day standing-room tickets for the Opera).

To get tickets to **Neuschwanstein Castle** (in Bavaria) during peak season, you can email, go online, or phone ahead to avoid the long lines (see page 337 for tips).

Because **airline carry-on restrictions** are always changing, visit the Transportation Security Administration's website (www.tsa.gov/travelers) for an up-to-date list of what you can bring on the plane with you...and what you have to check. Remember to arrive with plenty of time to get through security.

on Saturday (as early as 12:00 in towns and as late as 17:00 in cities), and are almost always closed on Sunday. Grocery stores in train stations are generally open daily until late. Banks in Vienna are open weekdays roughly from 8:00 until 15:00 (until 17:30 on Thu), but elsewhere in Austria, banks often close for lunch (open Mon–Fri 8:00–12:00 and 14:00–16:00). Many museums and sights are closed on Monday. Catholic regions, including Bavaria, shut down during religious holidays.

Shopping: For customs regulations and VAT refunds (the tax refunded on large purchases made by non-EU residents), see page 13.

Medical Help: If you get sick, do as the locals do and go to a pharmacist. They can help you with most any ailment. If a pharmacy is closed, a sign near the door indicates the nearest pharmacy that's open.

Watt's Up? Europe's electrical system is different from North America's in two different ways: the shape of the plug (two round prongs) and the voltage of the current (220 volts instead of 110 volts). For your North American plug to work in Europe, you'll need an adapter, sold inexpensively at travel stores in the US. As for the voltage, most newer electronics or travel appliances (such as hair dryers, laptops, and battery chargers) automatically convert the voltage—if you see a range of voltages printed on the item or its plug (such as "110–220"), it'll work in Europe. Otherwise, you can buy a converter separately in the US (about $20).

News: Americans keep in touch via the *International Herald Tribune* (published almost daily throughout Europe). Every Tuesday, the European editions of *Time* and *Newsweek* hit the stands with articles of particular interest to travelers. Sports addicts can get their daily fix online or from *USA Today*. Good websites include www.iht.com, http://news.bbc.co.uk, and www.europeantimes.com. Many hotels have CNN or BBC television channels available.

MONEY

Cash from ATMs

Throughout Europe, cash machines (ATMs) are the standard way for travelers to get local currency. Bring plastic—credit and/or debit cards—along with several hundred dollars in hard cash as an emergency backup. It's smart to bring two cards, in case one gets demagnetized or eaten by a temperamental machine.

Avoid using currency exchange booths (lousy rates and/or outrageous fees); if you have foreign currency to exchange, take it to a bank. Traveler's checks are a waste of time (long waits at slow banks) and a waste of money (in fees).

In Austria, the word for "cash machine" is *Bankomat* (*Geldautomat* in Germany). To use a cash machine to withdraw money from your account, you'll need a debit card (ideally with a Visa or MasterCard logo for maximum usability), plus a PIN code. Know your PIN code in numbers; there are only numbers—no letters—on European keypads.

Before you go, verify with your bank that your card will work overseas, and alert them that you'll be making withdrawals in

Exchange Rate

I list prices in euros for Austria.

1 euro (€) = about $1.40

To convert prices in euros to dollars, add about 40 percent:
€20 = about $28, €50 = about $70. Just like the dollar, the
euro is broken down into 100 cents. You'll find coins ranging
from 1 cent to 2 euros, and bills from 5 euros to 500 euros.

So that €12 visit to the café is about $17, and the €90 taxi
ride through Vienna is...uh-oh.

Europe; otherwise, the bank may not approve transactions if it
perceives unusual spending patterns. Also ask about international
fees; see "Credit and Debit Cards," next. Note that many ATMs
don't issue receipts with your transaction.

Try to take out large sums of money to reduce your per-
transaction bank fees. If the machine refuses your request, don't
take it personally. Just try again and select a smaller amount; some
cash machines won't let you take out more than about €150. If that
doesn't work, try a different machine.

To keep your cash safe, use a money belt—a pouch with a
strap that you buckle around your waist like a belt, and wear under
your clothes. Thieves target tourists. A money belt provides peace
of mind, allowing you to carry lots of cash safely. Don't waste time
every few days tracking down a cash machine—withdraw a week's
worth of money, stuff it in your money belt, and travel!

Credit and Debit Cards

For purchases, Visa and MasterCard are more commonly accepted
than American Express. Just like at home, credit and debit cards
work easily at larger hotels, restaurants, and shops, but smaller
businesses prefer payment in local currency (in small bills—break
large bills at a bank or larger store). Note that some receipts show
your credit-card number; don't toss these thoughtlessly.

Fees: Some credit and debit card transactions—whether for
purchases or ATM withdrawals—often come with tacked-on
"international transaction" fees of up to 3 percent plus $5 per trans-
action. To avoid unpleasant surprises, call your bank or credit-card
company before your trip to ask about these fees. If the fees are
too high, consider getting a card just for your trip: Capital One
(www.capitalone.com) and most credit unions have low-to-no
international transaction fees.

Damage Control for Lost Cards

If you lose your credit, debit, or ATM card, you can stop people from using it by reporting the loss immediately to the respective global customer-assistance centers. Call these 24-hour US numbers collect: Visa (410/581-9994), MasterCard (636/722-7111), and American Express (623/492-8427).

At a minimum, you'll need to know the name of the financial institution that issued you the card, along with the type of card (classic, platinum, or whatever). Providing the following information will allow for a quicker cancellation of your missing card: full card number, whether you are the primary or secondary cardholder, the cardholder's name exactly as printed on the card, billing address, home phone number, circumstances of the loss or theft, and identification verification (your birth date, your mother's maiden name, or your Social Security number—memorize this, don't carry a copy). If you are the secondary cardholder, you'll also need to provide the primary cardholder's identification-verification details. You can generally receive a temporary card within two or three business days in Europe.

If you promptly report your card lost or stolen, you typically won't be responsible for any unauthorized transactions on your account, although many banks charge a liability fee of $50.

Tipping

Tipping in Austria isn't as automatic and generous as it is in the US, but for special service, tips are appreciated, if not expected. As in the US, the proper amount depends on your resources, tipping philosophy, and the circumstance, but some general guidelines apply.

Restaurants: Tipping is an issue only at restaurants that have table service. If you order your food at a counter, don't tip.

At Austrian restaurants that have a wait staff, a service charge is generally included in the bill, although it's common to round up after a good meal (usually 5–10 percent; so, for an €18.50 meal, pay €20). Give the tip directly to your server. Rather than leaving coins, Austrians usually pay with paper, saying how much they'd like the bill to be (for example, for an €8.10 meal, give a €20 bill and say *"Neun Euro"*—"Nine euros"—to get €11 change).

Taxis: To tip the cabbie, round up. For a typical ride, round up about 5–10 percent (to pay a €4.50 fare, give €5; for a €28 fare, give €30). If the cabbie hauls your bags and zips you to the airport to help you catch your flight, you might want to toss in a little more. But if you feel like you're being driven in circles or otherwise ripped off, skip the tip.

Special Services: It's thoughtful to tip a couple of euros to someone who shows you a special sight and who is paid in no other way. Tour guides at public sites often hold out their hands for tips (€1–2) after they give their spiel; if I've already paid for the tour, I don't tip extra, though some tourists do give a euro, particularly for a job well done. I don't tip at hotels, but if you do, give the porter about a euro for carrying bags and leave a couple of euros in your room at the end of your stay for the maid if the room was kept clean. In general, if someone in the service industry does a super job for you, a tip of a euro or two is appropriate...but not required.

When in doubt, ask. If you're not sure whether (or how much) to tip for a service, ask your hotelier or the tourist information office; they'll fill you in on how it's done on their turf.

Getting a VAT Refund

Wrapped into the purchase price of your Austrian souvenirs is a Value-Added Tax (VAT) of 20 percent. If you make a purchase of more than a certain amount (€75.01 in Austria) at a store that participates in the VAT-refund scheme, you're entitled to get most of that tax back. Getting your refund is usually straightforward and, if you buy a substantial amount of souvenirs, well worth the hassle. If you're lucky, the merchant will subtract the tax when you make your purchase. (This is more likely to occur if the store ships the goods to your home.) Otherwise, you'll need to:

Get the paperwork. Have the merchant completely fill out the necessary refund document, called a "Tax-Free Shopping Cheque." You'll have to present your passport at the store.

Get your stamp at the border or airport. Process your cheque(s) at your last stop in the EU (e.g., at the airport) with the customs agent who deals with VAT refunds. It's best to keep your purchases in your carry-on for viewing, but if they're too large or dangerous (such as knives) to carry on, track down the proper customs agent to inspect them before you check your bag. You're not supposed to use your purchased goods before you leave. If you show up at customs wearing your new lederhosen, officials might look the other way—or deny you a refund.

Collect your refund. You'll need to return your stamped document to the retailer or its representative. Many merchants work with a service, such as Global Refund (www.globalrefund.com) or Premier Tax Free (www.premiertaxfree.com), which have offices at major airports, ports, or border crossings. These services, which extract a 4 percent fee, can refund your money immediately in your currency of choice or credit your card (within two billing cycles). If the retailer handles VAT refunds directly, it's up to you to contact the merchant for your refund. You can mail the documents from home, or quicker, from your point of departure (using a stamped, addressed envelope you've prepared or one that's been provided by the merchant)—and then wait. It could take months.

Customs for American Shoppers

You are allowed to take home $800 worth of items per person duty-free, once every 30 days. The next $1,000 is taxed at a flat 3 percent. After that, you pay the individual item's duty rate. You can also bring in duty-free a liter of alcohol (slightly more than a standard-size bottle of wine; you must be at least 21), 200 cigarettes, and up to 100 non-Cuban cigars. Food in cans or sealed jars is permissible, as long as no meat is included. Some, but not all, types of cheese are allowed. Fresh fruits and vegetables are prohibited. Note that you'll need to carefully pack any bottles of wine and other liquid-containing items in your checked luggage, due to the three-ounce limit on liquids in carry-on baggage. To check customs rules and duty rates before you go, visit www.cbp.gov, and click on "Travel," then "Know Before You Go."

SIGHTSEEING

Sightseeing can be hard work. Use these tips to make your visits to Austria's finest sights meaningful, fun, fast, and painless.

Plan Ahead

Set up an itinerary that allows you to fit in all your must-see sights. For a one-stop look at opening hours in Vienna and Salzburg, see the "At a Glance" sidebars on page 46 and page 228. Most sights keep stable hours, but you can easily confirm the latest by checking with the local TI.

Don't put off visiting a must-see sight—you never know when a place will close unexpectedly for a holiday, strike, or restoration. If you'll be visiting during a holiday, find out if a particular sight will be open by phoning ahead or checking its website.

When possible, visit major sights first thing (when your energy is best) and save other activities for the afternoon. Hit the highlights first, then go back to other things if you have the stamina and time.

Going at the right time can also help you avoid crowds. This book offers tips on specific sights, such as Schönbrunn Palace in Vienna and Neuschwanstein Castle in Bavaria. Try visiting very early, at lunch, or very late. Evening visits are usually peaceful, with fewer crowds.

At Sights

All sights have rules, and if you know about these in advance, they're no big deal.

Some important sights have metal detectors or conduct bag searches that will slow your entry.

At churches—which often offer interesting art (usually free) and a cool, welcome seat—a modest dress code (no bare shoulders or shorts) is encouraged.

Major museums and sights require you to check daypacks and coats. They'll be kept safely. If you have something you can't bear to part with, stash it in a pocket or purse. If you don't want to check a small backpack, carry it under your arm like a purse as you enter. From a guard's point of view, a backpack is generally a problem while a purse is not.

Photography is sometimes banned at major sights. Look for signs or ask. If cameras are allowed, flashes and tripods are usually not. Flashes damage oil paintings and distract others in the room. Even without a flash, a handheld camera will take a decent picture (or buy postcards or posters at the museum bookstore). Video cameras are generally allowed.

Some museums have special exhibits in addition to their permanent collection. Some exhibits are included in the entry price; others come at an extra cost (which you may have to pay even if you don't want to see the exhibit).

Many sights rent audioguides, which usually offer excellent recorded descriptions in English (about $7.50). If you bring along your own pair of headphones and a Y-jack, two people can sometimes share one audioguide and save. Guided tours in English are most likely to occur during peak season (some are free, while others can cost up to $13 and range widely in quality).

Expect changes—paintings can be on tour, on loan, out sick, or shifted at the whim of the curator. To adapt, pick up any available free floor plans as you enter, and ask museum staff if you can't find a particular painting.

Most important sights have an on-site café or cafeteria (usually a good place to rest and have a snack or light meal). The WCs are free and generally clean.

Key sights and museums have bookstores selling postcards and souvenirs. Before you leave, scan the postcards and thumb through the biggest guidebook (or skim its index) to be sure you haven't overlooked something that you'd like to see.

Most sights stop admitting people 30–60 minutes before closing time, and some rooms close early (generally about 45 minutes before the actual closing time). Guards usher people out, so don't save the best for last.

Every sight or museum offers more than what is covered in

this book. Use the information in this book as an introduction—not the final word.

SLEEPING

I favor accommodations (and restaurants) handy to your sight-seeing activities. Rather than list hotels scattered throughout a city, I choose two or three favorite neighborhoods and recommend the best accommodations values in each, from $25 bunk beds to fancy-for-my-book $250 doubles.

While accommodations in Austria are fairly expensive, they are normally very comfortable and come with breakfast. Plan on spending $100–150 per hotel double in Vienna and Salzburg, and $50–80 in towns and in private homes.

A triple is much cheaper than a double and a single. Single travelers save money at a B&B (called a *Pension* or *Gästehaus*, also advertised as *Privatzimmer*), where the single price is often little more than half the double-room price. Hotels, in contrast, charge almost as much for a single room as for a double. Hostels and dorms always charge per person.

I look for places that are friendly; clean; a good value; located in a central, safe, quiet neighborhood; English-speaking; and not mentioned in other guidebooks. I'm more impressed by a handy location and a fun-loving philosophy than hair dryers and shoe-shine machines.

I also like local character and simple facilities that don't cater to American "needs." Obviously, a place meeting every criterion is rare, and all of my recommendations fall short of perfection—sometimes miserably. But I've listed the best values for each price category, given the above criteria. The very best values are family-run places with showers down the hall and no elevator.

The prices listed in this book are generally valid for peak season, but may go up during festivals and major holidays (see "Major Holidays and Weekends" on page 8). Prices can soften off-season, for stays of two nights or longer, or for payment in cash (rather than by credit card). Always mention that you found the place through this book—many of the hotels listed offer special deals to our readers.

Unless I note otherwise, the cost of a room includes a breakfast (sometimes continental, but often buffet). The price is usually posted in the room. Before accepting, confirm your understanding of the complete price.

INTRODUCTION

Sleep Code

(€1 = about $1.40, country code: 43)

To help you sort easily through these listings, I've divided the rooms into three categories based on the price for a standard double room with bath:

$$$ **Higher Priced**
$$ **Moderately Priced**
$ **Lower Priced**

To give maximum information in a minimum of space, I use the following code to describe the accommodations. Prices listed are per room, not per person. When a price range is given for a type of room (such as double rooms listing for €100–150), it means the price fluctuates with the season, size of room, or length of stay.

S = Single room (or price for one person in a double).

D = Double or twin. Double beds are usually big enough for nonromantic couples.

T = Triple (generally a double bed with a single).

Q = Quad (usually two double beds).

b = Private bathroom with toilet and shower or tub.

s = Private shower or tub only (the toilet is down the hall).

According to this code, a couple staying at a "Db-€90" hotel would pay a total of €90 (about $125) for a double room with a private bathroom. Unless otherwise noted, breakfast is included, hotel staff speak basic English, and credit cards are accepted.

B&Bs

Compared to hotels, a bed-and-breakfast place *(Pension)* gives you double the cultural intimacy for half the price. Throughout Austria, people rent out rooms *(Zimmer)* in their homes to travelers. Look for *Zimmer Frei* or *Privatzimmer* signs. These are very common in areas popular with travelers (such as the Salzkammergut Lake District and Germany's Bavaria). Booking direct saves both you and your host the cut the TI takes. Especially in private homes, where the boss changes the sheets, people staying several nights are most desirable. One-night stays are sometimes charged extra.

You'll get your own key to a private room that's clean, comfortable, and simple, though usually homey. Some B&Bs are like mini-hotels, with a separate entrance and several rooms, each with a private bath. Other B&Bs are family homes with spare bedrooms (the rooms sometimes lack sinks, but you have free access to the bathroom and shower in the home). Most B&Bs include a hearty continental breakfast. Energy is expensive in this little country:

You'll endear yourself to B&B owners by turning off lights when you leave and avoiding excessively long showers.

*Gasthof*s are similarly priced small, family-run hotels. Don't confuse B&Bs with the German *Ferienwohnung*, which is a self-catering apartment rented out by the week or fortnight.

Hostels

Hostelers can take advantage of the wonderful network of hostels. Follow signs marked *Jugendherberge* (with triangles) or with the logo showing a tree next to a house. Generally, travelers without a membership card ($28 per year, sold at hostels in most US cities or online at www.hiusa.org, US tel. 202/783-6161) are admitted for an extra $4.

Hostels, including those in Austria, are open to members of all ages. For decades, Bavaria's official hostels were the only ones in Europe that enforced a maximum age limit of 26. But now, even this has been relaxed, and everyone is welcome (though some slow-to-change Bavarian hostels still place some restrictions or charge slightly higher rates for older travelers). Hostel bunks usually cost $10–20 per night (cheaper for those under 27, plus a possible $4 sheet-rental fee if you don't have your own—though many hostels now provide sheets). Many hostels serve good, cheap meals and/or provide kitchen facilities. If you plan to stay in hostels, bring your own sheet. While many hostels have a few doubles or family rooms available upon request for a little extra money, plan on gender-segregated dorms with 4 to 20 beds per room. Hostels can be idyllic and peaceful, but school groups can raise the rafters. School groups are most common on summer weekends and on school-year weekdays. I like small hostels best. While many hostels may say over the telephone that they're fully booked, most hold a few beds for people who drop in, or they can direct you to budget accommodations nearby.

Making Reservations

Given the quality of the places I've found for this book, I'd recommend that you reserve your rooms in advance, particularly during peak season. Book several weeks ahead, or as soon as you've pinned down your travel dates. Note that some holidays merit your making reservations far in advance (see "Major Holidays and Weekends," page 8).

To make a reservation, contact hotels directly by email, phone, or fax. Email is the clearest and most economical way to make a reservation. In addition, many hotel websites now have online reservation forms. If phoning from the US, be mindful of time zones (see page 8). Most hotels listed are accustomed to English-only speakers. To ensure you have all the information you need for your reservation, use the form in this book's appendix (also at www .ricksteves.com/reservation).

When you request a room for a certain time period, use the European style for writing dates: day/month/year. Hoteliers need to know your arrival and departure dates. For example, for a two-night stay in July, I would request "2 nights, arrive 16/07/2010, depart 18/07/2010." Consider carefully how long you'll stay; don't just assume you can extend your reservation for extra days once you arrive.

If you don't get a response within a few days, call to follow up. If the response from the hotel gives its room availability and rates, it's not a confirmation. You must tell them that you want that room at the given rate.

For more spontaneity, you can make reservations as you travel, calling hotels or B&Bs a few days to a week before your visit. If you prefer the flexibility of traveling without any reservations at all, you'll have greater success snaring rooms if you arrive at your destination early in the day. When you anticipate crowds (weekends are worst), call hotels at about 9:00 on the day you plan to arrive, when the hotel clerk knows who'll be checking out and just which rooms will be available.

Whether you're reserving from home or on the road, the hotelier will sometimes request your credit-card number for a one-night deposit. While you can email your credit-card information (I do), some people prefer to share that personal info via phone call, fax, or secure online reservation form (if the hotel has one on its website).

If you must cancel your reservation, it's courteous to do so with as much advance notice as possible (simply make a quick phone call or send an email). Family-run hotels and B&Bs lose money if they turn away customers while holding a room for someone who doesn't show up. Understandably, some hoteliers bill no-shows for one night. Hotels in larger cities such as Vienna and Salzburg sometimes have strict cancellation policies (for example, you might lose a deposit if you cancel within two weeks of your reserved stay, or you might be billed for the entire visit if you leave early). Ask about cancellation policies before you book.

Always reconfirm your room reservation a few days in advance from the road. If you'll be arriving after 17:00, let them know. Don't have the tourist office reconfirm rooms for you; they'll take a commission.

On the small chance that a hotel loses track of your reservation, bring along a hard copy of their emailed or faxed confirmation.

EATING

Traditional Austrian cuisine is heavy, hearty, and—by European standards—inexpensive. Though it's tasty, it can get monotonous if you fall into a schnitzel-filled rut. Be adventurous. Each region has its specialties, and all but the smallest towns have a restaurant serving non-Austrian cuisine.

For breakfast, expect fresh-baked bread and jam, plus cereal, cold cuts, and cheese. Austrians eat lunch and dinner about when we do, though they tend to eat a bigger lunch and smaller dinner.

Austrians are health-conscious, but many starchy, high-fat, high-calorie traditional foods remain staples on restaurant menus. As a new generation takes over their grandparents' restaurants and inns, however, it's becoming easier to find lighter versions of the meaty standards—and organic ingredients are getting more popular. Order house specials whenever possible.

The classic dish, a stand-by on menus across Austria, is Wiener schnitzel (breaded veal cutlet). Variations include Cordon bleu (filled with ham and cheese), and *Naturschnitzel* (not breaded, and served with rice and sauce). Chicken *(Huhn)* is usually served grilled or breaded and baked. Pork *(Schwein)* comes in all forms, including *Schweinsbraten* (roasted and served with dumplings and sauerkraut). Beef appears in goulash, as schnitzel, and in the Viennese *Tafelspitz* (boiled and served with vegetables). Fish dishes are generally very good.

Vegetarians will want to try *Eiernockerl* (egg gnocchi) and *Geröstete Knödel* (roasted dumplings). Noodles, potatoes, lettuce, and rice are standard side dishes. *Spargel* (giant white asparagus) is a must in early summer. For a meal-sized salad, order the *Salatteller.*

Treats include *Apfelstrudel, Topfenstrudel* (pastry filled with sweet cheese and raisins), and *Palatschinken* (filled crepes). The very Austrian *Kaiserschmarr'n* ("Emperor's crumbs") consists of fluffy, carmelized pancake strips, usually served with jam or raisins and nuts. Delectable, fancy specialty desserts, like Sacher torte, Vienna's famous chocolate cake, abound in city cafés.

Ethnic restaurants provide a welcome break from Austrian fare. Foreign cuisine is either the legacy of a crumbled empire (Hungarian and Bohemian, from which Austrian cuisine gets its goulash and dumplings) or a new arrival to feed recent immigrants. Italian, Turkish, Greek, and Asian food are good values.

Hotels often serve fine food. A *Gaststätte* is a simple, less-expensive restaurant. For smaller portions, order from the *kleine Hunger* (small hunger) section of the menu.

Most restaurants tack a menu onto their door for browsers and have an English menu inside. Only a rude waiter will rush

Austrian Wines

Austria's wine industry was scandalized in the 1980s when news broke of major vintners sweetening their wines with antifreeze. Already suffering from being characterized as "sweet and light," the local wine's reputation was scarred by this news. Austrians claim the practice was widespread in many countries, and believe Austria was just the scapegoat. Regardless, the local wine industry went into a tailspin.

Today, the Austrian wine industry no longer focuses on mass production, but instead specializes in fine boutique wines (generally not exported, and therefore not well-known). Locals order white or red Austrian wines expecting quality equal to French and Italian wines. When in Austria, I go for the better local wines when dining—well worth the cost (generally about €4 per small glass).

Some menus list wine prices by the tenth of a liter, or deciliter (dl); keep in mind that a normal-sized glass of wine (2 deciliters, often listed as "0,2 l") will cost twice what's listed. You can also order your wine by the *Viertel* (quarter-liter, 8 oz) or *Achtel* (eighth-liter, 4 oz).

When sampling Austrian wine, some vocabulary helps. You can say, "*Ein Viertel Weisswein* (white wine), *bitte* (please)." Order it *süss* (sweet), *halb trocken* (medium), or *trocken* (dry). *Rotwein* is red wine and *Sekt* is sparkling wine.

Try *Grüner Veltliner* if you like a dry white wine. *Traubenmost* is a heavenly grape juice—alcohol-free but on the verge of wine. *Most* is the same thing, but lightly alcoholic. *Sturm* is "new wine," stronger than *Most,* available only in autumn and part of the *Heuriger* phenomenon (described on page 162). The local red wine, called *Portugieser,* is pretty good. In fall, try the red "new" wine, *roter Sturm;* it's so fruity that locals say "Eat up!" when toasting with it. If you ask for a *gespritzter Wein,* you'll get a spritzer—white wine pepped up with a little sparkling water.

you. Good service is relaxed (slow to an American). You might be charged for bread you've eaten from the basket on the table; have the waiter take it away if you don't want it. To wish others "Happy eating!" offer a cheery *"Guten Appetit!"* When you want the bill, say, *"Rechnung* (REKH-nung), *bitte."* For tips on tipping, see page 12.

For most visitors, the rich pastries, wine, and beer provide the fondest memories of Austrian cuisine. The wine (85 percent white) from the Danube River Valley and eastern Austria is particularly good (see "Austrian Wines," above).

While better known for its wine than its beer, Austria offers plenty of fun for beer drinkers. Each region is proud of its local breweries—in Vienna, try Ottakringer; in Salzburg, look for Stiegl and Augustiner Bräu; and in Tirol, check out Frastanzer

Smoke Free? We'll See.

While many of its neighbors (including Italy, France, and many German states) have passed strict, extensive bans on smoking in public places, Austria has remained a haven for cigarette smokers. Diners, however, may start to see a change: Smoking is now supposed to be off-limits in all Austrian restaurants and cafés of at least 50 square meters (540 square feet); places at least 80 square meters big are allowed to build separate smoking rooms for their patrons. Most Austrian politicians favor the ban, but the two far-right parties say they're worried about the potential loss to businesses. While restaurant and café owners who ignore the new law can be fined up to €10,000, it's hard to say how seriously the law will be enforced (customers can be fined as well—up to €1,000). This means that some cafés and pubs may well remain under a thin blue cloud during your visit; fortunately, most offer plenty of outdoor seating.

and Fohrenburger. Lager (called *Märzen* here) is popular, as are *Pils* (barley-based), *Weissbier* (yeasty and wheat-based), and *Bock* (hoppy seasonal ale). A few more terms: *Flaschenbier* is bottled, *vom Fass* is on tap, and *Malzbier* is the malted soft drink that children learn on. *Radler* is half beer and half lemon soda. Dark beer *(Dunkles)* is uncommon in Austria, but easy to find if you make a foray into Bavaria. When you order beer, ask for *ein Pfiff* (a fifth-liter, about 7 oz), *ein Seidel* (third-liter, 10 oz), *ein Krügerl* (half-liter, 17 oz), or *eine Mass* (a whole liter—about a quart).

Tap water *(Leitungswasser)* is standard with a glass of wine, but otherwise an unusual request. Waiters would prefer that you buy *Mineralwasser* (*mit/ohne Gas,* with/without carbonation). Popular soft drinks include *Apfelsaft gespritzt* (half apple juice, half sparkling water), *Spezi* (Coke and orange soda), and the *über*-Austrian Almdudler (a ginger-ale-like soda). In cafés, look for *Himbeersoda* (raspberry soda) and the refreshing *Holunder gespritzt* (sparkling water flavored with elderberry blossoms).

Cheap Meals

In Austria, you're never far from a *Würstelstand* (sausage stand). Only a tourist puts the sausage in a bun like a hot dog. Munch alternately between the meat and the bread ("that's why you have two hands"), and you'll look like a native. Generally, the darker the weenie, the spicier it is. Here are the key words: *Weisswurst*—boiled white sausage; *Bosna*—with onions and curry; *Käsekrainer*—with melted cheese inside; *Debreziner*—spicy Hungarian; *Frankfurter*—our weenie; *frische*—fresh ("eat before the noon bells"); and *Senf*—

How Was Your Trip?

Were your travels fun, smooth, and meaningful? If you'd like to share your tips, concerns, and discoveries, please fill out the survey at www.ricksteves.com/feedback. I value your feedback. Thanks in advance—it helps a lot.

mustard (ask for *süss*—sweet; or *scharf*—sharp).

Most bakeries sell small, cheap sandwiches; look for *Leberkäsesemmel* (roll filled with Austrian meatloaf) as well as *Schnitzelsemmel* (schnitzel sandwich). *Stehcafés* (food counters) usually offer open-face finger sandwiches *(belegte Brote)* with a wide array of toppings. Other cheap eats include department-store cafeterias, *Schnell-Imbiss* (fast-food) stands, university cafeterias *(Mensas)*, hostels, and—especially in big cities—*Döner Kebab* kiosks (serving either sliced meat and vegetables, or falafel, in pita bread, as well as other Middle Eastern fast-food options). For a quick, cheap bite, have a deli make you a *Wurstsemmel*—a basic sausage sandwich.

TRAVELING AS A TEMPORARY LOCAL

We travel all the way to Europe to enjoy differences—to become temporary locals. You'll experience frustrations. Certain truths that we find "God-given" or "self-evident," such as cold beer, ice in drinks, bottomless cups of coffee, hot showers, and bigger being better, are suddenly not so true. One of the benefits of travel is the eye-opening realization that there are logical, civil, and even better alternatives.

Americans tend to be noisy in public places, such as restaurants and trains. My Austrian friends place a high value on speaking quietly in these same places. Listen while on the bus or in a restaurant—the place can be packed, but the decibel level is low. Try to remember this nuance, and soften your speaking voice as a way of respecting their culture.

If there is a negative aspect to the image Austrians have of Americans, it's that we are big, loud, aggressive, impolite, rich, superficially friendly, and a bit naive.

While Austrians look bemusedly at some of our Yankee excesses—and worriedly at others—they nearly always afford us individual travelers all the warmth we deserve. Judging from all the happy feedback I receive from travelers who have used this book, it's safe to assume you'll enjoy a great, affordable vacation—with the finesse of an independent, experienced traveler.

Thanks, and *gute Reise!*

BACK DOOR TRAVEL PHILOSOPHY
From *Rick Steves' Europe Through the Back Door*

Travel is intensified living—maximum thrills per minute and one of the last great sources of legal adventure. Travel is freedom. It's recess, and we need it.

Experiencing the real Europe requires catching it by surprise, going casual..."Through the Back Door."

Affording travel is a matter of priorities. (Make do with the old car.) You can travel—simply, safely, and comfortably—nearly anywhere in Europe for $120 a day plus transportation costs (allow more for bigger cities). In many ways, spending more money only builds a thicker wall between you and what you came to see. Europe is a cultural carnival, and, time after time, you'll find that its best acts are free and the best seats are the cheap ones.

A tight budget forces you to travel close to the ground, meeting and communicating with the people, not relying on service with a purchased smile. Never sacrifice sleep, nutrition, safety, or cleanliness in the name of budget. Simply enjoy the local-style alternatives to expensive hotels and restaurants.

Extroverts have more fun. If your trip is low on magic moments, kick yourself and make things happen. If you don't enjoy a place, maybe you don't know enough about it. Seek the truth. Recognize tourist traps. Give a culture the benefit of your open mind. See things as different but not better or worse. Any culture has much to share.

Of course, travel, like the world, is a series of hills and valleys. Be fanatically positive and militantly optimistic. If something's not to your liking, change your liking. Travel is addictive. It can make you a happier American as well as a citizen of the world. Our Earth is home to six and a half billion equally important people. It's humbling to travel and find that people don't envy Americans. Europeans like us, but, with all due respect, they wouldn't trade passports.

Globe-trotting destroys ethnocentricity. It helps you understand and appreciate different cultures. Regrettably, there are forces in our society that want you dumbed down for their convenience. Don't let it happen. Thoughtful travel engages you with the world—more important than ever these days. Travel changes people. It broadens perspectives and teaches new ways to measure quality of life. Rather than fear the diversity on this planet, travelers celebrate it. Many travelers toss aside their hometown blinders. Their prized souvenirs are the strands of different cultures they decide to knit into their own character. The world is a cultural yarn shop, and Back Door travelers are weaving the ultimate tapestry. Join in!

AUSTRIA

Österreich

During the grand old Habsburg days, Austria was Europe's most powerful empire. Its royalty built a giant kingdom (*Österreich* means "Eastern Empire") of more than 60 million people by making love, not war—having lots of children and marrying them into the other royal houses of Europe.

Today, this small, landlocked country clings to its elegant past more than any other nation in Europe. The waltz is still the rage. Music has long been a key part of Austria's heritage. The giants of classic music—Haydn, Mozart, Beethoven—were born here or moved here to write and perform their masterpieces. Music lovers flock to Salzburg every summer to attend its famous festival. But traditional folk music is also part of the Austrian soul. The world's best-loved Christmas carol, "Silent Night," was written by Austrians with just a guitar for accompaniment. Don't be surprised if you hear yodeling for someone's birthday—try joining in.

Austrians are very sociable—it's important to greet people in the breakfast room and those you pass on the streets or meet in shops. The Austrian version of "Hi" is a cheerful *"Grüss Gott"* (for more on the language, see "Hurdling the Language Barrier" on page 382 and "German Survival Phrases for Austria" on page 402).

Austria's capital city, Vienna, has enjoyed many progressive people-oriented programs that locals attribute to its socialistic city government. While Austria has gained recent notoriety for electing racist right-wingers, that attitude does not prevail everywhere. Large parts of the country may be conservative, but Vienna is extremely liberal. For 80 years (except for the Nazi occupation), Vienna has had a socialist government. Since the fall of the Soviet Union, the party changed its name to "Social Democrat"...but its people-oriented agenda is still the same.

While Vienna is in the flat Danube valley, much of Austria's

Austria Almanac

Official Name: Republik Österreich ("Eastern Empire"), or simply Österreich.

Population: Austria's 8.2 million people (similar population to the state of Georgia) are 91 percent ethnic Austrian, plus 4 percent from the former Yugoslavia. Three out of four Austrians are Catholic; about one in 20 is Muslim. German is the dominant language, but some provinces recognize other official languages for their Slavic- and Hungarian-descended citizens.

Latitude and Longitude: 47°N and 13°E. The latitude is the same as Minnesota or Washington state.

Area: With 32,400 square miles, Austria is similar in size to South Carolina or Maine.

Geography: The northeast is flat and well-populated; the less-populated southwest is mountainous, with the Alps rising up to the 12,450-foot Grossglockner. The 1,770-mile-long Danube River meanders west-to-east through the upper part of the country, passing through Vienna.

Biggest Cities: One in five Austrians lives in the capital of Vienna (1.7 million in the city; 2.2 million in the greater metropolitan area). Graz has 248,000, and Linz has 189,000.

Economy: Located at the crossroads of Europe and bordered by eight countries, Austria is well-integrated into the EU economy. The Gross Domestic Product is $322 billion (similar to Michigan's). It has a GDP per capita of $39,300—among Europe's highest. One of its biggest moneymakers is tourism. Austria produces wood, paper products (nearly half the land is forested)...and Red Bull Energy Drink. The country faces an aging population that increasingly collects social security—a situation that will strain the national budget in years to come.

Government: Austria has been officially neutral since 1955 and its citizens take a dim view of European unity. Although right-leaning parties made substantial gains in recent elections, the government continues to be a center-left coalition, currently headed by Federal President Heinz Fischer and Chancellor Werner Faymann (both Social Democrats). The resurgent right—buoyed by anti-immigrant and anti-EU sentiment—was dealt a blow in October 2008 when its "yuppie fascist" leader Jörg Haider died in a car accident. Austria is the only EU nation that lets 16- and 17-year-olds vote.

Flag: Three horizontal bands of red (top), white, and red.

The Average Austrian: A typical Austrian is 41 years old, has 1.36 children, and will live to be 79. He or she inhabits a 900-square-foot home, and spends leisure time with a circle of a few close friends. Chances are high that someone in that closely knit circle is a smoker—Austrians smoke more cigarettes per day than any other Europeans.

character is found in its mountains. Austrians excel in mountain climbing and winter sports such as alpine skiing. Innsbruck was twice the site of the Winter Olympics and Salzburg was a finalist for the 2014 games. When watching ski races, you'll often see fans celebrating with red-and-white flags at the finish line—Austria has won more Olympic medals in alpine skiing than any other country.

Austria lost a piece of its mountains after World War I, when the Tirol was divided between Austria and Italy. Many of Tirol's Italians still speak German and it is the first language in some of their schools. Though there was bitterness at the time of the division, today, with no border guards and a shared currency, you can hardly tell you're in a different country.

While Austrians speak German and talked about unity with Germany long before Hitler ever said *"Anschluss,"* they cherish their distinct cultural and historical traditions. They are not Germans. Austria is mellow and relaxed compared to Deutschland. *Gemütlichkeit* is the word most often used to describe this special Austrian cozy-and-easy approach to life. It's good living—whether engulfed in mountain beauty or bathed in lavish high culture. The people stroll as if every day were Sunday, topping things off with a cheerful visit to a coffee or pastry shop.

It must be nice to be past your prime—no longer troubled by being powerful, able to kick back and celebrate life in the clean, peaceful mountain air.

VIENNA
Wien

ORIENTATION

Vienna is the capital of Austria, the cradle of classical music, the home of the rich Habsburg heritage, and one of Europe's most livable cities. The city center is skyscraper-free, pedestrian-friendly, dotted with quiet parks, and traversed by quaint electric trams. Many buildings still reflect 18th- and 19th-century elegance, when the city was at the forefront of the arts and sciences. Compared with most modern European urban centers, the pace of life is slow.

For much of its 2,500-year history, Vienna (*Wien* in German—pronounced "veen") was on the frontier of civilized Europe. Located on the south bank of the Danube, it was threatened by Germanic barbarians (in Roman times), Mongol hordes (13th century), Ottoman Turks (the sieges of 1529 and 1683), and encroachment by the Soviet Empire after World War II.

Vienna reached its peak in the 19th century. Politically, it hosted Europe's diplomats at the 1814 Congress of Vienna, which reaffirmed Europe's conservative monarchy after the French Revolution and Napoleon. Vienna became one of Europe's cultural capitals, home to groundbreaking composers (Beethoven, Mozart, Brahms, Strauss), scientists (Doppler, Boltzmann), philosophers (Freud, Husserl, Schlick, Gödel, Steiner), architects (Wagner, Loos), and painters (Klimt, Schiele, Kokoschka). By the turn of the 20th century, Vienna sat on the cusp between stuffy Old World monarchy and subversive modern trends.

After the turmoil of the two world wars, Vienna has settled down into a somewhat sleepy, pleasant place where culture is still king. Classical music is everywhere. People nurse a pastry and coffee over the daily paper at small cafés. It's a city of world-class museums, big and small. Anyone with an interest in painting, music, architecture, beautiful objects, or Sacher torte with whipped cream will feel right at home.

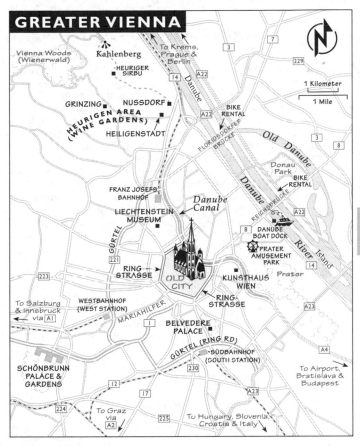

GREATER VIENNA

Vienna Woods (Wienerwald)
Kahlenberg
HEURIGER SIRBU
To Krems, Prague & Berlin
GRINZING
NUSSDORF
HEURIGEN AREA (WINE GARDENS)
HEILIGENSTADT
Danube
BIKE RENTAL
Old Danube
Donau Park
BIKE RENTAL
FRANZ JOSEFS BAHNHOF
LIECHTENSTEIN MUSEUM
Danube Canal
Danube River
Island
DANUBE BOAT DOCK
GÜRTEL
RING STRASSE
OLD CITY
PRATER AMUSEMENT PARK
KUNSTHAUS WIEN
Prater
To Salzburg & Innsbruck via A1
WESTBAHNHOF (WEST STATION)
MARIAHILFER
RING STRASSE
BELVEDERE PALACE
GÜRTEL (RING RD)
SÜDBAHNHOF (SOUTH STATION)
To Airport, Bratislava & Budapest
SCHÖNBRUNN PALACE & GARDENS
To Graz via A2
To Hungary, Slovenia, Croatia & Italy

1 Kilometer
1 Mile

Planning Your Time

For a big city, Vienna is pleasant and laid-back. Packed with sights, it's worth two days and two nights on the speediest trip. If you're visiting Vienna as part of a longer European trip, you could sleep on the train on your way in and out—Berlin, Kraków, Venice, Rome, the Swiss Alps (via Zürich), Paris, and the Rhine Valley are each handy night trains away. The Hofburg and Schönbrunn are both world-class palaces, but seeing both is redundant—with limited time or money, I'd choose just one. The Hofburg comes with the popular Sisi Museum and is right in the town center, making for an easy visit. With more time, a visit to Schönbrunn—set outside town amid a grand and regal garden— is also a great experience. (For efficient sightseeing, drivers should note that Schönbrunn Palace is conveniently on the way out of town toward Salzburg.)

Vienna Past and Present

Vienna is a head without a body. The capital of the once-grand Habsburg Empire for 640 years, Vienna started and lost World War I, and with it its far-flung holdings. Culturally, historically, and from a sightseeing point of view, this city is the sum of its illustrious past, ranking right up there with Paris, London, and Rome.

Vienna has always been the easternmost city of the West. In Roman times, it was Vindobona, on the Danube facing the Germanic barbarians. In the Middle Ages, Vienna was Europe's bastion against the Ottomans—a Christian breakwater against the riding tide of Islam (hordes of up to 200,000 Ottomans were repelled in 1529 and 1683). During this period, as the Ottomans dreamed of conquering what they called "the big apple" for their sultan, Vienna lived with a constant fear of invasion (and the Habsburg court ruled from safer Prague). You'll notice none of Vienna's great palaces were built until after 1683, when the Turkish threat was finally over.

The Habsburgs, who ruled the enormous Austrian Empire from 1273 to 1918, shaped Vienna. Some ad agency has convinced Vienna to make Elisabeth, wife of Emperor Franz Josef—with her narcissism and struggles with royal life—the darling of the local tourist scene. You'll see images of "Sisi" (SEE-see) all over town. But stay focused on the Habsburgs who mattered: Maria Theresa (ruled 1740-1780, see page 50) and Franz Josef (ruled 1848-1916, see page 115).

If you have two days for Vienna, here's a good way to spend them:

Day 1

9:00   Circle the Ringstrasse by tram, following my self-guided tram tour (page 101).

10:00   Drop by the TI for any planning and ticket needs, then see the sights in Vienna's old center (taking the Vienna City Walk, page 77): Monument Against War and Fascism, Kärntner Strasse, Kaisergruft crypt, St. Stephen's Cathedral (nave closed 11:30–13:30), and the Graben pedestrian zone.

12:00   Lunch of finger sandwiches at Buffet Trzesniewski.

13:00   Tour the Hofburg Palace and Treasury.

16:00   Hit one more museum, or shop, browse, and people-watch.

19:30   Choose classical music (concert or opera), Haus der Musik, *Heuriger* wine garden, or any sight listed under "Sightseeing After Dark." (See the "Music and Nightlife" chapter.)

After Napoleon's defeat and the Congress of Vienna in 1815 (which shaped 19th-century Europe), Vienna enjoyed its violin-filled belle époque, giving us our romantic image of the city: fine wine, chocolates, cafés, waltzes, and the good life.

In 1900, Vienna's 2.2 million inhabitants made it the world's fifth-largest city—after New York, London, Paris, and Berlin.

While Vienna's old walls had held out would-be invaders (including the Ottomans), they were no match for WWII bombs, which destroyed nearly a quarter of the city's buildings. In modern times, neutral Austria took a big bite out of the USSR's Warsaw Pact buffer zone. Today, Vienna is a springboard for newly popular destinations in Eastern Europe.

Vienna's population has dropped to 1.7 million, with dogs being the preferred "child" and the average Viennese mother having only 1.3 children. Even with fewer residents, Vienna is still a grand and elegant capital containing one-fifth of Austria's population.

The truly Viennese person is not Austrian, but rather a second-generation Habsburg cocktail, with grandparents from the distant corners of the old empire: Hungary, the Czech Republic, Slovakia, Poland, Slovenia, Croatia, Bosnia, Serbia, Romania, and Italy. Vienna is the melting-pot capital of a now-collapsed empire that, in its heyday, consisted of more than 60 million people—only eight million of whom were Austrian.

ORIENTATION

Day 2

Morning	Choose between Schönbrunn Palace (which could be redundant if you've seen the Hofburg Palace yesterday) or the Lipizzaner stallions. If you choose Schönbrunn Palace, arrive by 9:00 and return to central Vienna by noon. The Spanish Riding School's Lipizzaner stallions begin their practice at 10:00 (about March–June and mid-Aug–Dec Tue–Sat 10:00–12:00, no practice Sun–Mon or July–mid-Aug).
12:00	Have lunch at the Naschmarkt, and consider ducking into one or two sights (such as the Secession) on nearby Karlsplatz.
13:00	Tour the Opera (check red sign on door for today's schedule).
14:00	Visit the Kunsthistorisches Museum.
16:00	Choose from the many sights left to see in Vienna.
Evening	See Day 1 evening options. In summer, hit the City Hall food circus for dinner or a drink (on Rathausplatz).

Daily Reminder

Sunday: All sights are open, but shops are closed, including the Naschmarkt open-air market and the Dorotheum auction house. Most churches have restricted hours for sightseers. In spring and fall, the Spanish Riding School's Lipizzaner stallions perform at 11:00. The Wien Museum Karlsplatz is free.

Monday: Most of the major sights are open (such as St. Stephen's Cathedral, Opera, Hofburg Imperial Apartments, Schönbrunn Palace, and Belvedere Palace), but many sights are closed, including the Kunsthistorisches Museum, Secession, Augustinian Church, Academy of Fine Arts, Imperial Furniture Collection, Museum of Applied Art, Otto Wagner exhibit, Folkloric Museum, and Opera Museum. The Lipizzaner horses of the Spanish Riding School take the day off from practice. The KunstHausWien is half-price.

Tuesday: All sights are open, except the Hofburg Treasury, New Palace Museums, and the Natural History Museum. The Museum of Applied Art (MAK) stays open until 24:00.

Wednesday: All sights are open, except the Liechtenstein Museum. The Albertina and Natural History Museum stay open until 21:00.

Thursday: All sights are open, except the Liechtenstein Museum. The Kunsthistorisches and Leopold museums stay open until 21:00, and the Secession until 20:00.

Friday: All sights are open. The Spanish Riding School's Lipizzaner stallions often perform at 19:00 in spring and fall.

Saturday: All sights are open, except the Judenplatz Museum and Jewish Museum. The Spanish Riding School's Lipizzaner stallions often perform at 11:00 in spring and fall. The Museum of Applied Art (MAK) is free.

OVERVIEW

Vienna sits between the Vienna Woods (Wienerwald) and the Danube (Donau). To the southeast is industrial sprawl. The Alps, which arc across Europe from Marseille, end at Vienna's wooded hills, providing a popular playground for walking and sipping new wine. This greenery's momentum carries on into the city. More than half of Vienna is parkland, filled with ponds, gardens, trees, and statue-maker memories of Austria's glory days.

Think of the city map as a target with concentric sections: The bull's-eye is St. Stephen's Cathedral, the towering cathedral south of the Danube. Surrounding that is the old town, bound tightly by the circular road known as the Ringstrasse, marking what used to be the city wall. The Gürtel, a broader ring road, contains the rest of downtown. Outside the Gürtel lies the (uninteresting) sprawl of modern Vienna.

Addresses start with the district, or *Bezirk,* followed by the street and building number. The Ringstrasse (a.k.a. the Ring) circles the first *Bezirk.* Any address higher than the ninth *Bezirk* is beyond the Gürtel, far from the center. The middle two digits of Vienna's postal codes show the *Bezirk.* The address "7, Lindengasse 4" is in the seventh district, #4 on Linden street. Its postal code would be 1070.

Nearly all your sightseeing will be in the old town, located inside (and along) the Ringstrasse. To walk across this circular district takes about 30 minutes. St. Stephen's Cathedral sits in the center, at the intersection of the two main (pedestrian-only) streets: Kärntner Strasse runs north–south and Graben runs east–west. Within a few blocks of the cathedral is the Hofburg, a sprawling complex of palaces and museums. To the northwest of the cathedral is the "Bermuda Triangle" of pubs and cafés for nightlife.

Several sights lie on or just outside the Ringstrasse. A branch of the Danube River (*Donau* in German, DOH-now) borders the Ring to the north. On the south edge are the Opera, Karlsplatz, and the Kunsthistorisches and Natural History museums.

As a tourist, concern yourself only with this compact old center. When you do, sprawling Vienna suddenly becomes manageable.

Arrival in Vienna

For a comprehensive rundown on Vienna's two main train stations and nearby airports, as well as tips on arriving by car or boat—see Transportation Connections, page 174.

Tourist Information

Vienna's one real TI is a block behind the Opera at Albertinaplatz (daily 9:00–19:00, tel. 01/24555, press 2 for English info, www .vienna.info).

Confirm your sightseeing plans at the TI, and pick up the free and essential city map with a list of museums and hours (also available at most hotels), the monthly program of concerts (called *Wien-Programm*—details next), the *Vienna from A to Z* booklet (details later in this section), and the biannual city guide *(Vienna Journal).* The TI also books rooms for a €2.90 fee. While hotel and ticket-booking agencies at the train station and airport can answer questions and give out maps and brochures, I'd rely on the official TI if possible.

Wien-Programm: This monthly entertainment guide is particularly important, listing all of the events, including music, walks, expositions, and evening museum hours. It's organized this way: First you see the current month's festivals and live music goings-on (jazz, rock, and more). Next comes the schedule for the two big touristy draws: the Spanish Riding School and the Vienna Boys' Choir, followed by museums and exhibitions, and then the theater options, including the Opera schedule. The next section lists classical concerts (also organized by date, with phone numbers to call direct to check seat availability, and to save the 20 percent booking fees that you pay if you buy tickets through an agency). Last is the list of guided walks offered (*E* means "in English"). Note the key for abbreviations on the inside cover, which helps make this dense booklet useful even for non-German speakers.

Vienna from A to Z: Consider this handy booklet, sold by TIs for €3.60. Every major building in Vienna sports a numbered flag banner that keys into this booklet and into the TI's city map. If you get lost, find one of the "famous-building flags" and match its number to your map. If you're at a famous building, check the map to see what other key numbers are nearby, then check the *A to Z* book description to see if you want to go in. This system is especially helpful for those just wandering aimlessly among Vienna's historic charms.

Vienna Card: The much-promoted €18.50 Vienna Card is not worth the mental overhead for most travelers. It gives you a 72-hour transit pass (worth €13.60) and discounts of 10–40 percent at the city's museums. It might save the busy sightseer a few euros (though seniors and students will do better with their own discounts).

Helpful Hints

Internet Access: The TI has a list of Internet cafés. **BigNet** is the dominant outfit (www.bignet.at), with lots of computers at Hoher Markt 8–9 (daily 9:00–23:00). **Surfland Internet Café** is near the Opera (daily 10:00–23:00, Krugerstrasse 10, tel. 01/512-7701), and **Netcafe** is close to many of my recommended hotels (Mon–Fri 9:00–22:00, Sat 10:00–22:00, Sun 12:00–22:00, Mariahilfer Strasse 103, tel. 01/595-5558).

Post Offices: The main post office is near Schwedenplatz at Fleischmarkt 19 (Mon–Fri 7:00–22:00, Sat–Sun 9:00–22:00). Branch offices are at the Westbahnhof (Mon–Fri 7:00–22:00, Sat–Sun 9:00–20:00), near the Opera (Mon–Fri 7:00–19:00, closed Sat–Sun, Krugerstrasse 13), and scattered throughout town.

English Bookstore: Stop by the woody and cool **Shakespeare & Co.** (Mon–Sat 9:00–19:00 and sometimes later, generally closed Sun, north of Hoher Markt at Sterngasse 2, tel. 01/535-5053).

Keeping Up with the News: Don't buy newspapers. Read them for free in Vienna's marvelous coffeehouses. It's much classier.

Travel Agency: Ruefa is convenient, with good service for flights and train tickets. They'll waive the service charge for my readers (Mon–Fri 9:00–18:00, Sat 10:00–13:00, closed Sun, Spiegelgasse 15, tel. 01/513-4000).

Getting Around Vienna

By Public Transportation: Take full advantage of Vienna's simple, cheap, and super-efficient transit system, which includes trams

(a.k.a. streetcars), buses, U-Bahn (subway), and S-Bahn (faster suburban trains). The smooth, modern trams are Porsche-designed, with "backpack technology" that locates the engines and mechanical hardware on the roofs for a lower ride and easier entry. I generally stick to the tram to zip around the Ring and take the U-Bahn to outlying sights or hotels. Trams #1, #2, and #D all travel partway around the Ring. (To take a tram tour around the Ring, see page 101.)

The free Vienna map, available at TIs and hotels, includes a smaller schematic map of the major public transit lines, making the too-big €2.50 transit map unnecessary. (Transit maps are also posted conveniently on U-Bahn station walls.) As you study the map, note that tram lines are marked with numbers or letters (such as #38 or #D), while buses have numbers followed by an *A* (such as #38A). U-Bahn lines begin with U (e.g., U-1), and the directions are designated by the end-of-the-line stops. Blue lines are the speedier S-Bahns (transit info tel. 01/790-9100).

Trams, buses, the U-Bahn, and the S-Bahn all use the same tickets. Buy your tickets from *Tabak-Trafik* shops, station machines, marked *Vorverkauf* offices in the station, or—for trams only—on board (tickets only, more expensive). You have lots of choices:

- Single tickets (€1.70, €2.20 if bought on tram, good for one journey with necessary transfers);
- 24-hour transit pass (€5.70);
- 72-hour transit pass (€13.60);

- 7-day transit pass (*Wochenkarte*, €14, pass always starts on Mon); or
- 8-day card *(Acht Tage Karte)*, covering eight full days of free transportation for €27.20 (can be shared—for example, 4 people for 2 days each). With a per-person cost of €3.50/day (compared to €5.70/day for a 24-hr pass), this can be a real saver for groups.

Kids under 15 travel free on Sundays and holidays; kids under 6 always travel free.

Stamp a time on your ticket as you enter the Metro system, tram, or bus (stamp it only the first time for a multiple-use pass). Cheaters pay a stiff €70 fine, plus the cost of the ticket. Rookies miss stops because they fail to open the door. Push buttons, pull latches—do whatever it takes. Before you exit a U-Bahn station, study the wall-mounted street map. Choosing the right exit—signposted from the moment you step off the train—saves lots of walking.

Cute little electric buses wind through the tangled old center. Bus #1A is best for a joy ride—hop on and see where it takes you.

By Taxi: Vienna's comfortable, civilized, and easy-to-flag-down taxis start at €2.50. You'll pay about €10 to go from the Opera to the Westbahnhof. Pay only what's on the meter—any surcharges (other than the €2 fee added to fares when you telephone them, or €10 for the airport) are just crude cabbie rip-offs.

By Car with Driver: Consider the luxury of having your own car and driver. Johann (a.k.a. John) Lichtl is a kind, honest, English-speaking cabbie who can take up to four passengers in his car (€27/1 hr, €22/hr for 2 hrs or more, €27 to or from airport, mobile 0676-670-6750). Consider hiring gentle Johann for a day trip to the Danube Valley (see page 179; €140, up to 8 hrs), or to drive you to Salzburg with Danube sightseeing en route (€330, up to 14 hrs; other trips can be arranged). These special prices are valid with this book in 2010.

By Bike: Vienna is a great city for biking, though cheap bike-rental options are scarce in the city center (see recommendations below and get a list at the TI). The bike path along the Ring is wonderfully entertaining. Your best biking is likely up and down the traffic-free and people-filled Donauinsel (Danube Island).

Weather permitting from March through October, you can rent a bike all day (about 9:30 until dusk) from one of two shops near these bridges: **Floridsdorferbrücke** (€3.60/hr, €18/day, near tram #31 stop, tel. 01/278-8698) and **Reichsbrücke** (€5.40/hr, €27/day, tel. 01/263-5242, www.fahrradverleih.at).

American Rick Watts runs **Pedal Power,** and will deliver your bike to your hotel and pick it up when you're done (€32/day including delivery, Ausstellungsstrasse 3, tel. 01/729-7234, www.pedalpower.at). Rick also operates guided city tours on Segway scooters (2/day, see website for details) and by bike (see "Bike Tours," below).

Crazy Chicken bike rental, a short tram ride from the Westbahnhof, is less convenient, but a lot cheaper (€3/hr, €12/day, daily 8:30–19:00, near recommended Pension Fünfhaus at Grangasse 8—see page 150 for directions, tel. 01/892-2134, mobile 0664-421-4789).

Citybikewien, which has bikes parked in public racks all over town, is a clever program that works fine for locals, but can be headachy for tourists to figure out. The bikes lock in their stalls (50 of which are scattered through the city center) and are released when you insert a Citybike Tourist Card, sold for €2 at Pedal Power (listed earlier) and at Royal Tours (Herrengasse 1–3). Bikes cost €2 per hour (first hour free, fliers explain the process in English, www.citybikewien.at).

TOURS

Walking Tours—The TI's *Walks in Vienna* brochure describes Vienna's many guided walks. The basic 90-minute "Vienna at First Glance" introductory walk is offered daily throughout the summer (€13, leaves at 14:00 from near the Opera, in English and German, tel. 01/876-7111, mobile 0664-260-4388, www.wienguide.at). Various specialized tours go once a week and are listed on their website.

Bike Tours—Several companies offer city tours. **Pedal Power** runs two different three-hour tours daily from May to September (€23 per tour includes bike, €40 for both tours, departs at 9:45 and 14:15 in front of Opera at corner of Operngasse and the Kärntner Ring, also rents bikes, tel. 01/729-7234, www.pedalpower.at). **Wolfgang Höfler** leads bike tours as well as walking tours (€135/2 hrs, office@vienna-aktivtours.com, also listed on next page under "Private Guides").

Hop-On, Hop-Off Bus Tour—Vienna Sightseeing operates hop-on, hop-off bus tours (departures from the Opera 2–3/hr April–Oct 10:00–18:00, at top of each hour Nov–March 10:00–17:00, recorded commentary). The schedule is posted curbside (three different routes, €13 for 1 hr, €16 for 2 hrs). You could pay much more to get 24 hours of hop-on, hop-off privileges, but given the city's excellent public transportation and this outfit's meager frequency, I'd take this not to hop on and off, but only to get the narrated orientation drive through town.

Ring Tram Tour—The **Vienna Ring Tram,** a made-for-tourists streetcar, runs along the entire Ringstrasse (€6 for one loop, €9 for 24-hr hop-on, hop-off privileges, runs twice hourly 10:00–18:00,

ORIENTATION

July–Aug until 19:00, recorded narration).

You'll save money, however, by following my self-guided tram tour using city trams that circle the Ring. You'll need to make one transfer, but the trams run frequently and you'll sit alongside real *Wieners* (see Ringstrasse Tram Tour chapter).

City Bus Tour—Vienna Sightseeing offers a basic three-hour city tour, including a tour of Schönbrunn Palace (€36, 3/day April–Oct, 2/day Nov–March, call 01/7124-6830 or go to www.viennasight seeingtours.com, which also lists their many other tours).

Horse and Buggy Tour—These traditional horse-and-buggies, called *Fiakers*, take rich romantics on clip-clop tours lasting 20 minutes (€40–old town), 40 minutes (€65–old town and the Ring), or one hour (€95–all of the above, but more thorough). You can share the ride and cost with up to five people. Because it's a kind of guided tour, talk to a few drivers before choosing a carriage, and pick a driver who's fun and speaks English (tel. 01/401-060).

Private Guides—The tourist board's website (www.vienna.info) has a long list of local guides with their specialties and contact information. **Lisa Zeiler** is an excellent English-speaking guide (2-hr walks for €130—if she's booked, she can set you up with another guide, tel. 01/402-3688, lisa.zeiler@gmx.at). **Ursula Klaus** is an art scholar specializing in turn-of-the-20th-century Vienna, music, art, and architecture (also €130/2 hrs, mobile 0676-421-4884, ursula.klaus@aon.at). Lisa and Ursula are both top-notch, bring art museums to life masterfully, and can tailor tours to your interests. **Wolfgang Höfler** focuses on Vienna's 20th-century history (€135/2 hrs, also leads bike tours—see previous page, www.vienna-aktivtours.com, office@vienna-aktivtours.com).

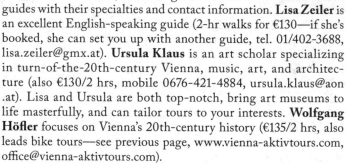

SIGHTS IN VIENNA

The sights listed in this chapter are arranged by neighborhood for handy sightseeing. When you see a ✪ in a listing, it means the sight is covered in much more depth in my Vienna City Walk or one of my self-guided tours. This is why Vienna's most important attractions get the least coverage in this chapter—we'll explore them later in the book.

For tips on sightseeing, see page 14 in the Introduction. For a self-guided walk connecting many of central Vienna's top sights, see the Vienna City Walk on page 77.

Inside the Ring

▲▲▲**St. Stephen's Cathedral (Stephansdom)**—This massive Gothic church with the skyscraping spire sits at the center of Vienna. Its highlights are the impressive exterior, the view from the top of the south tower, a carved pulpit, and a handful of quirky sights associated with Mozart and the Habsburg rulers.

Cost: Entering the church is free (except July–mid-Oct, when it costs €3 to get past the rear of the nave). Going up the towers costs €3 (by stairs, south tower, better view, entrance outside the church) or €4.50 (by elevator, north tower, entrance inside the church).

Hours: The church doors are open Mon–Sat 6:00–22:00, Sun 7:00–22:00, but the nave is open for tourists only Mon–Sat 9:00–11:30 & 13:30–16:30, Sun 13:30–16:30. The south-tower stairs are open daily 9:00–17:30. The north-tower elevator runs daily July–Aug 8:30–18:00, April–June and Sept–Oct 8:30–17:30, Nov–March 8:30–17:00, last elevator ascends 20 min before closing.

✪ See the St. Stephen's Cathedral Tour on page 91.

▲▲▲**Opera (Staatsoper)**—The Opera, facing the Ring and near the TI, is a central point for any visitor. Vienna remains one of the world's great cities for classical music, and this building still belts

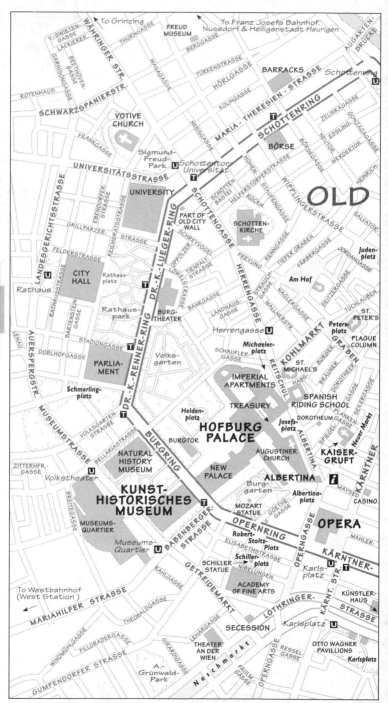

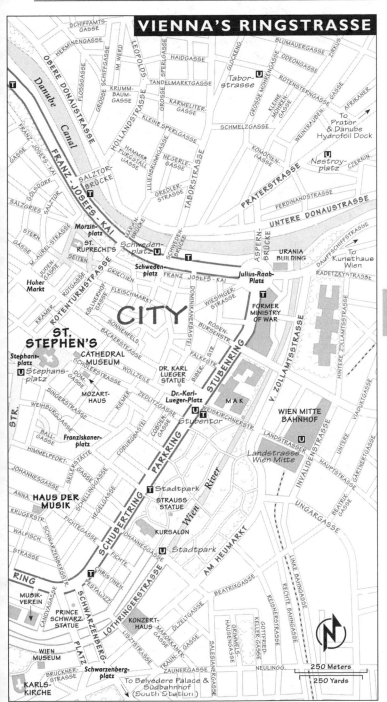

VIENNA'S RINGSTRASSE

out some of the finest opera, both classic and cutting-edge. While the critical reception of the building 130 years ago led the architect to commit suicide, and though it's been rebuilt since its destruction by WWII bombs, it's still a sumptuous place. The interior has a chandeliered lobby and carpeted staircases perfect for making the scene. The theater itself features five wrap-around balconies, gold and red decor, and a bracelet-like chandelier.

Depending on your level of tolerance for opera, you can simply admire the Neo-Renaissance building from the outside, take a guided tour of the lavish interior, visit the Opera Museum, or attend a performance.

Performances: For information on attending a performance, see page 169.

Tours: Unless you're attending a performance, you can enter the Opera only with a guided 50-minute tour, offered nearly daily in English (€6.50; generally July–Aug at 11:00, 13:00, 14:00, 15:00, and often at 10:00 and 16:00; Sept–June fewer tours, afternoons only; tel. 01/514-442-624). Tour times are often changed or cancelled due to rehearsals and performances. The opera posts a monthly schedule (blue, on the wall), but the more accurate schedule is the daily listing (red, posted on the door on the Operngasse side of building, farthest from St. Stephen's Cathedral). Tour tickets include the tiny and disappointing Opera Museum (across the street toward the Hofburg), except on Monday, when the museum is closed.

Opera Museum: New and included in your opera tour ticket (whether you like it or not), the Opera Museum is a let-down, with descriptions only in German and rotating six-month-long special exhibits (€3, or included in the €6.50 tour ticket, Tue–Sun 10:00–18:00, closed Mon, a block away from the Opera, near Albertina Museum, tel. 01/514-442-100).

Habsburg Sights in and near the Hofburg Palace

The complex, confusing, and imposing Imperial Palace, with 640 years of architecture, demands your attention. This first Habsburg residence grew with the family empire from the 13th century until 1913, when the last "new wing" opened. The winter residence of the Habsburg rulers until 1918, it's still the home of the Spanish Riding School, the Vienna Boys' Choir, the Austrian president's office, 5,000 government workers, and several important museums. For an overview of the palace layout, see page 111. Don't get confused by the Hofburg's myriad courtyards and many museums. Focus on three sights: the Imperial Apartments, Treasury, and the museums at the New Palace (Neue Burg).

The section below also covers Habsburg sights located near—but not inside—the Hofburg (including the Albertina Museum,

Kaisergruft, and Augustinian Church).

Eating at the Hofburg: Down the tunnel to Heroes' Square is a tiny but handy sandwich bar called **Hofburg Stüberl** (same €2.50 sandwich price whether you sit or go, Mon–Fri 7:00–18:00, Sat–Sun 10:00–16:00). For a cheap, quick meal, duck into **Restaurant zum Alten Hofkeller** in a cellar under the palace (€5 plates, Mon–Fri 7:30–14:30, closed Sat–Sun and in Aug, cafeteria-style, mod and efficient, Schauflergasse 7).

▲▲▲**Imperial Apartments (Kaiserappartements)**—These lavish, Versailles-type, "wish-I-were-God" royal rooms are the downtown version of the grander Schönbrunn Palace. If you're rushed and have time for only one palace, do this. Palace visits are a one-way romp through three sections: the luxurious Imperial Apartments themselves, the Sisi Museum dedicated to the troubled empress, and a porcelain and silver collection.

The Imperial Apartments are a mix of Old World luxury and modern 19th-century convenience. Here, Emperor Franz Josef I lived and worked along with his wife, Sisi. The Sisi Museum traces the development of her legend, analyzing how her fabulous but tragic life created a 19th-century Princess Diana. You'll read bits of her poetic writing, see exact copies of her now-lost jewelry, and learn about her escapes, dieting mania, and chocolate bills.

Cost, Hours, Location: €10, includes well-done audioguide, daily July–Aug 9:00–18:00, Sept–June 9:00–17:00, last entry 30 min before closing, from courtyard through St. Michael's Gate— just off Michaelerplatz, tel. 01/533-7570, www.hofburg-wien.at.

✪ See the Hofburg Imperial Apartments Tour, page 109.

▲▲▲**Hofburg Treasury (Weltliche und Geistliche Schatzkammer)**—One of the world's most stunning collections of royal regalia, the Hofburg Treasury shows off sparkling crowns, jewels, gowns, and assorted Habsburg bling in 21 darkened rooms. The treasures, well-explained by an audioguide, include the crown of the Holy Roman Emperor, Charlemagne's saber, a unicorn horn, and more precious gems than you can shake a scepter at.

Cost, Hours, Information: €10, €18 combo-ticket with Kunsthistorisches Museum, Wed–Mon 10:00–18:00, closed Tue; from the Hofburg's central courtyard, follow *Schatzkammer* signs to the Schweizerhof; tel. 01/525-240, www.khm.at. While no English descriptions are provided within the Treasury, the well-produced, €3 audioguide provides a wealth of information and is worth renting.

✪ See the Hofburg Treasury Tour, page 121.

▲▲**Hofburg New Palace Museums: Armor, Music, and Ancient Greek Statues**—The New Palace (Neue Burg) houses three separate collections, all included in a single ticket price—an armory (with a killer collection of medieval weapons), historical

Vienna at a Glance

▲▲▲**St. Stephen's Cathedral** Enormous, historic Gothic cathedral in the center of Vienna. **Hours:** Church doors open Mon–Sat 6:00–22:00, Sun 7:00–22:00; nave open for tourists only Mon–Sat 9:00–11:30 & 13:30–16:30, Sun 13:00–16:30. South tower climbable daily 9:00–17:30; elevator up shorter north tower runs daily July–Aug 8:30–18:00, April–June and Sept–Oct 8:30–17:30, Nov–March 8:30–17:00. See page 41.

▲▲▲**Opera** Dazzling, world-famous opera house. **Hours:** Visit the Opera by guided 50-minute tour only, nearly daily in English; generally July–Aug at 11:00, 13:00, 14:00, 15:00, and often at 10:00 and 16:00; Sept–June fewer tours, afternoon only; call ahead to confirm tour times or check out daily schedule in red on door. Opera Museum open Tue–Sun 10:00–18:00, closed Mon. See page 41.

▲▲▲**Hofburg Palace's Imperial Apartments** Lavish main residence of the Habsburgs. **Hours:** Daily July–Aug 9:00–18:00, Sept–June 9:00–17:00. See page 45.

▲▲▲**Hofburg Palace's Treasury** The Habsburgs' collection of jewels, crowns, and other valuables—the best on the Continent. **Hours:** Wed–Mon 10:00–18:00, closed Tue. See page 45.

▲▲▲**Kunsthistorisches Museum** World-class exhibit of the Habsburgs' art collection, including Raphael, Titian, Caravaggio, Bosch, and Brueghel. **Hours:** Tue–Sun 10:00–18:00, Thu until 21:00, closed Mon. See page 55.

▲▲▲**Schönbrunn Palace's Royal Apartments** Spectacular summer residence of the Habsburgs, similar in grandeur to Versailles. **Hours:** Daily July–Aug 8:30–18:00, April–June and Sept–Oct 8:30–17:00, Nov–March 8:30–16:30, reservations recommended. See page 72.

▲▲**Hofburg's New Palace Museums** Uncrowded collection of armor, musical instruments, and ancient Greek statues, in the elegant halls of a Habsburg palace. **Hours:** Wed–Mon 10:00–18:00, closed Tue. See page 45.

▲▲**Albertina Museum** Habsburg residence with decent apartments and world-class temporary exhibits. **Hours:** Daily 10:00–18:00, Wed until 21:00. See page 48.

▲▲**Kaisergruft** Crypt for the Habsburg royalty. **Hours:** Daily 10:00–18:00. See page 49.

▲▲**Haus der Musik** Modern museum with interactive exhibits on Vienna's favorite pastime. **Hours:** Daily 10:00–22:00. See page 52.

▲▲**Belvedere Palace** Elegant palace of Prince Eugene of Savoy, with a collection of 19th- and 20th-century Austrian art (including Klimt). **Hours:** Daily 10:00–18:00. See page 63.

▲**Spanish Riding School** Prancing white Lipizzaner stallions. **Hours:** Spring and fall only, performances Sun at 11:00 and either Sat at 11:00 or Fri at 19:00, practice sessions Tue–Sat 10:00–12:00. See page 51.

▲**Natural History Museum** Big building facing Kunsthistorisches Museum, featuring the ancient *Venus of Willendorf*. **Hours:** Wed-Mon 9:00–18:30, Wed until 21:00, closed Tue. See page 55.

▲**Karlskirche** Baroque church with close-up look at restoration. **Hours:** Mon–Sat 9:00–18:00, Sun 13:00–18:00. See page 57.

▲**Academy of Fine Arts** Small but exciting collection by 15th- to 18th-century masters. **Hours:** Tue–Sun 10:00–18:00, closed Mon and Aug 2009–Sept 2010 or later. See page 58.

▲**The Secession** Art Nouveau exterior and Klimt paintings *in situ*. **Hours:** Tue–Sun 10:00–18:00, Thu until 20:00, closed Mon. See page 59.

▲**Naschmarkt** Sprawling, lively, people-filled outdoor market. **Hours:** Mon–Fri 6:00–18:30, Sat 6:00–17:00, closed Sun, closes earlier in winter. See page 62.

▲**Imperial Furniture Collection** Eclectic collection of Habsburg furniture. **Hours:** Tue–Sun 10:00–18:00, closed Mon. See page 68.

▲**Liechtenstein Museum** Impressive Baroque collection. **Hours:** Fri–Tue 10:00–17:00, closed Wed–Thu. See page 69.

▲**KunstHausWien** Modern art museum dedicated to zany local artist/environmentalist Hundertwasser. **Hours:** Daily 10:00–19:00. See page 69.

▲**Prater** Beloved amusement park with landmark Ferris wheel. **Hours:** Rides operate daily until late. See page 74.

SIGHTS IN VIENNA

musical instruments, and classical statuary from ancient Ephesus. The included audioguide brings the exhibits to life and lets you hear the collection's fascinating old instruments being played. An added bonus is the chance to wander alone among the royal Habsburg halls, stairways, and painted ceilings.

The Arms and Armor Collection displays weaponry and body armor from all over the vast Habsburg empire, including exotic Turkish suits of armor. Long after gunpowder had rendered medieval weaponry obsolete, the Habsburgs staunchly maintained the knightly code of chivalry, and celebrated family events with tournaments and jousts.

The Ancient Musical Instruments Collection shows instruments through the ages, especially the rapid evolution from harpsi-

chord to piano. In the 19th century, Vienna was the world's musical capital. Admire Beethoven's (supposed) clarinet, Leopold Mozart's violin, a keyboard perhaps played by Wolfgang Mozart, and Brahms' piano.

The Ephesus Museum has Greek artifacts from the bustling ancient city of 300,000 people (located in modern-day Turkey, near Kuşadası on the southwestern coast). The *Bronze Statue of an Athlete* is a jigsaw of 234 shattered pieces meticulously put back together. Look at the scale model of the city of Ephesus; you can make out the theater, the stadium, and—in the middle of an open plain—the Temple of Artemis that is now in the museum's collection. The *Statue of Artemis* from the temple, representing a fertility goddess, is draped with round objects—which may have symbolized breasts, eggs, fruits, or bulls' testicles (€8, Wed–Mon 10:00–18:00, closed Tue, last entry 30 min before closing, almost no tourists, tel. 01/525-240, www.khm.at).

▲▲**Albertina Museum**—This building, at the southern tip of the Hofburg complex (near the Opera), was the residence of Maria Teresa's favorite daughter: Maria Christina, who was the only one allowed to marry for love rather than political strategy. Her many sisters were jealous. (Marie-Antoinette had to marry the French king...and lost her head over it.) Maria Christina's husband, Albert of Saxony, was a great collector of original drawings, and amassed an enormous assortment of works by Dürer, Rembrandt, Rubens, Schiele, and others. Today, reproductions of some of these works hang in the Albertina's elegant French-Classicist–style state rooms *(Prunkräume)*. Head here first—this offers a great opportunity to wander freely under the chandeliers of a Habsburg palace, unconstrained by velvet ropes. Then browse the modern galleries, which hold a rotating exhibit from the museum's Batliner collection of modern art (with minor works by major artists—Monet, Picasso, Chagall, Matisse), along with temporary exhibits. Though the entry fee is a bit steep, the Albertina's temporary exhibits are often top-notch—if you're unsure whether it's worth the admission fee, check flyers and posters around town to see what's on.

Cost, Hours, Location: €9.50, price can vary based on special exhibits, audioguide-€4, daily 10:00–18:00, Wed until 21:00, overlooking Albertinaplatz across from the TI and Opera, tel. 01/534-830, www.albertina.at.

▲▲**Kaisergruft, the Remains of the Habsburgs**—Visiting the imperial remains is not as easy as you might imagine. These original organ donors left their bodies—about 150 in all—in the unassuming Kaisergruft (the Imperial Crypt at the Capuchin Church), their hearts in the Augustinian Church (described below; church open long hours daily), and their entrails in the crypt below St. Stephen's Cathedral. Don't tripe.

Cost, Hours, Location: €4, daily 10:00–18:00, last entry at 17:40, behind the Opera on Neuer Markt, tel. 01/512-6853. As you enter, be sure to buy the €0.50 map with a Habsburg family tree and a chart locating each coffin.

Highlights: The double coffin of **Maria Theresa** (1717–1780) and her husband, **Franz I** (1708–1765), is worth a close look for its artwork. Maria Theresa outlived her husband by 15 years—which she spent in mourning. Old and fat, she installed a special lift enabling her to get down into the crypt to be with her dear, departed Franz (even though he had been far from faithful). The couple recline—Etruscan-style—atop their fancy lead coffin. At each corner are the crowns of the Habsburgs—the Holy Roman Empire, Hungary, Bohemia, and Jerusalem. Notice the contrast between the Rococo splendor of Maria Theresa's tomb and the simple box holding her more modest son, **Josef II** (at his parents' feet; for more on Maria Theresa and Joe II, see the sidebar on the following page, and the Habsburg family tree on page 367).

Franz Josef (1830–1916; see sidebar on page 115) is nearby,

in an appropriately austere military tomb. Flanking Franz Josef are the tombs of his son, the archduke **Rudolf,** and Empress Elisabeth. Rudolf and his teenage mistress supposedly committed suicide together in 1889 at Mayerling hunting lodge and—since the Church figured he forced her and was therefore a murderer—it took considerable legal

Empress Maria Theresa (1717–1780) and Her Son, Emperor Josef II (1741–1790)

Maria Theresa was the only woman to officially rule the Habsburg Empire in that family's 640-year reign. She was a strong and effective empress (r. 1740–1780). People are quick to remember Maria Theresa as the mother of 16 children (10 survived into adulthood). Imagine that the most power-ful woman in Europe either was pregnant or had a newborn for most of her reign. Maria Theresa ruled after the Austrian defeat of the Ottomans, when Europe recognized Austria as a great power. (Her rival, the Prussian emperor, said, "When at last the Habsburgs get a great man, it's a woman.") For an abridged Habsburg family tree, see page 367.

The last of the Baroque imperial rulers, and the first of the modern rulers of the Age of Enlightenment, Maria Theresa marked the end of the feudal system and the beginning of the era of the grand state. She was a great social reformer. During her reign, she avoided wars and expanded her empire by skill-fully marrying her children into the right families. For instance, after daughter Marie-Antoinette's marriage into the French Bourbon family (to Louis XVI), a country that had been an enemy became an ally. (Unfortunately for Marie-Antoinette, Maria Theresa's timing was off.)

To stay in power during the age of revolution, Maria Theresa had to be in tune with her age. She taxed the Church and the nobility, provided six years of obligatory education to all children, and granted free health care to all in her realm. Maria Theresa also welcomed the boy genius Mozart into her court.

The empress' legacy lived on in her son, Josef II, who ruled as emperor himself for a decade (1780–1790). He was an even more avid reformer, building on his mother's accom-plishments. An enlightened monarch, Josef mothballed the too-extravagant Schönbrunn Palace, secularized the monas-teries, established religious tolerance within his realm, freed the serfs, made possible the founding of Austria's first general hospital, and promoted relatively enlightened treatment of the mentally ill. Josef was a model of practicality (for example, reusable coffins à la *Amadeus,* and no more than six candles at funerals)—and very unpopular with other royals. But his policies succeeded in preempting the revolutionary anger of the age, enabling Austria to avoid the turmoil that shook so much of the rest of Europe.

hair-splitting to win Rudolf this spot (after examining his brain, it was determined that he was mentally disabled and therefore incapable of knowingly killing himself and his girl). *Kaiserin* Elisabeth (1837–1898), a.k.a. **Sisi,** always gets the "Most Flowers" award (see sidebar on page 112).

In front of those three are the two most recent Habsburg tombs. **Empress Zita** was laid to rest here in 1989, followed by her son, **Karl Ludwig,** in 2007. The funeral procession for Ludwig, the fourth son of the last Austrian emperor, was probably the last such Old Regime event in European history. The monarchy died hard in Austria. Today there are about 700 living Habsburg royals, mostly living in exile. When they die, they get buried in their countries of exile.

Body parts and ornate tombs aside, the real legacy of the Habsburgs is the magnificence of this city. Step outside. Pan up. Watch the clouds glide by the ornate gables of Vienna.

▲**Spanish Riding School**—Seats for performances by Vienna's renowned Lipizzaner stallions book up months in advance, but standing room is sometimes available the same day (tickets-€35–165, standing room-€20–28, March–June and Sept–Dec Sun at 11:00 and either Sat at 11:00 or Fri at 19:00, fewer shows in Feb, none in Jan or July–Aug, tel. 01/533-9031, www.srs.at). Luckily for the masses, training sessions with music in a chandeliered Baroque hall are open to the public (€12 at the door, roughly March–June and mid-Aug–Dec Tue–Sat 10:00–12:00—but only when the horses are in town).

Tourists line up early at Josefsplatz (the large courtyard between Michaelerplatz and Albertinaplatz), at the door marked *Spanische Hofreitschule.* If you want to hang out with tour groups, get there early and wait for the doors to open at 10:00. Better yet, simply show up late. Almost no one stays for the full two hours— except for the horses. As people leave, new tickets are printed continuously, so you can just prance in with no wait at all. Don't have high expectations, as the horses often do little more than trot and warm up.

▲**Augustinian Church (Augustinerkirche)**—This is the Gothic and Neo-Gothic church where the Habsburgs latched, then buried, their hearts (weddings took place here, and the royal hearts are in the vault). Don't miss the exquisite, tomb-like Canova memorial (Neoclassical, 1805) to Maria Theresa's favorite daughter, Maria Christina, with its incredibly sad white-marble procession. The church's 11:00 Sunday Mass is a hit with music-lovers—both a Mass and a concert, often with an orchestra accompanying the choir. To pay, contribute to the offering plate and buy a CD afterwards. Programs are posted by the entry (church open long hours daily, Augustinerstrasse 3).

The church faces Josefsplatz, with its statue of the great reform emperor Josef II. Next to the Augustinian Church, the **National Library** and its State Hall are impressive (€7, Tue–Sun 10:00–18:00, Thu until 21:00, closed Mon).

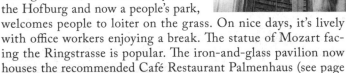

Burggarten (Palace Garden)— This greenbelt, once the backyard of the Hofburg and now a people's park, welcomes people to loiter on the grass. On nice days, it's lively with office workers enjoying a break. The statue of Mozart facing the Ringstrasse is popular. The iron-and-glass pavilion now houses the recommended Café Restaurant Palmenhaus (see page

158) and a small but fluttery butterfly exhibit (€5.50; April–Oct Mon–Fri 10:00–16:45, Sat–Sun 10:00–18:15; Nov–March daily 10:00–15:45). The butterfly zone is delightfully muggy on a brisk off-season day, and trippy any time of year. If you tour it, notice the butterflies hanging out on the trays with rotting slices of banana. They lick the fermented banana juice as it beads, and then just hang out there in a stupor...or fly giddy loop-de-loops.

More Sights Inside the Ring

▲▲**Haus der Musik**—Vienna's "House of Music" has a small first-floor exhibit on the Vienna Philharmonic, and upstairs you'll enjoy fine audiovisual exhibits on each of the famous hometown boys (Haydn, Mozart, Beethoven, Strauss, and Mahler). But the museum is unique for its effective use of interactive touch-screen computers and headphones to explore the physics of sound. You can twist, dissect, and bend sounds to make your own musical language, merging your voice with a duck's quack or a city's traffic roar. Wander through the "sonosphere" and marvel at the amazing acoustics—I could actually hear what I thought only a piano tuner could hear. Pick up a virtual baton to conduct the Vienna Philharmonic Orchestra (each time you screw up, the musicians put their instruments down and ridicule you). Really experiencing the place takes time. It's open late and makes a good evening activity (€10, €15 combo-ticket with Mozarthaus, daily 10:00–22:00, last entry 1 hr before closing, 2 blocks from the Opera at Seilerstätte 30, tel. 01/51648, www.hdm.at).

▲**Vienna's Auction House, the Dorotheum**—For an aristocrat's flea market, drop by Austria's answer to Sotheby's, the Dorotheum. Its five floors of antique furniture and fancy knick-knacks have been put up either for immediate sale or auction, often by people who inherited old things they don't have room for. Wandering through here, you feel like you're touring a museum with exhibits you can buy (Mon–Fri 10:00–18:00, Sat 9:00–17:00, closed Sun, classy little café on second floor, between the Graben pedestrian street and Hofburg at Dorotheergasse 17, tel. 01/51560, www.dorotheum.com). The info desk on the ground floor has a building map and schedule of upcoming auctions. Labels on each item predict the auction value. Continue your hunt for the perfect curio on the streets around the Dorotheum, lined with many fine antique shops.

St. Peter's Church (Peterskirche)—Baroque Vienna is at its best in this gem, tucked away a few steps from the Graben.

Admire the rose-and-gold, oval-shaped Baroque interior, topped with a ceiling fresco of Mary kneeling to be crowned by Jesus and the Father, while the dove of the Holy Spirit floats way up in the lantern. Taken together, the church's elements—especially the organ, altar painting, pulpit, and coat of arms (in the base of the dome) of church founder Leopold I—make St. Peter's one of the city's most beautiful and ornate churches.

To the right of the altar, a dramatic golden statue shows the martyrdom of St. John Nepomuk (c. 1340–1393). The Czech saint defied the heretical King Wenceslas, so he was tossed to his death off the Charles Bridge in Prague. In true Baroque style, we see the dramatic peak of his fall, when John has just passed the point of no return. The Virgin Mary floats overhead in a silver cloud.

The present church (from 1733) stands atop earlier churches dating back 1,600 years. On either side of the nave are glass cases containing skeletons of Christian martyrs from Roman times. Above the relic on the left is a painting of the modern saint Josemaria Escriva, founder of the conservative Catholic organization Opus Dei, of *Da Vinci Code* notoriety (free, church open Mon–Fri 7:00–19:00, Sat–Sun 9:00–19:00; organ concert Mon–Fri at 15:00, Sat–Sun at 20:00; just off the Graben between the Plague Monument and Kohlmarkt, tel. 01/533-6433).

Mozarthaus—Opened in 2006 to commemorate Wolfgang's 250th birthday, this museum is easy to get excited about, but it disappoints. Exhibits fill the only surviving Mozart residence in

Vienna, where he lived from 1784 to 1787, when he had lots of money. You'll learn his life story, with an emphasis on his most creative years...when he lived here. Included is a rundown on the Vienna music scene during the Mozart years, a quirky look at his gambling habits and his interest in crudely erotic peep shows, and a four-minute montage of his most famous arias in a mini-theater. Unfortunately, visiting the museum is like reading a book standing up—rather than turning pages, you climb stairs. There are almost no real artifacts. Wolfie would have found the audioguide dreadful. While the museum might be worth the time and money for Mozart enthusiasts, both Mozart sights in Salzburg (the Birthplace and the Residence—see Salzburg chapter) are more gratifying. In Vienna, I enjoy the Haus der Musik (described previously) much more (€9, €15 combo-ticket with Haus der Musik, daily 10:00–19:00, a block behind the cathedral, go through arcade at #5 and walk 50 yards to Domgasse 5, tel. 01/512-1791, www.mozarthausvienna.at).

Judenplatz Memorial and Museum—The classy square called Judenplatz marks the location of Vienna's 15th-century Jewish community, one of Europe's largest at the time. The square, once filled with a long-gone synagogue, is now dominated by a blocky memorial to the 65,000 Austrian Jews killed by the Nazis. The memorial—a library turned inside out—symbolizes Jews as "people of the book" and causes viewers to ponder the huge loss of culture, knowledge, and humanity that took place between 1938 and 1945.

The Judenplatz Museum, while sparse, has displays on medi-eval Jewish life and a well-done video re-creating the ghetto as it looked five centuries ago. (If you're skipping the museum, at least pop into its entry hall to check the model of Vienna as it was in the 1500s.) Wander the scant remains of the medieval synagogue below street level—discovered during the construction of the Holocaust memorial. This was the scene of a medieval massacre. Since Christians weren't allowed to lend money, Jews were Europe's moneylenders. As so often happened in Europe, when Viennese Christians fell too deeply into debt, they found a convenient excuse to wipe out the local ghetto—and their debts at the same time. In 1421, 200 of Vienna's Jews were burned at the stake. Others who refused a forced conversion committed mass suicide in the synagogue (€4, Sun–Thu 10:00–18:00, Fri 10:00–14:00, closed Sat, Judenplatz 8, tel. 01/535-0431, www.jmw.at).

Kunsthistorisches Museum and Nearby

▲▲▲**Kunsthistorisches Museum**—This exciting museum, across the Ring from the Hofburg Palace, showcases the grandeur and opulence of the Habsburgs' collected artwork in a grand building (built as a museum in 1888). There are European masterpieces galore, all well-hung on one glorious floor, plus a fine display of Egyptian, classical, and applied arts.

Cost, Hours, Location: €10, €18 combo-ticket with the Hofburg Treasury, audioguide-€3, Tue–Sun 10:00–18:00, Thu until 21:00, closed Mon, on the Ringstrasse at Maria-Theresien-Platz, U-2 or U-3: Volkstheater/Museumsplatz, tel. 01/525-240, www.khm.at.

✪ See the Kunsthistorisches Museum Tour on page 129.

▲**Natural History Museum**—In the twin building facing the Kunsthistorisches Museum, you'll find moon rocks, dinosaur stuff, and the fist-sized *Venus of Willendorf*—at 25,000 years old, the world's oldest sex symbol. Even though the museum is not glitzy or high-tech, it's a hit with children and scientifically curious grown-ups.

For a quick visit, head first to the *Venus of Willendorf*—she's on the mezzanine level, in Room 11 (from the entrance lobby, climb the stairs, head for the back, and turn left). The four-inch-tall, chubby stone statuette, found in the Danube Valley, is a generic female (no face or feet) resting her hands on her ample breasts. The statue's purpose is unknown, but she may have been a symbol of fertility for our mammoth-hunting ancestors. In Room 10 nearby are big dinosaur skeletons.

For a more chronological visit, start upstairs on the first floor (in Room 21), and follow hundreds of millions of years of evolution—from single cells to sea creatures, reptiles, birds, mammals, and primates. Finish with the hairless primate—man—downstairs in Rooms 11–14.

The collection of rocks (mezzanine, Rooms 1–5, to the right of the entrance lobby) is also impressive, and includes one of the largest collections of meteorites in the world. Of the museum's 20 million objects, you're sure to find something interesting.

Cost, Hours, Information: €8, Wed–Mon 9:00–18:30, Wed until 21:00, closed Tue, on the Ringstrasse at Maria-Theresien-Platz, U-2 or U-3: Volkstheater/Museumsplatz, tel. 01/521-770, www.nhm-wien.ac.at.

MuseumsQuartier—The vast grounds of the former imperial stables now corral several impressive, cutting-edge museums. Walk

into the complex from the Hofburg side, where the main entrance (with visitors center) leads to a big court-yard with cafés, fountains, and ever-changing "installation lounge furniture," all surrounded by the quarter's various museums (behind Kunsthistorisches Museum, U-2 or U-3: Volkstheater/Museumsplatz). Various combo-tickets are available for those interested in more than just the Leopold and Modern Art museums (visit www.mqw.at).

The **Leopold Museum** features several temporary exhibits of modern Austrian art, and a top floor that holds the largest collection of works by Egon Schiele (1890–1918; these works make some people uncomfortable—Schiele's nudes are *really* nude) and a few paintings by Gustav Klimt, Kolo Moser, and Oskar Kokoschka (€10, €3 audioguide—worth it only for enthusiasts, daily 10:00–18:00, Thu until 21:00, tel. 01/525-700, www.leopoldmuseum.org). Note that for these artists, you'll do better in the Belvedere Palace (described on page 63).

The **Museum of Modern Art** (Museum Moderner Kunst Stiftung Ludwig, a.k.a. "MUMOK") is Austria's leading modern-art gallery. It's the striking lava-paneled building—three stories tall and four stories deep, offering seven floors of far-out art that's hard for most visitors to appreciate. This huge, state-of-the-art museum displays revolving exhibits showing off art of the last generation—including Paul Klee, Pablo Picasso, and Pop artists (€9, €2 audioguide has more than you probably want to hear, daily 10:00–18:00, Thu until 21:00, tel. 01/52500, www.mumok.at).

Rounding out the sprawling MuseumsQuartier are an architecture museum, Transeuropa, Electronic Avenue, children's museum, and the Kunsthalle Wien—an exhibition center for contemporary art (€7.50, daily 10:00–19:00, Thu until 22:00, tel. 01/521-8933, www.kunsthallewien.at).

Karlsplatz and Nearby

These sights cluster around Karlsplatz, just southeast of the Ringstrasse (U-1, U-2, or U-4: Karlsplatz). From the U-Bahn station's passageway, it's a 30-minute walk around the sights on Karlsplatz: the Karlskirche, Secession, and Naschmarkt (allow more time to actually visit these sights).

Karlsplatz—This picnic-friendly square, with its Henry Moore sculpture in the pond, is ringed with sights. The massive, domed

Karlskirche and its twin spiral columns dominate the square. The small green, white, and gold pavilions near the church are from the late 19th-century municipal train system *(Stadtbahn)*. One of Europe's first subway systems, this precursor to today's U-Bahn was built with a military purpose in mind: to move troops quickly in time of civil unrest—specifically, out to Schönbrunn Palace. With curvy iron frames, decorative marble slabs, and painted gold trim, these are pioneering works in the *Jugendstil* style, designed by Otto Wagner, who influenced Klimt and the Secessionists. One of the pavilions is open as an exhibit on Otto Wagner (€2, April–Oct Tue–Sun 9:00–18:00, closed Mon and Nov–March, near the Ringstrasse).

▲Karlskirche (St. Charles' Church)—Charles Borromeo, a 16th-century bishop from Milan, was an inspiration during plague

times. This "votive church" was dedicated to him in 1713, when an epidemic spared Vienna. The church offers the best Baroque in Vienna, with a unique combination of columns (showing scenes from the life of Charles Borromeo, à la Trajan's Column in Rome), a classic pediment, and an elliptical dome. But this church is especially worthwhile for the chance (probably through 2010) to see restoration work in progress.

Inside, the fresco in the dome shows Signor Borromeo (in red and white bishops' robes) gazing up into heaven, spreading his arms wide and pleading with Christ to spare Vienna from the plague. The colorful 13,500-square-foot fresco was painted in the 1730s by Johann Michael Rottmayr.

To get a closer look, ride the industrial lift to a platform at the base of the 235-foot dome. (Consider that the church was built

and decorated with a scaffolding system essentially the same as this one.) Once up there, you'll climb stairs to the steamy lantern at the extreme top of the church. At that dizzying height, you're in the clouds with cupids and angels.

Many details that appear smooth and beautiful from ground level—such as gold leaf, paintings, and fake marble—look rough and sloppy up close. It's surreal to observe the 3-D figures from an unintended angle—

check out Christ's leg, which looks dwarf-sized up close. Faith, Hope, and Charity triumph and inspire. Borromeo lobbies heaven for plague relief. Meanwhile, a Protestant's Lutheran Bible is put to the torch by angels. At the very top, you'll see the tiny dove representing the Holy Ghost, surrounded by a cheering squad of nipple-lipped cupids.

Cost and Hours: €6, includes audioguide, visit to renovation site, and skippable one-room museum; Mon–Sat 9:00–18:00, Sun 13:00–18:00, last entry 30 min before closing. The entry fee may seem steep, but remember that it funds the restoration.

Wien Museum Karlsplatz—This underappreciated museum walks you through the history of Vienna with fine historic arti-

facts. You'll work your way up, chronologically: The ground floor exhibits Roman artifacts and original statues from St. Stephen's Cathedral (c. 1350), with various Habsburgs showing off the slinky hip-hugging fashion of the day. The first floor features old city maps, booty from an Ottoman siege, and an 1850 city model showing the town just before the wall was replaced by the Ring. Finally, the second floor displays a city model from 1898 (with the new Ringstrasse), sentimental Biedermeier paintings and objets d'art, and early 20th-century paintings (including some by Gustav Klimt). The museum is worth the €6 admission (free Sun, open Tue–Sun 9:00–18:00, closed Mon, www.wienmuseum.at).

▲Academy of Fine Arts (Akademie der Bildenden Künste) The exciting regular collection goes back on display in Fall 2010, with works by Bosch, Botticelli, and Rubens (quick, sketchy cartoons used to create his giant canvases); a Venice series by Guardi; and a self-portrait by a 15-year-old van Dyck. It's all magnificently lit and well-described by the €2.50 audioguide, and comes with comfy chairs.

The fact that this is a working art academy gives it a certain realness. As you wander the halls of the academy, ponder how history might have been different if Hitler—who applied to study architecture here but was rejected—had been accepted as a student. Before leaving, peek into the ground floor's central hall—textbook Historicism, the Ringstrasse style of the late 1800s.

Cost, Hours, Location: Likely €7 (price may change when museum reopens in Fall 2010 after a two-year renovation), Tue–Sun 10:00–18:00, closed Mon, 3 blocks from the Opera at Schillerplatz 3, tel. 01/588-162-222, www.akademiegalerie.at.

▲The Secession—This little building, behind the Academy

of Fine Arts, was created by the Vienna Secession movement, a group of nonconformist artists led by Gustav Klimt, Otto Wagner,

and friends. (For more on the art movement, see the sidebar on the next page.)

The young trees carved into the walls and its bushy "golden cabbage" rooftop (see photo, next page) are symbolic of a renewal cycle. Today, the Secession continues to showcase cutting-edge art, as well as one of Gustav Klimt's most famous works, the *Beethoven Frieze*.

Cost, Hours, Location: €3.50, but temporary exhibits often boost the price to €6, Tue–Sun 10:00–18:00, Thu until 20:00, closed Mon, Friedrichstrasse 12, tel. 01/587-5307, www .secession.at.

◑ Self-Guided Tour: While the staff hopes you take a look at the temporary exhibits (and the ticket includes this price whether you like it or not), most tourists head directly for the basement, home to a small exhibit about the history of the building and the museum's highlight: Klimt's classic *Beethoven Frieze* (a.k.a. the "Searching Souls").

One of the masterpieces of Viennese Art Nouveau, this 105-foot-long fresco was the multimedia centerpiece of a 1902 exhibition honoring Ludwig van Beethoven. Sit down and read the free flier, which explains Klimt's still-powerful work, inspired by Beethoven's Ninth Symphony. Working clockwise around the room, follow Klimt's story:

Left Wall: Floating female figures drift and weave and search—like we all do—for happiness. Unfortunately, their aspirations are dashed and brought to earth, leaving them kneeling and humble. They plead for help from heroes stronger than themselves—represented by the firm knight in gold, who revives their hopes and helps them carry on.

Center Wall: The women encounter many obstacles in their pursuit of happiness—the three dangerous Gorgons (naked ladies), the gorilla-faced monster of fear, and the three seductive women of temptation. These obstacles can leave us bent over with grief (like the woman on the right) while our hopes pass by overhead.

Right Wall: But we can still find happiness through art, thanks to Lady Poetry (with the lyre) and the great hero of

Art Nouveau (a.k.a. *Jugendstil* or the Vienna Secession), c. 1896–1914

As Europe approached the dawn of a new *(nouveau)* century, it embraced a new art: Art Nouveau.

On the one hand, it was very forward-looking and modern, embracing the new technology of iron and glass. But Art Nouveau was also a reaction against the sheer ugliness of the mass-produced, boxy, rigidly geometrical art of the Industrial Age. Art Nouveau artists returned to nature (which abhors a straight line), and were inspired by the curves of plants. And as in nature, no two objects are exactly the same, leaving the artist free to make his work unique.

Art Nouveau street lamps twist and bend like flower stems. Ironwork fountains sprout buds that squirt water. Dining rooms are paneled with leafy garlands of carved wood. Advertising posters feature flowery typefaces and beautiful young women rendered in pure, curving lines. A hit with interior decorators, Art Nouveau was a total "look" that could be applied to furniture, jewelry, paintings, and the building itself.

Though the Art Nouveau movement began in Paris and Belgium, each country gave it its own spin. In German-speaking lands (including Austria), Art Nouveau was called *Jugendstil* (meaning "youth style").

The innovators in Vienna called their particular *Jugendstil* movement The Secession, named for the daring artists who "seceded" from tradition. They turned their backs on Vienna's centuries-long love affair with Baroque, Rococo, and Neoclassical styles. They preferred buildings that were simple and geometrically pure, which they then decorated with a few unadulterated Art Nouveau touches. Various artists were part of this movement. Architects, painters, and poets had no single unifying style, except a commitment to what was new. The Secessionist motto was: "To each age its art, and to art its liberty."

The TI has a brochure laying out Vienna's 20th-century architecture. Here are some of the best of Vienna's scattered *Jugendstil* sights:

The Secession: This clean-lined building at the Ring end of the Naschmarkt (see previous page) was the headquarters of the

the arts: Beethoven. In the original 1902 exhibition, a statue of Beethoven appeared at this crucial turning point in the narrative, where the blank space is today. Klimt's painting was displayed on separate screens, and visitors could look through a gap to catch glimpses of the star of the exhibition, Beethoven.

Beethoven's presence inspires the yearning souls to carry on, and they finally reach true happiness, represented by Mr. Poetry. At the climax of the frieze, a naked couple embraces in ecstasy as a heavenly choir sings the "Ode to Joy" from the Ninth Symphony:

group of artists calling them-selves The Secession. It's nick-named the "golden cabbage" for its bushy gilded rooftop (actually, those are the lau-rel leaves of Apollo, the God of Poetry) designed by the painter Gustav Klimt. It was here that young artists first exhibited their "youth-style" art in 1897. In the basement is Klimt's *Beethoven Frieze*.

Belvedere Palace: This museum's collection includes work by Secessionist leader and poster boy Gustav Klimt (1862–1917). He gained fame painting slender young women entwined together in florid embrace, exploring the highly charged erotic terrain of his contemporary, Sigmund Freud. Klimt took the decorative element of Art Nouveau to extremes. In many of his paintings, only the face and bits of body show through gilded ornamental friezes. The two lovers of *The Kiss* are wrapped up in the colorful gold-and-jeweled cloak of bliss (for more about the palace, see page 63).

The Anchor Clock on Hoher Markt: This mosaic-decorated clock (1911–1917) spans two buildings and does a musical act at noon. The clock honors 12 great figures from Vienna's history, from Marcus Aurelius to Joseph Haydn. While each gets his own top-of-the-hour moment, all parade by at high noon. A plaque on the left names each figure. Notice the novel way to mark the time.

Karlsplatz: Otto Wagner (1841–1918), Vienna's premier *Jugendstil* architect, designed several structures for Vienna's subway system, including the original arched entrances (see page 56).

"Joy, you beautiful spark of the gods...under thy gentle wings, all men shall become brothers."

Glass Cases: These show sketches Klimt did in preparation for this work. Klimt embellished the painting with painted-on gold (his brother and colleague was a goldsmith), and by gluing on reflecting glass and mother-of-pearl for the ladies' dresses and jewelry. The adjacent room tells the history of this masterpiece (transferred from screens to the Secession walls), and how the building was damaged in World War II.

▲**Naschmarkt**—In 1898, the city decided to cover up its Vienna River. The long, wide square they created was filled with a lively pro-

duce market that still bustles most days (closed Sun). It's long been known as *the* place to get exotic faraway foods. In fact, locals say, "From here start the Balkans."

From near the Opera, the Naschmarkt (roughly, "Munchies Market") stretches along Wienzeile street. This "Belly of Vienna" comes with two parallel lanes— one lined with fun and reasonable

eateries, and the other featuring the town's top-end produce and gourmet goodies. This is where top chefs like to get their ingredients. At the gourmet vinegar stall, you sample the vinegar like perfume—with a drop on your wrist (see photo). Farther from the center, the Naschmarkt becomes likeably seedy and surrounded by sausage stands, Turkish *Döner Kebab* stalls, cafés, and theaters. At the market's far end is a line of buildings with fine Art Nouveau facades. Each Saturday, the Naschmarkt is infested by a huge flea market where, in olden days, locals would come to hire a monkey to pick little critters out of their hair (Mon–Fri 6:00–18:30, Sat 6:00–17:00, closed Sun, closes earlier in winter; U-1, U-2, or U-4: Karlsplatz). For a picnic in the park, pick up your grub here and walk over to Karlsplatz (described on page 56).

Museum of Applied Art

The Österreichisches Museum für Angewandte Kunst, or MAK, is Vienna's answer to London's Victoria and Albert Museum. It shows off the fancies of local aristocratic society, including a fine *Jugendstil* collection.

The MAK is more than just another grand building on the Ringstrasse. It was built to provide models of historic design for Ringstrasse architects, and is a delightful space in itself (many locals stop in to enjoy a coffee on the plush couches in the main lobby). Each wing is dedicated to a different era. Exhibits, well-described in English, come with a playful modern flair—notable modern designers were assigned various spaces.

Cost, Hours, Location: €8, €10 includes a hefty English guidebook, free on Sat, open Tue–Sun 10:00–18:00, Tue until 24:00, closed Mon, Stubenring 5, tel. 01/711-360, www.mak.at.

The associated **Restaurant Österreicher im MAK** is named for a chef renowned for his classic and modern Viennese cuisine. Classy and mod, it's trendy for locals (open daily, reserve for evening, €10–15 plates).

Beyond the Ring

The following museums are located outside the Ringstrasse but inside the Gürtel, or outer ring road.

▲▲**Belvedere Palace**—This is the elegant palace of Prince Eugène of Savoy (1663–1736), the still-much-appreciated conqueror of the Ottomans. Eugène, a Frenchman considered too short and too ugly to be in the service of Louis XIV, offered his services to the Habsburgs. While he was indeed short and ugly, he became the greatest military genius of his age and the toast of Viennese society. When you conquer cities, as Eugène did, you get really rich.

He had no heirs, so the state got his property and Emperor Josef II established the Belvedere as Austria's first great public art gallery.

You can tour the lavish palace, see sweeping views of the gardens and the Vienna skyline, and enjoy world-class art starring Gustav Klimt, French Impressionism, and a grab-bag of other 19th- and early-20th-century artists.

Cost, Hours, Information: €9.50 for Upper Belvedere Palace only, €12.50 for Upper and Lower palaces—not worth it, audio-guide-€3, daily 10:00–18:00, no photos allowed inside, entrance at Prinz-Eugen-Strasse 27, tel. 01/7955-7134, www.belvedere.at.

Location: The palace is a 15-minute walk south of the Ring. To get there from the center, catch tram #D at the Opera (direction Südbahnhof; it stops at the palace gate).

○ Self-Guided Tour: The Belvedere Palace is actually two grand buildings—the Upper Palace and Lower Palace—separated by a fine garden. For our purposes, the Upper Palace is what matters. The palace's eclectic collection is tailor-made for browsing. Here's a plan to get you started:

First Floor—Marble Hall: From the entrance, climb the staircase to the first floor and enter the grand red-and-gold, chandeliered Marble Hall. This was Prince Eugène's party room. The ceiling fresco shows Eugène (in the center, wearing blue and pink) about to be crowned with a laurel wreath for his military victories and contributions to Vienna.

View from the Marble Hall: *Belvedere* means "beautiful view." Look over the Baroque gardens, the mysterious sphinxes (which symbolized solving riddles and the finely educated mind of your host, Eugène), the Lower Palace, and the city. Left to right, find the dome of Karlskirche (through the trees on the left), the green dome of St. Peter's church, the spire of St. Stephen's (where

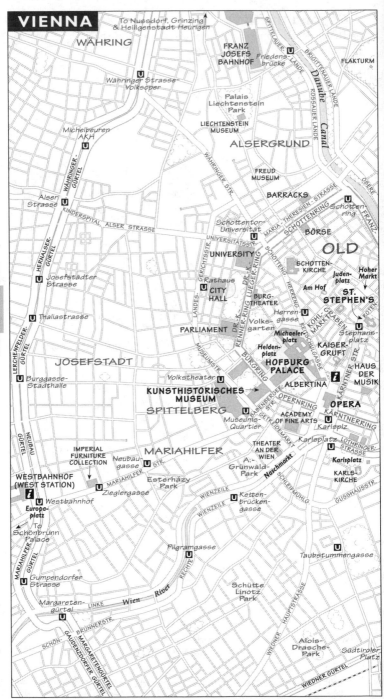

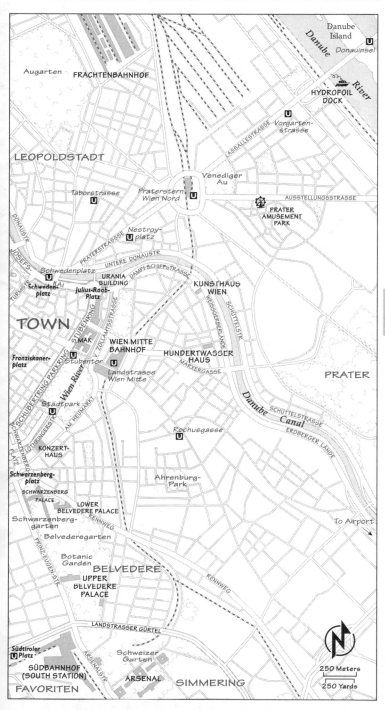

Gustav Klimt
(1862–1918)

Klimt, a noted womanizer, made a career painting the female form as beautiful, seductive, and dangerous. His erotic paint-

ings scandalized official Vienna, and he was a founding member of the Secessionist artists who "seceded" from bourgeois constraints. He dedicated his later years to works commissioned by the liberal elite.

Klimt explored multimedia. Besides oil paints, he painted with gold leaf or applied bright objects to the canvas/panel for decorative effect. He often worked in a square-frame format. (He occasionally made the frames themselves, along with his brother, a gold engraver.) There's no strong 3-D in his paintings; the background and foreground are merged together into a decorative pattern. His women are clearly drawn, emerging from the complex design. With their come-hither looks and erotic poses, they capture the over-ripe beauty and edgy decadence of turn-of-the-century Vienna.

Eugene is buried, see page 41), and the black dome of the Silesian Church. St. Stephen's spire is 400 feet tall, and no other tall buildings are allowed inside the Ringstrasse. The hills— covered with vineyards—are where the Viennese love to go to sample new wine. Beyond the spire you can see Kahlenberg, from where you can walk down to several recommended *Heurigen* (wine gardens—see

page 162). These hills are the beginnings of the Alps, which stretch from here all the way to Marseille, France. The square you're overlooking was filled with people on May 15, 1955, as local leaders stood on the balcony and proclaimed Austrian independence following a decade-long Allied occupation after World War II.

First Floor—East Wing: Alongside Renoir's ladies, Monet's landscapes, and Van Gogh's rough brushstrokes, you'll find similar works by their lesser-known Austrian counterparts. Around

Restitution of Art Stolen by Nazis

The Austrian government has worked diligently to fairly reimburse victims of the Nazis, whose buildings, businesses, personal belongings, and art were taken after the 1938 *Anschluss* (when Germany annexed Austria).

A fund of more than $200 million was established by both the Austrian government and corporations who profited through their collaboration with the Nazis. Surviving locals (mostly Jews) who paid a *Reichsfluchtsteuer* ("tax for fleeing the country") were located and given some money. Former slave laborers were also tracked down and given €5,000 each. (Imagine what an amazing windfall that would be for an 80-year-old Romanian peasant woman.)

Most significantly for sightseers, great art was returned to its rightful owners. The big news for the Vienna art world was the return of several Gustav Klimt paintings, most notably his *Golden Adele,* from Vienna's Belvedere Palace collection to a Jewish woman in California. In 2006, *The Golden Adele* was auctioned off for $135 million, one of the highest prices ever paid for a painting. While the Austrian government wanted to buy it back, it figured she was asking too much for the art and refused to get into a bidding war. Fortunately for art lovers, the most famous Klimt *(The Kiss)* was not involved in the restitution and remains in Vienna's Belvedere Palace.

1900, Austrian artists come to the fore, soaking up Symbolism, Expressionism, and other Modernist trends.

In the two rooms full of sumptuous paintings by Klimt you can get caught up in his fascination with the beauty and danger he saw in women. To Klimt, all art was erotic art. He painted during the turn-of-the-century, when Vienna was a splendid laboratory of hedonism. For Klimt, Eve was the prototypical woman; her body, not the apple, provided the seduction. Frustrated by the censorship of his age, Klimt refused every form of state support. Even fully clothed, his women have a bewitching eroticism in a world full of pollen and pistils.

The famous painting of *Judith I* (1901) shows no biblical heroine—Klimt paints her as a high-society Vienna woman with an ostentatious dog-collar necklace. With half-closed eyes and slightly parted lips, she's dismissive...yet mysterious and bewitching. Holding the head of her biblical victim, she's the modern femme fatale.

In what is perhaps his most well-known painting, *The Kiss,* Klimt's woman is no longer dominating, but submissive, abandoning herself to her man in a fertile field and a vast universe. In a glow emanating from a radiance of desire, the body she presses against is a self-portrait of the artist himself.

Klimt nurtured the next generation of artists, especially Egon Schiele. Don't miss the poignant Schiele family portrait from 1918—his wife died while he was still working on it. (Schiele and his child were soon taken by the influenza epidemic that swept through Europe after World War I.)

The Rest of the Upper Palace: The Belvedere's collection goes through the whole range of 19th- and 20th-century art: Historicism, Romanticism, Impressionism, Realism, tired tourism, Expressionism, Art Nouveau, and early Modernism.

The **second floor** shows off early 19th-century paintings in the Biedermeier style. This was the period (1815–1848) when conservative elements in Central Europe clamped down on Napoleon's Revolutionary ideas. Paintings are realistic portraits, landscapes, and scenes from everyday life and from history. The style is soft-focus, hypersensitive, super-sweet, and sentimentally Romantic—the poor are happy, things are lit impossibly well, and folk life is idealized. (Then came the democratic revolutions of 1848, the invention of the camera, Realism and Impressionism...and all hell broke loose.)

With a combo-ticket, you could also visit the **gardens** and the Austrian Baroque and medieval art in the **Lower Palace.** Prince Eugène lived in that palace, but he's long gone, and I wouldn't bother to visit.

▲**Imperial Furniture Collection (Kaiserliches Hofmobiliendepot)**—Bizarre, sensuous, eccentric, or precious, this collection is your peek at the Habsburgs' furniture—from grandma's wheelchair to the emperor's spittoon—all thoughtfully described in English. The Habsburgs had many palaces, but only the Hofburg was permanently furnished. The rest were furnished on the fly—set up and taken down by a gang of royal roadies called the "Depot of Court Movables" (Hofmobiliendepot). When the monarchy was dissolved in 1918, the state of Austria took possession of the Hofmobiliendepot's inventory—165,000 items. Now this royal storehouse is open to the public in a fine and sprawling museum. Don't go here for the *Jugendstil* furnishings. The older Baroque, Rococo, and Biedermeier pieces are the most impressive and tied most intimately to the royals. Combine a visit to this museum with a stroll down the lively shopping boulevard, Mariahilfer Strasse.

Cost, Hours, Location: €7, Tue–Sun 10:00–18:00, closed Mon, Mariahilfer Strasse 88, U-3: Zieglergasse, tel. 01/5243-3570.

▲**Liechtenstein Museum**—The noble Liechtenstein family (who own only a tiny country, but whose friendship with the Habsburgs goes back generations) amassed an incredible private art collection. Their palace was long a treasure for Vienna art lovers. Then, in 1938—knowing Hitler was intent on plundering artwork to create an immense "Führer Museum"—the family fled to their tiny homeland with their best art. Since the museum reopened in 2004, attendance has been disappointing, but the problem is its location (and perhaps its steep price)...not its worthiness.

The Liechtensteins' "world of Baroque pleasures" includes the family's rare "Golden Carriage" which was used for their grand entry into Paris in 1738. It was carted to the edge of town and assembled there. It's a rare example of the French Rococo style, as nearly all such carriages were destroyed in the French Revolution. The museum also has a plush Baroque library, an inviting English Garden, and an impressive collection of paintings, including a complete cycle of early Rubens.

Cost, Hours, Location: €10, audioguide €1, Fri–Tue 10:00–17:00, last entry 30 min before closing, closed Wed–Thu, tram #D to Bauernfeldplatz, Fürstengasse 1, tel. 01/319-5767-252, www.liechtensteinmuseum.at. The gardens are free and open until 20:30 (but aren't worth the trip on their own).

▲**KunstHausWien: Hundertwasser Museum**—This "make yourself at home" museum and nearby apartment complex are

a hit with lovers of modern art, mixing the work and philosophy of local painter/environmentalist Friedensreich Hundertwasser (1928–2000). Stand in front of the colorful checkerboard building and consider Hundertwasser's style. He was against "window racism": Neighboring houses allow only one kind of window, but 100H$_2$O's windows are each different—and he encouraged residents in the Hundertwasserhaus (a 5–10 minute walk away, see below) to personalize them. He recognized "tree tenants" as well as human tenants. His buildings are spritzed with a forest and topped with dirt and grassy little parks—close to nature and good for the soul.

Floors and sidewalks are irregular—to "stimulate the brain" (although current residents complain it just causes wobbly furniture and sprained ankles). Thus 100H$_2$O waged a one-man fight—during the 1950s and 1960s, when concrete and glass ruled—to save the human soul from the city. (Hundertwasser claimed that "straight lines are godless.")

Inside the museum, start with his interesting biography.

His fun paintings are half psychedelic *Jugendstil* and half just kids' stuff. Notice the photographs from his 1950s days as part of Vienna's bohemian scene. Throughout the museum, keep an eye out for the fun philosophical quotes from an artist who believed, "If man is creative, he comes nearer to his creator."

Cost, Hours, Location: €9 for Hundertwasser Museum, €12 combo-ticket includes special exhibitions, half-price on Mon, open daily 10:00–19:00, extremely fragrant and colorful garden café, Untere Weissgerberstrasse 13, tram #1: Hetzgasse or U-3: Landstrasse—but the tram stop is much closer than the U-Bahn stop, tel. 01/712-0491, www.kunsthauswien.com. To get here from the Landstrasse U-Bahn stop, walk 10 minutes downhill (north) along Untere Viaduktgasse (a block east of the station), or ride tram #0 three stops to Radetzskyplatz; from there signs point to the museum.

Hundertwasserhaus: The KunstHausWien provides by far the best look at Hundertwasser, but for an actual lived-in apart-

ment complex by the green master, walk five minutes to the one-with-nature Hundertwasserhaus (at Löwengasse and Kegelgasse). This complex of 50 apartments was built in the 1980s as a breath of architectural fresh air in a city of boring, blocky apartment complexes. While not open to visitors, it's worth a look from the outside. Don't miss the view from Kegelgasse to see the "tree tenants" and the internal winter garden that residents enjoy.

Hundertwasser detractors—of which there are many—remind visitors that $100H_2O$ was a painter, not an architect. They point out that the Hundertwasserhaus was designed without any real concern about the environment, communal living, or even practical comfort. Almost all of the original inhabitants got fed up with the novelty and moved out.

Sigmund Freud Museum—Freud enthusiasts enjoy seeing the humble apartment and workplace of the man who fundamentally changed our understanding of the human psyche. Dr. Sigmund Freud (1856–1939), a graduate of Vienna University, established his practice here in 1891. For the next 47 years, he received troubled patients who hoped to find peace

by telling him their dreams, life traumas, and secret urges. It was here that he wrote his influential works, including the landmark *Interpretation of Dreams* (1899).

Today, you can walk through his three-room office (but not the apartments next door, where Freud lived with his large family).

The rooms are tiny and disappointingly bare. Freud, who was Jewish, fled Vienna when the Nazis came to power. He took most of his furniture with him, including the famous couch (now in a London museum).

In the entryway, you can see Freud's cane, hat, pocket flask, and a few other objects. The waiting room is the most furnished, with original furniture, his books, and his collection of primitive fertility figurines. The consulting room and study are lined with old photos and documents that trace Freud's fascinating (if Vienna-centric) life: a happy childhood; medical school in the then-pioneering field of psychology; research into the effects of cocaine; a happy marriage, large family, and wholesome middle-class lifestyle; use of hypnosis as therapy; years of self-analysis and first patients in analysis; publication of controversial works on dreams and sexuality; association with other budding psychologists such as the Swiss Carl Jung; and, finally, his hard-earned recognition and worldwide fame.

In other rooms of the museum, you'll find plenty of papers, photos, videos, and temporary exhibits about Freud and cutting-edge psychotherapy. All in all, the museum is quite old-fashioned—tediously described in a three-ring binder loaned to visitors, which complements the more general audioguide.

Cost, Hours, Location: €7, audioguide-€2, daily July–Sept 9:00–18:00, Oct–June 9:00–17:00, cool shop, half a block downhill from the Schlickgasse tram #D stop, Berggasse 19, tel. 01/319-1596, www.freud-museum.at.

Schönbrunn Palace (Schloss Schönbrunn)

Among Europe's palaces, only Schönbrunn rivals Versailles. This former summer residence of the Habsburgs is big, with 1,441 rooms. But don't worry—only 40 rooms are shown to the pub-

lic. Of the plethora of sights at the palace, the highlight is a tour of the Royal Apartments—the chandeliered rooms where the Habsburg nobles lived. You can also stroll

SCHÖNBRUNN PALACE

SIGHTS IN VIENNA

the gardens, tour the coach museum, and visit a handful of lesser sights nearby.

Getting There: Take U-4 to Schönbrunn and walk 400 yards (just follow the crowds). The main entrance is in the left side of the palace as you face it.

▲▲▲**Royal Apartments**—While the exterior is Baroque, the interior was finished under Maria Theresa in let-them-eat-cake Rococo. The chandeliers are either of Bohemian crystal or of hand-carved wood with gold-leaf gilding. Thick walls hid the servants as they ran around stoking the ceramic stoves from the back, and attending to other behind-the-scenes matters. When WWII bombs rained on the city and the palace grounds, the palace itself took only one direct hit. Thankfully, that bomb, which crashed through three floors—including the sumptuous central ballroom—was a dud. Most of the public rooms are decorated in Neo-Baroque, as they were under Franz Josef (r. 1848–1916). The rest of the palace has been converted to simple apartments and rented to the families of 260 civil servants, who enjoy rent control and governmental protections so they can't be evicted.

Cost: The admission price is based on which route you select (each one includes an audioguide): the 22-room **Imperial Tour** (€9.50, 45 min, Grand Palace rooms plus apartments of Franz Josef and Elisabeth—mostly 19th-century and therefore least interesting) or the 40-room **Grand Tour** (€13, 60 min, includes Imperial Tour plus Maria Theresa's apartments—18th-century Rococo). A combo-ticket called the **Schönbrunn Pass Classic** includes the Grand Tour, as well as other sights on the grounds: the Gloriette viewing terrace, maze, privy garden, and court bakery—complete with *Apfelstrudel* demo and tasting (€16, available April–Oct only). I'd go for the Grand Tour.

Hours: Daily July–Aug 8:30–18:00, April–June and Sept–Oct 8:30–17:00, Nov–March 8:30–16:30. Information: www.schoen brunn.at.

Crowd-Beating Tips: Schönbrunn suffers from crowds. It can be a jam-packed sauna in the summer. It's busiest from 9:30 to 11:30, especially on weekends and in July and August; it's least crowded from after 14:00, when there are no groups. To avoid the long delays in summer, make a reservation by telephone a few days in advance (tel. 01/8111-3239, answered daily 8:00–17:00, wait through the long message for the operator). You'll get an appointment time and a ticket number. Check in at least 30 minutes early. Upon arrival, go to the "Group and Reservations" desk (immediately inside the gate on the left at the gate house—long before the actual palace), give your number, pick up your ticket, and jump in ahead of the masses. If you show up in peak season without calling first, you deserve the frustration. (In this case, you'll have to wait in line, buy your ticket, and wait until the listed time to enter—which could be tomorrow.) If you have any time to kill, spend it exploring the gardens or Coach Museum.

Palace Gardens—Unlike the gardens of Versailles, meant to shut out the real world, Schönbrunn's park was opened to the public in 1779 while the monarchy was in full swing. It was part of Maria Theresa's reform policy, making the garden a celebration of the evolution of civilization from autocracy into real democracy.

Most of the park itself is free, as it has been since the 1700s (open daily sunrise to dusk, entrance on either side of the palace). The small side gardens are the most elaborate. The Kammergarten on the left was a fancy private garden for the Habsburgs (now restored and with a fee). The so-called Sisi Gardens on the right are free. Inside are several other sights, including a **palm house** (€4, daily May–Sept 9:30–18:00, Oct–April 9:30–17:00, last entry 30 min before closing); Europe's oldest **zoo**, or *Tiergarten*, built by Maria Theresa's husband for the entertainment and education of the court in 1752 (€12, April–Sept daily 9:00–18:30, closes earlier off-season, tel. 01/877-9294); and—at the end of the gardens—the

Gloriette, a purely decorative monument celebrating an obscure Austrian military victory and offering a fine city view (viewing terrace-€2, included in €16 Schönbrunn Pass Classic, daily April–Sept 9:00–18:00, July–Aug until 19:00, Oct 9:00–17:00, closed Nov–March). A touristy choo-choo train makes the rounds all day, connecting Schönbrunn's many attractions.

Wagenburg Coach Museum—The Schönbrunn coach museum is a 19th-century traffic jam of 50 impressive royal carriages and sleighs. Highlights include silly sedan chairs, the death-black hearse carriage (used for Franz Josef in 1916, and most recently for Empress Zita in 1989), and an extravagantly gilded imperial carriage pulled by eight Cinderella horses. This was rarely used other than for the coronation of Holy Roman Emperors, when it was disassembled and taken to Frankfurt for the big event (€4.50; daily April–Oct 9:00–18:00, Nov–March 10:00–16:00; last entry 30 min before closing, 200 yards from palace, walk through right arch as you face palace, tel. 01/525-24-3470).

ACTIVITIES

People-Watching and Strolling

These activities allow you to take it easy and enjoy the Viennese good life.

▲**Stadtpark (City Park)**—Vienna's major park is a waltzing world of gardens, memorials to local musicians, ponds, peacocks, music in bandstands, and Viennese escaping the city. Notice the *Jugendstil* entrance at the Stadtpark U-Bahn station. The Kursalon, where Strauss was the violin-toting master of waltzing ceremonies, hosts daily touristy concerts in three-quarter time.

▲**Prater**—Since the 1780s, when the reformist Emperor Josef II gave his hunting grounds to the people of Vienna as a public park, this place has been Vienna's playground. While tired and a bit rundown these days, Vienna's sprawling amusement park still tempts visitors with its huge 220-foot-tall, famous, and lazy Ferris wheel *(Riesenrad)*, roller coaster, bumper cars, Lilliputian railroad, and endless eateries. Especially if you're traveling with kids, this is a fun, goofy place to share the evening with thousands of Viennese (rides run May–Sept 9:00–24:00—but quiet after 22:00, March–April and Oct 10:00–22:00, Nov–Dec 10:00–20:00, grounds always open, U-1: Praterstern). For a local-style family dinner, eat at Schweizerhaus (good food, great Czech Budvar—the original "Budweiser"—beer, classic conviviality).

Donauinsel (Danube Island)—In the 1970s, the city dug a canal parallel to the mighty Danube River, creating both a flood barrier and a much-loved island escape from the city (easy U-Bahn access on U-1 to Donauinsel). This skinny, 12-mile long island provides a natural wonderland. All along the traffic-free, grassy park you'll find locals—both Viennese, and especially immigrants and those who can't afford their own cabin or fancy vacation—at play. The swimming comes tough, though, with rocky entries rather than sand. The best activity here is a bike ride (see "Getting Around Vienna—By Bike," page 38). Note that if you venture far from the crowds, you're likely to encounter nudists on inline skates.

▲▲**Cafés**—A break for *Kaffee und Kuchen* (coffee and cake) in one of the city's historical cafés is a must on any Viennese visit (for a list of cafés, see page 161).

▲*Heurigen* **Wine Gardens**—Locals and tourists alike enjoy lingering in these rustic wine gardens in rural neighborhoods, easily accessible by public transportation from downtown Vienna (see page 162).

A Walk in the Vienna Woods (Wienerwald)—For a quick side-trip into the woods and out of the city, catch the U-4 to Heiligenstadt, then bus #38A to Kahlenberg, where you'll enjoy great views and a café overlooking the city. From there, it's a peaceful 45-minute downhill hike to the *Heurigen* of Nussdorf or Grinzing to enjoy some new wine (see "Vienna's Wine Gardens," page 162). Your free TI-produced city map can be helpful...just go downhill.

For the very best views, stay on bus #38A to Leopoldsberg (if your #38A bus goes only to Kahlenberg—see the destination marked on the front of the bus or ask the driver—hop off in Kahlenberg and wait for the next bus to Leopoldsberg, leaves 2/hr). There you'll find a lovely Baroque church, a breezy *Weinstube* (wine pub), and shady tables with expansive panoramas of the city and the Danube. While it seems like a long way to go for a big view, buses are cheap (or free with a transit pass) and run frequently (2/hr to Leopoldsberg, last bus around 17:30; buses that end at Kahlenberg run 3–6/hr, 2/hr after 21:00, last bus around 22:30). For an overview of this area, see the map on page 31.

Naschmarkt—Vienna's busy produce market is a great place for people-watching (see page 62).

Shopping

Traditional Austrian Clothing—If you're interested in picking up a classy felt suit or dirndl, you'll find shops all over town. Most central is the fancy **Loden Plankl** shop (across from the Hofburg, at Michaelerplatz 6). But the **Tostmann Trachten** shop is the ultimate for serious shopping. Frau Tostmann powered the resurgence of this style. Her place is like a shrine to traditional Austrian and folk clothing (called *Tracht*)—handmade and very expensive (Schottengasse 3A, 3-min walk from Am Hof, tel. 01/533-5331, www.tostmann.at).

Artsy Gifts—Vienna's museum shops are some of Europe's best. The design store in the Museum of Applied Art (MAK) is a delight; the shops of the Albertina Museum, Kunsthistorisches Museum, Belvedere Palace, KunstHausWien, and the MuseumsQuartier museums are also particularly good.

Window Shopping—The narrow streets north and west of the cathedral are sprinkled with old-fashioned shops that seem to belong to another era, carrying a curiously narrow range of items for sale (old clocks, men's ties, gloves, and so on). Dedicated window-shoppers will enjoy the Dorotheum auction house (see page 53).

VIENNA CITY WALK

This walk connects the top three sights in Vienna's old center: the Opera, St. Stephen's Cathedral, and the Hofburg Palace. Along the way, you'll see sights covered elsewhere in the book, and get an overview of Vienna's past and present.

ORIENTATION

Length of This Walk: Allow one hour, and more time if you plan to stop into any of the major sights along the way.

Opera: A visit is possible only with a 50-min guided tour (€6.50, generally July–Aug at 11:00, 13:00, 14:00, 15:00, and often at 10:00 and 16:00; Sept–June fewer tours, afternoons only; tel. 01/514-442-624). For information on attending a performance, see page 41.

Café Sacher: Daily 8:00–24:00, Philharmoniker Strasse 4, tel. 01/51456.

Albertina Museum: €9.50, price can vary based on special exhibits, audioguide-€4, daily 10:00–18:00, Wed until 21:00, overlooking Albertinaplatz across from the TI and the Opera, tel. 01/534-830, www.albertina.at.

Kaisergruft: €4, daily 10:00–18:00, last entry at 17:40, behind the Opera on Neuer Markt, tel. 01/512-6853.

St. Stephen's Cathedral: Free (except July–mid-Oct, when it's €3 to get past the rear of the nave). Church open Mon–Sat 6:00–22:00, Sun 7:00–22:00; nave open for tourists only Mon–Sat 9:00–11:30 & 13:30–16:30, Sun 13:00–16:30. South tower climbable daily 9:00–17:30; elevator up shorter north tower runs daily July–Aug 8:30–18:00, April–June and Sept–Oct 8:30–17:30, Nov–March 8:30–17:00.

St. Peter's Church: Free, Mon–Fri 7:00–19:00, Sat–Sun 9:00–19:00, just off the Graben between the Plague Monument and Kohlmarkt, tel. 01/533-6433.

Hofburg Imperial Apartments: €10, daily July–Aug 9:00–18:00, Sept–June 9:00–17:00, last entry 30 min before closing, tel. 01/533-7570, www.hofburg-wien.at.

Hofburg Treasury: €10, €18 combo-ticket with Kunsthistorisches Museum, Wed–Mon 10:00–18:00, closed Tue, tel. 01/525-240, www.khm.at.

THE WALK BEGINS

• *Begin at the square outside Vienna's landmark Opera House. (The Opera's entrance faces the Ringstrasse; we're starting at the busy pedestrian square that's to the right of the entrance as you're facing it.)*

Opera

If Vienna is the world capital of classical music, this building is its throne room, one of the planet's premier houses of music. It's typical of Vienna's 19th-century buildings in that it features a revival style—Neo-Renaissance—with arched windows, half-columns, and the sloping copper roof typical of French Renaissance châteaux (see "Historicism" sidebar, page 106).

Since the structure was built in 1869, almost all of opera's luminaries have passed through here. Its former musical directors include Gustav Mahler, Herbert von Karajan, and Richard Strauss. Luciano Pavarotti, Maria Callas, Placido Domingo, and many other greats have sung from its stage.

In the pavement along the side of the Opera (and all along Kärntner Strasse, the bustling shopping street we'll visit shortly), you'll find star plaques forming a Hollywood-style walk of fame. These are the stars of classical music—famous composers, singers, musicians, and conductors.

If you're a fan, take a guided tour of the Opera (see page 41). If you're not, you still might consider springing for an evening performance (standing-room tickets are surprisingly cheap; see page 169). Check the Wien Ticket

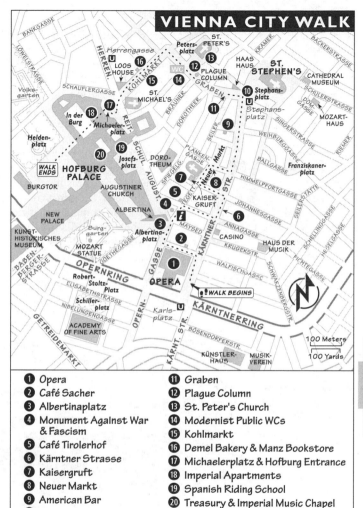

VIENNA CITY WALK

① Opera
② Café Sacher
③ Albertinaplatz
④ Monument Against War & Fascism
⑤ Café Tirolerhof
⑥ Kärntner Strasse
⑦ Kaisergruft
⑧ Neuer Markt
⑨ American Bar
⑩ Stephansplatz
⑪ Graben
⑫ Plague Column
⑬ St. Peter's Church
⑭ Modernist Public WCs
⑮ Kohlmarkt
⑯ Demel Bakery & Manz Bookstore
⑰ Michaelerplatz & Hofburg Entrance
⑱ Imperial Apartments
⑲ Spanish Riding School
⑳ Treasury & Imperial Music Chapel

kiosk in the booth on this square for information on this and other entertainment options during your visit.

The Opera marks a busy intersection in Vienna, where Kärntner Strasse meets the Ring. The Karlsplatz U-Bahn station in front of the Opera is a huge underground shopping mall with fast food, newsstands, lots of pickpockets, and even a Vienna Opera Toilet experience (€0.60, *mit Musik*).

• *Walk behind the Opera and across the street toward the dark red awning to find the famous...*

Café Sacher

This is the home of the world's classiest chocolate cake, the Sacher torte: two layers of cake separated by apricot jam and covered in

dark-chocolate icing, usually served with whipped cream. It was invented in a fit of improvisation in 1832 by Franz Sacher, dessert chef to Prince Metternich (the mastermind diplomat who redrew the map of post-Napoleon Europe). The cake became world-famous when the inventor's son served it next door at his hotel (you may have noticed the fancy doormen). Many locals complain that the cakes have gone downhill, and many tourists are surprised by how dry they are—you really need that dollop of *Schlagobers*. Still, coffee and a slice of cake here can be €8 well invested for the historic ambience alone. While the café itself is grotesquely touristy, the adjacent Sacher Stube has ambience and natives to spare. For maximum elegance, sit inside.

• *Head to the left of Hotel Sacher (as you face the café). At the end of the street is a small square where you'll find the TI (see page 35), an equestrian statue, and a building with a huge modern overhang.*

Albertinaplatz

The tan-and-white Neoclassical building with the statue alcoves

marks the tip of the Hofburg Palace—the sprawling complex of buildings that was long the seat of Habsburg power (we'll end this walk at the palace's center). The balustraded terrace up top was originally part of Vienna's defensive rampart. Later, it was the balcony of Empress Maria Theresa's daughter Maria Christina, who lived at this end of the palace. And today, her home houses the **Albertina Museum,** topped by a sleek, controversial titanium canopy (called the "diving board" by critics). Most of the museum's stunning permanent collection isn't on display, but visitors can enjoy first-rate temporary exhibits (see page 48).

Albertinaplatz is filled with statues that make up the powerful, thought-provoking **Monument Against War and Fascism,** which remembers the dark years when Austria came under Nazi rule (1938–1945).

VIENNA CITY WALK

The statue-group has four parts. The split white monument, *The Gates of Violence*, remembers victims of all wars and violence.

Standing directly in front of it, you're at the gates of a concentration camp. Step into a montage of wartime images: clubs and WWI gas masks, a dying woman birthing a future soldier, and chained slave laborers sitting on a pedestal of granite cut from the infamous quarry at Mauthausen Concentration Camp (see page 192). The hunched-over figure on the ground behind is a Jew forced to scrub anti-Nazi graffiti off a street with a toothbrush. The statue with its head buried in the stone is Orpheus entering the underworld, meant to remind Austrians (and the rest of us) of the victims of Nazism...and the consequences of not keeping our governments on track. Behind that, the 1945 declaration that established Austria's second republic—and enshrined human rights—is cut into the stone.

The experience gains emotional impact when you realize this monument stands on the spot where several hundred people were buried alive when the cellar they were hiding in was demolished during a WWII bombing attack (see photo to right of park, English description of memorial on the left).

Austria was led into World War II by Germany, which annexed the country in 1938, saying Austrians were wannabe Germans anyway. But Austrians are not Germans—never were, never will be. They're quick to tell you that Austria was founded in the 10th century, whereas Germany wasn't born until 1870. For seven years just before and during World War II (1938–1945), there was no Austria. In 1955, after 10 years of joint occupation by the victorious Allies, Austria regained total independence on the condition that it would be forever neutral (and never join NATO or the Warsaw Pact). To this day, Austria is outside of NATO (and Germany).

Behind the monument is **Café Tirolerhof**, a classic Viennese café full of things that time has passed by: chandeliers, marble tables, upholstered booths, waiters in tuxes, and newspapers. For more on Vienna's cafés, see page 161.

• *From the café, turn right on Führichsgasse, passing the cafeteria-style Rosenberger Markt Restaurant (listed on page 158). Walk one block until you hit...*

Kärntner Strasse

This grand, mall-like street (traffic-free since 1974) is the people-watching delight of this in-love-with-life city. Today's Kärntner

Strasse (KAYRNT-ner SHTRAH-seh) is mostly a crass commercial pedestrian mall—its famed elegant shops long gone. But

locals know it's the same road
Crusaders marched down
as they headed off from St.
Stephen's Cathedral for the
Holy Land in the 12th century. Its name indicates that it
leads south, toward the region
of Kärnten (Carinthia, a province divided between Austria
and Slovenia). Today it's full of shoppers and street musicians.

Where Führichsgasse meets Kärntner Strasse, note the city
Casino (across the street and a half-block to your right, at #41)—
once venerable, now tacky, it exemplifies the worst of the street's
evolution. Turn left to head up Kärntner Strasse, going away from
the Opera. As you walk along, be sure to look up, above the modern storefronts, for glimpses of the
street's former glory. On the left
at #26, **J & L Lobmeyr Crystal**
("Founded in 1823") still has
its impressive brown storefront
with gold trim, statues, and the
Habsburg double-eagle. Inside,
breathe in the classic Old World
ambience as you climb up to the
glass museum. In the market for

some $400 napkin rings? Lobmeyr's your place.

• *At the end of the block, turn left on Marco d'Aviano Gasse to make
a short detour to the square called Neuer Markt. Straight ahead is
an orange-ish church with a triangular roof and cross, the Capuchin
Church. In its basement is the...*

Kaisergruft

Under the church sits the Imperial Crypt, filled with what's left

of Austria's emperors, empresses, and
other Habsburg royalty. For centuries,
Vienna was the heart of a vast empire
ruled by the Habsburg family, and here
is where they lie buried in their fancy
coffins. You'll find all the Habsburg
greats, including Maria Theresa, her
son Josef II (Mozart's patron), Franz Josef,
and Empress Sisi. Before moving on,
consider paying your respects here (see
page 49).

see
page 49).

VIENNA CITY WALK

Neuer Markt

In the center of Neuer Markt square is the **four rivers fountain**
showing Lady Providence surrounded
by figures symbolizing the rivers that
flow into the Danube. The statues,
originally nude, were replaced with
more modest versions by Maria
Teresa. The buildings all around you
were rebuilt after World War II. Half
of the city's inner center was inten-
tionally destroyed by Churchill to
demoralize the Viennese, who were
disconcertingly enthusiastic about
the Nazis.

• *Lady Providence's one bare breast
points back to Kärntner Strasse (50 yards away). Before you head back
to the busy shopping street, you could stop for a sweet treat at the heavenly Kurkonditorei Oberlaa (look for the vertical sign at the far corner
of the square; see page 159). Leave the square by returning to Kärntner
Strasse and turn left. Two blocks along, on the left, is the...*

American Bar

Over the door, the jutting American-flag sign (in red, white, and

blue glass) is one of the few ornaments
on this minimalist building. This is
the first of several structures along
this walk designed by the architect
Adolf Loos (see sidebar on next page).
Inside it's dark, plush, and small, with
great €8 cocktails (note that gawkers
are discouraged in this still-hip bar).

• *Continue down Kärntner Strasse to
the main square. As you approach the cathedral, you're likely to first
see it as a reflection in the round-glass
windows of the modern Haas Haus
(described next). Pass the U-Bahn station (which has WCs), where the street
spills into...*

Stephansplatz

The cathedral's massive spire looms
overhead, worshippers and tourists
pour inside the church, and shoppers and top-notch street entertain-
ers buzz around the outside. You're
at the center of Vienna.

Adolf Loos
(1870–1933)

"Decoration is a crime," wrote Adolf Loos, the turn-of-the-20th-century architect who was Vienna's answer to Frank Lloyd Wright. Foreshadowing the Modernist style of "less is more" and "form follows function," Loos stripped buildings down to their structural skeleton.

In his day, most buildings were plastered with fake Greek columns, frosted with Baroque balustrades, and studded with statues. Even the newer buildings featured flowery Art Nouveau additions. Loos' sparse, geometrical style stood out at the time—and it still does a century later. Loos was convinced that unnecessary ornamentation was a waste of workers' valuable time and energy, and was a symbol of an unevolved society. (He even went so far as to compare decoration on a facade with a lavatory wall smeared with excrement.) On this walk, you'll see four examples of his work:

American Bar (Kärntner Durchgang 10): Built the same year that Loos published his famous essay *Ornament and Crime,* this tiny bar features Loos' specialties. The facade is cubical, with square columns and crossbeams (and no flowery capitals). The interior is elegant and understated, with rich marble and mirrors that appear to expand the small space. The best way to admire the interior is to sit down and order a drink.

Public WCs on Graben: Yes, these modern loos are by Loos.

Manz Bookstore: The facade is a perfect cube, divided into other simple, rectangular shapes.

Loos House on Michaelerplatz: The facade is a perfectly geometrical grid of square columns and windows. Compare it with the Hofburg's ornate, Neo-Rococo look (done only a few decades earlier) to see how revolutionary Loos was. This anti–Art Nouveau statement (inspired by Frank Lloyd Wright and considered Vienna's first "modern" building) was considered shocking. The building's trapezoidal footprint makes no attempt to hide the awkward street corner it's placed on. This "house without eyebrows" features windows without the customary cornice framing the top. The 10 flower boxes beneath the windows (the "moustaches") were added by Loos with reluctance, only after citizens protested that the building was just too stark.

The Gothic church (c. 1300–1450) is known for its 450-foot south tower, its colorful roof, and its place in Viennese history. When it was built, it was a huge church for what was then a tiny town, and it helped put the fledgling city on the map.

At this point, you may want to take a break from the walk to tour the church (❍ see St. Stephen's Cathedral Tour, page 91). Even if you don't go inside, you can check out some of the exterior sights: the south tower, remnants of earlier churches, the old facade, and World War II–era photos that show the destruction during the war (to the right of the church).

Surrounding the church are buildings featuring centuries of architectural styles. Start at the cathedral and pan the square clockwise. To the right of the Gothic cathedral, the upper floors of the **International Building/Bank of Austria** have decorative Art Nouveau elements. Where Kärntner Strasse hits Stephansplatz (at #3), the **Equitable Building** (filled with lawyers, bankers, and insurance brokers) is a fine example of Neoclassicism from the turn of the 20th century. Look up and imagine how slick Vienna must have felt in 1900.

Facing St. Stephen's is the sleek concrete-and-glass **Haas Haus,** a postmodern building by noted Austrian architect Hans Hollein (finished in 1990). The curved facade is supposed to echo the Roman fortress of Vindobona (its ruins were found near here). The Viennese initially protested having this stark modern tower right next to their beloved cathedral, but since then, it's become a fixture of Vienna's main square. Notice how the smooth, rounded glass reflects St. Stephen's pointy architecture, providing a great photo opportunity. The café and pricey restaurant inside offer a nice perch, complete with a view of Stephansplatz below.

At the north end of the square is the (somewhat run-down) Modernist **J.F. Kennedy Haus,** named for the popular American president—who came to Vienna for a summit hoping (but failing) to halt the construction of the Berlin Wall.

To the left of the church, the **Manner** store is known for its wafer cookies with the church logo. For a quick detour, turn right at the Manner store and walk past the touristy horse carts to the doorway at #6. This leads to a picturesque **lane** lined with shops and restaurants (it's also where you'll find the Cathedral Museum—see page 234). Behind the church, a block away (but not worth the detour) is **Mozarthaus,** where the composer lived while writing the opera *The Marriage of Figaro.*

• *Exit the square with your back to the cathedral entrance. Walk past the Haas Haus, down the street called...*

Graben

This was once a *Graben,* or ditch—originally the moat for the Roman military camp. Back during Vienna's 19th-century heyday, there were nearly 200,000 people packed into the city's inner center (inside Ringstrasse), walking through dirt streets. Today this area houses 20,000. Graben was a busy street with three lanes of traffic until the 1970s, when it was turned into one of Europe's first pedestrian-only zones.

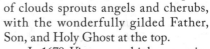

As you walk down Graben, you'll reach Dorotheergasse (two blocks on your left after leaving Stephansplatz), which leads to the **Dorotheum** auction house (consider poking your nose in here later for some fancy window-shopping—see page 53).

In the middle of this pedestrian zone is the extravagantly blobby **Holy Trinity plague column** *(Pestsäule).* The 70-foot pillar of clouds sprouts angels and cherubs, with the wonderfully gilded Father, Son, and Holy Ghost at the top.

In 1679, Vienna was hit by a massive epidemic of bubonic plague. Around 75,000 Viennese died—about a third of the city. Emperor Leopold I dropped to his knees (something emperors never did in public) and begged God to save the city. (Find Leopold about a quarter of the way up the monument. Hint: The typical inbreeding of royal families left him with a gaping underbite.) His prayer was heard by Lady Faith (the statue below Leopold, carrying a cross). With the help of a heartless little cupid, she tosses an old naked woman—symbolizing the plague—into the abyss and saves the city. In gratitude, Leopold vowed to erect this monument, which became a model for other cities ravaged by the same plague.

• *Just past the plague monument, look down the short street to the right, which frames a Baroque church with a stately green dome.*

St. Peter's Church

Leopold I also ordered this church to be built as a thank-you for surviving the 1679 plague. The church stands on the site of a much older church that may have been Vienna's first (or second) Christian church. Inside, St. Peter's shows Vienna at its Baroque best (see page 53).

• *Continue west on Graben, where you'll immediately find some stairs leading underground to two...*

Public WCs

In about 1900, a local chemical-maker needed a publicity stunt to prove that his chemicals really got things clean. He purchased two wine cellars under Graben and had them turned into classy WCs in the Modernist style (designed by Adolf Loos, see sidebar on page 84), complete with chandeliers and finely crafted mahogany. The restrooms remain clean to this day—in fact, they're so inviting that they're used for poetry readings. Locals and tourists happily pay €0.50 for a quick visit.

• *Graben dead-ends at the aristocratic supermarket Julius Meinl am Graben (see page 158). From here, turn left. In the distance is the big green and gold dome of the Hofburg, where we'll end this walk. The street leading up to the Hofburg is...*

Kohlmarkt

This is Vienna's most elegant and unaffordable shopping street—Tiffany, Cartier, Giorgio Armani—with the emperor's palace at the end. Strolling Kohlmarkt, daydream about the edible window displays at **Demel** (#14, daily 10:00–19:00). Demel is the ultimate

Viennese chocolate shop. The room is filled with Art Nouveau boxes of Empress Sisi's choco-dreams come true: *Kandierte Veilchen* (candied violet petals), *Katzenzungen* (cats' tongues), and so on. The cakes here are moist (compared to the dry Sacher tortes). The enticing window displays change monthly, reflecting current happenings in Vienna. Inside, an impressive cancan of cakes is displayed to tempt visitors into springing for the €10 cake-and-coffee deal (point to the cake you want). You can sit inside, with a view of the cake-making, or outside, with the street action. (Upstairs is less crowded.) Shops like this boast "K.u.K."—good enough for the *König und Kaiser* (king and emperor—same guy).

Next to Demel, the **Manz Bookstore** has a Loos-designed facade (see sidebar on page 84). Just beyond Demel and across the street, at #1152, you can pop in to a charming little Baroque **carriage courtyard,** with the surviving original carriage garages.

• *Kohlmarkt ends at the square called...*

Michaelerplatz

This square is dominated by the impressive facade of the Hofburg Palace. Opposite the facade, notice the modern **Loos House** (now a bank) built at about the same time as the palace's grandiose facade (see sidebar on Loos on page 84). In the center of this square, a scant bit of Roman Vienna lies exposed just beneath street level. On the left is the fancy Loden Plankl shop, with traditional Austrian formal wear. Next door (at #6), pop through the passageway to find a quiet courtyard with a big wooden carving of Jesus praying in Gethsemane. Across Augustinerstrasse, to the left of the Hofburg entrance, is the wing of the palace that houses the Spanish Riding School and its famous white Lipizzaner stallions (see page 51). Farther down this street lies Josefsplatz, with its Augustinian Church (see page 51), and at the end of the street, Albertinaplatz and the Opera (where we started this walk).

• *We'll finish up our tour where Austria's glorious history began—at the...*

Hofburg

This is the complex of palaces where the Habsburg emperors lived (except in summer, when they lived out at Schönbrunn Palace). Study the grand entry facade to the Hofburg Palace—it's Neo-Baroque from about 1900. The four heroic giants illustrate Hercules wrestling with his great challenges (much like the late-empire Habsburgs, I'm sure).

Enter the Hofburg through the gate, where you immediately find yourself beneath a big rotunda (the netting is there to keep birds from perching). The doorway on the right is the entrance to the **Imperial Apartments,** where the Habsburg emperors once lived in chandeliered elegance. Today you can tour its lavish rooms, as well as a museum on Empress Sisi, and a porcelain and silver collection (❂ see Hofburg Imperial Apartments Tour on page 109). To the left is the ticket office for the **Spanish Riding School** (see page 51).

Continuing on, you emerge from the rotunda into the main courtyard of the Hofburg, called **In der Burg.** The Caesar-like statue is of Habsburg Emperor Franz II (1768–1835), grandson of Maria Theresa, grandfather of Franz Josef, and father-in-law of Napoleon. Behind him is a tower with three kinds of clocks (the yellow disk shows the phase of the moon tonight). To the right of Franz are the Imperial Apartments, and to the left are the offices of Austria's mostly ceremonial president (the more powerful chancellor lives in a building just behind this courtyard).

Franz faces the oldest part of the palace. The colorful red, black, and gold gateway (behind you), which used to have a drawbridge, leads to the 13th-century Swiss Court (Schweizerhof), named for the Swiss mercenary guards once stationed there. Here you'll find the **Treasury** (Schatzkammer; ❂ see Hofburg Treasury Tour on page 121) and the **Imperial Music Chapel** (Hofmusikkapelle, see page 167) where the Boys' Choir sings the Mass.

Back at In der Burg, face Franz and turn left, passing through the **tunnel,** with a few tourist shops and restaurants (see Hofburg Stüberl on page 45).

The tunnel spills out into spacious **Heldenplatz** (Heroes' Square). On the left is the impressive curved facade of the **New Palace** (Neue Burg). This vast wing was built in the early 1900s to be the new Habsburg living quarters (and was meant to have a matching building facing it). But in 1914, the heir-to-the-throne Archduke Franz Ferdinand—while waiting politely for his long-lived uncle, Emperor Franz Josef, to die—was assassinated in Sarajevo. The archduke's death sparked World War I and the eventual end of eight centuries of Habsburg rule.

This impressive building saw even sadder days a few decades later, when Adolf Hitler addressed adoring throngs from the New Palace balcony in 1938, after Austria was annexed.

Inside the building nowadays are the **New Palace Museums,** an eclectic collection of weaponry, suits of armor, musical instruments, and ancient Greek statues (see page 45). The two equestrian statues are Prince Eugene of Savoy (1663–1736), who battled the Ottoman Turks, and Archduke Charles (1771–1847), who battled Napoleon. Eugene gazes to the far distance at the prickly spires of Vienna's City Hall (see page 107).

The Hofburg's **Burggarten** (with the much-photographed Mozart statue) is not visible from here, but it's just behind the New Palace. If you were to continue on through the Greek-columned passageway (the Äussere Burgtor), you'd reach the

Ringstrasse, the Kunsthistorisches Museum (see page 129), and the MuseumsQuartier (see page 56).

Walk Over

You're in the heart of Viennese sightseeing. The Hofburg contains some of Vienna's best sights and museums. From the Opera to the Hofburg, from chocolate to churches, from St. Stephen's to Sacher torte—Vienna waits for you.

ST. STEPHEN'S CATHEDRAL TOUR

Stephansdom

This massive church is the Gothic needle around which Vienna spins. According to the medieval vision of its creators, it stands like a giant jeweled reliquary, offering praise to God from the center of the city. The church and its towers, especially the 450-foot south tower, give the city its most iconic image. (Check your pockets for 10-cent euro coins; ones minted in Austria feature the south tower on the back.) The cathedral has survived Vienna's many wars and today symbolizes the city's freedom.

ORIENTATION

Cost: Entering the church is free (except July–mid-Oct, when it's €3 to get past the rear of the nave). Going up the towers costs €3 (by stairs, south tower) or €4.50 (by elevator, north tower).

Hours: The church doors are open Mon–Sat 6:00–22:00, Sun 7:00–22:00, but the nave is open for tourists only Mon–Sat 9:00–11:30 & 13:30–16:30, Sun 13:30–16:30. During services, you can't enter the main nave (unless you're attending Mass), but you can go into the back of the church to reach the north tower elevator (see below).

Information: Tel. 01/515-523-526, www.stephanskirche.at.

Tours: The €4 tours in English are entertaining (daily April–Oct at 15:45, check information board inside entry to confirm schedule). The €2 audioguide is well-done, but for most, the information in this chapter will be enough.

Climbing the Towers: The iconic **south tower** rewards a tough climb up a claustrophobic, 343-step staircase with dizzying views (possibly obscured by scaffolding, which may still surround the tower during your visit). You can reach it via the entrance outside the church, around the right as you face the west facade (€3, daily 9:00–17:30).

The **north tower** holds the famous "Pummerin" bell and is easier to ascend, but it's much shorter and not as exciting, with lesser views (no stairs, elevator-€4.50, daily July–Aug 8:30–18:00, April–June and Sept–Oct 8:30–17:30, Nov–March 8:30–17:00, last elevator ascends 20 min before closing, entrance inside the church on the left side of the nave).

THE TOUR BEGINS

• *Find a spot in the square where you can take in the sheer magnitude of this massive church, with its skyscraping spire.*

Exterior

The church we see today dates mainly from 1300–1450, when builders expanded on an earlier structure and added two huge towers at the end of each transept.

The impressive 450-foot south tower took two generations to build (65 years), and was finished in 1433. The tower is a rarity among medieval churches in that it was completed before the Gothic style—and the age of faith— petered out. (See if you can find the Turkish cannonball stuck in the tower, a remnant of one of several Ottoman sieges of the city. Hint: It's on the southwest corner of the tower, about 50 feet up.) Consider climbing the tower now, or wait until after your cathedral visit (see "Climbing the South Tower," at the end of this chapter).

The half-size north tower (223 feet), around the other side of the church, was meant to be a matching steeple but was abandoned mid-construction when they ran out of money.

The sharply pitched roof stands 200 feet tall and is covered in 230,000 colorful ceramic tiles. The zigzag pattern on the south side is purely decorative, with no special symbolism. On the north are the twin eagles of the Habsburg coat of arms.

When it was built, St. Stephen's—covering almost an acre of land—was a huge church for what was then just a modest town of 10,000. The ruler who built the church copied a church in Prague— and made it bigger—in order to impress his father-in-law. It helped convince the region's religious authorities that Vienna deserved a bishop, thus making St. Stephen's a "cathedral." Politically, this helped Vienna become a city to be reckoned with, and it soon replaced Prague as the seat of the Holy Roman Empire.

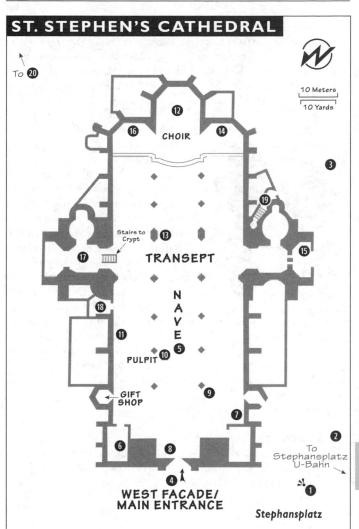

ST. STEPHEN'S CATHEDRAL

To **20**

10 Meters
10 Yards

12

16   CHOIR   **14**

3

19

Stairs to
Crypt   **13**

17   TRANSEPT   **15**

18

11   N
A
V
E

5

PULPIT   **10**

9

7

GIFT
SHOP

6   **8**

4   **2**

To
Stephansplatz
U-Bahn

1

WEST FACADE/
MAIN ENTRANCE

Stephansplatz

ST. STEPHEN'S CATHEDRAL

1 Exterior View
2 Footprint of Earlier Church
3 Old Photos
4 West Facade & Main Entrance
5 Nave
6 Chapel of Prince Eugene of Savoy
7 Maria Pócs Icon
8 Organ
9 Pillar Statues (Madonna with the Protective Mantle)
10 Pulpit with Self-Portrait

11 Second Self-Portrait
12 High Altar
13 Plaque of Rebuilding
14 Tomb of Frederick III
15 Mozart Plaque
16 Wiener Neustädter Altar
17 North Transept (Crypt & "Christ with a Toothache")
18 North Tower Elevator
19 South Tower Stairs
20 To Cathedral Museum

This is the third church to stand on this spot. You can see the footprint of the **earlier church** in the pavement, to the right of the main entrance. The remains of a **still-older church** are on display underground, in the U-Bahn station. (To see them, head down the stairs into the station and turn left, following *Virgilkapelle* signs—no transit ticket necessary.)

The cathedral was heavily damaged at the end of World War II. To the right of the cathedral (along the building with the

Austrian flags and *Churhaus* plaque) are **old photos** showing the destruction. In 1945, Vienna was caught in the chaos between the occupying Nazis and the approaching Soviets. Allied bombs sparked fires in nearby buildings. The embers leapt to the cathedral rooftop. The original timbered Gothic roof burned and collapsed into the nave, the cathedral's huge bell crashed to the ground, and the fire raged for two days. Civic pride prompted a financial outpouring, and the roof was rebuilt to its original splendor by 1952. Locals who contributed to the postwar reconstruction each had a chance to "own" one tile for their donation. The photos show the WWII damage...with replacement bricks neatly stacked and ready for the reconstruction.

• *Approach the main entrance and the...*

West Facade

The church's main entrance is the oldest part of the church (c. 1240), done in the Romanesque style. Two stubby octagonal

towers flank the large main doorway, and Christ looks down from the tympanum over the door.

Before Christians occupied Vienna, there was a pagan Roman temple here, and the facade pays homage to that ancient heritage. Roman-era statues are embedded in the facade, and the two octagonal towers are dubbed the "heathen towers" because they're built with a few Roman stones (flipped over to hide the pagan inscriptions and expose the smooth sides).

The cathedral was central to the city when Austria was under Nazi rule. To the right of the doorway, find where anti-Nazi rebels carved **"O5"** into the wall, about chest high (behind the Plexiglas, under the first plaque). The story goes that Hitler—who'd actually grown up in Austria—spurned his roots. When he attained power, he refused to call the country "Österreich" (UHR-stair-rike), its true name, insisting on the Nazi term "Ostmark." Austrian patriots wrote the code "O5" to keep the true name alive: The "5" stands for the fifth letter of the alphabet (E), which often stands in for an umlaut, giving the "O" its correct pronunciation for "Österreich."

• *Enter the church.*

Interior

Nave

Find a spot to look down the immense nave—more than a football field long and nine stories tall. It's lined with clusters of slender pil-

lars that soar upward to support the ribbed crisscross arches of the ceiling. Stylistically, the nave is Gothic with a Baroque overlay. It's a spacious, glorious venue that's often used for high-profile concerts.

On the left (north) side of the nave, near the gift shop, is the gated entrance to the **Chapel of Prince Eugene of Savoy.** Prince Eugene (1663–1736), a teenage seminary student from France, arrived in Vienna in 1683 as the city was about to be overrun by the Ottoman Turks. He volunteered for the army and helped save the city, launching his career as a military man for the Habsburgs. His specialty was conquering the Turks. When he died, the grateful Austrians buried him in the chapel, marked by a ceremonial plaque in the floor. Later, this chapel is where Mozart's funeral service was held.

Near the opposite (south) wall, in a gold-and-silver sunburst frame, is the Byzantine-style **Maria Pócs Icon** (Pötscher Madonna). The picture of Mary and Child is said to have wept real tears in 1697, as Central Europe was once again being threatened by the Turks. Prince Eugene saved the day at the stunning Battle of Zenta (in modern-day Serbia), a victory that broke the back of the Ottoman army. If you see crowds of pilgrims leaving flowers or lighting candles around the icon, they're most likely Hungarians thanking the Virgin for helping Prince Eugene liberate their homeland.

Over the church entrance is the choir loft, with the 10,000-pipe **organ,** a 1960 replacement for the famous one destroyed during World War II. The replacement is also one of Europe's biggest, framed by a backdrop of red and blue stained glass.

· *Looking back down the nave, note the statues on the columns (about 30–40 feet above the ground).*

Pillar Statues

The nave's columns are richly populated with 77 life-size stone and ceramic statues, making a saintly parade to the high altar.

Check out the first pillar on the right. Facing the side wall is the **Madonna with the Protective Mantle,** shown giving ref-

uge to people of all walks of life. Also on that same pillar, find Moses with the Ten Commandments. Near Moses is the church's namesake, St. Stephen (facing the entrance), holding the stones he was martyred with. Nearby is Christ as the Man of Sorrows, and (higher up) St. Christopher carrying the Christ child on his shoulders.

These are just a few. On other columns, Bible students can find their favorite characters and saints—more Madonnas, St. George (killing the dragon), Francis of Assisi, arrow-filled St. Sebastian, and so on.

· *Start down the nave toward the altar. At the second pillar on the left is the...*

Pulpit

The Gothic sandstone pulpit (c. 1515) is a masterpiece carved from three separate blocks (see if you can find the seams). A spiral stairway winds up to the lectern, surrounded and supported

by the four church "doctors," whose writings influenced early Catholic dogma. Each has a very different and very human facial expression: Ambrose (daydreamer), Jerome (skeptic), Gregory (explainer), and Augustine (listener).

The pulpit is as crammed with religious meaning as it is with beautifully realistic carvings. The top of the stairway's railing swarms with lizards as animals of light and toads as animals of darkness. The "Dog of the Lord" stands at the top, making sure none of those toads pollutes the sermon. Below the toads, wheels with three parts (the Trinity) roll up, while wheels with four spokes (the four seasons, symbolizing mortal life) roll down.

Find the guy peeking out from under the stairs. This may be a **self-portrait** of the artist. In medieval times, art was done for

the glory of God, and artists worked anonymously. But this pulpit was carved as humanist Renaissance ideals were creeping in from Italy—and individual artists were becoming famous. So the artist included what may be a rare self-portrait bust in his work. He leans out from a window, sculptor's compass in hand, to observe the world and his work. The artist's identity, however, is disputed. Long thought to be Hungarian mason Anton Pilgram, many scholars now believe it's Dutch sculptor Nicolaes Gerhaert van Leyden; both worked extensively on the cathedral.

A few steps farther ahead (past the next column), on the left wall of the church is a **similar self-portrait** of Pilgram (or is it Gerhaert?) in color, taken from the original organ case. He holds a compass and L-square and symbolically shoulders the heavy burden of being a master builder of this huge place.

• *Continue up the nave to the altar.*

High Altar

The tall, ornate, black marble altarpiece (1641, by Tobias and Johann Pock) is topped with a statue of Mary. It frames a large

painting of the Stoning of St. Stephen, painted on copper. Stephen (at the bottom), having refused to stop professing his faith, is pelted with rocks by angry pagans. As he lies dying, he gazes up to see a vision of Christ, the cross, and the angels of heaven. The stained glass behind the painting—some of the oldest in the church—creates a kaleidoscopic jeweled backdrop.

• *On the third column from the altar (left side of the nave), about 10 feet above the ground, is the...*

Plaque of Rebuilding

St. Stephen's is proud to be Austria's national church. The plaque explains how each region contributed to the rebuilding after

World War II: "Die Glocke" (the bell) was financed by the state of Upper Austria. "Das Tor" (the entrance portal) was from Steiermark, the windows from Tirol, the pews from Vorarlberg, the floor from Lower Austria, and so on.

During World War II, many of the city's top art treasures were hidden safely in cellars and salt mines—hidden by both the Nazi occupiers (to protect against war damage) and by citizens (to protect against Nazi looters). The stained-glass windows behind the high altar were meticulously dismantled and packed away. The pulpit was encased in a shell of brick. As the war was drawing to a close, it appeared St. Stephen's would escape major damage. But as the Nazis were fleeing, the bitter Nazi commander in charge of the city ordered that the church be destroyed. Fortunately, his underlings disobeyed. Unfortunately, the church accidentally caught fire during Allied bombing shortly thereafter, and the roof collapsed. Among the other losses, the nave's precious stained-glass windows were blown out in the big fire—and had to be replaced with lesser-quality, Tupperware-colored glass. Before the fire, the entire church was lit with windows like the richly colored ones behind the altar.

• To the right of the altar is the impressive Tomb of Frederick III. Unfortunately, it's usually fenced off, except for guided tours.

Tomb of Frederick III

This imposing, red-marble tomb is like a big king-size–bed coffin with an effigy of Frederick lying on top, surrounded by his coat of arms. It's likely by the same Nicolaes Gerhaert van Leyden who may have done the pulpit.

Frederick III (1415–1493) is considered the "father" of Vienna for turning the small village into a royal town with a cosmopolitan feel. Frederick secured a bishopric, turning the newly completed St. Stephen's church into a cathedral. The emperor's major contribution to Austria, however, was in fathering Maximilian I and marrying him off to Mary of Burgundy, instantly making the Habsburg Empire a major player in European politics. The simple, dense, no-frills tomb (made of marble from Salzburg) is as long-lasting as Frederick's legacy. To make sure it stayed that way, locals saved his tomb from damage during World War II by encasing it, like the pulpit, in a shell of brick.

• Make your way to the south transept, which is on your left as you face the church entrance. On the wall to the left of the door, look for a white plaque in German, the...

Mozart Plaque

Wolfgang Amadeus Mozart (1756–1791) was married in St. Stephen's, attended Mass here, and baptized two of his children here.

Mozart spent most of his adult life in Vienna. Born in Salzburg, Mozart was a child prodigy who toured Europe. He performed for Empress Maria Theresa's family in Vienna when he was eight. At age 25, he left Salzburg in a huff (freeing himself from his domineering father) and settled in Vienna. Here he found instant fame as a concert pianist and freelance composer, writing *The Marriage of Figaro, Don Giovanni*, and *The Magic Flute*. He married Constanze Weber in St. Stephen's, and they set up house in a lavish apartment a block east of the church (this house is now the lackluster Mozarthaus museum). Mozart lived at the epicenter of Viennese society—among musicians, actors, and aristocrats. He played in a string quartet with Joseph Haydn. At church, he would have heard Beethoven's teacher playing the organ. (Mozart may have met the star-struck young Beethoven in Vienna—or maybe not; accounts vary.)

After his early success, Mozart fell on hard times, and the couple had to move to the suburbs. When Mozart died at age 35 (in 1791), he was not buried at St. Stephen's, because the cemetery that once surrounded the church had been cleared out a decade earlier as an anti-plague measure. Instead, his remains (along with most Viennese of his day) were dumped into a mass grave outside of town. But he was honored with a funeral service in St. Stephen's—held in the Prince Eugene of Savoy Chapel, where they played his famous (unfinished) Requiem.

• *Cross the nave. To the left of the main altar, you'll find the large...*

Wiener Neustädter Altar

The triptych altarpiece—the symmetrical counterpart of Frederick III's tomb—was commissioned by Frederick in 1447. It's certainly impressive...if you arrange a guided tour to get up close to see it. Otherwise, admire the painted saints on the outer doors (visible when the triptych is closed) or the gilded wooden statues on the inside (when open).

North Transept

In the north transept, you can descend into the **crypt** (for a fee), which holds the bodies (or at least the innards) of 72 Habsburgs, including that of Rudolf IV, the man who began building the south tower. This is where Austria's rulers were buried before the Kaisergruft was built (see page 49). Along the west side of the transept wall is a statue of Christ on the cross. With his doleful expression, he's been nicknamed the **"Christ with a Toothache."**

• Head back toward the entrance. Stick to the north side of the nave if you're interested in...

Ascending the North Tower

The cramped north tower elevator (look for the *Aufzug zur Pummerin* sign) takes you to a mediocre view and a big bell. Nicknamed "the Boomer" (Pummerin), it's old (first cast in 1711), big (nearly 10 feet across), and very heavy (21 tons). By comparison, the Liberty Bell is four feet across and weighs one ton. It's supposedly the second-biggest bell in the world that rings by swinging. A physical symbol of victory over the Ottoman Turks in 1683, the Pummerin was cast from cannons (and cannon balls) captured from the Ottomans when Vienna was liberated from the siege. During the WWII fire that damaged the church, the Pummerin fell to the ground and cracked. It had to be melted down and recast. These days, locals know the Pummerin as the bell that rings in the Austrian New Year.

• Exit the church. Make a U-turn to the left if you're up for...

Climbing the South Tower

The 450-foot-high south tower, once key to the city's defense as a lookout point, is still dear to Viennese hearts. (It's long been affectionately nicknamed "Steffl," Viennese for "Stevie.") No church spire in (what was) the Austro-Hungarian Empire is taller—by Habsburg decree. It offers a far better view than the north tower, but you'll earn it by hiking 343 tightly wound steps up the spiral staircase (this hike burns about one Sacher torte worth of calories). From the top, use your city map to locate the famous sights. There are great views of the colorful church roof, the low-level Viennese skyline (major skyscrapers are regulated in the city center), and—in the distance—the Viennese Woods.

*• Your tour is over. Some may wish to visit the forlorn **Cathedral Museum**, located outside the north transept, past the horses. It gives a close-up look at piles of religious paintings, statues, stained-glass windows, illuminated manuscripts, and a treasury (€7, Tue–Sat 10:00–17:00, closed Sun–Mon, Stephansplatz 6, tel. 01/515-523-689).*

For the rest, you're at the very center of Vienna. Explore.

RINGSTRASSE TRAM TOUR

In the 1860s, Emperor Franz Josef had the city's ingrown medieval wall torn down and replaced with a grand boulevard 190 feet wide. The road, arcing nearly three miles around the city's core, predates all the buildings that line it—so what you'll see is very "Neo": Neoclassical, Neo-Gothic, and Neo-Renaissance. One of Europe's great streets, the Ringstrasse is lined with many of the city's top sights.

This self-guided tram tour gives you a fun orientation and a ridiculously quick glimpse of some major sights as you glide by. Vienna's red trams (a.k.a. streetcars) circle the Ring. Most of them are sleek and new, with a few lovably clickety-clackety older ones still running. Neither tram #1 nor #2 make the entire loop around the Ring, but you can see it all by making one transfer between them. It's a no-stress way to sit shoulder-to-shoulder with ordinary Wieners and see their city.

If you have a transit pass (instead of a ticket), you can—and should—jump on and off as you go, seeing sights that interest you. Some of the best stops are: Weihburggasse (Stadtpark), Stubentor (Museum of Applied Art, a.k.a. MAK), Rathausplatz (City Hall and its summertime food circus), and Burgring (Kunsthistorisches Museum and Hofburg Palace).

You'll find that the tram goes faster than you can read. It's best to look through this chapter ahead of time, then ride with an eye out for the various sights described here.

ORIENTATION

Cost: €1.70 (one transit ticket), €2.20 if bought on tram. A single ticket can be used to cover the whole route, including the transfer between trams (you're not allowed to interrupt your

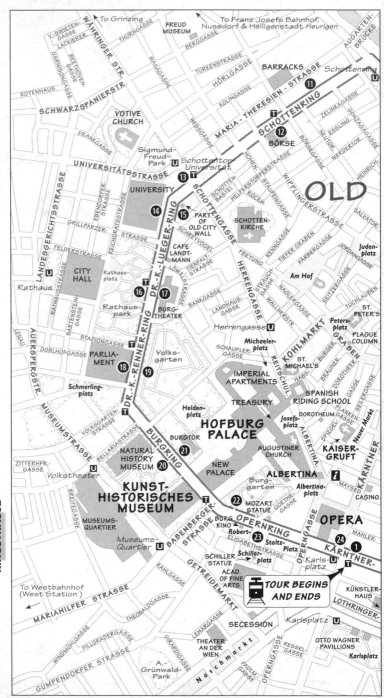

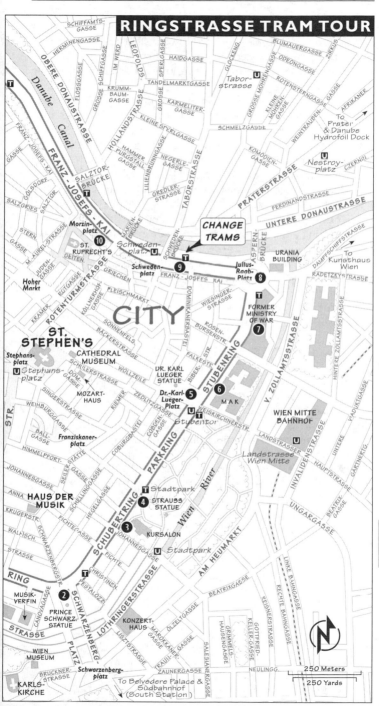

RINGSTRASSE TRAM TOUR

trip, except to transfer). A transit pass (e.g., a 24-hr pass for €5.70, or a 72-hr pass for €13.60) works better for this ride—with a pass you're free to hop on and off as you like; another tram will be along in a few minutes. For more on riding Vienna's trams, see page 37.

When to Go: While this tour works best in the daylight, the tram ride is still worthwhile after dark, when nearly every sight on the route is well-lit.

Getting Started: Start with tram #2, going counter-clockwise around the Ring. Catch it at the Opera (or, if you're coming from Mariahilfer Strasse, at the U-3 stop at the Volkstheater). Change at Schwedenplatz to tram #1, which brings you back to where you began.

Pricier Option: A just-for-tourists tram circles the Ring without requiring a transfer—but it costs more and runs less often (€6 for one loop, €9 for 24-hr hop-on, hop-off privileges, 2/hr 10:00–18:00, July–Aug until 19:00). An excellent bike path circles the whole route, too (see "Getting Around Vienna—By Bike," page 38).

Length of This Tour: About 30 minutes; allow more time if you hop off along the way.

THE TOUR BEGINS

Catch tram #2 just across the street from the Opera; take the underpass and follow signs with the tram symbol. You want the tram going against the direction of car traffic (direction Friedrich-Engels-Platz). If you can, grab a seat on the right—if it's an old-fashioned tram, try to grab the front seat of the front car.

Let's go:

❶ **Look left:** Just next to the Opera, the city's main pedestrian drag, Kärntner Strasse, leads to the zigzag-mosaic roof of **St. Stephen's Cathedral.** This tram tour makes a 360-degree circle around the cathedral, staying about this same distance from it.

❷ **Look right:** At the first bend (before the first stop), you'll see a tall fountain and a guy on a horse. Schwarzenbergplatz shows off its **equestrian statue** of Prince Charles Schwarzenberg, who fought Napoleon. Behind that is the Russian monument (behind the fountain with the Soviet soldier holding a flag), which was built in 1945 as a forced thank-you to the Soviets for liberating Austria from the Nazis. Formerly a sore point, now it's just ignored. Beyond that (out of sight, on tram D route) is Belvedere

RINGSTRASSE

Palace (see page 63).

❸ **Look right:** Going down Schubertring, you reach the huge **Stadtpark** (City Park), which honors many great Viennese musicians and composers with statues. At the beginning of the park, the gold-and-cream concert hall behind the trees is the **Kursalon,** opened in 1867 by the Strauss brothers, who directed many waltzes here. Touristy Strauss concerts are held in this building (for details, see page 168). If the weather's nice, hop off here for a stroll in the park.

❹ **Look right:** Immediately after the next stop, in the same park, the gilded statue of "Waltz King" **Johann Strauss** holds a violin as he did when he conducted his orchestra, whipping his fans into a three-quarter-time frenzy.

❺ **Look left:** Just after the next stop, at end of the park, a green statue of **Dr. Karl Lueger** honors the popular man who was mayor of Vienna until 1910.

❻ **Look right:** Coming up, the big red-brick building is the **Museum of Applied Art** (MAK, showing furniture and design through the ages). Consider hopping off here for a coffee in its beautiful lobby. Its unique gift shop also makes for a fun diversion (free to see lobby; museum admission-€8, free on Sat; open Tue–Sun 10:00–18:00, Tue until 24:00, closed Mon; museum described on page 62).

❼ **Look right:** At next bend, the big white building with decorative military helmets above the windows was the **Austrian Ministry of War**—back when that was a major operation. Field Marshal Radetzky, a military big shot in the 19th century under Franz Josef, still sits on his high horse. He's pointing toward the Post Office Savings Bank (left), the only Art Nouveau building facing the Ring.

❽ **Look right:** At the next corner, the white-domed building over your right shoulder as you turn is the **Urania,** Franz Josef's 1910 observatory. Lean forward and look behind it for a peek at the huge red cars of the giant 100-year-old Ferris wheel in Vienna's Prater amusement park (fun and characteristically Viennese, described on page 74).

Historicism

The architecture along the Ring is known as "Historicism" because it's all Neo-this and Neo-that. It takes design elements from the past—Greek columns, Renaissance arches, Baroque frills—and plasters them on the facade to simulate a building from the past.

Generally, the style fits the purpose of the particular building. For example, the Neoclassical parliament building celebrates ancient Greek notions of democracy. The Neo-Gothic City Hall recalls when medieval burghers ran the city government in Gothic days. Neo-Renaissance museums, such as the Kunsthistorisches and Natural History Museums, celebrate learning. And the Neo-Baroque National Theater recalls the age when opera and theater flourished.

❾ **Prepare to get off:** Your next stop is Schwedenplatz. Get off the tram here and wait for tram #1 (heading in the same direction you've been going; trams come along every 5–10 minutes). Gelato fans may want to prolong the wait a little with a stop at the Eissalon am Schwedenplatz (daily 10:00–23:00).

While you wait, notice the waterway next to you, and how blue it isn't: It's the **Danube Canal** (a.k.a. the "Baby Danube"), one

of the many small arms of the river that once made up the Danube at this location. The rest have been gathered together in a mightier modern-day Danube, farther away. This area was once the center of the original Roman town, Vindobona, located on the banks of the Danube—beyond which lay the barbarian Germanic lands.

If some of the buildings across the canal seem a bit drab, that's because this neighborhood was thoroughly bombed in World War II. These postwar buildings were constructed on the cheap, and are now being replaced by sleek, futuristic buildings. They include the OPEC headquarters, where oil ministers often meet to set prices. Get ready—here comes tram #1.

❿ **Look left:** Now that you're on tram #1, keep an eye toward the old city center. After three long blocks, opposite the BP station (be ready—it passes fast), you'll see the ivy-covered walls and round Romanesque arches of **St. Ruprecht's** (Ruprechtskirche), the oldest church in Vienna. It was built in the 11th century on a bit of Roman ruins. Remember, medieval Vienna was defined by that long-gone wall that you're tracing on this tour. Relax for a few stops (or marvel at the public-transit infrastructure Vienna enjoys) until the corner.

⓫ Look right: Leaving the canal, the tram turns left up Schottenring. A block after the first corner, you can see a huge red-brick castle—actually high-profile **barracks** built here at the command of a nervous Emperor Franz Josef (who found himself on the throne as an 18-year-old in 1848, the same year people's revolts against autocracy were sweeping across Europe).

⓬ Look left: At the next stop, the orange-and-white, Neo-Renaissance temple of money—the **Börse**—is Vienna's stock exchange.

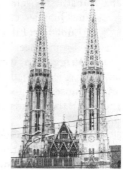

⓭ Look right: At the next stop, on the corner, the huge, frilly, Neo-Gothic church on the right is a **"votive church,"** a type of church built to fulfill a vow in thanks for God's help—in this case, when an 1853 assassination attempt on Emperor Franz Josef failed.

⓮ Look right: Just before the next tram stop is the **Vienna University** building (Universität). Established in 1365, it has no real campus as the buildings are scattered around town.

⓯ Look left: Immediately opposite the university is a chunk of the old **city wall** (behind a gilded angel). Beethoven lived and composed in the building just above the piece of wall.

⓰ Look right: At next stop, flying the flag of Europe, the Neo-Gothic **City Hall** (Rathaus) towers over Rathausplatz. This square is a festive site in summer, with a thriving food circus and a huge screen showing outdoor movies, operas, and concerts. If you're here in summer, come back for lunch or dinner—or, if you're hungry and it's thriving, hop off now (July–mid-Sept 11:00–late; see page 171 and page 159). In December, the City Hall becomes a huge Advent calendar, with 24 windows opening—one each day—as Christmas approaches.

⓱ Look left: Immediately across the street from City Hall is the **Burgtheater,** Austria's national theater. Next door is Café Landtmann (the only café built with the Ringstrasse buildings, and one of the city's finest).

⓲ Look right: Just before the next stop, the Neo-Greek temple of democracy houses the **Austrian Parliament.** The lady with the golden helmet is Athena, goddess of wisdom.

⓳ Look left: Across the street from the Parliament is the imperial park called the **Volksgarten,** with a fine rose garden (free and open to the public).

⑳ Look right: After the next stop is the **Natural History Museum** (Naturhistorisches Museum), which faces its twin, the **Kunsthistorisches Museum,** containing the city's greatest collection of paintings (see page 55). The **MuseumsQuartier** behind them completes the ensemble with a collection of mostly modern art museums (see page 56). A hefty statue of Empress Maria Theresa squats between the museums, facing the grand gate to the Hofburg Palace.

㉑ Look left: The arched gate (the Burgtor) leads to the **Hofburg,** the emperor's palace (described on page 44). Of the five arches, the center one was used only by the emperor. Your tour is nearly finished, so consider hopping off here to see the Hofburg, the Kunsthistorisches Museum, or one of the museums in the MuseumsQuartier.

㉒ Look left: Fifty yards after the next stop, through a gate in the black-iron fence, is a statue of Mozart. It's one of many charms in the **Burggarten,** which until 1918 was the private garden of the emperor. Vienna had more than its share of intellectual and creative geniuses. A hundred yards farther (also on the left, just out of the park), the German philosopher Goethe sits in a big, thought-provoking chair.

㉓ Look right: Goethe seems to be playing trivia with German poet Schiller across the street (on your right). Behind the statue of Schiller is the **Academy of Fine Arts** (described on page 58; next to it is the Burg Kino, which plays the movie *The Third Man* three times a week in English—see page 172).

㉔ Look left...and get off: Hey, there's the **Opera** again. Jump off the tram and see the rest of the city. (To join me on a walking tour of Vienna's center, which starts here at the Opera, see page 77.)

RINGSTRASSE

HOFBURG IMPERIAL APARTMENTS TOUR

Silberkammer • Sisi Museum • Kaiserappartements

In this tour of the Hofburg Imperial Apartments, see the lavish, Versailles-like rooms that were home to the hardworking Emperor Franz Josef I and his reclusive, eccentric empress, known as "Sisi." From here, the Habsburgs ruled their vast empire.

Franz Josef was (for all intents and purposes) the last of the Habsburg monarchs, and these apartments straddle the transition from old to new. You'll see chandeliered luxury alongside office furniture and electric lights.

Franz Josef and Sisi were also a study in contrasts. Where Franz was earnest, practical, and spartan, Sisi was poetic, high-strung, and luxury-loving. Together, they lived their lives in the cocoon of the Imperial Apartments, seemingly oblivious to how the world was changing around them.

ORIENTATION

Cost: €10, includes well-done audioguide.

Hours: Daily July–Aug 9:00–18:00, Sept–June 9:00–17:00, last entry 30 min before closing.

Getting There: Enter under the rotunda at the Hofburg entrance between Michaelerplatz and the palace's central courtyard (In der Burg).

Information: You'll find some helpful posted information in English, and the included audioguide brings the exhibit to life. With those tools and this chapter, you won't need the €8 *Imperial Apartments/Sisi Museum/Silver Collection* guidebook. Tel. 01/533-7570, www.hofburg-wien.at.

THE TOUR BEGINS

Your ticket grants you admission to three separate exhibits, which you'll visit on a pretty straightforward one-way route. The first floor holds a collection of precious porcelain and silver knickknacks *(Silberkammer)*. You then go upstairs to the Sisi Museum, which has displays about her life. This leads into the 20-odd rooms of Imperial Apartments *(Kaiserappartements)*, starting in Franz Josef's rooms, which lead into the dozen rooms where his wife Sisi lived.

IMPERIAL PORCELAIN AND SILVER COLLECTION

Your visit (and the excellent audioguide) starts on the ground floor, with the Habsburg court's vast tableware collection, which the audioguide actually manages to make fairly interesting. Browse the collection to gawk at the opulence and to take in some colorful Habsburg trivia (who'd have thunk that the court had an official way to fold a napkin—and that the technique remains a closely guarded secret?).

• *Once you're through all those rooms of dishes, climb the stairs—the same staircase used by the emperors and empresses who lived here. At the top is a timeline of Sisi's life. Pass through the turnstile, consider the WC, and enter the room with the...*

Model of the Hofburg

Circle to the far side to find where you're standing right now, near the smallest of the Hofburg's three domes.

The Hofburg was the epicenter of one of Europe's great political powers. Six hundred years of Habsburgs lived here in the winter and at Schönbrunn Palace in the heat of summer. The Hofburg started as a 13th-century medieval castle (near where you are right now) and expanded over the centuries to today's 240,000-square-meter (60-acre) complex, now owned by the state.

To the left of the dome (as you face the facade) is the steeple of the Augustiner church. It was there, in 1854, that Franz Josef married 16-year-old Elisabeth of Bavaria, and their story began.

• *Now enter a darkened room at the beginning of the...*

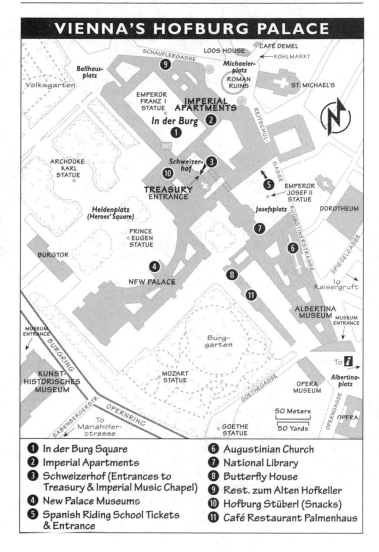

VIENNA'S HOFBURG PALACE

① In der Burg Square
② Imperial Apartments
③ Schweizerhof (Entrances to Treasury & Imperial Music Chapel)
④ New Palace Museums
⑤ Spanish Riding School Tickets & Entrance
⑥ Augustinian Church
⑦ National Library
⑧ Butterfly House
⑨ Rest. zum Alten Hofkeller
⑩ Hofburg Stüberl (Snacks)
⑪ Café Restaurant Palmenhaus

SISI MUSEUM

Empress Elisabeth (1837–1898)—a.k.a. "Sisi" (SEE-see)—was Franz Josef's mysterious, beautiful, and narcissistic wife. This museum traces her fabulous but tragic life.

Sisi's Death

The exhibit starts with Sisi's sad end, showing her **death mask**, photos of her **funeral procession** (by the Hercules statues facing Michaelerplatz), and an **engraving** of a grieving Franz Josef. It

Sisi
(1837–1898)

Empress Elisabeth—Franz Josef's beautiful wife—was the 19th-century equivalent of Princess Diana. Known as "Sisi" since childhood, she became an instant celebrity when she married Franz Josef at the age of 16.

Sisi's main goals in life seem to have been preserving her reputation as a beautiful empress, maintaining her Barbie-doll figure, and tending to her fairy-tale, ankle-length hair. In the 1860s, she was considered one of the most beautiful women in the world. But, in spite of severe dieting and fanatic exercise, age took its toll. After turning 30, she refused photographs and portraits and was generally seen in public with a delicate fan covering her face (and bad teeth).

Complex and influential, Sisi was adored by Franz Josef, whom she respected. Although Franz Josef was supposed to have married her sister Helene (in an arranged diplomatic marriage), he fell in love with Sisi instead. It was one of the Habsburgs' few marriages for love.

Sisi's personal mission and political cause was promoting Hungary's bid for autonomy within the empire. Her personal tragedy was the death of her son Rudolf, the crown prince, in an apparent suicide (an incident often dramatized as the "Mayerling Affair," after the royal hunting lodge where it happened). Disliking Vienna and the confines of the court, Sisi traveled more and more frequently. (She spent so much time in Budapest, and with Hungarian statesman Count Andrássy, that many believe her third daughter to be the count's.) As the years passed, the restless Sisi and her hardworking husband became estranged. In 1898, while visiting Geneva, Switzerland, she was murdered by an Italian anarchist.

Sisi's beauty, bittersweet life, and tragic death helped create her larger-than-life legacy. However, her importance is often inflated by melodramatic accounts of her life. The Sisi Museum seeks to tell a more accurate story.

was at her death that the obscure, private empress' legend began to grow.

• *Continue into the corridor.*

The Sisi Myth

Newspaper clippings of the day make it clear that the empress was not a major public figure in her lifetime. She was often absent from public functions and the censored press was gagged from reporting on her eccentricities. After her death, however, her image quickly became a commodity, and began appearing on everyday items such as **candy tins** and **beer steins.**

The plaster-cast **statue** captures the one element of her persona everyone knew: her petite beauty. Sisi was nearly 5'8" (a head taller than her husband), had a 20-inch waist, and weighed only about 100 pounds. (Her waistline eventually grew...to 21 inches. That was at age 50, after giving birth to four children.) This statue, a copy of one of 30 statues that were erected in her honor in European cities, shows her holding one of her trademark fans. It doesn't show off her magnificent hair, however, which reached down to her ankles.

Sisi-mania really got going in the 1950s with a series of **movies** based on her life (starring Romy Schneider), depicting the empress as beautiful and innocent.

• *Round the corner into the next room.*

Sisi's Childhood

Sisi grew up on a noble estate in Bavaria, amid horses and countryside, far from sophisticated city life. (See her **baby shoes** and the picture of her **childhood palace.**) At 15, Franz Josef—who'd been engaged to someone else—spied Sisi and fell in love. They married. At the wedding reception, Sisi burst into tears, the first sign that something was not right.

The Ballroom: Sisi at Court

Big portraits of Sisi and Franz Josef show them in their royal finery. **Jewels** (actually, replicas) reproduce some of the finery she wore as empress—but to her, they were her "chains." She hated official court duties, being the center of attention, and the constraints of public life. Sisi's mother-in-law dominated her child-rearing, her first-born died, and she complained that she couldn't sleep or eat. However, she did participate in one political cause—championing rights for Habsburg-controlled Hungary (see her **bust** and **portrait as Queen of Hungary**).

• *Head into the next, darkened room.*

Sisi's Beauty

Sisi longed for the carefree days of her youth. She began to withdraw from public life, passing time riding horses (see **horse** statuettes and pictures) and tending obsessively to maintaining her physical beauty. Her **recipes for beauty preparations** included creams and lotions as well as wearing a raw-meat face mask while she slept. Sisi weighed herself obsessively on her gold-trimmed **scale,** and tried all types of diets, including bouillon made with a **duck press.** (She never gave up pastries and ice cream, however.) After she turned 30, Sisi refused all portraits or photographs, preferring that only her more youthful depictions be preserved. Appreciate the **white nightgown, white gloves,** and **ivory fan,** because her life was about to turn even more dark.

• *Then enter the darkest room.*

Death of Sisi's Son

A mannequin wears a replica of Sisi's **black dress.** In 1889, Sisi and Franz Josef's son, Prince Rudolf—whose life had veered into sex, drugs, and liberal politics—killed his lover and himself in a suicide pact. Sisi was shattered, and retreated further from public life.

• *Stroll through several more rooms.*

Escape

Sisi consoled herself with **poetry** (the museum has quotes on the walls) that expresses a longing to escape into an ideal world. She also consoled herself with travel. (See a reconstruction of her **rail car;** a step above a *couchette.*) The **map** shows her visits to Britain, Eastern Europe, and her favorite spot, Greece.

Final Room: Assassination

Sisi met her fate while traveling. While walking along a street in Geneva, Sisi was stalked and attacked by an Italian anarchist who despised royal oppressors and wanted notoriety for his cause. (He'd planned on assassinating a less-famous French prince that day—whom he'd been unable to track down—but quickly changed plans when word got out that Sisi was in town.) The **murder weapon** was this small, crude knife. It made only a small wound, but it proved fatal.

• *After the Sisi Museum, a one-way route takes you through a series of royal rooms. The first room—as if to make clear that there was more to the Habsburgs than Sisi—shows a family tree tracing the Habsburgs from 1273 to their messy WWI demise. From here, you enter the private apartments of the royal family (Franz Josef's first, then Sisi's).*

IMPERIAL APARTMENTS

These were the private apartments and public meeting rooms for the emperor and empress. Franz Josef I lived here from 1857 until his death in 1916. (He had hoped to move to new digs in the New Palace, but that was not finished until after his death.)

Franz Josef was the last great Habsburg ruler. (For an abridged Habsburg family tree, see page 367.) In these rooms, he presided over defeats and liberal inroads, as the world was changing and the monarchy became obsolete. Here he met with advisors and welcomed foreign dignitaries, hosted lavish, white-gloved balls and stuffy formal dinners, and raised three children. He slept (alone)

Emperor Franz Josef
(1830–1916)

Franz Josef I—who ruled for 68 years (1848–1916)—was the embodiment of the Habsburg Empire as it finished its six-century-long ride. Born in 1830, Franz Josef had a stern upbringing that instilled in him a powerful sense of duty and—like so many men of power—a love of things military.

His uncle, Ferdinand I, suffered from profound epilepsy, which prevented him from being an effective ruler. As the revolutions of 1848 rattled royal families throughout Europe, the Habsburgs forced Ferdinand to abdicate and put 18-year old Franz Josef on the throne. Ironically, as one of his first acts as emperor, Franz Josef—whose wife would later become closely identified with Hungarian independence—put down the 1848 revolt in Hungary with bloody harshness. He spent the first part of his long reign understandably paranoid, as social discontent continued to simmer.

Franz Josef was very conservative. But worse, he wrongly believed that he was a talented military tactician, and led Austria into catastrophic battles against Italy (which was fighting for its unification and independence) in the 1860s. As his army endured severe, avoidable casualties, it became clear: Franz Josef was a disaster as a general.

Wearing his uniform to the end, he never saw what a dinosaur his monarchy was becoming, and never thought it strange that the majority of his subjects didn't even speak German. Franz Josef had no interest in democracy and pointedly never set foot in Austria's parliament building. But, like his contemporary Queen Victoria, he was a microcosm of his empire—old-fashioned but sacrosanct. His passion for low-grade paperwork earned him the nickname "Joe Bureaucrat." Mired in these petty details, he missed the big picture. In 1914, he helped start a Great War that ultimately ended the age of monarchs. The year 1918 marked the end of Europe's big royal families: Hohenzollerns (Prussia), Romanovs (Russia), and Habsburgs (Austria).

on his austere bed while his beloved wife Sisi retreated to her own rooms. He suffered through the assassination of his brother, the suicide of his son and heir, the murder of his wife, and the assassination of his nephew, Archduke Ferdinand, which sparked World War I and spelled the end of the Habsburg monarchy.

The Emperor's Rooms
Waiting Room for the Audience Room

Mannequins from the many corners of the Habsburg realm illustrate the multi-ethnic nature of the vast empire. (Also see the

map of the empire, by the window.) Every citizen had the right to meet privately with the emperor, and people traveled fairly far to do so. While they waited nervously, they had these **three huge paintings** to stare at—propaganda showing crowds of commoners enthusiastic about their Habsburg rulers.

The painting on the right shows an 1809 scene of Emperor Franz II (Franz Josef's grandfather) returning to Vienna, celebrating the news that Napoleon had begun his retreat.

In the central painting, Franz II makes his first public appearance to adoring crowds after recovering from a life-threatening illness (1826).

In the painting on the left, Franz II returns to Vienna (see the Karlskirche in the background) to celebrate the defeat of Napoleon. The 1815 Congress of Vienna that followed was the greatest assembly of diplomats in European history. Its goal: to establish peace by shoring up Europe's monarchies against the rise of democracy and nationalism. It worked for about a century, until a colossal war—World War I—wiped out the Habsburgs and the rest of Europe's royal families.

This room's **chandelier**—considered the best in the palace—is Baroque, made of Bohemian crystal. It lit things until 1891, when the palace installed electric lights.

Audience Room

This is the room where Franz Josef received commoners from around the empire. They came from far and wide to show gratitude or to make a request. Imagine you've traveled for days to have your say before the emperor. You're wearing your new fancy suit—Franz Josef required that men coming before him wear a tailcoat, women a black gown with a train. You've rehearsed what you want to say. You hope your hair looks good.

Suddenly, you're face-to-face with the emp himself. (The **portrait** on the easel shows Franz Josef in 1915, when he was more than 80 years old.) Despite your efforts, you probably weren't in this room long. He'd stand at the **high table** (far left) as the visiting commoners had their say. (Standing kept things moving.) You'd hear a brief response from him (quite likely the same he'd given all day), and then you'd back out of the room while bowing (also required). On the table, you can read a partial **list** of 56 appointments he had on January 3, 1910 (three columns: family name, meeting topic, and *Anmerkung*—the emperor's "action log").

Conference Room

The emperor presided here over the equivalent of cabinet meetings. An ongoing topic was what to do with unruly Hungary. After 1867, Franz Josef granted Hungary a measure of independence (thus creating the "Austro-Hungarian Empire"). Hungarian diplomats attended meetings here, watched over by **paintings** on the wall showing Austria's army suppressing the popular Hungarian uprising...subtle.

Emperor Franz Josef's Study

This room evokes how seriously the emperor took his responsibilities as the top official of a vast empire. Famously energetic, Franz Josef lived a spartan life dedicated to duty. The **desk** was originally between the windows. Franz Josef could look up from his work and see his lovely, long-haired, tiny-waisted Empress Elisabeth's reflection in the mirror. Notice the **trompe l'oeil paintings** above each door, giving the believable illusion of marble relief. Notice also all the **family photos**—the perfect gift for the dad/uncle/hubby who has it all.

The walls between the rooms are wide enough to hide servants' corridors (the hidden door to his valet's room is in the back left corner). The emperor lived with a personal staff of 14: "three valets, four lackeys, two doormen, two manservants, and three chambermaids."

Emperor's Bedroom

Franz Josef famously slept on this no-frills **iron bed,** and used the **portable washstand** until 1880 (when the palace got running water). He typically rose at 3:30, and started his day in prayer, kneeling at the **prayer stool** against the far wall. After all, he was a "Divine Right" ruler. While he had a typical emperor's share of mistresses, his dresser was always well-stocked with **photos** of Sisi. Franz Josef lived here after his estrangement from Sisi. An **etching** shows the empress—a fine rider and avid hunter—sitting sidesaddle while jumping a hedge.

Large Salon

This room was for royal family gatherings, and went unused after Sisi's death. The big, ornate **stove** in the corner was fed from behind (this remained a standard form of heating through the 19th century).

Small Salon

This room is dedicated to the memory of Franz Josef's brother (see the **bearded portrait**), the Emperor Maximilian of Mexico, who was assassinated in 1867. It was also a smoking room. This was a necessity in the early 19th century, when smoking was newly fashionable for men, and was never done in the presence of women.

After the birth of their last child in 1868, Franz Josef and Sisi began to drift further apart. Left of the door is a small **button** the

IMPERIAL APTS

emperor had to buzz before entering his estranged wife's quarters. You, however, can go right in.

• *Climb a few steps and enter Sisi's wing.*

Empress' Rooms

Empress' Bedroom and Drawing Room

This was Sisi's room, refurbished in the Neo-Rococo style in 1854. There's the red **carpet,** covered with oriental rugs. There were always lots of fresh flowers. She not only slept here, but also lived here—the bed was rolled in and out daily—until her death in 1898. The **desk** is where she sat and wrote her letters and poems.

Sisi's Dressing/Exercise Room

Servants worked three hours a day on Sisi's famous hair, while she passed the time reading. She'd exercise on the **wooden structure** and on the **rings** suspended from the doorway to the left. Afterward, she'd get a massage on the red-covered **bed.** You can psychoanalyze Sisi from the **portraits and photos** she chose to hang on her walls. They're mostly her favorite dogs, her Bavarian family, and several portraits of the romantic and anti-monarchist poet Heinrich Heine. Her infatuation with the liberal Heine caused a stir in royal circles.

Sisi's Bathroom

Detour into the behind-the-scenes palace. In the narrow passage-way, you'll walk by Sisi's hand-painted porcelain, dolphin-head **WC** (on the right). In the main bathroom, you'll see her huge copper tub (with the original wall coverings behind it) where servants washed her hair—an all-day affair. Sisi was the first Habsburg to have running water in her bathroom (notice the hot and cold faucets). You're walking on the first linoleum ever used in Vienna (c. 1880).

Servants' Quarters

Next, enter the servants' quarters, with hand-painted **tropical scenes.** Take time to enjoy the playful details. As you leave these rooms and re-enter the imperial world, look back to the room on the left.

Empress' Great Salon

The room is **painted** with Mediterranean escapes, the 19th-century equivalent of travel posters. The **statue of Polyhymnia** (the mythical Muse of poetry) is by the great Neoclassical master Antonio Canova. It has the features of Elisa, Napoleon's oldest sister, who hobnobbed with the Habsburgs. A **print** shows how

Franz Josef and Sisi would—on their good days—share breakfast in this room.

Small Salon

The portrait is of **Crown Prince Rudolf,** Franz Josef and Sisi's only son. On the morning of January 30, 1889, the 30-year-old Rudolf and a beautiful baroness were found shot dead in his hunting lodge in Mayerling. An investigation never came up with a complete explanation, but Rudolf had obviously been cheating on his wife, and the affair ended in an apparent murder-suicide. The scandal shocked the empire and tainted the Habsburgs, Sisi retreated further into her fantasy world, and Franz Josef carried on stoically with a broken heart. The mysterious "Mayerling Affair" has been dramatized in numerous movies, plays, opera, and even a ballet.

• *Leaving Sisi's wing, turn the corner into the white-and-gold rooms occupied by the czar of Russia during the 1814–1815 Congress of Vienna. Sisi and Franz Josef used the rooms for formal occasions and public functions.*

Alexander Apartments

Red Salon

The **Gobelin wall** hangings were a 1776 gift from Marie-Antoinette and Louis XVI in Paris to their Viennese counterparts.

Dining Room

It's dinnertime, and Franz Josef has called his extended family together. The settings are modest...just silver. Gold was saved for

formal state dinners. Next to each name card was a menu naming the chef responsible for each dish. (Talk about pressure.) While the Hofburg had tableware for 4,000, feeding 3,000 was a typical day. The cellar was stocked with 60,000 bottles of wine. The kitchen was huge—50 birds could be roasted at once on the hand-driven spits.

The emperor sat in the center of the long table. "Ladies and gentlemen" alternated in the seating. The green glasses were for Rhenish wine. Franz Josef enforced strict protocol at mealtime: No one could speak without being spoken to by the emperor, and no one could eat after he was done. While the rest of Europe was growing democracy and expanding personal freedoms, the Habsburgs preserved their ossified worldview to the bitter end.

IMPERIAL APTS

In 1918, World War I ended, Austria was created as a modern nation-state, the Habsburgs were tossed out...and the Hofburg Palace was destined to become a museum.

• *Drop off your audioguide, zip through the shop, go down the stairs, and you're back on the street. Two quick lefts take you back to the palace square (In der Burg), where the Treasury awaits just past the black, red, and gold gate on the far side (see the next chapter).*

HOFBURG TREASURY TOUR

Weltliche und Geistliche Schatzkammer

This Hofburg Palace's "Secular and Religious Treasure Room" contains the best jewels on the Continent. Slip through the vault doors and reflect on the glitter of 21 rooms filled with scepters, swords, crowns, orbs, weighty robes, double-headed eagles, gowns, gem-studded bangles, and a unicorn horn.

There are plenty of beautiful objects here—I've highlighted those that have the most history behind them. But you could spend days in here marveling at the riches of the bygone empire.

The Treasury's audioguide is excellent and makes up for the lack of written English descriptions. Use this chapter to get the lay of the land, then explore the Treasury in detail with the audioguide.

ORIENTATION

Cost: €10, €18 combo-ticket with Kunsthistorisches Museum.

Hours: Wed–Mon 10:00–18:00, closed Tue.

Audioguide: €3, and well worth it.

Getting There: The Treasury is tucked away in the Hofburg Palace complex. From the Hofburg's central courtyard (called In der Burg), salute the Caesar-esque statue and turn about-face. Pass through the black, red, and gold gate, following *Schatzkammer* signs, which lead into a small courtyard; the Treasury is in the far right corner (see map on page 111).

Information: Tel. 01/525-240, www.khm.at.

Starring: The Imperial Crown and other accessories of the Holy Roman Emperors, plus many other crowns, jewels, robes, and priceless knickknacks.

THE TOUR BEGINS

The Habsburgs saw themselves as the successors to the ancient Roman emperors, and they wanted crowns and royal regalia to match the pomp of the ancients. They used these precious objects for coronation ceremonies, official ribbon-cutting events, and their own personal pleasure. You'll see the prestigious crowns and accoutrements of the rulers of the Holy Roman Empire (a medieval alliance of Germanic kingdoms so named because it wanted to be considered the continuation of the Roman Empire). Other crowns belonged to Austrian dukes and kings, and some robes and paraphernalia were used by Austria's religious elite. And many costly things were created simply for the enjoyment of the wealthy (but not necessarily royal) Habsburgs.

From the First Habsburg to Napoleon
Room 1
Start your tour with a look at the underwhelming **crown of Rudolf IV,** the one stripped of jewels, with an orb-and-cross on the top,

located near the doorway leading into Room 2. (This particular crown is actually a 1764 simulation of the original.) Rudolf IV (1339–1365) was the founder of the Habsburg dynasty, and the first to be crowned the Archduke of Austria. Some of his descendants would later be crowned not only as rulers of Austria, but also as Holy Roman Emperors. (See the Habsburg family tree on page 367.) They copied elements of Rudolf's crown when designing their own, trying to capture some of his reflected glory.

Room 2
The personal **crown of Rudolf II** (1602) occupies the center of the room along with its accompanying scepter and orb; a bust of Rudolf II (1552–1612) sits nearby.

The crown's design symbolically merges a bishop's miter ("Holy"), the arch across the top of a Roman emperor's helmet ("Roman"), and the typical medieval king's crown ("Emperor"). Accompanying the crown is the matching **scepter** (made from the ivory tusk of a narwhal), and the **orb** holding four diamonds to symbolize the four corners of the world, which the emperor ruled. Orbs have been royal symbols of the world since ancient Roman times. They seem to indicate that, even in pre-Columbus days, Europe's intelligentsia assumed the world was round.

This crown was Rudolf's personal one. He wore a different crown (which we'll see later) in his official role as Holy Roman Emperor. In many dynasties, a personal crown like this was dismantled by the next ruler to custom-make his own. But Rudolf's crown was so well-crafted that it was passed down through the generations, even inspiring crown-shaped church steeples as far

away as Amsterdam (when it was under Habsburg control).

Two centuries later (1806), this crown and scepter became the official regalia of Austria's rulers, as seen in the large **portrait of Franz I** (the one behind you). Napoleon Bonaparte had just conquered Austria and dissolved the Holy Roman Empire. Franz (ruled 1792–1835) was allowed to remain in power, but he had to downgrade his title from "Franz II, Holy Roman Emperor" to "Franz I, Emperor of Austria."

Rooms 3 and 4

These rooms contain some of the **coronation vestments and regalia** needed for the new Austrian (not Holy Roman) emperor. There was a different one for each of the emperor's subsidiary titles, e.g., King of Hungary or King of Lombardy. So many crowns and kingdoms in the Habsburg's vast empire! Those with ermine collars are modeled after Napoleon's coronation robes.

• *For more on how Napoleon had an impact on Habsburg Austria, pass through Room 9 and into...*

Room 5

Ponder the **Cradle of the King of Rome,** once occupied by Napoleon's son, who was born in 1811 and made King of Rome. The little eagle at the foot is symbolically not yet able to fly, but glory-bound. Glory is symbolized by the star, with dad's big *N* raised high.

Napoleon Bonaparte (1769–1821) was a French commoner who rose to power as a charismatic general in the Revolution. While pledging allegiance to democracy, he in fact crowned himself Emperor of France and hobnobbed with Europe's royalty. When his wife Josephine could not bear him a male heir, Napoleon divorced her and married into the Habsburg family.

Portraits show Napoleon and his new bride, Marie Louise, Franz I/II's daughter (and Marie-Antoinette's great-niece). Napoleon gave her a **jewel chest** decorated with the bees of industriousness, his personal emblem. With the birth of the baby King of Rome, Napoleon and Marie Louise were poised to start a new dynasty of European rulers...but then Napoleon met his Waterloo, and the Habsburgs remained in power.

Miscellaneous Wonders

Room 6

For Divine Right kings, even child-rearing was a sacred ritual that needed elaborate regalia for public ceremonies. The 23-pound **gold basin and pitcher** were used to baptize noble children, who were dressed in the **hooded baptismal dresses** displayed nearby.

Room 7

These jewels are the true "treasures," a cabinet of wonders used by Habsburgs to impress their relatives (or to hock when funds got low). The irregularly shaped, 2,680-karat **emerald** is rough-cut, as the cutter wanted to do only the minimum to avoid making a mistake and shattering the giant gem. Check out the milky **opal,** the **"hair amethyst,"** and a 492-karat **aquamarine.** The helmet-like jewel-studded **crown** was a gift from Muslim Turks supporting a Hungarian king who, as a Protestant, was a thorn in the side of the Catholic Habsburgs (who eventually toppled him).

Room 8

The eight-foot-tall, 500-year-old **"unicorn horn"** (a narwhal tusk), was considered to have magical healing powers bestowed from on high. This one was owned by the Holy Roman Emperor—clearly a divine monarch. The huge **agate bowl,** cut from a single piece, may have been made in ancient Roman times and eventually found its way into the collection of their successors, the Habsburgs.

Religious Rooms

After Room 8, you enter several rooms of **religious objects**—crucifixes, chalices, mini-altarpieces, reliquaries, and bishops' vestments. Habsburg rulers mixed the institutions of church and state, so these precious religious accoutrements were also part of their display of secular power.

• *Browse these rooms, then backtrack, passing by the Cradle of the King of Rome, and eventually reaching...*

Regalia of the Holy Roman Empire
Room 10

The next few rooms contain some of the oldest and most venerated objects in the Treasury—the robes, crowns, and sacred objects of the Holy Roman Emperor.

The big red-silk and gold-thread **mantle,** nearly 900 years old, was worn by Holy Roman Emperors at their coronation.

Notice the oriental imagery: a palm tree in the center, flanked by lions subduing camels. The hem is written in Arabic (wishing its wearer "great wealth, gifts, and pleasure"). This robe, brought back from the East by Crusaders, gave the Germanic emperors an exotic look that recalled great Biblical kings such as Solomon. Many Holy Roman Emperors were crowned by the pope himself. That fact, plus this Jerusalem-looking mantle, helped put the "Holy" in Holy Roman Emperor.

Room 11

The collection's highlight is the 10th-century **crown of the Holy Roman Emperor.** It was probably made for Otto I (c. 960), the first king to call himself Holy Roman Emperor.

Charlemagne (Karl der Grosse) and the Holy Roman Empire

The title Holy Roman Emperor conveyed three important concepts:

Holy = The emperor ruled by divine authority (and not as a pagan Roman).

Roman = He was a successor to the empire that fell in A.D. 476.

Emperor = He was a ruler over many different nationalities.

Charlemagne (747–1814) briefly united much of Western Europe—that is, the former Roman Empire. On Christmas Eve in the year 800, he was crowned "Roman Emperor" by the pope in St. Peter's Basilica in Rome. After Charlemagne's death, the empire split apart. His successors (who ruled only a portion of Charlemagne's empire) still wanted to envision themselves as inheritors of Charlemagne's greatness. They took to calling themselves Roman Emperors, and added the "Holy" part in the 11th century to emphasize that they ruled by divine authority.

It was an elected, not necessarily hereditary, office. Each province had important rulers, called Electors, who would gather to pick the new ruler. The practice lasted through medieval and Renaissance times, with many of the HREs being members of the Habsburg family.

At the empire's peak around 1520, it truly was great, stretching from Vienna to Spain, from Holland to Sicily, and from Bohemia to Bolivia in the New World. But throughout much of its existence, the HRE consisted of little more than petty dukes, ruling a loose coalition of independent nobles. It was Voltaire who quipped that the HRE was "neither holy, nor Roman, nor an empire."

Napoleon ended the title in 1806. The last emperors (including Franz Josef) were merely emperors of Austria and Hungary.

The Imperial Crown swirls with symbolism "proving" that the emperor was both holy and Roman: The cross on top says the HRE ruled as Christ's representative on earth, and the jeweled arch over the top is reminiscent of the parade helmet of ancient Romans. The jewels themselves allude to the wearer's kinghood in the here and now. Imagine the impression this priceless, glittering crown must have made on the

emperor's medieval subjects.

King Solomon's portrait on the crown (to the right of the cross) is Old Testament proof that kings can be wise and good. King David (next panel) is similar proof that they can be just. The crown's eight sides represent the celestial city of Jerusalem's eight gates. The jewels on the front panel symbolize the 12 apostles.

On the forehead of the crown, notice that beneath the cross there's a pale-blue heart-shaped sapphire. Look a little small for the prime spot? That's because this is a replacement for a long-lost opal said to have had almost mythical, magical powers.

In another glass case is the 11th-century **Imperial Cross** that preceded the emperor in ceremonies. Encrusted with jewels, it had a hollow compartment (its core is wood) that carried substantial chunks thought to be from *the* **cross** and *the* **Holy Lance** used to pierce the side of Jesus when he was crucified (both pieces are displayed in the same glass case). Holy Roman Emperors actually carried the lance into battle in the 10th century. Look behind the cross to see how it was a box that could be clipped open and shut, used for holding holy relics. You can see bits of the "true cross" anywhere, but this is a prime piece—with the actual nail hole.

The other case has additional objects used in the coronation ceremony—the **orb** (orbs were modeled on late-Roman ceremonial objects, then topped with the cross) and **scepter** (the one with the oak leaves) and the sword, carried ahead of the emperor in the procession. In earlier times, these objects were thought to have belonged to Charlemagne himself, the greatest ruler of medieval Europe, but in fact they're mostly from 300 to 400 years later (c. 1200).

Yet another glass case contains more objects said to belong to Charlemagne. Some of these may actually be authentic, since they're closer to his era. You'll see the jeweled, purse-like **reliquary of St. Stephen** and the **saber of Charlemagne.** The gold-covered **Book of the Gospels** was the Bible that HREs placed their hand on to swear the oath of office. On the wall nearby, the **tall painting** depicts Charlemagne modeling the Imperial Crown—although

the crown wasn't made until a hundred years after he died.

Room 12

Now picture all this regalia used together. The **painting** shows the coronation of Maria Theresa's son Josef II as Holy Roman

Emperor in 1764. Set in a church in Frankfurt (filled with the bigwigs—literally—of the day), Josef is wearing the same crown and royal garb that you've just seen.

Emperors followed the same coronation ritual that originated in the 10th century. The new emperor would don the mantle. The entourage paraded into a church for Mass, led by the religious authorities carrying the Imperial Cross. The emperor placed his hand on the Book of the Gospels and swore his oath. Then he knelt before the three Electors (or sometimes even the pope himself), who placed the Imperial Crown on his head. The new emperor rose, accepted the orb and scepter, and—dut dutta dah!—you had a new ruler.

The Rest of the Treasury

Room 12 also displays the **leather cases** used to store and transport the crowns, crosses, and other objects. Another glass case contains **relics**—such as a fragment of Jesus' manger, a piece of Christ's loincloth, and a shred of the Last Supper tablecloth.

Rooms 13–15 have (among other things) **portraits of important Habsburgs,** such as Maximilian I and Mary of Burgundy. Room 16 contains the **royal vestments** (15th century), which display perhaps the most exquisite workmanship in the entire Treasury. Look closely— they're "painted" with gold and silver threads. But after seeing so much bling, by the time you view these vestments, they can seem downright understated—just another example of the pomp and circumstance of the majestic Habsburgs.

KUNSTHISTORISCHES MUSEUM TOUR

The Kunsthistorwhateveritis Museum—let's just say "Koonst"—houses the family collection of Austria's luxury-loving Habsburg rulers. Their joie de vivre is reflected in this collection—some of the most beautiful, sexy, and fun art from two centuries (c. 1450–1650). At their peak of power in the 1500s, the Habsburgs ruled Austria, Germany, northern Italy, the Netherlands, and Spain—and you'll see art from all these places and beyond.

The building itself is huge, lavishly decorated, and features grand marble staircases and lobbies glittering with gold-leaf splendor. Despite its palatial feel, it was originally designed for the same purpose it serves today—to showcase its treasures while impressing visitors with the grandeur of the empire.

ORIENTATION

Cost: €10, €18 combo-ticket with the Hofburg Treasury.
Hours: Tue–Sun 10:00–18:00, Thu until 21:00, closed Mon.
Location: It's on the Ringstrasse at Maria-Theresien-Platz, U-2 or U-3: Volkstheater/Museumsplatz.
Information: The audioguide costs €3. Tel. 01/525-240, www.khm.at.
Starring: The world's best collection of Breughels, plus Titian, Caravaggio, a Vermeer gem, and Rembrandt self-portraits.

THE TOUR BEGINS

Of the museum's many exhibits, we'll tour only the Painting Gallery (Gemäldegalerie) on the first floor. Climb the main staircase, featuring Antonio Canova's statue of *Theseus Clubbing the Centaur*. Italian Art is in the right half of the building (as you face Theseus), and Northern Art to the left. Notice that the museum labels the largest rooms with Roman numerals (Saal I, II, III), and the smaller rooms around the perimeter with Arabic (Rooms 1, 2, 3).

• *Enter Saal I and walk right into the High Renaissance.*

Venetian Renaissance (1500–1600)—Titian, Veronese, Tintoretto

About the year 1500, Italy had a renaissance, or "rebirth," of interest in the art and learning of ancient Greece and Rome. In painting, that meant that ordinary humans and Greek gods joined saints and angels as popular subjects.

Saal I spans the long career of **Titian** the Venetian (it rhymes). He painted portraits, Christian Madonnas, and sexy Venuses with equal ease. He seemed par-

ticularly intimate with the pre-Christian gods and their antics. In *Mars, Venus, and Amor,* a busy cupid oversees the goddess of love, making her case that war is not the answer. Mars—his weapons blissfully discarded—sees her point.

Danae with Nursemaid (usually in Saal I, but may be out for restoration during your visit) features more pre-Christian mythology. Zeus, the king of the gods, was always zooming to earth in the form of some creature or other to fool around with mortal women. Here, he descends as a shower of gold to consort with the willing Danae. You can almost see the human form of Zeus within the cloud. Danae is helpless with rapture, opening her legs to receive him, while her servant tries to catch the heavenly spurt with a towel. Danae's rich, luminous flesh on the left of the canvas is set off by the dark servant at right and the threatening sky above. The white sheets beneath her make her glow even more. This is not just a classic nude—it's a Renaissance Miss August. How could ultra-conservative Catholic emperors have tolerated such a downright pagan and erotic painting? Apparently, without a problem.

In the large *Ecce Homo,* Titian tackles a Christian theme. A crowd mills about, when suddenly there's a commotion. They nudge each other and start to point. Follow their gaze diagonally up the

KUNSTHISTORISCHES MUSEUM

To Opera

VAN DER WEYDEN, BOSCH & VAN EYCK

COREGGIO & PARMIGIANINO

DÜRER

EARLY NORTHERN

MANTEGNA

RAPHAEL

17 16 14 1 2 3 4

Saal XI

Saal X

BRUEGEL

Saal IX

WC

WC

THESEUS STATUE

TITIAN
TOUR BEGINS

Saal I

VERO-NESE
Saal II

TINTO-RETTO
Saal III

MAIN STAIRCASE

MORE NORTHERN ART

NORTHERN ART

ITALIAN ART

MORE ITALIAN ART

RINGSTRASSE

RUBENS

Saal XIII

Saal XIV

Saal XV

BAROQUE
Saal VI

CARA-VAGGIO
Saal V

VERMEER

21 22 23 STEEN

VELÁZ-QUEZ 10

i

REMBRANDT
TOUR ENDS

BOOKS

Not to Scale

ENTRANCE
(on ground level)

MARIA-THERESIEN-PLATZ

KUNSTHISTORISCHES

stairs to a battered figure entering way up in the corner. "Ecce Homo!" says Pilate. "Behold the man." And he presents Jesus to the mob. For us, as for the unsympathetic crowd, the humiliated Son of God is not the center of the scene, but almost an afterthought.

• *Enter Saal II.*

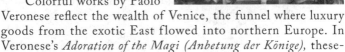

Colorful works by Paolo Veronese reflect the wealth of Venice, the funnel where luxury goods from the exotic East flowed into northern Europe. In Veronese's *Adoration of the Magi (Anbetung der Könige)*, these-Three-Kings-from-Orient-are dressed not in biblical costume, but in the imported silks of Venetian businessmen.

• *In Saal III...*

Tintoretto's many portraits give us a peek at the movers and shakers of the Venetian Empire.

• *The following paintings are generally found in Rooms 1–4, the smaller rooms that adjoin Saals I, II, and III.*

Italian Renaissance and Mannerism

St. Sebastian (Der Hl. Sebastian), by **Andrea Mantegna,** is shot through with arrows. Sebastian was an early Christian martyr, but he stands like a Renaissance statue—on a pedestal, his weight on one foot, displaying his Greek-god anatomy. Mantegna places the three-dimensional "statue" in a three-dimensional setting, using floor tiles and roads that recede into the distance to create the illusion of depth.

In **Correggio**'s *Jupiter and Io,* the king of the gods appears in a cloud—see his foggy face and hands?—to get a date with a beautiful nymph named Io. ("Io, Io, it's off to earth I go.") Correggio tips Renaissance "balance"—the enraptured Io may be perched vertically in the center of the canvas right now, but she won't be for long.

Find the little round painting nearby. In his *Self-Portrait in a Convex Mirror (Selbstbildnis im Konvexspiegel),* 21-year-old **Parmigianino** (like the cheese) gazes into a convex mirror and perfectly reproduces the curved reflection on a convex piece of wood. Amazing.

The 22-year-old **Raphael** (roff-eye-EL) captured the spirit of the High Renaissance, combining symmetry, grace, beauty, and emotion. His *Madonna of the Meadow (Die Madonna im Grünen)* is a mountain of motherly love— Mary's head is the summit and her flowing robe is the base—enfolding baby Jesus and John the Baptist. The geometric perfection, serene landscape, and Mary's adorable face make this a masterpiece of sheer grace...but then you get smacked by an ironic fist: The cross the little tykes play with foreshadows their gruesome deaths.

Farther along, through the small rooms along the far end of this wing, find the cleverly deceptive portraits by **Giuseppe Arcimboldo.** His *Summer*—a.k.a "Fruit Face"—is one of four paintings the Habsburg court painter did showing the seasons (and elements) as people. With a pickle nose, pear chin, and corn-husk ears, this guy literally is what he eats.

• *Find Caravaggio in Saal V.*

Caravaggio

Caravaggio (kah-rah-VAH-jee-oh) shocked the art world with brutally honest reality. Compared with Raphael's super-sweet *Madonna of the Meadow*, Caravaggio's *Madonna of the Rosary (Die Rosenkranzmadonna*, the biggest canvas in the room) looks perfectly ordinary, and the saints kneeling around her have dirty feet.

In *David with the Head of Goliath (David mit dem Haupt des Goliath)*—in the corner near the window—Caravaggio turns a third-degree-interrogation light on a familiar Bible story. David shoves the dripping head of the slain giant right in our noses. The painting, bled of color, is virtually a black-and-white crime-scene photo—slightly overexposed. Out of the deep darkness shine only a few crucial details. This David is not a heroic Renaissance man like Michelangelo's famous statue, but a homeless teen that Caravaggio paid to portray God's servant. And the severed head of Goliath is none other than Caravaggio himself, an in-your-face self-portrait.

• *Find Room 10, in the corner of the museum.*

Velázquez

When the Habsburgs ruled both Austria and Spain, cousins kept in touch through portraits of themselves and their kids. Diego Velázquez (veh-LOSS-kehs) was the greatest of Spain's "photojournalist" painters: heavily influenced by Caravaggio's realism, capturing his subjects without passing judgment, flattering, or glorifying them.

Watch little Margarita Habsburg grow up in three different *Portraits of Margarita Theresa (Die Infantin Margarita Teresa)*, from

age two to age nine. Margarita was destined from birth to marry her Austrian cousin, the future Emperor Leopold I. Pictures like these, sent from Spain every few years, let her pen-pal/fiancé get to know her. Also see a portrait of Margarita's little brother, *Philip Prosper*, looking like a tiny priest. The kids' oh-so-serious faces, regal poses, and royal trappings are contradicted by their cuteness. No wonder Velázquez was so popular.

• *Return to the main Saals and continue on, past glimpses of Baroque art, featuring large, colorful canvases showcasing over-the-top emotions and the surefire mark of Baroque art: pudgy, winged babies. If you don't have time to get out to Schönbrunn Palace on this visit, you can get a good look at it here—find Canaletto's* Schloss Schönbrunn *in Saal VII, which also shows the Viennese skyline in the distance. When you reach the stairwell, head kitty-corner across it to the east wing, opposite the Titian Room. Make your way to Room 14 to see some...*

Early Northern Art

The "Northern Renaissance," brought on by the economic boom of Dutch and Flemish trading, was more secular and Protestant than Catholic-funded Italian art. We'll see fewer Madonnas, saints, and Greek gods and more peasants, landscapes, and food. Paintings are smaller and darker, full of down-to-earth objects. Northern artists sweated the details, encouraging the patient viewer to appreciate the beauty in everyday things.

In the three sections of Room 14 are three early northern painters. **Rogier van der Weyden**'s *Triptych: The Crucifixion (Kreuzigungsaltar)* strips the Crucifixion down to the essential characters, set in a sparse landscape. The agony

is understated, seen in just a few solemn faces and dramatically creased robes. To the left, in the painstakingly detailed *Portrait of Cardinal Niccolò Albergati*, **Jan van Eyck** refuses to airbrush out the jowls and wrinkles, showcasing the quiet dignity of an ordinary man.

And in the freestanding case, **Hieronymus Bosch**'s *Christ Carrying the Cross (Kreuztragung Christi)* is crammed with puny humans, not supermen.

• *Saal X contains the largest collection of Bruegels in captivity. Linger. If you like it, linger longer.*

Pieter Bruegel—Norman Rockwell of the 16th Century

The undisputed master of the slice-of-life village scene was Pieter Bruegel the Elder (c. 1525–1569). (His name is pronounced "BROY-gull," and is sometimes spelled *Brueghel*. Don't confuse Pieter Bruegel the Elder with his sons, Pieter Brueghel the Younger and Jan Brueghel, who added luster and an "h" to the family name.) Despite his many rural paintings, Bruegel was actually a cultivated urbanite who liked to wear peasants' clothing to observe country folk at play (a trans-fest-ite?). He celebrated their simple life, but he also skewered their weaknesses—not to single them out as hicks, but as universal examples of human folly.

The *Peasant Wedding (Bauernhochzeit)*, Bruegel's most famous work, is less about the wedding than the food. It's a farmers' feed-

ing frenzy as the barnful of wedding guests scrambles to get their share of free cats. Two men bring in the next course, a tray of fresh pudding. The bagpiper pauses to check it out. A guy grabs bowls and passes them down the table, taking our attention with them. Everyone's going at it, including a kid in an oversize red cap who licks the bowl with his fingers. In the middle of it all, look who's been completely forgotten—the demure bride sitting in front of the blue-green cloth. (One thing: The guy carrying the front end of the food tray—is he stepping forward with his right leg, or with his left, or with...all three?)

Speaking of two left feet, Bruegel's *Peasant Dance (Bauerntanz)* shows peasants happily clogging to the tune of a lone bagpiper who wails away while his pit crew keeps him lubed with wine. The three Bruegel landscape paintings are part of an

original series of six "calendar" paintings, depicting the seasons of the year. *The Gloomy Day (Der düstere Tag)* opens the cycle, as winter turns to spring...slowly. The snow has melted, flooding the distant river, the trees are still leafless, and the villagers stir, cutting wood and mending fences. We skip ahead to autumn in *The Return of the Herd (Heimkehr der Herde)*—still sunny, but winter's storms are fast approaching. We see the scene from above, emphasizing the landscape as much as the people. Finally, in *Hunters in Snow (Jäger im Schnee)* it's the dead of winter, and three dog-tired hunters with their tired dogs trudge along with only a single fox to show for their efforts. As they crest the hill,

the grove of bare trees opens up to a breathtaking view—they're almost home, where they can join their mates playing hockey. Birds soar like the hunters' rising spirits—emerging from winter's work and looking ahead to a new year.

• *Linger among the Breugels, then head for the nearby Room 16.*

Albrecht Dürer

As the son of a goldsmith and having traveled to Italy, Dürer (DEW-rer) combined meticulous Northern detail with Renaissance symmetry. So his *Landauer Altarpiece of the Trinity*

(Allerheiligenbild) may initially look like a complex pig-pile of saints and angels, but it's perfectly geometrical. The crucified Christ forms a triangle in the center, framed by triangular clouds and flanked by three-sided crowds of people—appropriate for a painting about the Trinity. Dürer practically invented the self-portrait as an art form, and he included himself, the lone earthling in this heavenly vision (bottom right), with a plaque announcing that he, Albrecht Dürer, painted this in 1511.

This end of the Kunst is sprinkled with more gems of Northern Renaissance art—as you stroll from Room 17 to 20, note what these works have in common: small canvases, small themes, and extreme attention to detail. For more on some of the highlights, see the "More Northern Art" sidebar.

• *Before you reach the end of the hall, head left to reenter the big-canvas, bright-colored world of Baroque in Saal XIII.*

Peter Paul Rubens

Stand in front of Rubens' *Self-Portrait (Selbstbildnis)* and admire the darling of Catholic-dominated Flanders (Belgium) in

More Northern Art

If you like fine details and straightforward realism, seek out these works in Rooms 17-21.

Contrast Dürer's powerful Renaissance Christ with **Lucas Cranach**'s all-too-human *Crucifixion (Die Kreuzifixion)*—twisted, bleeding, scarred, and vomiting blood, as the storm clouds roll in.

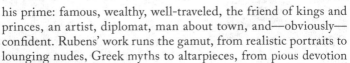

Albrecht Altdorfer's garish *Resurrection (Die Auferstehung Christi*—see photo on right) looks like a poster for a bad horror film: "Easter Sunday III. He's back from the dead... and he's ticked!" A burning Christ ignites the dark cave, tingeing the dazed guards.

Hans Holbein painted *Jane Seymour*, wife number III of the VI wives of Henry VIII. The former lady in waiting— timid and modest—poses stiffly (see photo on left), trying very hard to look the part of Henry's queen. Next.

In *Flowers in a Wooden Vessel (Der Grosse Blumenstrauss)*, **Jan Brueghel,** son of the famous Pieter Bruegel, puts meticulously painted flowers from different seasons together in one artfully arranged vase.

his prime: famous, wealthy, well-traveled, the friend of kings and princes, an artist, diplomat, man about town, and—obviously—confident. Rubens' work runs the gamut, from realistic portraits to lounging nudes, Greek myths to altarpieces, from pious devotion to violent sex. But, can we be sure it's Baroque? Ah yes, I'm sure you'll find a pudgy, winged baby somewhere.

The 53-year-old Rubens married Hélène Fourment, this dimpled girl of 16. She pulls the fur around her ample flesh, simultaneously covering herself and exalting her charms. Rubens called this painting *The Little Fur (Das Pelzchen)*—and used the same name for his young bride. Hmm. Hélène's sweet cellulite was surely an inspiration to Rubens—many of his female figures have Helene's gentle face and dimpled proportions.

In the large *Ildefonso Altarpiece*, a glorious Mary appears (with her entourage of p.w.b.'s) to reward the grateful Spanish saint with a chasuble (priest's smock).

• *Saal XIV features more big Rubens canvases.*

How could Rubens paint all these enormous canvases in one lifetime? He didn't. He kept a workshop of assistants busy painting backgrounds and minor figures, working from Rubens' small sketches (often displayed in Room 14 or nearby). Then the master stepped in to add the finishing touches.

• *From there, find Room 22.*

Jan Vermeer

In his small canvases, the Dutch painter Jan Vermeer quiets the world down to where we can hear our own heartbeat, letting us appreciate the beauty in common things.

The curtain opens and we see *The Art of Painting (Die Malkunst)*, a behind-the-scenes look at Vermeer at work. He's

painting a model dressed in blue, starting with her laurel-leaf headdress. The studio is its own little dollhouse world framed by a chair in the foreground and the wall in back. Then Vermeer fills this space with the few gems he wants us to focus on—the chandelier, the map, the painter's costume. Everything is lit by a crystal-clear light, letting us see these everyday items with fresh eyes.

The painting is also called *The Allegory of Painting*. The model has the laurel leaves, trumpet, and book that symbolize fame. The artist—his back to the public—earnestly tries to capture fleeting fame with a small sheet of canvas.

• *Finish your tour in the corner room.*

Rembrandt van Rijn

Rembrandt became wealthy by painting portraits of Holland's upwardly mobile businessmen, but his greatest subject was himself. In the *Large Self-Portrait (Grosses Selbstbildnis)* we see the hands-on-hips, defiant, open-stance determination of a man who will do what he wants, and if they don't like it, tough.

The Case of the Salt Cellar Stealer

In the middle of the night of May 11, 2003, someone broke into the Kunsthistorisches Museum, smashed the glass case containing Benvenuto Cellini's delightful *Salt Cellar (Saliera)*, and set off the alarm. The thief grabbed the $60 million, gold-plated salt bowl and ran, scrambling through a second-story window and down some construction scaffolding. The security guard, assuming it was a false alarm, simply turned it off and went back to sleep.

For two years, the *Salt Cellar* vanished from sight. Police looked everywhere—including a foray into Italy, chasing a tip from a prankster—but came up empty. Meanwhile, the 10-inch-high masterpiece lay hidden right nearby, tucked under a bed in a Vienna apartment.

Then, in October of 2005, a ransom note arrived at the insurance company: Pay $12 million and the statue will be returned. The thief even sent proof he really had it, enclosing the tiny pickle-fork trident held by Neptune. An exchange was arranged, but on the appointed day, the thief suddenly got suspicious. He called it off by sending a text message from his mobile phone. Crafty police traced the call, and located the Vienna store where the phone had been purchased. They pored over the store's security camera footage until they found who had bought it. When they published the images in the media, the thief turned himself in. He was an otherwise ordinary security-alarm salesman who'd almost pulled off the art crime of the century.

Police found the salt bowl carefully wrapped, boxed, and buried in the woods near Vienna, with only a few scratches on it. The 1,000-day ordeal was over, and Cellini's one-of-a-kind masterpiece was home.

In typical Rembrandt style, most of the canvas is a dark, smudgy brown, with only the side of his face glowing from the darkness. (Remember Caravaggio? Rembrandt did.) Unfortunately, the year this was painted, Rembrandt's fortunes changed. Looking at the *Small Self-Portrait (Kleines Selbstbildnis)* from 1657, consider Rembrandt's last years. His wife died, his children died young, and commissions for paintings dried up as his style veered from the common path. He had to auction off paintings to pay his debts, and he died a poor man. Rembrandt's numerous

self-portraits painted from youth until old age show a man always changing—from wide-eyed youth to successful portraitist to this disillusioned, but still defiant, old man.

The Rest of the Kunst

We've seen only the *Kunst* (art) half of the Kunsthistorisches ("art history") Museum. The collections on the ground floor are among Europe's best, filled with ancient treasures and medieval curios. Highlights include a statue of the Egyptian pharaoh Thutmosis III, and the Gemma Augustea, a Roman cameo kept by Julius Caesar on his private desk. Happily, the *Salt Cellar*, one of the glittering jewels in the museum's crown is now back, after being stolen several years ago (see sidebar). The divine golden salt bowl by Renaissance sculptor Benvenuto Cellini is the centerpiece of the "Kunstkammer"—a section dedicated to Habsburg medieval and Renaissance jeweled wonders.

SLEEPING IN VIENNA

As you move out from the center, hotel prices drop. My listings are in the old center (figure at least €100 for a decent double), along the likeable Mariahilfer Strasse (about €90), and near the Westbahnhof (about €70).

Book ahead for Vienna if you can, particularly for holidays (see "Major Holidays and Weekends" on page 8, and "Making Reservations" on page 18). Business hotels have their highest rates in September and October, when it's peak convention time. Prices are also high right around New Year's Eve.

While few accommodations in Vienna are air-conditioned, you can generally get fans on request. Places with elevators often have a few stairs to climb, too.

These hotels lose big and you pay more if you find a room through Internet booking sites. Book direct by phone, fax, or email and save. For tips on reaching these hotels upon arrival in Vienna, see page 18.

Within the Ring, in the Old City Center

You'll pay extra to sleep in the atmospheric old center, but if you can afford it, staying here gives you the best classy Vienna experience.

$$$ Hotel am Stephansplatz is a four-star business hotel with 56 rooms. It's plush but not over-the-top, and reasonably priced for its incredible location—facing the cathedral—and sleek comfort. Every detail is modern and quality; breakfast is superb, with a view of the city waking up around the cathedral; and the staff is always ready with a friendly welcome (Sb-€160–180, Db-€210–250, prices vary with season and room size, prices shoot up during conventions—most often in Sept–Oct, €20 less July–Aug and in winter, €15 less Fri–Sun, extra bed-€50, children free

---

Sleep Code

(€1 = about $1.40, country code: 43, area code: 01)
S = Single, **D** = Double/Twin, **T** = Triple, **Q** = Quad, **b** = bathroom, **s** = shower only. English is spoken at each place. Unless otherwise noted, credit cards are accepted, rooms have no air conditioning, and breakfast is included.

To help you sort easily through these listings, I've divided the rooms into three categories, based on the price for a standard double room with bath:

$$$ Higher Priced—Most rooms €120 or more.
  $$ Moderately Priced—Most rooms between €75–120.
    $ Lower Priced—Most rooms €75 or less.

---

or very cheap, air-con, free Internet access, Wi-Fi in lobby, sauna, elevator, Stephansplatz 9, U-1 or U-3: Stephansplatz, tel. 01/534-050, fax 01/5340-5710, www.hotelamstephansplatz.at, office @hotelamstephansplatz.at).

$$$ Hotel Pertschy, circling an old courtyard, is big and hotelesque. Its 56 huge rooms are elegantly creaky, with chandeliers and Baroque touches. Those on the courtyard are quietest (Sb-€95–114, Db-€139–169 depending on room size, €20–30 cheaper off-season, extra bed-€36, non-smoking rooms, free Internet terminal in lobby, free Wi-Fi, elevator, Habsburgergasse 5, U-1 or U-3: Stephansplatz, tel. 01/534-490, fax 01/534-4949, www.pertschy.com/cms/index.html, pertschy@pertschy.com).

$$$ Pension Aviano is another peaceful place, with 17 comfortable rooms on the fourth floor above lots of old-center action (Sb-€104, Db-€148–169 depending on size, roughly €20 cheaper per room in July–Aug and Nov–March, extra bed-€33, non-smoking rooms, fans, elevator, between Neuer Markt and Kärntner Strasse at Marco d'Avianogasse 1, tel. 01/512-8330, fax 01/5128-3306, www.secrethomes.at, aviano@secrethomes.at).

$$$ Hotel Schweizerhof is classy, with 55 big rooms, all the comforts, shiny public spaces, and a formal ambience. It's centrally located midway between St. Stephen's Cathedral and the Danube Canal (Sb-€80–100, Db-€115–150, Tb €135–175, extra bed-€35, low prices are for July–Aug and slow times, with cash and this book get your best price and then claim a 10 percent discount, free Wi-Fi, elevator, Bauernmarkt 22, U-1 or U-3: Stephansplatz, tel. 01/533-1931, fax 01/533-0214, www.schweizerhof.at, office@schweizerhof.at). Since this is in the "Bermuda Triangle" nightclub area (see page 171), it can be noisy on weekends (Thu–Sat). If you'll be here then, ask for a quiet room when you reserve.

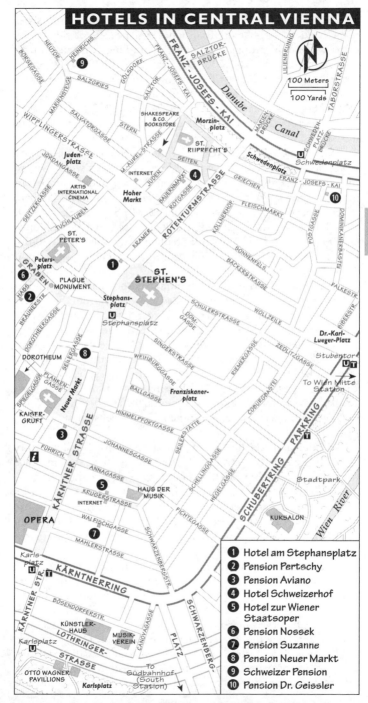

HOTELS IN CENTRAL VIENNA

SLEEPING IN VIENNA

1. Hotel am Stephansplatz
2. Pension Pertschy
3. Pension Aviano
4. Hotel Schweizerhof
5. Hotel zur Wiener Staatsoper
6. Pension Nossek
7. Pension Suzanne
8. Pension Neuer Markt
9. Schweizer Pension
10. Pension Dr. Geissler

$$$ Hotel zur Wiener Staatsoper, the Schweizerhof's sister hotel, is quiet, with a more traditional elegance. Its 22 tidy rooms come with high ceilings, chandeliers, and fancy carpets on parquet floors (tiny Sb-€80–100, Db-€115–150, Tb-€135–175, extra bed-€25, cheaper prices are for July–Aug and Dec–March, fans on request, elevator, a block from the Opera at Krugerstrasse 11; U-1, U-2, or U-4: Karlsplatz; tel. 01/513-1274, fax 01/513-127-415, www .zurwienerstaatsoper.at, office@zurwienerstaatsoper.at, manager Claudia).

$$ At Pension Nossek, an elevator takes you above any street noise into Frau Bernad and Frau Gundolf's world, where the children seem to be placed among the lace and flowers by an interior designer. With 30 rooms right on the wonderful Graben, this is a particularly good value (S-€52–60, Ss-€62, Sb-€76–80, Db-€120, €30 extra for sprawling suites, extra bed-€35, cash only, elevator, Graben 17, U-1 or U-3: Stephansplatz, tel. 01/5337-0410, fax 01/535-3646, www.pension-nossek.at, reservation@pension -nossek.at).

$$ Pension Suzanne, as Baroque and doily as you'll find in this price range, is wonderfully located a few yards from the Opera. It's small, but run with the class of a bigger hotel. The 25 rooms are packed with properly Viennese antique furnishings and paintings (Sb-€81, Db-€103–124 depending on size, 4 percent discount with this book and cash, extra bed-€25, spacious apartment for up to 6 also available, discounts in winter, fans on request, elevator, free Internet access, free Wi-Fi, Walfischgasse 4; U-1, U-2, or U-4: Karlsplatz and follow signs for Opera exit; tel. 01/513-2507, fax 01/513-2500, www.pension-suzanne.at, info@pension-suzanne.at, manager Michael).

$$ Pension Neuer Markt is family-run, with 37 quiet, comfy rooms in a perfectly central locale. Its hallways have the ambience of a cheap cruise ship (Ss-€60–77, Sb-€90–130, smaller Ds-€80– 96, Db-€110–135, prices vary with season and room size, extra bed-€20, request a quiet room when you reserve, fans, fee to use lobby Internet terminal, elevator, Seilergasse 9, tel. 01/512-2316, fax 01/513-9105, www.hotelpension.at/neuermarkt, neuermarkt @hotelpension.at).

$$ Schweizer Pension has been family-owned for three generations. Anita runs an extremely tight ship, offering 11 homey rooms for a great price, with parquet floors and lots of tourist info (S-€42–51, big Sb-€65–78, D-€60–75, Db-€82–93, Tb-€105–119, prices depend on season and room size, cash only, entirely non-smoking, elevator, laundry-€18/load, Heinrichsgasse 2, U-2 or U-4: Schottenring, tel. 01/533-8156, fax 01/535-6469, www.schweizerpension.com, schweizer.pension@chello.at). She also rents a quad with bath (€125–132—too small for 4 adults but

SLEEPING IN VIENNA

great for combos of 2 adults/2 kids or 3 adults/1 kid).

$$ Pension Dr. Geissler has 23 plain-but-comfortable rooms in a modern, nondescript apartment building about 10 blocks northeast of St. Stephen's, near the canal (S-€48, Ss-€68, Sb-€76, D-€65, Ds-€77, Db-€95, 20 percent less in winter, elevator, Postgasse 14, U-1 or U-4: Schwedenplatz—Postgasse is to the left as you face Hotel Capricorno, tel. 01/533-2803, fax 01/533-2635, www.hotelpension.at/dr-geissler, dr.geissler@hotelpension.at).

Hotels and Pensions on or near Mariahilfer Strasse

Lively Mariahilfer Strasse connects the Westbahnhof (West Station) and the city center. The U-3 line, starting at the Westbahnhof, goes down Mariahilfer Strasse to the cathedral. This tourist-friendly, vibrant area is filled with shopping malls, simpler storefronts, and cafés. Its smaller hotels and private rooms are generally run by people from the non-German-speaking part of the former Habsburg Empire (i.e., Eastern Europe). Most hotels are within a few steps of a U-Bahn stop, just one or two stops from the Westbahnhof (direction from the station: Simmering). The nearest place to do laundry is **Schnell & Sauber Waschcenter** (wash-€4.50 for small load or €9 for large load, plus a few euros to dry, daily 6:00–23:00, a few blocks north of Westbahnhof on the east side of Urban-Loritz-Platz).

$$$ NH Hotels, a Spanish chain, runs two stern, stylish-but-passionless business hotels a few blocks apart on Mariahilfer Strasse. Both rent ideal-for-families suites, each with a living room, two TVs, bathroom, desk, and kitchenette (rack rate: Db suite-€118–237, going rate usually closer to €130, plus €16 per person for optional breakfast, apartments for 2–3 adults, 1 kid under 12 free, non-smoking rooms, elevator, free Internet access, fee for Wi-Fi). The 78-room **NH Atterseehaus** is at Mariahilfer Strasse 78 (U-3: Zieglergasse, tel. 01/524-5600, fax 01/524-560-015, nh atterseehaus@nh-hotels.com), and the slightly pricier **NH Wien** has 106 rooms at Mariahilfer Strasse 32 (usually around Db-€145, U-3: Neubaugasse—follow *Stiftgasse* signs to exit and turn left from top of escalator; from Mariahilferstrasse, enter through shop passageway between Nordsee and Edusco—or from Lindengasse 9, tel. 01/521-720, fax 01/521-7215, nhwien@nh-hotels.com). The website for both is www.nh-hotels.com.

$$ Hotel Pension Corvinus is bright, modern, and proudly and warmly run by a Hungarian family: Miklós, Judit, Anthony, and Zoltan. Its 12 comfortable rooms are spacious, and some are downright sumptuous (Sb-€59–69, Db-€95–105, Tb-€109–119, get these special Rick Steves prices with this book, extra bed-€26, also has apartments with kitchens, most rooms non-smoking, air-con,

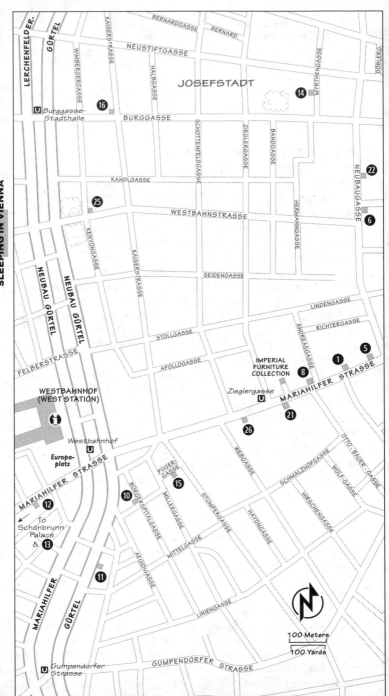

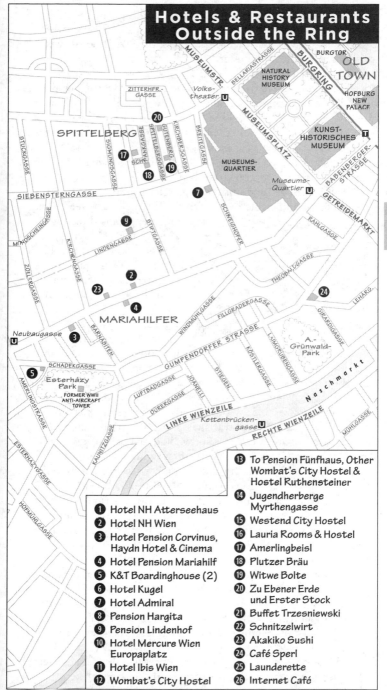

Hotels & Restaurants Outside the Ring

1. Hotel NH Atterseehaus
2. Hotel NH Wien
3. Hotel Pension Corvinus, Haydn Hotel & Cinema
4. Hotel Pension Mariahilf
5. K&T Boardinghouse (2)
6. Hotel Kugel
7. Hotel Admiral
8. Pension Hargita
9. Pension Lindenhof
10. Hotel Mercure Wien Europaplatz
11. Hotel Ibis Wien
12. Wombat's City Hostel
13. To Pension Fünfhaus, Other Wombat's City Hostel & Hostel Ruthensteiner
14. Jugendherberge Myrthengasse
15. Westend City Hostel
16. Lauria Rooms & Hostel
17. Amerlingbeisl
18. Plutzer Bräu
19. Witwe Bolte
20. Zu Ebener Erde und Erster Stock
21. Buffet Trzesniewski
22. Schnitzelwirt
23. Akakiko Sushi
24. Café Sperl
25. Launderette
26. Internet Café

elevator, free Internet access and Wi-Fi, parking garage-€15/day with this book, on the third floor at Mariahilfer Strasse 57–59, U-3: Neubaugasse, tel. 01/587-7239, fax 01/587-723-920, www .corvinus.at, hotel@corvinus.at).

$$ Hotel Pension Mariahilf's 12 rooms are clean, well-priced, and good-sized (if outmoded), with a slight Art Deco flair. Book direct and ask for a Rick Steves discount (Sb-€60–75, twin Db-€78–98, Db-€88–115, Tb-€110–138, 5–6-person apartment with kitchen-€115–160, lower prices are for off-season or longer stays, elevator, free Wi-Fi, parking-€15, Mariahilfer Strasse 49, U-3: Neubaugasse, tel. 01/586-1781, fax 01/586-178-122, www .mariahilf-hotel.at, office@mariahilf-hotel.at).

$$ K&T Boardinghouse rents spacious, comfortable, good-value rooms at both of its two locations. The first has three bright

and airy rooms three flights above lively Mariahilfer Strasse (no elevator). The second location, just across the street, has five newly furnished units on the first floor (Db-€79, Tb-€99, Qb-€119, 2-night minimum, no breakfast, air-con-€10/day, cash only but reserve with credit card, non-smoking, free Internet access and Wi-Fi, coffee in rooms, first location: Mariahilfer Strasse 72, second location: Chwallagasse 2; for either, get off at U-3: Neubaugasse; tel. 01/523-2989, mobile 0676-553-6063, fax 01/522-0345, www.ktboardinghouse.at, k.t@chello .at, Tina). To reach the Chwallagasse location from Mariahilfer Strasse, turn left at Café Ritter and walk down Schadekgasse one short block; tiny Chwallagasse is the first right.

$$ Haydn Hotel is big and formal, with masculine public spaces and 50 spacious rooms (Sb-€80–90, Db-€110–120, suites and family apartments, extra bed-€30, ask for 10 percent Rick Steves discount, all rooms non-smoking, air-con, elevator, free Internet access, fee for Wi-Fi, parking-€15/day, Mariahilfer Strasse 57–59, U-3: Neubaugasse, tel. 01/5874-4140, fax 01/586-1950, www.haydn-hotel.at, info@haydn-hotel.at, Nouri).

$$ Hotel Kugel is run with pride and attitude. "Simple quality and good value" is the motto of the hands-on owner, Johannes Roller. It's a big 34-room hotel with simple Old World charm, offering a fine value (Db-€85, supreme Db with canopy beds-€105–115, cash only, completely non-smoking, Siebensterngasse 43, at corner with Neubaugasse, U-3: Neubaugasse, tel. 01/523-3355, fax 01/5233-3555, www.hotelkugel.at, office@hotelkugel.at). Herr Roller also offers several cheaper basic rooms for backpackers.

$$ Hotel Admiral is huge and prac-
tical, with 80 large, workable rooms (Sb-
€70, Db-€94, extra bed-€25, mention
this book for these special prices, cheaper
in winter, breakfast-€6 per person,
free Internet access and Wi-Fi, limited
free parking if you call to reserve it—
otherwise €10/day, a block off Maria-
hilfer Strasse at Karl-Schweighofer-
Gasse 7, U-2 or U-3: Volkstheater,
tel. 01/521-410, fax 01/521-4116, www
.admiral.co.at, hotel@admiral.co.at).

$ Pension Hargita rents 24 gener-
ally small, bright, and tidy rooms (mostly twins) with Hungarian
decor. This spick-and-span, well-located place is a great value
(S-€40, Ss-€47, Sb-€57, D-€54, Ds-€60, Db-€68, Ts-€75, Tb-€82,
Qb-€112, extra bed-€12, breakfast-€5, completely non-smoking,
reserve with credit card but pay with cash to get these rates, corner
of Mariahilfer Strasse and Andreasgasse, Andreasgasse 1, U-3:
Zieglergasse, tel. 01/526-1928, fax 01/526-0492, www.hargita
.at, pension@hargita.at, Erika and Tibor). While the pension is
directly on bustling Mariahilfer Strasse, its windows block noise
well.

$ Pension Lindenhof rents 19 very basic, very worn but clean
rooms. It's a dark and mysteriously dated time warp filled with
plants (and a fun guest-generated postcard wall); the stark rooms
have outrageously high ceilings and teeny bathrooms (S-€32,
Sb-€40, D-€54, Db €72, T-€81, Tb-€108, Q-€108, Qb-€144, hall
shower-€2, cash only, elevator, Lindengasse 4, U-3: Neubaugasse,
tel. 01/523-0498, fax 01/523-7362, www.pensionlindenhof.at,
pensionlindenhof@yahoo.com, run by Gebrael family; Zara,
Keram, and his father speak English).

Near the Westbahnhof (West Station)

$$$ Hotel Mercure Wien Europaplatz offers high-rise modern
efficiency and comfort in 211 air-conditioned rooms, directly across
from the Westbahnhof (Db-€130–170 depending on season, online
deals as cheap as Db-€70 if you book well in advance, break-
fast-€14, free Internet access, fee for Wi-Fi, elevator, parking-€15/
day, Matrosengasse 6, U-3: Westbahnhof, tel. 01/5990-1181, fax
01/597-6900, www.mercure.com, h1707@accor.com).

$$ Hotel Ibis Wien, a modern high-rise hotel with American
charm, is ideal for anyone tired of quaint old Europe. Its 340
cookie-cutter rooms are bright, comfortable, and modern, with
all the conveniences (Sb-€72, Db-€89, Tb-€106, breakfast-€9.50,
air-con, elevator, free Internet access and Wi-Fi in lobby, parking

garage-€11/day; exit Westbahnhof to the right and walk 400 yards, Mariahilfer Gürtel 22–24, U-3: Westbahnhof; tel. 01/59998, fax 01/597-9090, www.ibishotel.com, h0796@accor.com).

$ Pension Fünfhaus is big, plain, clean, and bare bones—almost institutional. The neighborhood is rundown (with a few ladies loitering late at night) and the floors are tile, but this 47-room pension offers the best doubles you'll find for about €50 (S-€37, Sb-€45, D-€50–53, Db-€60–63, T-€73–79, Tb-€88–94, 4-person apartment-€100-110, cash only, closed mid-Nov–Feb, Sperrgasse 12, U-3: Westbahnhof, tel. 01/892-3545 or 01/892-0286, fax 01/892-0460, www.pension5haus.at, pension5haus@tiscali.at, Frau Susi Tersch). Half the rooms are in the main building and half are in the annex, which has good rooms but is near the train tracks and a bit scary on the street at night. From the station, ride tram #52 or #58 two stops down Mariahilfer Strasse away from center, and ask for Sperrgasse. Crazy Chicken bike rental, listed on page 39, is just a block farther down Sperrgasse.

Cheap Dorms and Hostels near Mariahilfer Strasse

$ Jugendherberge Myrthengasse is your classic huge and well-run youth hostel, with 260 beds (€17–21 per person in 2- to 6-bed rooms, includes sheets and breakfast, non-members pay €3.50 extra, fee for Internet access, free Wi-Fi, always open, no curfew, lockers and lots of facilities, Myrthengasse 7, tel. 01/523-6316, fax 01/523-5849, hostel@chello.at).

$ Westend City Hostel, just a block from the Westbahnhof and Mariahilfer Strasse, is well-run and well-located, with 180 beds in 4- to 12-bed dorms (€21–25 per person, depending on how many in the room, D-€62–68, €4 cheaper Nov–mid-March—except around New Year's, includes sheets, breakfast, and locker; cash only, fee for Internet access, free Wi-Fi, laundry-€7, Fügergasse 3, tel. 01/597-6729, fax 01/597-672-927, www.westendhostel.at, info@westendhostel.at).

$ Lauria Rooms and Hostel is a creative little place run by friendly Gosha, with two 10-bed coed dorms with lockers for travelers ages 17 to 30 (€16/bed), plus several other rooms sleeping two to four each (any age, €22–25/bed, Ds-€62, Ts-€78, Qs-€96; Kaiserstrasse 77, tram #5 or a 10-min walk from Westbahnhof, tel. 01/522-2555, www.lauria-vienna.at, lauria_vienna@hotmail.com).

$ *More Hostels:* Other hostels with €17–19 beds and €50 doubles near Mariahilfer Strasse are **Wombat's City Hostel** (2 locations: one near tracks behind the station at Grangasse 6, another even closer to station at Mariahilfer Strasse 137, tel. 01/897-2336, www.wombats-hostels.com, office@wombats-vienna.at) and

Hostel Ruthensteiner (smoke-free; leave the Westbahnhof to the right and follow Mariahilfer Strasse behind the station, then left on Haidmannsgasse for a block, then turn right and find Robert-Hamerling-Gasse 24; tel. 01/893-4202, www.hostelruthensteiner .com, info@hostelruthensteiner.com).

EATING IN VIENNA

The Viennese appreciate the fine points of life, and right up there with waltzing is eating. The city has many atmospheric restaurants. As you ponder the Eastern European specialties on menus, remember that Vienna's diverse empire may be no more, but its flavors linger.

While cuisines are routinely named for countries, Vienna claims to be the only *city* with a cuisine of its own: Vienna soups come with fillings (semolina dumpling, liver dumpling, or pancake slices). *Gulasch* is a beef ragout of Hungarian origin (spiced with onion and paprika). Of course, Wiener schnitzel is traditionally a breaded and fried veal cutlet (though pork is more common these days). Another meat specialty is boiled beef *(Tafelspitz)*. While you're sure to have *Apfelstrudel,* try the sweet cheese strudel, too *(Topfenstrudel*—wafer-thin strudel pastry filled with sweet cheese and raisins). The *dag* you see in some prices stands for "decigram" (10 grams). Therefore, *10 dag* is 100 grams, or about a quarter-pound. For some background on Austria's excellent wines, see page 21.

On nearly every corner, you can find a colorful *Beisl* (BYE-zul). These uniquely Viennese taverns are a characteristic cross between an English pub and a French brasserie—filled with poetry teachers and their students, couples loving without touching, housewives on their way home from cello lessons, and waiters who enjoy serving hearty food and drinks at an affordable price. Ask at your hotel for a good *Beisl.* (Beware: If Austrians ignore their new non-smoking laws, *Beisls* may still be quite smoky; fortunately, most have outdoor seating.)

Many restaurants offer a "menu," a fixed-price bargain meal at lunchtime.

Near St. Stephen's Cathedral

Each of these eateries is within about a five-minute walk of the cathedral.

Gigerl Stadtheuriger offers a friendly near-*Heuriger* wine cellar experience (à la Grinzing—see "Vienna's Wine Gardens," page 162), often with accordion or live music, without leaving the city center. Just point to what looks good. Food is sold by the weight; 100 grams *(10 dag)* is about a quarter-pound (cheese and cold meats cost about €3 per 100 grams, salads are about €2 per 100 grams; price sheet is posted on the wall to right of buffet line). The *Karree* pork with herbs is particularly tasty and tender. They also have menu entrées, spinach strudel, quiche, *Apfelstrudel*, and, of course, casks of new and local wines (sold by the *Achtel*). Meals run €7–12 (daily 15:00–24:00, indoor/outdoor seating, behind cathedral, a block off Kärntner Strasse, a few cobbles off Rauhensteingasse on Blumenstock, tel. 01/513-4431).

Zu den Drei Hacken, another fun and typical wine cellar, famous for its local specialties (€10 plates, Mon–Sat 11:00–23:00, closed Sun, indoor/outdoor seating, Singerstrasse 28, tel. 01/512-5895). A third recommended *Stadtheuriger,* the Melker Stiftskeller, sits between Am Hof square and the Ring (listed on page 158).

Buffet Trzesniewski is an institution—justly famous for its elegant and cheap finger sandwiches and small beers (€1 each). Three different sandwiches and a *kleines Bier (Pfiff)* make a fun, light lunch. Point to whichever delights look tasty (or grab the English translation sheet and take time to study your 22 sandwich options). The classic favorites are *Geflügelleber* (chicken liver), *Matjes mit Zwiebel* (herring with onions), and *Speck mit Ei* (bacon and eggs). Pay for your sandwiches and a drink. Take your drink tokens to the lady on the right. Sit on the bench and scoot over to a tiny table when a spot opens up. Trzesniewski has been a Vienna favorite for a century...and many of its regulars seem to have been here for the grand opening (Mon–Fri 8:30–19:30, Sat 9:00–17:00, closed Sun; 50 yards off the Graben, nearly across from brooding Café Hawelka, Dorotheergasse 2; tel. 01/512-3291). In the fall, this is a good opportunity to try the fancy grape juices—*Most* or *Traubenmost* (described in "Austrian Wines" sidebar on page 21). Their other location, at Mariahilfer Strasse 95, serves the same sandwiches with the same menu in the same ambience, and is near many recommended hotels (Mon–Fri 8:30–19:00, Sat 9:00–18:00, closed Sun).

Reinthaler's Beisl is a time warp that serves simple, traditional *Beisl* fare all day. It's handy for its location (a block off the Graben, across the street from Buffet Trzesniewski) and because it's a rare restaurant in the center that's open on Sunday. Its fun, classic interior winds way back (use the handwritten daily menu

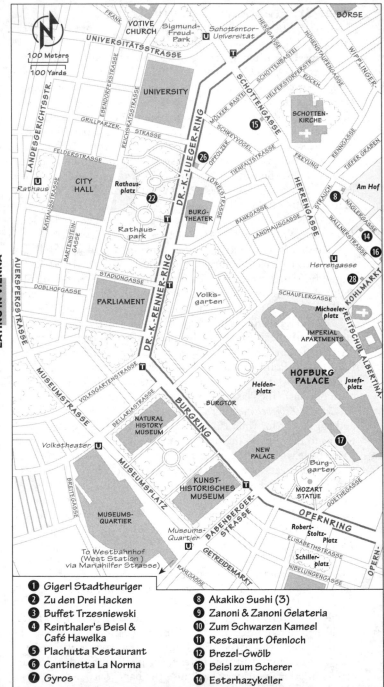

EATING IN VIENNA

1 Gigerl Stadtheuriger
2 Zu den Drei Hacken
3 Buffet Trzesniewski
4 Reinthaler's Beisl & Café Hawelka
5 Plachutta Restaurant
6 Cantinetta La Norma
7 Gyros

8 Akakiko Sushi (3)
9 Zanoni & Zanoni Gelateria
10 Zum Schwarzen Kameel
11 Restaurant Ofenloch
12 Brezel-Gwölb
13 Beisl zum Scherer
14 Esterhazykeller

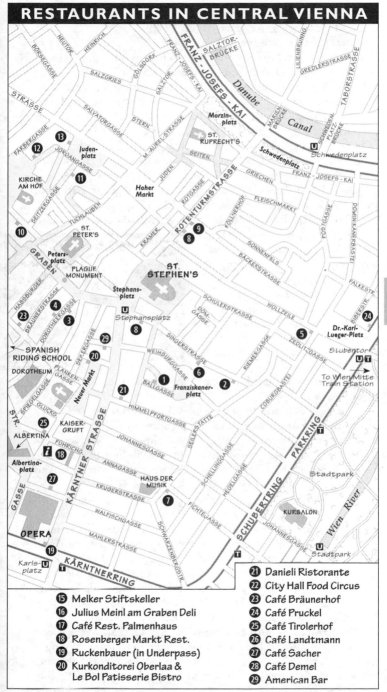

RESTAURANTS IN CENTRAL VIENNA

15 Melker Stiftskeller
16 Julius Meinl am Graben Deli
17 Café Rest. Palmenhaus
18 Rosenberger Markt Rest.
19 Ruckenbauer (in Underpass)
20 Kurkonditorei Oberlaa &
   Le Bol Patisserie Bistro

21 Danieli Ristorante
22 City Hall Food Circus
23 Café Bräunerhof
24 Café Pruckel
25 Café Tirolerhof
26 Café Landtmann
27 Café Sacher
28 Café Demel
29 American Bar

rather than the printed English one, €6–12 plates, daily 11:00–22:30, at Dorotheergasse 4, tel. 01/513-1249).

Plachutta Restaurant, with a stylish green-and-cream, elegant-but-comfy interior and breezy covered terrace, is famous for the best beef in town. You'll find an enticing menu with all the classic Viennese beef dishes, fine desserts, attentive service, and an enthusiastic and sophisticated local clientele. They've developed the art of beef to the point of producing popular cookbooks. Their specialty is a page-long list of *Tafelspitz*—a traditional copper pot of boiled beef with broth and vegetables. Treat the broth as your soup course. A chart on the menu lets you choose your favorite cut. Make a reservation for this high-energy Vienna favorite (€16–21 per pot, daily 12:00–22:30, 10-min walk from St. Stephen's Cathedral to Wollzeile 38, U-3: Stubentor, tel. 01/512-1577).

Cantinetta La Norma, a short walk from the cathedral, serves fresh, excellent Italian dishes amid a cozy, yet energetic ambience. Even on weeknights the small dining area is abuzz with friendly chatter among its multinational, extremely loyal regulars. Owner Paco and his staff Hany and Novka will happily show you their snapshots of the notables who've dined here (€7–18 entrées,  daily 11:00–24:00, outdoor seating, Franziskaner Platz 3, tel. 01/512-8665).

Gyros is a humble little Greek/Turkish joint run by Yilmaz, a fun-loving Turk from Izmir. He simply loves to feed people—the food is great, the price is cheap, and you almost feel like you took a quick trip to Turkey (Mon–Sat 10:00–24:00, Sun 10:00–18:00, a long block off Kärntner Strasse at corner of Fichtegasse and Seilerstätte, tel. 01/228-9551).

Akakiko Sushi is a small chain of Japanese restaurants with an easy sushi menu that's worth considering if you're just schnitzeled out. The €9 bento box meals are a decent value. Three locations have no charm but are fast, reasonable, and convenient (€7–10 meals, all open daily 10:30–23:30): Singerstrasse 4 (a block off Kärntner Strasse near the cathedral), Rotenturmgasse 6 (also near the cathedral), Heidenschuss 3 (near other recommended eateries just off Am Hof), and Mariahilfer Strasse 42–48 (fifth floor of Kaufhaus Gerngross, near many recommended hotels).

Ice Cream!: **Zanoni & Zanoni** is a very Italian *gelateria* run by an Italian family. They're mobbed by happy Viennese hungry for their huge €2 cones to go. Or, to relax and watch the thriving people scene, lick your gelato in their fun outdoor area (daily 7:00–

Wieners in Wien

For hardcore Viennese cuisine, drop by a *Würstelstand*. The local hot-dog stand is a fixture on city squares throughout the old center, serving a variety of hot dogs and pickled side dishes with a warm corner-meeting-place atmosphere. The *Wiener* we know is named for Vienna, but the guy who invented the weenie studied in Frankfurt. Out of nostalgia for his school years, he named his fun fast food for that city...a Frankfurter. Only in Vienna are *Wieners* called *Frankfurters*. (Got that?)

Explore the fun menus. Be adventurous. The many varieties of hot dogs cost €2–3 each. *Kren* is horseradish. Check out the sausage terms on page 22. You'll find particularly good stands on Hoher Markt, the Graben, and in front of the Albertina Museum.

24:00, 2 blocks up Rotenturmstrasse from cathedral at Lugeck 7, tel. 01/512-7979).

Near Am Hof Square

The square called Am Hof (U-3: Herrengasse) is surrounded by a maze of atmospheric medieval lanes; the following eateries are all within a block of the square.

Zum Schwarzen Kameel ("The Black Camel") is popular for its two classy but very different scenes: a tiny, elegant restaurant and a trendy wine bar. The small, dark-wood, 12-table, Art Nouveau restaurant serves fine gourmet Viennese cuisine (three-course dinner-€60–75 plus pricey wine). The wine bar is filled with a professional local crowd enjoying small plates from the same kitchen at a better price. This is *the* place for horseradish and thin-sliced ham (*Beinschinken mit Kren*, €7 a plate, *Achtung*—the horseradish is *hot*). I'd order the *Vorspeisenteller* (a great antipasti dish that comes with ham and horseradish) and their *Tafelspitz* (€16). Stand, grab a stool, or sit anywhere you can—it's customary to share tables in the wine-bar section. Fine Austrian wines are sold by the *Achtel* (eighth-liter glass) and listed on the board; Aussie bartender Karl can help you choose. They also have a buffet of tiny €1–2 sandwiches (daily 8:30–24:00, Bognergasse 5, tel. 01/533-8125).

Restaurant Ofenloch serves good, old-fashioned Viennese cuisine with friendly service, both indoors and out. This 300-year-old eatery, with great traditional ambience, is dressy (with white tablecloths) but intimate and woodsy. It's central but not overrun with tourists (€13–19 main dishes, Mon–Sat 11:00–22:30, closed Sun, Kurrentgasse 8, tel. 01/533-8844).

Brezel-Gwölb, a Tolkienesque wine cellar with outdoor dining on a quiet square, serves delicious light meals, fine *Krautsuppe* (cabbage soup), and old-fashioned Viennese dishes. It's ideal for a romantic late-night glass of wine (daily 11:30–23:30; leave Am Hof on Drahtgasse, then take first left to Ledererhof 9; tel. 01/533-8811).

Beisl zum Scherer, around the corner, is untouristy and serves traditional plates for €10–15. Sitting outside, you'll face a stern Holocaust memorial. Inside comes with a soothing woody atmosphere and intriguing decor (Mon–Sat 11:30–22:00, closed Sun, Judenplatz 7, tel. 01/533-5164).

Esterhazykeller, both ancient and popular, has traditional fare deep underground. For a cheap and sloppy buffet, climb down to the lowest cellar. For table service on a pleasant square, sit outside (Mon–Sat 11:00–23:00, Sun 16:00–23:00, may close for lunch in Aug–Sept and/or in bad weather, just below Am Hof at Haarhof 1, tel. 01/533-3482).

Melker Stiftskeller is an untouristy *Stadtheuriger* in a deep and rustic circa-1626 cellar with hearty, inexpensive meals and new wine (Tue–Sat 17:00–24:00, closed Sun–Mon and mid-July–mid-Aug, between Am Hof and Schottentor U-Bahn stop at Schottengasse 3, tel. 01/533-5530).

Julius Meinl am Graben, a posh supermarket right on the Graben, has been famous since 1862 as a top-end delicatessen with all the gourmet fancies. Along with the picnic fixings on the shelves, there's a café with light meals and great outdoor seating, a stuffy and pricey restaurant upstairs, and a take-away counter (shop open Mon–Fri 8:00–19:30, Sat 9:00–18:00, closed Sun; restaurant open Mon–Sat until 24:00, closed Sun; Am Graben 19, tel. 01/532-3334).

Near the Opera

Café Restaurant Palmenhaus overlooks the Palace Garden (Burggarten—see page 52). Tucked away in a green and peaceful corner two blocks behind the Opera in the Hofburg's backyard, this is a world apart. If you want to eat modern Austrian cuisine surrounded by palm trees rather than tourists, this is it. And, since it's at the edge of a huge park, it's great for families. Their fresh fish with generous vegetables specials are on the board (€8.50 two-course lunches available Mon–Fri, €15–18 entrées, open daily 10:00–24:00, serious vegetarian dishes, fish, extensive wine list, indoors in greenhouse or outdoors, tel. 01/533-1033).

Rosenberger Markt Restaurant is mobbed with tour groups. Still, if you don't mind a freeway-cafeteria ambience in the center of the German-speaking world's classiest city, this self-service eatery is fast and easy. It's just a block toward the cathedral from the Opera. The best cheap meal here is a small salad or veggie plate stacked high (daily 10:30–23:00, lots of fruits, veggies, fresh-squeezed juices, addictive banana milk, ride the glass elevator downstairs, Maysedergasse 2, tel. 01/512-3458).

Ruckenbauer, a favorite for a quick bite, is a fast-food kiosk in a transit underpass under the street in front of the Opera, between the entryways marked *U2/U4* and *U1* (Mon–Fri 6:00–20:00, Sat–Sun 9:00–20:00). Their €1.60 *Tramezzini* sandwiches and fine pastries make a classy, quick picnic lunch or dinner before the Opera, just 100 yards away.

Kurkonditorei Oberlaa may not have the royal and plush fame of Demel (see page 87), but this is where Viennese connoisseurs serious about the quality of their pastries go to get fat. With outdoor seating on Neuer Markt, it's particularly nice on a hot summer day (€10 daily three-course lunches, great selection of cakes, daily 8:00–20:00, Neuer Markt 16, other locations about town, including the Naschmarkt, tel. 01/5132-9360). Next door, **Le Bol Patisserie Bistro** satisfies your need for something French. The staff speaks to you in French, serving fine €8 salads, baguette sandwiches, and fresh croissants (Mon–Sat 8:00–22:00, Sun 10:00–20:00, Neuer Markt 14).

Danieli Ristorante is your best classy Italian bet in the old center. White-tablecloth dressy, but not stuffy, it has reasonable prices (€10–18 pizza and pastas, fresh fish, open daily, 30 yards off Kärntner Strasse opposite Neuer Markt at Himmelpfortgasse 3, tel. 01/513-7913).

City Hall (Rathausplatz) Food Circus

During the summer, scores of outdoor food stands and hundreds of picnic tables are set up in the park in front of the City Hall. Local mobs enjoy mostly ethnic meals for decent-but-not-cheap prices, and classical entertainment on a big screen (see page 171). The fun thing here is the energy of the crowd, and a feeling that you're truly eating as the Viennese do...not schnitzel and quaint traditions, but trendy "world food" with young people out having fun in a fine Vienna park setting (July–mid-Sept daily from 11:00 until late, in front of City Hall on the Ringstrasse), see map on page 107.

Spittelberg Quarter

A charming cobbled grid of traffic-free lanes and Biedermeier apartments has become a favorite neighborhood for Viennese wanting a little dining charm between the MuseumsQuartier and Mariahilfer Strasse (handy to many recommended hotels; take Stiftgasse from Mariahilfer Strasse, or wander over here after you close down the Kunsthistorisches Museum). Tables tumble down sidewalks and into breezy courtyards filled with appreciative natives enjoying dinner or a relaxing drink. It's only worth the trip on a balmy summer evening, as it's dead in bad weather. Stroll Spittelberggasse, Schrankgasse, and Gutenberggasse and pick your favorite. Don't miss the vine-strewn wine garden at Schrankgasse 1. To locate these restaurants, see the map on pages 146–147.

Amerlingbeisl, with a casual atmosphere both on the cobbled street and in its vine-covered courtyard, is a great value (€7 plates, €6–8 daily specials, salads, veggie dishes, traditional specialties, daily 9:00–2:00 in the morning, Stiftgasse 8, tel. 01/526-1660).

Plutzer Bräu, next door, is also good (ribs, burgers, traditional dishes, Tirolean beer from the keg, daily 11:00–2:00 in the morning, food until 24:00, Schrankgasse 4, tel. 01/526-1215).

Witwe Bolte is classier and a good choice for uninspired Viennese cuisine with tablecloths. Its tiny square has wonderful leafy ambience (daily 11:30–23:30 except closed 15:00–17:30 mid-Jan–mid-March, Gutenberggasse 13, tel. 01/523-1450).

Zu Ebener Erde und Erster Stock is a charming little restaurant with a near-gourmet menu. The upstairs is Biedermeier-style, with violet tablecloths and seating for about 20. The downstairs is more casual and woody. Reservations are smart (traditional three-course fixed-price meal–€30, Mon–Fri 7:00–20:30, closed Sat–Sun, Burggasse 13, tel. 01/523-6254).

Near Mariahilfer Strasse

Mariahilfer Strasse (see map on pages 146–147) is filled with reasonable cafés serving all types of cuisine. For a quick yet traditional bite, consider the venerable **Buffet Trzesniewski** sandwich bar at Mariahilfer Strasse 95 (see page 153).

Schnitzelwirt is an old classic with a 1950s patina and a clientele to match. In this once-smoky, still-working-class place, no one finishes their schnitzel ("to-go" for the dog is wrapped in newspaper, "to-go" for you is wrapped in foil). You'll find no tourists, just cheap €6 schnitzel meals (Mon–Sat 10:00–23:00, closed Sun, Neubaugasse 52, tel. 01/523-3771).

The **Naschmarkt** (described on page 62) is Vienna's best Old World market, with plenty of fresh produce, cheap local-style eateries, cafés, *Döner Kebab* and sausage stands, and the best-value sushi in town (Mon–Fri 6:00–18:30, Sat 6:00–17:00, closed Sun, closes earlier in winter; U-4: Karlsplatz, follow *Karlsplatz* signs out of the station). Survey the lane of eateries at the end of the market nearest the Opera. The circa-1900 pub is inviting. Picnickers can buy supplies at the market and eat on nearby Karlsplatz (plenty of chairs facing the Karlskirche).

Viennese Coffee: From Ottomans to Starbucks

The story of coffee in Vienna is steeped in legend. In the 17th century, the Ottomans (invaders from the Turkish Empire) were laying siege to Vienna. A spy working for the Austrians who infiltrated the Ottoman ranks got to know the Turkish lifestyle...including their passion for a drug called coffee. After the Austrians persevered, the ecstatic Habsburg emperor offered the spy anything he wanted. The spy asked for the Ottomans' spilled coffee beans, which he gathered up to start the first coffee shop in town. (It's a nice story. But actually, there was already an Armenian in town running a coffeehouse.)

In the 18th century, coffee boomed as an aristocratic drink. In the 19th-century Industrial Age, people were expected to work 12-hour shifts, and coffee became a hit with the working class, too. By the 20th century, the Vienna coffee scene became so refined that old-timers remember when waiters brought a sheet with various shades of brown (like paint samples) so a customer could make clear exactly how milky she wanted her coffee.

In 2003, Vienna's first Starbucks boldly opened next to the Opera—across the street from the ultimate Old World coffeehouse, the Café Sacher. The locals like the easy-chair ambience and quality of Starbucks coffee, but think it's over-priced. Viennese coffee connoisseurs aren't impressed by quantity, can't relate to flavored coffee, and think drinking out of a paper cup is really trashy. The consensus: For the same price, you can have an elegant and traditional experience in a top Vienna-style coffee shop instead. While the "coffee-to-go" trend has been picked up by many bakeries and other joints, the Starbucks invasion has stalled, with nowhere near as many outlets as the Seattle-based coffee empire had planned.

Vienna's Cafés

In Vienna, the living room is down the street at the neighborhood coffeehouse. This tradition is just another example of Viennese expertise in good living. Each of Vienna's many long-established (and sometimes even legendary) coffeehouses has its individual character (and characters). These classic cafés are a bit tired, with a shabby patina and famously grumpy waiters who treat you like an uninvited guest invading their living room. Still, it's a welcoming place. They offer newspapers, pastries, sofas, quick and light workers' lunches, elegant ambience, and "take all the time you want" charm for the price of a cup of coffee. Order it *melange* (like a cappuccino), *brauner* (strong coffee with a little milk), or *schwarzer* (black). Americans who ask for a latte are mistaken for Italians and given a cup of hot milk. Rather than buy the *International Herald Tribune* ahead of time, spend the money on a cup of coffee and read the paper for free, Vienna-style, in a café.

These are my favorites:

Café Hawelka has a dark, "brooding Trotsky" atmosphere, paintings by struggling artists who couldn't pay for coffee, a saloon-wood flavor, chalkboard menu, smoked velvet couches, an international selection of newspapers, and a phone that rings for regulars. Mrs. Hawelka died just a couple weeks after Pope John Paul II. Locals suspect the pontiff wanted her much-loved *Buchteln* (marmalade-filled doughnuts) in heaven. Mr. Hawelka, now alone and understandably a bit forlorn, still oversees the action (Wed–Mon 8:00–2:00 in the morning, Sun from 10:00, closed Tue, just off the Graben, Dorotheergasse 6).

Café Sperl dates from 1880, and is still furnished identically to the day it opened—from the coat tree to the chairs (Mon–Sat 7:00–23:00, Sun 11:00–20:00 except closed Sun July–Aug, just off Naschmarkt near Mariahilfer Strasse, Gumpendorfer 11, tel. 01/586-4158).

Café Bräunerhof, between the Hofburg and the Graben, offers a classic ambience with no tourists and live music on weekends (light classics, no cover, Sat–Sun 15:00–18:00), and a practical menu with daily specials (open long hours daily, Stallburgasse 2).

Other Classics in the Old Center: All of these places are open long hours daily: **Café Pruckel** (at Dr.-Karl-Lueger-Platz, across from Stadtpark at Stubenring 24); **Café Tirolerhof** (2 blocks from the Opera, behind the TI on Tegetthoffstrasse, at Führichgasse 8); and **Café Landtmann** (directly across from the City Hall on the Ringstrasse at Dr.-Karl-Lueger-Ring 4). The Landtmann is unique, as it's the only grand café built along the Ring with all the other grand buildings.

Wein in Wien: Vienna's Wine Gardens (Heurigen)

The *Heuriger* (HOY-rih-gur) is a uniquely Viennese institution. When the Habsburgs let Vienna's vintners sell their own new wine (called *Sturm*) tax-free, several hundred families opened *Heurigen* (HOY-rih-gehn)—wine-garden restaurants clustered around the edge of town. A tradition was born. Today, they do their best to maintain the old-village atmosphere, serving the homemade new wine (the last vintage, until November 11, when a new vintage year begins) with small meals and strolling musicians. Most *Heurigen* are decorated with enormous antique presses from their vineyards. Wine gardens might be closed on any given day; call ahead to confirm if you have your heart set on a particular place. (For a near-*Heuriger* experience in downtown Vienna, drop

The *Heurigen* Experience

There are more than 1,700 acres of vineyards within Vienna's city limits, and countless *Heuriger* taverns. For a *Heuriger*

evening, rather than go to a particular place, take a tram to the wine-garden district of your choice and wander around, choosing the place with the best ambience.

At any *Heuriger*, fill your plate at a self-serve cold cut buffet (€6–9 for dinner). Food is sold by the *"10 dag"* unit. (A *dag* is a decigram, so *10 dag* is 100 grams—about a quarter-pound.)

Dishes to look for...or look out for: *Stelze* (grilled knuckle of pork), *Fleischlaberln* (fried ground-meat patties), *Schinkenfleckerln* (pasta with cheese and ham), *Schmalz* (a spread made with pig fat), *Blunzen* (black pudding...sausage made from blood), *Presskopf* (jellied brains and innards), *Liptauer* (spicy cheese spread), *Kornspitz* (whole-meal bread roll), and *Kummelbraten* (crispy roast pork with caraway).

Waitresses will then take your wine order (€2.50 per quarter-liter, about 8 oz). Many locals claim it takes several years of practice to distinguish between the *Sturm* wine and vinegar.

EATING IN VIENNA

by Gigerl Stadtheuriger—see page 153.)

I've listed three good *Heuriger* neighborhoods, plus one rural *Heuriger*, on the outskirts of Vienna (see the map on page 31). To reach the neighborhoods from downtown Vienna, it's best to use public transportation (cheap, 30 min, runs late in the evening, directions given per listing below), or you can take a 15-minute taxi ride from the Ring.

Nussdorf—An untouristy district, characteristic and popular with the Viennese, Nussdorf has plenty of *Heuriger* ambience. Right at the last stop on tram #D's route (Beethovengang), you'll find three long and skinny places side by side. Of these, **Schübel-Auer Heuriger** is my favorite (Tue–Sat 16:00–24:00, closed Sun–Mon, Kahlenberger Strasse 22, tel. 01/370-2222). Also consider **Heuriger Kierlinger** (daily 15:30–24:00, Kahlenberger Strasse 20, tel. 01/370-2264) and **Steinschaden** (daily 15:00–24:00, Kahlenberger Strasse 18, tel. 01/370-1375). Walk through any of these and you pop out on Kahlenberger Strasse, where a walk 20 yards uphill takes you to some more eating and drinking fun: **Bamkraxler** ("Tree Jumper"), the only *Biergarten* amid all these vineyards. It's a fun-loving, youthful place with fine keg beer and a regular menu—traditional, ribs, veggie, kids' menu—rather than the *Heuriger* cafeteria line (€8–12 meals, kids' playground, Tue–Sat 16:00–24:00, Sun 11:00–24:00, closed Mon, Kahlenberger Strasse 17, tel. 01/318-8800).

Getting to the Nussdorf Heurigen: Take tram #D from the Ringstrasse (stops include the Opera, Hofburg/Kunsthistorisches Museum, and City Hall) to its endpoint (the stop labeled *Nussdorf* isn't the end—stay on for one more stop to Beethovengang). If you're not starting from somewhere near tram #D's route, take the U-4 to Heiligenstadt, then catch tram #D from in front of the U-Bahn station. Tram #D runs every 5–10 minutes (fewer trams after 23:00, last tram around 24:30).

Grinzing—Of the many *Heuriger* suburbs, Grinzing is the most famous, lively...and touristy. If you're looking to avoid tour groups, head elsewhere.

Getting to the Grinzing Heurigen: From the Heiligenstadt U-4 station, take bus #38A and get off at Himmelstrasse, just past the green onion-top dome (runs every 10–20 min, 2/hr after 21:00, last bus around 22:30). Bus #38A also runs way above Grinzing to the Kahlenberg and Leopoldsberg viewpoints—many people precede their visit to Grinzing with a visit to one or both of the viewpoints, then ride 20 minutes back into the *Heuriger* action (see "A Walk in the Vienna Woods," page 75). Note: Don't confuse bus #38A with tram #38—which also goes to Grinzing, but starts at the Ring (at Schottentor).

From the Grinzing tram stop, follow Himmelgasse uphill toward the green onion-top dome. You'll pass plenty of wine gardens—and tour buses—on your way up. Just past the dome, you'll find the heart of the *Heurigen*.

Heiligenstadt (Pfarrplatz)—Between Nussdorf and Grinzing, this neighborhood features several decent spots, including the famous and touristy **Mayer am Pfarrplatz** (a.k.a. Beethovenhaus, Mon–Sat 16:00–24:00, Sun 11:00–23:00, Pfarrplatz 2, tel. 01/370-1287). This place has a charming inner courtyard with an accordion player and a sprawling backyard with a big children's play zone. Beethoven lived—and began work on his Ninth Symphony—here in 1817; he'd previously written his Sixth Symphony *(Pastorale)* while staying in this then-rural district. He hoped the local spa would cure his worsening deafness. **Weingut and Heuriger Werner Welser,** a block uphill from Beethoven's place, is lots of fun, with music nightly from 19:00 (open daily 15:30–24:00, Probusgasse 12, tel. 01/318-9797).

Getting to the Heiligenstadt Heurigen: From the Heiligenstadt U-4 station, take bus #38A (runs every 10–20 min, 2/hr after 21:00, last bus around 22:30). Get off at Fernsprechamt/Heiligenstadt, walk uphill, and take the first right onto Nestelbachgasse, which leads to Pfarrplatz and the Beethovenhaus. Bus #38A also runs uphill from here, past the Grinzing *Heurigen,* to the Kahlenberg viewpoint (see "Grinzing," above).

If you want to connect the Grinzing and Heiligenstadt areas with the Nussdorf neighborhood, use bus #38A and tram #D (transfer at Grinzinger Strasse).

Heuriger Sirbu—This option is actually in the vineyards, high above Vienna with great city and countryside views, a top-notch buffet, a glass veranda, and a traditional interior for cool weather. It's a bit touristy, and dinner reservations are often required, since it's more upmarket and famous as "the ultimate setting" (May–mid-Oct from 15:00, closed Sun, big play zone for kids, Kahlenberger Strasse 210, tel. 01/320-5928). It's high above regular transit service, but fun to incorporate with a little walking. Ideally, ride bus #38A to Kahlenberg (some buses turn around here, others continue on to Leopoldsberg viewpoint), and walk behind the buildings to find Kahlenberger Strasse—then follow it downhill for 15 minutes. (If you're starting with Nussdorf, then going on to Sirbu, follow directions to Bamkraxler—see Nussdorf listing, page 163—then follow Kahlenberger Strasse uphill for 35 min).

MUSIC AND NIGHTLIFE

Vienna—the birthplace of what we call classical music—still thrives as a music capital. On any given evening, you'll have your choice of opera, Strauss waltzes, Mozart chamber concerts, the famous Boys' Choir, and lighthearted musicals. If techno or rock are more your scene, you'll find plenty in the pubs and clubs of the "Bermuda Triangle" neighborhood near St. Stephen's Cathedral and along the Gürtel. Besides music, you can spend an evening enjoying art, watching a classic film, or sipping Viennese wine in a village wine garden. Save some energy for Vienna after dark.

MUSIC

As far back as the 12th century, Vienna was a mecca for musicians—both sacred and secular (troubadours). The Habsburg emperors of the 17th and 18th centuries were not only generous supporters of music, but fine musicians and composers themselves. (Maria Theresa played a mean double bass.) Composers such as Haydn, Mozart, Beethoven, Schubert, Brahms, and Mahler gravitated to this music-friendly environment. They taught each other, jammed together, and spent a lot of time in Habsburg palaces. Beethoven was a famous figure, walking—lost in musical thought—through Vienna's woods. In the city's 19th-century belle époque, "Waltz King" Johann Strauss and his brothers kept Vienna's 300 ballrooms spinning.

This musical tradition continues into modern times, leaving some prestigious Viennese institutions for today's tourists to enjoy: the Opera (see page 41), the Boys' Choir (see next page), and the great Baroque halls and churches, all busy with classical and waltz concerts. As you poke into churches and palaces, you may hear groups practicing. You're welcome to sit and listen.

Vienna is Europe's music capital. It's music *con brio* (with brilliance) from October through June, reaching a symphonic climax during the Vienna Festival each May and June. Sadly, in July and August, the Boys' Choir, the Opera, and many more music companies are—like you—on vacation. But Vienna hums year-round with live classical music. Except for the Boys' Choir, the musical events listed below are offered in summer.

The best-known entertainment venues are the Staatsoper (for straight-up opera), the Volksoper (for musicals and "operettas"), the Wiener Musikverein (home of the Vienna Philharmonic Orchestra), and the Wiener Konzerthaus (various events).

Vienna Boys' Choir—The boys sing (from a high balcony, where they are heard but not seen) at the 9:15 Sunday Mass from September through June in the Hofburg's Imperial Music Chapel (Hofmusikkapelle). The entrance is at Schweizerhof; you can get there from In der Burg square or go through the tunnel from Josefsplatz.

Reserved seats must be booked two months in advance (€5–29; reserve by fax, email, or mail: fax from the US 011-431-533-992-775, whmk@chello.at, or write Hofmusikkapelle, Hofburg-Schweizerhof, 1010 Wien; call 01/533-9927 for information only—they can't book tickets at this number).

Much easier, standing room inside is free and open to the first 60 who line up. Even better, rather than line up early, you can simply swing by and stand in the narthex just outside, where you can hear the boys and see the Mass on a TV monitor.

Boys' Choir concerts are also given Fridays at 16:00 in late April, May, June, September, and October on stage at the Musikverein, near the Opera and Karlskirche (€36–56, around 30 standing-room tickets go on sale at 15:30 for €15, Karlsplatz 6; U-1, U-2, or U-4: Karlsplatz; tel. 01/5880-4173).

They're talented kids, but, for my taste, not worth all the commotion. Remember, many churches have great music during Sunday Mass. Just 200 yards from the Boys' Choir chapel, Augustinian Church has a glorious 11:00 service each Sunday (see page 51).

Touristy Mozart and Strauss Concerts—If the music comes to you, it's touristy—designed for flash-in-the-pan Mozart fans. Powdered-wig orchestra performances are given almost nightly in grand traditional settings (€25–50). Pesky wigged-and-powdered Mozarts peddle tickets in the

MUSIC

streets. They rave about the quality of the musicians, but you'll get second-rate chamber orchestras, clad in historic costumes, performing the greatest hits of Mozart and Strauss. These are casual, easygoing concerts with lots of tour groups. While there's not a Viennese person in the audience, the tourists generally enjoy the evening.

To sort through all your options, check with the ticket office in the TI (same price as on the street, but with all venues to choose from). Savvy locals suggest getting the cheapest tickets, as no one seems to care if cheapskates move up to fill unsold pricier seats. Critics explain that the musicians are actually very good (often Hungarians, Poles, and Russians working a season here to fund an entire year of music studies back home), but that they haven't performed much together so aren't "tight."

Of the many fine venues, the Mozarthaus might be my favorite—a small room richly decorated in Venetian Renaissance style with intimate chamber-music concerts (€35–42, Thu–Fri at 19:30, Sat at 18:00, near St. Stephen's Cathedral at Singerstrasse 7, tel. 01/911-9077).

Strauss Concerts in the Kursalon—For years, Strauss concerts have been held in the Kursalon, where the "Waltz King" himself directed wildly popular concerts 100 years ago (€39–56, concerts nightly generally at 20:15, tel. 01/512-5790 to reserve). Shows last 1.75 hours and are a mix of ballet, waltzes, and a 15-piece orchestra. It's touristy—tour guides holding up banners with group numbers wait out front after the show. Even so, the per-formance is playful, visually fun, fine quality for most, and with a tried-and-tested, crowd-pleasing format. The conductor welcomes the crowd in German (with a wink) and English; after that...it's English only.

Serious Concerts—These events, including the Opera, are listed in the monthly *Wien-Programm* (available at TI, described on page 36). Most tickets run €40–55 (plus a stiff booking fee when booked in advance or through a box office like the one at the TI). A few venues charge as little as €25; look around if you're not set on any particular concert. While it's easy to book tickets online long in advance, spontaneity is also workable, as there are invariably people selling their extra tickets at face value or less outside the door before concert time. If you call a concert hall directly, they can advise you on the availability of (cheaper) tickets at the door. Vienna takes care of its starving artists (and tourists) by offering

cheap standing-room tickets to top-notch music and opera (generally an hour before each performance).

The Opera—The Vienna State Opera (Staatsoper)—with musicians provided by the Vienna Philharmonic Orchestra in the

pit—is one of the world's
top opera houses. They put
on 300 performances a year,
but in July and August the
singers rest their voices (or
go on tour). Since there
are different operas nearly
nightly, you'll see big trucks
out back and constant action
backstage—all the sets need

to be switched each day. Even though the expensive seats normally
sell out long in advance, the opera is perpetually in the red and
subsidized by the state.

Opera Tickets: To buy tickets in advance, call 01/514-440
or 01/513-1513 (phone answered daily 10:00–21:00, www.wiener
-staatsoper.at). The theater's box office is open from 9:00 until two
hours before each performance. Unless Placido Domingo is in
town, it's easy to get one of 567 **standing-room tickets** (*Stehplätze*,
€3 up top or €4 downstairs). While the front doors open one hour
before the show starts, a side door (middle of building, on the
Operngasse side) opens 80 minutes before curtain time, giving
those in the know an early grab at standing-room tickets (tickets
sold until 20 min after curtain time). Just walk straight in, then
head right until you see the ticket booth marked *Stehplätze* (tel.
01/514-447-880). If fewer than 567 people are in line, there's no
need to line up early. If you're one of the first 160 in line, try for
the "Parterre" section and you'll end up dead-center at stage level,
directly under the Emperor's Box (otherwise, you can choose
between the third floor—*Balkon*, or the fourth floor—*Galerie*).
Dress is casual (but do your best) at the standing-room bar. Locals
save their spot along the rail by tying a scarf to it.

The excellent "electronic libretto" translation screens help
make the experience worthwhile for opera newbies. (Press the
button to turn yours on; press again for English.)

Rick's Crude Tips: For me, three hours is a lot of opera. But
just to see and hear the Opera in action for half an hour is a treat.
You can buy a standing-room spot and just drop in for part of the
show. Ending time is posted in the lobby—you could stop by for
just the finale. If you go at the start or finish, you'll see Vienna
dressed up. Of the 567 people with cheap standing-room tickets,
invariably many will not stand through the entire performance. If
you drop by after show-time, you can wait for tourists to leave and

bum their tickets off them—be sure to ask them for clear directions to your spot. (While it's perfectly legal to swap standing-room spots, be discreet if finding your spot mid-performance—try to look like you know where you're going.) Even those with standing-room tickets are considered "ticket-holders," and are welcome to explore the building. As you leave, wander around the first floor (fun if leaving early, when halls are empty) to enjoy the sumptuous halls (with prints of famous stage sets and performers) and the grand entry staircase. The last resort (and worst option) is to drop into the Café Oper Vienna inside the Opera, and watch the opera live on TV screens (reasonable menu and drinks).

Vienna Volksoper: For less-serious operettas and musicals, try Vienna's other opera house, located along the Gürtel, west of the city center (see *Wien-Programm* brochure or ask at TI for schedule, Währinger Strasse 78, tel. 01/5144-4360, www.volksoper.at).

Theater an der Wien—Considered the oldest theater in Vienna, this venue was designed in 1801 for Mozart operas—intimate, with just a thousand seats. Reopened in 2006 for Mozart's 250th birthday, it treats Vienna's music lovers to a different opera every month—generally Mozart with a contemporary setting and modern interpretation—with the excellent Vienna Radio Orchestra in the pit. With the reopening of Theater an der Wien, Vienna now supports three opera companies. This one is the only company playing through the summer (facing the Naschmarkt at Linke Wienzeile 6, tel. 01/5883-0660 for information, tickets available at www.theater-wien.at).

Musicals—The Wien Ticket pavilion sells tickets to contemporary American and British musicals performed in the German language (€10–100, €5 standing-room tickets available 2 hrs before curtain time), and offers these tickets at half-price from 14:00 until 17:00 the day of the show. Or you can reserve (full-price) tickets for the musicals by phone (call Wien Ticket at tel. 01/58885).

Films of Concerts—To see free films of great concerts in a lively, outdoor setting near City Hall, see "Nightlife," next.

Dance Evening—If you'd like to dance (waltz and ballroom), or watch people who are really good at it, consider the Dance Evening at the Tanz Café in the Volksgarten (€5–6, May–Sept Sat from 19:00 and Sun from 18:00, www.volksgarten.at).

Classical Music to Go—To bring home Beethoven, Strauss, or the Wiener Philharmonic on a top-quality CD, shop at Gramola on the Graben or EMI on Kärntner Strasse.

NIGHTLIFE

If powdered wigs and opera singers in Viking helmets aren't your thing, Vienna has plenty of alternatives. For an up-to-date rundown on fun after dark, check www.viennahype.at.

City Hall Open-Air Classical-Music Cinema and Food Circus—A thriving people scene erupts each evening in summer (July–early Sept) at the park in front of City Hall (Rathaus, on the Ringstrasse). Thousands of people keep a food circus of 24 simple stalls busy. There's not a plastic cup anywhere, just real plates and glasses— Vienna wants the quality of eating to be as high as the music that's about to begin. About 3,000 folding chairs face a 60-foot-wide  screen up against the City Hall's Neo-Gothic facade. When darkness falls, an announcer explains the program, and then the music starts. The program is different every night—mostly movies of opera and classical concerts, with some films. The TI has the schedule (programs generally last about 2 hrs, starting when it's dark—between 21:30 in July and 20:30 in Aug and early Sept).

Since 1991, the city has paid for 60 of these summer event nights each year. Why? To promote culture. Officials know that the City Hall Music Festival is mostly a "meat market" where young people come to hook up. But they believe many of these people will develop a little appreciation of classical music and high culture on the side.

Heurigen—Viennese wine gardens, called *Heurigen*, are a great way to enjoy new wine, a light meal, and a festive local atmosphere. Eat and drink in intimate taverns or leafy courtyards, surrounded by antique wine presses, friendly *Wieners*, strolling musicians, and fellow tourists. Most gardens are located on the outskirts of town—in the legendary Vienna Woods—but they're easy to reach by tram, bus, taxi, or tourist "train." For more on the *Heurigen*, including recommendations and transportation information, see page 162.

Bermuda Triangle (Bermuda Dreleck)—The area known as the "Bermuda Triangle"—north of St. Stephen's Cathedral, between Rotenturmstrasse and Judengasse—is the hot local nightspot. You'll find lots of music clubs and classy pubs, or *Beisl* (such as Krah Krah, Salzamt, Bermuda Bräu, and First Floor—for cocktails with a view of live fish). The serious-looking guards have

Sightseeing After Dark

Every night in Vienna some sights stay open late. Here's the scoop from Monday through Sunday:

St. Stephen's Cathedral: Nightly until 22:00 (but nave closes earlier). See page 41.

KunstHausWien: Nightly until 19:00. See page 69.

Haus der Musik: Nightly until 22:00. See page 52.

Museum of Applied Art (MAK): Tue until 24:00. See page 62.

Albertina Museum: Wed until 21:00. See page 48.

Natural History Museum: Wed until 21:00. See page 55.

The Secession: Thu until 20:00. See page 59.

Kunsthistorisches Museum: Thu until 21:00. See page 55.

Leopold Museum: Thu until 21:00. See page 56.

Museum of Modern Art (MUMOK): Thu until 21:00. See page 56.

Other late-night activities include: going to an opera or concert (see "Music" on page 166); a free, open-air cultural event outside City Hall (see page 171); or a fun outing at the Prater amusement park (see page 74). Also remember that Vienna's coffee shops (see page 161) and wine gardens (see page 162) are generally open late.

nothing to do with the bar scene—they're guarding the synagogue nearby.

Gürtel—The Gürtel is Vienna's outer ring road. The arches of a lumbering viaduct (which carries a train track) are now filled with trendy bars, sports bars, dance clubs, strip clubs, antique shops, and restaurants. To experience—or simply see—the latest scene in town, head out here. The people-watching—the trendiest kids on the block—makes the trip fun even if you're looking for exercise rather than a drink. Ride U-6 to Nussdorfer Strasse or Thaliastrasse and hike along the viaduct.

English Cinema—Two great theaters offer three or four screens of English movies nightly (€6–9): **English Cinema Haydn,** near my recommended hotels on Mariahilfer Strasse (Mariahilfer Strasse 57, tel. 01/587-2262, www.haydnkino.at); and **Artis International Cinema,** right in the town center a few minutes from the cathedral (Schultergasse 5, tel. 01/535-6570).

***The Third Man* at Burg Kino**—This movie, voted the best British film ever by the British Film Institute, takes place in 1949 Vienna—when it was divided, like Berlin, between the four victorious Allies. With a dramatic Vienna cemetery scene, coffeehouse culture surviving amid the rubble, and Orson Welles being chased through the sewers, the tale of a divided city about to fall under Soviet rule and rife with smuggling is an enjoyable two-hour experience while in Vienna (€8, in English with German subtitles; 3 or 4 showings weekly: Fri at 22:45, Tue and Sun afternoons depending on other film times; Opernring 19, tel. 01/587-8406, www.burgkino.at).

TRANSPORTATION CONNECTIONS

This chapter covers Vienna's major train stations and its airport, and includes tips for connections to/from Vienna by car and boat.

BY TRAIN

Long home to two bustling main train stations, Vienna is currently building one central station (Hauptbahnhof) that will replace both by 2013. Until then, the Westbahnhof (West Station) continues to serve trains to/from Germany, Switzerland, and Hungary, but the Südbahnhof (South Station)—the locus of the new central station—is mostly closed (though trains to/from Bratislava now run from a provisional eastern "Ostbahn" section of the Südbahnhof). Most other international trains are now served by the Wien-Meidling Bahnhof (southbound trains to/from Italy, Slovenia, and Croatia, as well as northbound trains to/from the Czech Republic and Poland). Trains don't always adhere to these generalizations, so confirm which station your train leaves from. For general train information in Austria, call 051-717 (to get an operator, dial 2, then 2).

Westbahnhof: The Reisebüro am Bahnhof desk has maps, books hotels (for a pricey fee), sells the Vienna Card (described on page 36), and answers questions (Mon–Fri 8:00–19:00, Sat 8:00–13:00, closed Sun). This station is also under construction, so its many services are now scattered throughout a provisional hall—including a train info desk (daily 7:30–21:00), grocery store (daily 5:30–23:00), ATMs, change offices, a post office, and storage facilities. To reach airport buses and taxis, from the platforms head outside and left.

To get to the city center (and most likely, your hotel), take the U-Bahn (subway) on the U-3 line (buy your ticket or transit pass—described on page 37—from a machine). Follow U-3 signs to the tracks (direction: Simmering). If your hotel is along Mariahilfer Strasse, your stop is on this line. If you're sleeping in the center—or just can't wait to start sight-seeing—ride five stops to Stephansplatz, at the very center of town. From there, the TI is a five-minute stroll down pedestrian Kärntner Strasse.

Wien-Meidling Bahnhof: This once-small suburban station has been souped up to accommodate the traffic that once passed through the Südbahnhof. It has a train info desk, ATMs, luggage lockers (underground, near track 7), as well as airport bus services. To reach the hotels on Mariahilfer Strasse, or to head to Stephansplatz, take the U-Bahn on the U-6 line (direction: Floridsdorf) to the Westbahnhof, then change to the U-3 line (see "Westbahnhof," above). If you're staying near the Opera, you can catch the direct tram #62 (direction: Karlsplatz); to Schwedenplatz take the U-6 (direction: Floridsdorf) two stops to Längenfeldgasse, then change to the U-4 (direction: Heiligenstadt). To get here from the center, take the U-Bahn or tram to Philadelphiabrücke.

Südbahnhof (Ostbahn): If you're coming from or going to Bratislava, you'll find yourself at the busy construction zone that was once the Südbahnhof. To reach the city center from here, take tram #D to the Ring; to reach Mariahilfer Strasse, hop on bus #13A.

Franz Josefs Bahnhof: This small station serves Krems and other points on the north bank of the Danube (including Český Krumlov). The station doesn't have a U-Bahn stop—but convenient tram #D connects it to the city center. If you're headed elsewhere in town, get off at Spittelau (one stop early), which is on the U-4 and U-6 lines (or, if you're headed out of town from somewhere not near the tram #D route, take the U-Bahn to Spittelau and catch your train there).

From Vienna by Train to: Melk (2/hr, 1.25 hrs, some with change in St. Pölten), **Krems** (at least hourly, 1 hr), **Mauthausen** (about hourly until 17:30, 2 hrs, change in St. Valentin), **Bratislava** (2–3/hr, 1 hr; or try the boat trip described on page 217), **Salzburg** (1–2/hr, 2.5–3 hrs), **Hallstatt** (hourly, 4 hrs, change in Attnang-Puchheim), **Innsbruck** (every 2 hrs, 5 hrs), **Budapest** (every 2 hrs direct, 3 hrs; more with transfers), **Prague** (5/day direct, 4.5 hrs; more with 1 change, 5–6 hrs), **Český Krumlov** (6/day with at least one change, 5–6 hrs, connections from all three Vienna stations depending on time of day), **Munich** (4/day direct, 4.25 hrs; otherwise about hourly, 5–5.75 hrs, transfer in Salzburg), **Berlin** (8/day, most with 1 change, 9.5 hrs, some via Czech Republic; longer on night train), **Dresden** (2/day, 7 hrs; plus 1 night train/day, 9 hrs), **Zürich** (nearly hourly, 9–10 hrs, 1 with changes in Innsbruck and Feldkirch, night train), **Ljubljana** (1 convenient early-morning direct train, 6 hrs; otherwise 6/day with change in Villach, Maribor, or Graz, 6–7 hrs), **Zagreb** (4/day, 5.5–7 hrs, 2 direct, others with 1–2 changes), **Kraków** (3 decent daytime options, 6.25 hrs direct or 7–8.5 hrs with 1–3 changes, plus a night train), **Warsaw** (2/day direct including 1 night train, 7.75–8.5 hrs), **Rome** (3/day, 13–15 hrs, plus several overnight options), **Venice** (3/day, 8 hrs with changes—some may involve bus connections; plus 1 direct night train, 11 hrs), **Frankfurt** (7/day direct, 7 hrs), **Paris** (7/day, 12–17 hrs, 1–3 changes, night train), **Strasbourg** (9/day, 9–11 hrs, 2–3 changes, direct night train, 10 hrs), **Amsterdam** (3/day, 11.25–12.5 hrs, 1–2 changes; longer night-train options via Hannover).

To Prague and Budapest: Vienna is the springboard for a quick trip to these two magnificent cities—it's three hours by train to Budapest and 4.5 hours to Prague (or 8 hours via Prague night train, sleeper car only—no *couchettes*, leaves Westbahnhof around 22:00). Americans and Canadians do not need visas to enter the Czech Republic or Hungary.

BY PLANE

Vienna International Airport

The airport, 12 miles from the center, has easy connections to Vienna's various train stations (airport tel. 01/700-722-233, www.viennaairport.com).

To get from the airport to the center of town, your cheapest option is taking the S-Bahn commuter train to the central Wien-Mitte Bahnhof, on the east side of the Ring (S-7 yellow, buy 2-zone ticket from machines on the platform, price includes any bus or S- or U-Bahn transfers, 2/hr, 24 min, €3.40, generally departs at :09 and :39, 24 min). You can also take the newer City Airport Train to the Wien-Mitte Bahnhof (CAT, follow green signs, 2/hr, usually departs at :05 and :35, 16 min, €10, www.cityairporttrain.com). From Wien-Mitte you can take the U-Bahn to Mariahilfer Strasse or other neighborhoods.

Express airport buses (parked immediately in front of the arrival hall, €6, 2/hr, 30 min, buy ticket from driver, note time to destination on curbside TV monitors) go conveniently to the Schwedenplatz U-Bahn station (for city-center hotels), Westbahnhof (for Mariahilfer Strasse hotels), and Südbahnhof, where it's easy to continue by taxi or public transportation (see "Trains," earlier in this chapter).

Taxis into town cost about €35 (including the €11 airport surcharge); taxis also wait at the downtown terminus of each airport transit service. Hotels arrange for fixed-rate car service to the airport (€30, 30-min ride).

Bratislava Airport

The airport in nearby Bratislava, Slovakia—a hub for some low-cost flights—is just an hour away from Vienna (see page 217 in the Bratislava chapter).

BY CAR

Route Tips for Drivers

Approaching Vienna: Navigating your way into Vienna is straight-forward, but study your map first. Approaching Vienna on the A-1 from **Melk** or **Salzburg,** it's simple: You'll pass Schönbrunn Palace before hitting the Gürtel (the city's outer ring road); turn left onto the Gürtel to reach Mariahilfer Strasse hotels, or continue on to reach hotels inside the Ringstrasse (the city's inner ring; clockwise traffic only). If you're approaching from **Krems,** stay on the A-22 as it follows the Danube, and cross the river at the fourth bridge (Reichsbrücke). At the big roundabout, take the second right onto Praterstrasse, which leads directly to the Ringstrasse. Circle around until you reach the "spoke" street you need.

From **Budapest,** get on the A-4 at Nickelsdorf; from there it's a straight shot into Vienna along the Danube Canal. From the canal, turn left at the Aspernbrücke bridge and cross the canal, which puts you directly on the Ringstrasse.

In Vienna: The city has deliberately created an expensive hell for cars in the center. Don't even try to drive here. If you must bring a car into Vienna, leave it at an expensive garage.

Leaving Vienna: To leave Vienna for points west (such as the Danube Valley and Salzburg), circle the Ringstrasse clockwise until just past the Opera. Then follow the blue signs past the Westbahnhof to *Schloss Schönbrunn* (Schönbrunn Palace), which is directly on the way to the West A-1 autobahn to Linz. If you stop at the palace for a visit, leave the palace by 15:00 and you should beat rush hour.

BY BOAT

High-speed boats connect Vienna to the nearby capitals of Bratislava (Slovakia) and Budapest (Hungary). While it's generally cheaper and faster to take the train—and the boat is less scenic and romantic than you might imagine—some travelers enjoy the Danube riverboat experience.

To Bratislava: For the details on this connection, see page 217 in the Bratislava chapter.

To Budapest: In the summer, the Budapest-based Mahart line runs daily high-speed hydrofoils down the Danube to Budapest. The boat leaves Vienna late April through early October daily at 9:00 and arrives in Budapest at 14:30 (Budapest to Vienna: 9:00–15:30). The trip costs €89 one-way. On any of these boats, you can also stop in the Slovak capital, Bratislava (explained on page 217 in Bratislava, Slovakia chapter). In Vienna, you board at the DDSG Blue Danube dock at the Reichsbrücke (Handelskai 265, U-1: Vorgartenstrasse). To confirm times and prices, and to buy tickets, contact DDSG Blue Danube in Vienna (Austrian tel. 01/58880, www.ddsg-blue-danube.at) or Mahart in Budapest (Hungarian tel. 1/484-4010, www.mahartpassnave.hu).

DANUBE VALLEY

Melk • Mauthausen

From the Black Forest in Germany to the Black Sea in Romania, the Danube flows 1,770 miles through 10 countries. Western Europe's longest river (the Rhine is only half as long), it's also the only major river flowing west to east, making it invaluable for commercial transportation.

The Danube is at its romantic best just west of Vienna. Mix a cruise with a bike ride through the Danube's Wachau Valley, lined with ruined castles, beautiful abbeys, small towns, and vineyard upon vineyard. After touring the glorious Melk Abbey, douse your warm, fairy-tale glow with a bucket of Hitler at the Mauthausen concentration camp memorial.

Planning Your Time

The Danube Valley is worth two days: Allow one day to visit Melk's abbey and to cruise the river valley by boat or bike; a second day gives you time to get to Mauthausen. Visiting this concentration camp, though a little difficult for non-drivers, is unforgettable and worthwhile, even if you've already seen other camps. Mauthausen should be seen en route to or from Salzburg or Hallstatt.

For drivers starting in Vienna, it's best to visit the Danube Valley, Mauthausen, and Hallstatt before Salzburg, but train travelers coming from the Danube Valley and Mauthausen should head straight to Salzburg to avoid arriving in the evening in Hallstatt, when the boat stops running (see "Arrival in Hallstatt" on page 278).

Day Trip from Vienna: If you want to day trip to the Danube, catch the early train to Melk, tour the Abbey, eat lunch, and take an afternoon trip along the river from Melk to Krems. Note that the boat goes much faster downstream (eastbound, from Melk to Krems) than vice versa. From Krems, catch the train back to

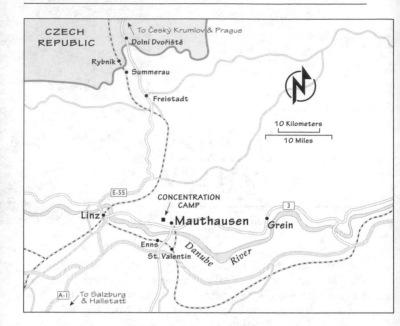

Vienna. Try a boat/bike combination or consider the Austrian railway's convenient Kombi-ticket. This special package includes the train trip from Vienna to Melk, entry to the Melk Abbey, a boat cruise to Krems, and the return train trip to Vienna for a total of €45 (buy at any of Vienna's train stations).

Getting to the Danube Valley

By Train: Melk is on the autobahn and just off the Salzburg–Vienna train line (transfer in Amstetten or St. Pölten). Because Melk and Krems are on opposite sides of the river, trains from Vienna to Krems and Melk run on different lines (trains to Melk depart from Vienna's Westbahnhof; Krems-bound trains depart from Vienna's Franz Josefs Bahnhof; see "Transportation Connections" on page 174).

By Car: See "Route Tips for Drivers" at the end of this chapter for advice on how to connect Vienna, the Danube Valley, Mauthausen, and Hallstatt.

Getting Around the Danube Valley

By car, bike, bus, or boat, the 24-mile stretch of the Danube between Melk and Krems is as pretty as they come. You'll cruise the Danube's wine road, passing wine gardens all along the river. Keep an eye out for wreaths of straw or greenery, hung out as an invitation to come in and taste. In local slang, someone who's feeling his wine is "blue." (Blue Danube?) Note that in German,

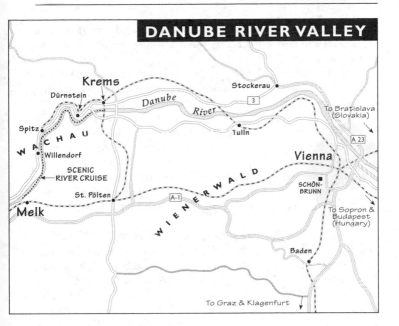

DANUBE RIVER VALLEY

Danube is *Donau* (DOH-now), as you'll see by the signs.

Biking and boating are the most enjoyable ways to enjoy the stretch from Melk to Krems. Your transportation options for the return trip, however, require some advance thought. You can ride the boat in both directions, but because of the river current, it takes twice as long coming upstream. You can ride a bike in both directions, but given that it's 48 miles round-trip, and slightly uphill all the way back, coming back via boat or train may be the better option. Buses run on both sides of the river, but views are more limited; they are a good rainy-day option (no bikes allowed on board).

Your best non-bike option if the weather is good and time is short: Ride the boat from Melk downriver to Krems in the morning, and take a train-bus combination back to Melk, transferring in the village of Spitz.

By Boat: Two different companies run boats between Melk

and Krems: **DDSG** (3/day in each direction May–Sept, 1/day late April and Oct, tel. 01/58880, www .ddsg-blue-danube.at) and **Brandner** (2/day in each direction May–Sept, 1/day late April and Oct, tel. 07433/259-021, www.brandner .at). Both charge the same amount: €19 one-way, €24 round-trip ticket allowing stopovers (bikes ride for €2); railpass-holders get a 20 percent discount with DDSG and a 10 percent discount with Brandner.

In peak season (May–Sept), boats depart daily from Melk at 8:25, 11:00, 13:50 (two different boats), and 16:15 (1.75-hour ride downstream). Boats depart from Krems at 10:10, 10:15, 13:00, 15:40, and 15:45 (because of the 6-knot flow of the Danube, the same ride upstream takes nearly twice as long—3 hours). The 16:15 departure from Melk and the 15:45 departure from Krems require an easy transfer in Spitz; the rest are direct. Confirm these times by calling the boat companies (see above), the Melk TI (see page 183), or the Krems TI (see page 188). Both companies also offer longer cruises that start or end in Vienna (check their websites for more info).

By Bike: See the "Melk-to-Krems Danube Valley Bike Ride" described on page 187. Ask any local TI or your hotel for the latest on bike-rental options. Some hotels rent or loan bikes; in Melk, try Hotel zur Post (€9/half-day, €12/day, free for guests) or Gasthof Goldener Stern (€10/day for guests). For a bike/boat combination, consider Wachau Touristik Bernhardt. It has bike-rental depots at the Melk boat dock and by the train station at Spitz. For a €3 service fee, you can pick up your bike at one station and leave it at the other (€9 after 12:30, €12 for all day, June–Oct daily 10:00–16:30 at Melk, depot in Spitz is often unstaffed—call and they'll meet you there in about 10 min, returns until 18:00, ID for deposit—they make a copy so you have the drop-off option, Melk mobile 0664/222-2070, Spitz tel. 02713/2222).

By Bus and Train Along the North Bank: While you can take the bus between Melk and Krems on either side of the river, the easiest option is to travel on the north side, combining buses and trains that run frequently every day of the week. Ride the bus between Melk and Spitz and the train between Spitz and Krems (nearly hourly connections until 19:00, 1 hour total, €8.30).

By Bus Along the South Bank: It's less convenient to ride on the south side, where buses aren't as frequent (Melk–Krems: Mon–Fri 4/day—1 direct bus, Sat 2/day—1 direct bus; Krems–Melk: Mon–Fri 5/day—2 direct, Sat 3/day—all direct; no bus in either direction on Sun, 1 hr, €7).

In Melk, buses leave from the Hauptplatz stop, near Hotel Stadt Melk. In Krems, they leave from the Bahnhofplatz stop in front of the train station. For the best views, sit on the driver's side from Melk to Krems or the passenger's side from Krems to Melk, (tel. 051-717—to get an operator, dial 2 then 2, www.postbus.at).

By Train: While tiny, one-car, milk-run trains chug along from village to village up the river, these trains don't stop at Melk. Cyclists with tired legs can, however, return by train from Krems to Melk via St. Pölten (this route offers no river views; see "Melk-to-Krems Danube Valley Bike Ride" on page 187).

By Car and Driver: Johann Lichtl, based in Vienna, can take you on a day tour of the Danube Valley (see page 38).

Melk

Sleepy and elegant under its huge abbey, which seems to police the Danube, the town of Melk offers a pleasant stop.

ORIENTATION

Tourist Information

The TI, run by helpful Manfred Baumgartner, is a block off the main square (look for green signs) and has info on nearby castles,

the latest on bike rental, specifics on bike rides along the river, Internet access (€1/15 min), a free town map with a self-guided walking tour, and a list of Melk hotels and *Zimmer* in private homes (July–Aug Mon–Sat 9:00–19:00, Sun 10:00–12:00 & 17:00–19:00; May–June and Sept Mon–Fri 9:00–12:00 & 14:00–18:00, Sat–Sun 10:00–12:00 & 16:00–18:00; April and Oct shorter hours and closed Sun; closed Nov–March; good picnic garden with WC behind TI, Babenbergerstrasse 1, tel. 02752/5230-7410, www.niederoesterreich.at/melk).

Arrival in Melk

By Train: Walk straight out of the station (lockers-€2–3.50) and continue ahead for several blocks; at the curve, keep straight and go down the stairs, following the cobbled alley that dumps you into the center of the village. Access to Melk Abbey is up on your right (follow signs to *Zum Stift* or *Fussweg Stift Melk*), and the TI is a block off the end of the square to your right.

By Boat: Turn right as you leave the boat dock and follow the canalside bike path toward the big yellow abbey (the village is beneath its far side). In about five minutes, you'll come to a flashing light (at intersection with bridge); turn left and you're steps from downtown.

To reach the boat dock from Melk, leave the town toward the river, with the abbey on your right. Turn right when you get to the busy road and follow the canal (at the fork just before the gas station, it's quicker to jog left onto the bike path than to follow the main road). Follow signs for *Linienschifffahrt–Scheduled Trips–Wachau.*

SIGHTS AND ACTIVITIES

▲▲Melk Abbey (Benediktinerstift Melk)

Melk's newly restored abbey, beaming proudly over the Danube Valley, is one of Europe's great sights. Established as a fortified Benedictine abbey in the 11th century, it was destroyed by fire. What you see today is 18th-century Baroque. Architect Jakob Prandtauer made the building one with nature. The abbey church, with its 200-foot-tall dome and symmetrical towers, dominates the complex—emphasizing its sacred purpose.

Freshly painted and gilded throughout, it's a Baroque dream, a lily alone. The grand restoration project—financed in part by the sale of the abbey's Gutenberg Bible to Harvard—was completed by 1996 to celebrate the 1,000th anniversary of the first reference to a country named Österreich (Austria).

Cost and Hours: €7.70, includes entrance to Abbey Park, daily May–Sept 9:00–17:30, April and Oct 9:00–16:30, last entry 30 min before closing; Nov–March the abbey is open only for tours in German with a little English at 11:00 and 14:00; tel. 02752/555-232, www.stiftmelk.at.

Tours: English tours of the abbey are offered daily (April–Oct at 14:55, €9.50 ticket includes tour and admission). A private guide can be reserved at least one day in advance (€45 plus the €7.70 per-person entrance fee).

➲ **Self-Guided Tour:** Although you can take a guided tour, it's easiest just to wander through on your own. Each room is described in English.

• *Go through the first passageway and approach the grand entry to the...*

East Facade: Imagine the abbot on the balcony greeting you as he used to greet important guests. Flanking him are statues of Peter and Paul (leaders of the apostles and patron saints of the abbey church) and the monastery's coat of arms (crossed keys). High above are the Latin words "Glory only in the cross" and a huge copy of the Melk Cross (one of the abbey's greatest treasures—the original is hiding in the treasury and viewable only with special permission).

MELK

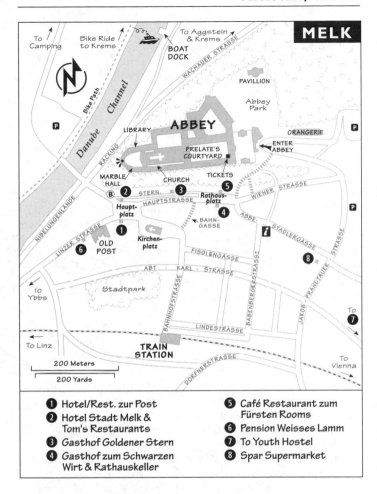

MELK

To Camping
Bike Ride to Krems
To Aggstein & Krems
WACHAUER STRASSE
BOAT DOCK
PAVILLION
Abbey Park
Danube Channel
Bike Path
LIBRARY
ABBEY
ORANGERIE
PACKING
PRELATE'S COURTYARD
ENTER ABBEY
MARBLE HALL
CHURCH
TICKETS
STERN
Rathaus-platz
WIENER STRASSE
B
Haupt-platz
HAUPTSTRASSE
BAHN-GASSE
ABBE-
STADLERGASSE
NIBELUNGENLÄNDE
LINZER STRASSE
OLD POST
Kirchen-platz
FISOLENGASSE
BABENBERGERSTRASSE
JAKOB · PRANDTAUER · STRASSE
To Ybbs
ABT · KARL · STRASSE
Stadtpark
BAHNHOFSTRASSE
LINDESTRASSE
To
To Linz
TRAIN STATION
DORFMERSTRASSE
To Vienna

200 Meters
200 Yards

1 Hotel/Rest. zur Post
2 Hotel Stadt Melk & Tom's Restaurants
3 Gasthof Goldener Stern
4 Gasthof zum Schwarzen Wirt & Rathauskeller
5 Café Restaurant zum Fürsten Rooms
6 Pension Weisses Lamm
7 To Youth Hostel
8 Spar Supermarket

• *Pass into the main courtyard.*

Prelate's Courtyard: This is more than a museum. For 900 years, monks of St. Benedict have lived and worked here. Their task: bringing and maintaining Christianity and culture to the region. (Many of the monks live outside the abbey in the community.) They run a high school with about 800 students, a small boarding school, and a busy retreat center.

There have been low points. During the Reformation (1500s), only eight monks held down the theological fort. Napoleon made his headquarters here in 1805 and 1809. And in 1938, when Hitler annexed Austria, the monastery was squeezed into one end of the complex and nearly dissolved. But today, the institution survives—that's the point of the four modern frescoes gracing the courtyard—funded by agriculture (historically, monasteries are big

MELK

landowners) and your visit.

• *In the far left-hand corner, climb the stairs to the...*

Imperial Corridor and Abbey Museum: This 640-foot-long corridor, lined with paintings of Austrian royalty, is the spine of the Abbey Museum. Duck into the first room of the museum (on the left, near beginning of hall). Art treasures and a recently updated exhibit (with creepy sound-and-light effects and some English explanations) fill several rooms.

• *Continue through the museum—walking parallel to the corridor, passing through the trippy mirrored room and around a beautifully preserved Northern Renaissance altarpiece—and go through the room at the end, with the big rotating model of the abbey.*

Marble Hall: While the door frames are real marble, most of this large dining room/ballroom is stucco. The treasure here

is the ceiling fresco (by Tirolean Paul Troger, 1731), best appreciated from the center of the room. Notice three themes: 1) The Habsburgs liked to be portrayed as Hercules; 2) Athena, the goddess of wisdom, is included, because the Habsburgs were smart as well as strong; and 3) The Habsburgs were into art and culture. This is symbolized by angels figuratively reining in the forces of evil, darkness, and brutality. Through this wise moderation, goodness, beauty, art, and science can rule. Look up again as you leave the room to see how the columns were painted at an angle to give the illusion of a curved ceiling.

Balcony: Here, we enjoy dramatic views of the Danube Valley, the town of Melk, and the facade of the monastery church. The huge statue above everything shows the risen Christ, cross in hand and victorious over death—the central message of the entire place.

Library: For the Benedictine monks, the library was—except for the church itself—the most important room in the abbey. Consider how much money they must have invested in its elabo-

rate decor.

In the Middle Ages, monasteries controlled information and hoarded it in their libraries. At a time when most everyone else was illiterate, monks were Europe's educated elite, and had the power to dictate

MELK

what was true...and what wasn't.

The inlaid bookshelves, matching bindings, and another fine Troger fresco combine harmoniously to create the Marble Hall's thematic counterpart. This room celebrates not wise politics, but faith. The ceiling shows a woman surrounded by the four cardinal virtues (wisdom, justice, fortitude, and recycling)—natural traits that lead to a supernatural faith. The statues flanking the doors represent the four traditional university faculties (law, medicine, philosophy, and theology).

There would be a Gutenberg Bible in this room...but it was sold to Harvard University to raise money to restore the library and glittering church.

Church: The finale is the church, with its architecture, ceiling frescoes, stucco marble, grand pipe organ, and sumptuous chapels adorned with chubby cherubs (how many can you count?). All these ele-ments combine in full Baroque style to make the theological point: A just battle leads to victory. The ceil-ing shows St. Benedict's triumphant entry into heaven (on a fancy carpet). In the front, below the huge papal crown, the saints Peter and Paul shake hands before departing for their final battles, martyrdom, and ultimate victory. And, high above, the paint-ing in the dome shows that victory:  the Holy Trinity, surrounded by saints of particular importance to Melk, happily in heaven.

Other Abbey Sights: Near the entrance (and exit) to the abbey, you'll find the Abbey Park (included in abbey ticket, or €3 for just the park, May–Oct daily 9:00–18:00, closed Nov–April)—home to a picturesque Baroque pavilion housing some fine fres-coes by Johann Wenzel Bergel and a café. Nearby, in the former orangerie, is the abbey's expensive restaurant.

Near Melk, in the Danube Valley

▲▲**Melk-to-Krems Danube Valley Bike Ride**—The three- to four-hour pedal from Melk to Krems takes you through the Wachau Valley—steeped in tradition, blanketed with vineyards, and orna-mented with cute villages. Bicyclists rule here, and you'll find all the amenities that make this valley so popular with Austrians on two wheels. For bike-rental info in Melk, see page 182.

Bike routes are clearly marked with green *Donau–Radweg* signs. The local TIs give out a *Donauradweg* brochure with a help-ful if basic route map. As you study it, note that the north bank has the best and most popular trail; it's paved all the way, winds through picturesque villages, and runs near, though not directly beside, the river. But consider the south bank, which has less car traffic. Although the bike trail merges with the actual road about half the time,

it comes with better river views. (Note: The bike-in-a-red-border signs mean "no biking.")

Pedal downstream toward Krems to enjoy a gradual slope in your favor. Then catch the boat back, but be prepared—this makes for a much longer day (it's slow upstream—about 3 hours). From Krems, you and your bike can also head back to Melk by train via St. Pölten, but that route takes you out of the scenic valley (roughly hourly, 1.25 hours).

If you prefer, you can go half-and-half by cruising to Spitz—a good midway point—and then hopping on a bike (or vice versa). Spitz has a boat station and train station (the bike path between Spitz and Krems is more interesting than between Melk and Spitz). Little ferries shuttle bikers and vacation-goers regularly across the river at three points.

Krems—Krems is a gem. Stroll the traffic-free, shopper's-wonderland old town. Pick up a map from the TI (from the boat dock,

go inland to second roundabout, turn right on Steiner Donaulände, walk 3 blocks after overhead railroad tracks to a park, then turn left on Utzstrasse—the TI's on the right after you pass Fischergasse; TI hours: May–Oct Mon–Fri 9:00–18:00, Sat 11:00–17:00, Sun 11:00–16:00; Nov–April Mon–Fri 9:00–17:00, closed Sat–Sun; Utzstrasse 1, tel. 02732/82676, krems tourismus@pegasus.at). If nothing else, it's a pleasant 20-minute walk from the dock to the train station. For information on train connections between Krems and Vienna, see "Transportation Connections" on page 174.

Sleeping in Krems: **$ Melanie Stasny's Gästezimmer** is a super place to stay—friendly, and with a proud vineyard and wine cellar (€23 per person in Db, Tb, or Qb; big Db-€52, 300 yards from dock at Steiner Landstrasse 22, tel. 02732/82843). When her place is booked, she sends travelers to her son's place down the street. The TI can usually find you a bed in a private home (D-€40,

Db-€50, cheap rooms harder to come by in Sept–Oct).

Dürnstein—This touristic flypaper lures hordes of tour bus and cruise ship visitors with its traffic-free quaintness and its one claim to fame (and fortune): Richard the Lionhearted was imprisoned here in 1193. You can probably sleep in his bedroom. Still, the town is a delight, and the ruined castle above can be reached by a good hike with great river views.

Willendorf—This is known among prehistorians as the town where the oldest piece of European art was found. There's a tiny museum in the village center (free, limited hours). A block farther uphill (follow the signs to *Venus*, just under tracks, follow stairs to right), you can see the monument where the well-endowed, 25,000-year-old fertility symbol, the *Venus of Willendorf*, was discovered. (The fist-sized original is now in Vienna's Natural History Museum—see page 55.)

SLEEPING

In Melk

Melk makes a fine overnight stop. Except during August, you shouldn't have any trouble finding a good room at a reasonable rate. The TI has a long list of people renting rooms for about €20 per person. Most of these are a few miles from the center.

$$$ Hotel zur Post is Melk's most modern-feeling hotel—professional and well-run by the Ebner family, with 28 comfy and tidy rooms over a good restaurant (Sb-€60–70, Db-€96–110 depending on size, Db suite-€145, has bigger suites that sleep 3–5 people, 8 percent discount with cash and this book, closed Jan–mid-Feb, elevator, sauna, Linzer Strasse 1, tel. 02752/52345, fax 02752/234-550, www.hotelpost-melk.at, info@hotelpost-melk.at). Hotel zur Post has free bikes for guests, and rents them to non-guests (€9/half-day, €12/day).

$$$ Hotel Stadt Melk, a block below the main square, has pink halls and drab, outmoded rooms. Melk's moderately priced options (listed next) offer better rooms for lower prices, but this will do in a pinch (Sb-€58–65, Db-€93, Hauptplatz 1, tel. 02752/524-750, fax 02752/524-7519, www.hotelstadtmelk.com, hotel.stadt melk@netway.at).

$$ Gasthof Goldener Stern's 11 rooms have barn-flavored elegance and flowers on every pillow. The pricier canopy-bed rooms are very romantic. This lively place buzzes with locals eating in the atmospheric old restaurant—and with Regina and Kurt Schmidt's five children. It's on the small alley that veers off the main square above the twin turrets (D-€42–56, Db-€58–80, Db suite-€104, prices depend on room size, rooms for up to 6 also available, cash only, all rooms non-smoking, €10/day bike rental

---

Sleep Code

(€1 = about $1.40, country code: 43, area code: 02752)

S = Single, **D** = Double/Twin, **T** = Triple, **Q** = Quad, **b** = bathroom, **s** = shower only. Breakfast is included and everyone speaks at least some English. Credit cards are accepted unless otherwise noted.

To help you sort easily through these listings, I've divided the rooms into three categories, based on the price for a standard double room with bath:

$$$ **Higher Priced**—Most rooms €75 or more.

$$ **Moderately Priced**—Most rooms between €50–75.

$ **Lower Priced**—Most rooms €50 or less.

---

for guests, Sterngasse 17, tel. 02752/52214, fax 02752/522-144, www.sternmelk.at, goldenerstern.melk@aon.at).

$$ Gasthof zum Schwarzen Wirt offers classy, clean, basic rooms with nice floors and decor with a modern, African touch, right in the middle of town (Db-€63, Tb-€75, Qb-€90, cash only, Rathausplatz 13, tel. & fax 02752/52257, www.schwarzer wirt.at, addo@schwarzerwirt.at, Addo family). They also run a restaurant—see "Eating."

$$ Cafe Restaurant zum Fürsten rents 10 clean rooms over its creaky restaurant. Run by the Madar family, it's right on the traffic-free main square, with a fountain outside the door and the Melk Abbey hovering overhead (Sb-€41–47, small Db-€62, big Db with bathtub-€78, cash only, Rathausplatz 3–5, tel. 02752/52343, fax 02752/523-434, www.tiscover.at/cafe-madar, cafe.madar@net way.at).

$ Pension Weisses Lamm has the cheapest beds in the center—and absentee management. All but two of the seven (very) worn-but-clean rooms have bathrooms (Db-€50, Tb-€75, cash only, Linzer Strasse 7, look for namesake white lamb on sign, tel. 0664/231-5297, fax 02752/51224, www.pension-weisses-lamm -melk.at, pension.weisses.lamm@hotmail.com).

$ *Hostel:* The modern, institutional **youth hostel** is a 10-minute walk from the station; go straight out from the station down Bahnhofstrasse, then turn right at the next corner onto Abt-Karl-Strasse (24 4-bed rooms, one 8-bed room; beds-€20, Sb or Db-€10 extra, €2 less if staying 3 or more nights, includes sheets and breakfast, no curfew, reception open daily 16:00–21:00, reception desk staffed intermittently Nov–March—call ahead, Abt-Karl-Strasse 42, tel. 02752/52681, fax 02752/526-815, http://melk.noejhw.at, melk@noejhw.at).

MELK

EATING

Restaurants at the recommended hotels **Gasthof Goldener Stern** (closed day varies) and **Café Restaurant zum Fürsten** (open daily) have fine, inexpensive local cuisine.

Hotel Restaurant zur Post, classier and pricier, is worth the few extra euros. Downstairs is a fun and atmospheric wine cellar, with both local and international wines (daily 11:30–21:30, closed Jan–mid-Feb, good local dishes, courtyard and fine streetside seating with an abbey view, Linzer Strasse 1, tel. 02752/52345).

Tom's Gourmet, located in Hotel Stadt Melk, serves the city's most elegant cuisine, with delicate nouvelle cuisine–type fixed-price meals (€75 for standard, €100 for 7-course blowout). A second restaurant in the same place, **Tom's Leger,** offers typical Austrian specialties for much less (€15–18 entrées, both restaurants open Thu–Tue 12:00–14:00 & 18:00–21:00, closed Wed, terrace seating, reservations smart, Hauptplatz 1, tel. 02752/524-7530). **Tom's Café,** right at the hotel entrance, has homemade goodies and a rare (for Austria) treat: coffee to go.

Locals swear by the food at **Rathauskeller Gasthof zum Schwarzen Wirt,** with good Austrian dishes. It's run by the Ghanaian-Austrian Addo family (€8–11 for most meals, lunch specials; May–Oct usually daily 10:00–22:00; Nov–April closed 14:30–16:30, Thu, and Sun evenings; Rathausplatz 13, tel. 02752/52257). They sometimes cook West African dinners—if interested, call or stop by to ask if it's on tonight's menu, and reserve your meal.

Supermarket: Pick up picnic supplies at the easy-to-reach **Spar** (Mon–Fri 7:00–18:30, Sat 7:00–17:00, closed Sun, behind TI on Jakob-Prandtauer-Strasse).

MELK

TRANSPORTATION CONNECTIONS

Both Melk and Krems are connected to Vienna by frequent trains.

From Melk by Train to: Vienna's Westbahnhof (2/hr, 1.25 hrs, some with transfer in St. Pölten), **Salzburg** (at least hourly, 2.5–3 hrs, transfer in Amstetten or St. Pölten), **Mauthausen** (hourly, 1.5 hrs, transfer in Amstetten and St. Valentin).

From Krems by Train to: Vienna (hourly, 1–1.5 hrs, see next paragraph), **Melk** (roughly hourly, 1.5 hrs, via St. Pölten; for train/bus connections along river, see "By Bus and Train Along the

North Bank," page 182).

Krems trains leave from/arrive at Vienna's Franz Josefs Bahnhof (a small station on the north edge of the city). It's connected to the city center by convenient tram #D, but lacks a U-Bahn stop. If you're trying to connect Krems to a spot in Vienna best reached by U-Bahn, consider departing from or arriving at Vienna's Spittelau train/U-Bahn station instead of Franz Josef (it's the train's first stop after the Franz Josefs Bahnhof if leaving Vienna; the next-to-last stop if arriving).

By Car to/from the Danube Valley: See "Route Tips for Drivers" at the end of this chapter.

Mauthausen Concentration Camp

In the beautiful rolling hills flanking the Danube River, just upstream from Vienna, stands the notorious former concentration camp at Mauthausen (MOWT-how-zehn). This slave-labor and death camp functioned from 1938 to 1945 for the exploitation and extermination of Hitler's opponents. More than half of its 206,000 quarry-working prisoners died here, mostly from starvation or exhaustion.

The Nazis' camps, scattered across much of Europe by the early 1940s, were of two types: extermination camps, where people were simply exterminated en masse (such as at Auschwitz), and concentration camps such as Mauthausen, where people were essentially worked to death. In these camps, your ability to endure forced labor amounted to a stay of execution.

Mauthausen, like many camps, was located at a quarry. Inmates generally labored for the German armaments industry or quarried stone for vast Nazi building projects. The long stairway that connected the quarry with the Mauthausen camp and its stone depot earned the name "stairway of death" for good reason.

With Nazi efficiency in mind, people were fed the bare minimum to continue working. If you couldn't carry slabs of rocks on your back up the stairway all day long—under the harshest of conditions and on this starvation diet—you were shot on the spot.

Most died within a year of their arrival.

Today the barracks of Mauthausen—which held as many as 80,000 slave-laborers at a time—tell the story of this camp. Outside the barracks is a park area where each home country of the camp's victims has erected a gripping memorial to their citizens who perished here. Many yellowed photos have fresh flowers to honor loved ones who are still not forgotten.

Allow two hours to tour the camp completely. You can borrow a free, 45-minute audioguide (leave ID as deposit). The barracks house a worthwhile museum at the far end of the camp on the right (no English, but the excellent €2.60 English guidebook has descriptions for every display case). The most emotionally moving rooms and the gas chamber are downstairs. The spirits of the victims of these horrors can still be felt.

Mauthausen rivals Dachau as the most powerful concentration-camp experience a traveler can have in Western Europe (€2, daily 9:00–17:30, last entry one hour before closing, some exhibits are at new visitors center near the car park—but tickets for the camp must be purchased inside camp at ticket booth, tel. 07238/2269, TI tel. 07238/3860, www.mauthausen-memorial .at; for directions, see "Transportation Connections" on the next page). A graphic 45-minute movie is shown at the top of each hour between 9:00 and 16:00. There are several film rooms—check in at the visitors center to request an English showing.

Back outside the camp, find the barbed-wire memorial overlooking the quarry and the "stairway of death" *(Todesstiege)*. Hike

down and back up the sad stairway to ponder the vast quarry from its ground level; you'll be left with a lasting and poignant impression. (If you have a car and want to see the quarry but avoid the hike, turn right as you leave the main parking lot and park at the quarry.)

By visiting a concentration camp and putting ourselves through this emotional wringer, we heed and respect the fervent wish of the victims of this fascism—that we never forget. Many people forget by choosing not to know.

MAUTHAUSEN

SLEEPING

Near Mauthausen

$$ Hotel zum Goldenen Schiff is a decent value, with 20 comfy rooms and a quaint location. It faces the delightful main square of Enns. This village, just off the autobahn—less than four miles southwest of Mauthausen and 62 miles west of Vienna—calls itself Austria's oldest town (Sb-€47, Db-€68, family rooms, fee for Internet access and free Wi-Fi, free parking, Hauptplatz 23, tel. 07223/86086, fax 07223/860-8615, www.hotel-brunner.at, wolfgang.brunner@liwest.at).

EATING

Moststube Frellerhof, a farmhouse 50 yards below the Mauthausen parking lot, offers a refreshing, peaceful break after your visit. They serve *Most* (grape juice ready to become wine), homemade schnapps, and light, farm-fresh meals (May–mid-Sept daily from 13:00, April and mid-Sept–Oct Sat–Sun only, closed Nov–March, playground, tel. 07238/2789).

TRANSPORTATION CONNECTIONS

Getting to Mauthausen

Most trains stop at St. Valentin, midway between Salzburg and Vienna, where sporadic trains make the 15-minute ride to the Mauthausen station (get map from station attendant, camp is #9 on map). While there are no lockers at the station, the camp's visitor center will keep an eye on your bags during your visit.

Getting from Mauthausen Station to Mauthausen Camp: To cover the three miles between the camp and station, you can **hike** (1 hour, follow signs to *Ehemaliges KZ-Gedenkstätte Lager*) or take a **taxi** (minibus taxis available, about €10 one-way, ask taxi to pick you up in 2 hours, share the cost with other tourists, tel. 07238/2439). Train info: tel. 051-717 (to get an operator, dial 2 then 2).

From Vienna by Train to Mauthausen: You can reach Mauthausen direct from Vienna's Südbahnhof, but the connection is infrequent (once daily), leaves early (at about 7:30), and takes five hours. Far better are the frequent connections from the Westbahnhof, which involve a transfer in St. Valentin (about hourly until 17:30, 2 hrs).

From Mauthausen by Train via St. Valentin to: Salzburg (hourly, 2 hrs, allow extra 20 min to get from camp memorial to station), **Vienna** (nearly hourly, 2 hrs), **Hallstatt** (nearly hourly, 3 hrs, transfer at St. Valentin and Attnang-Puchheim—be sure to arrive in Hallstatt in time for the last boat—see page 278).

Route Tips for Drivers

Vienna to Hallstatt, via the Wachau Valley, Melk, and Mauthausen (210 miles): The most scenic stretch of the Danube is the Wachau Valley between Krems and Melk. Leave Vienna by crossing the Danube to reach the A-22 autobahn. Head north (following *Praha*/Prague signs) to Stockerau, then take exit #30 to the S-5 highway, which leads to Krems. After Krems, take Route 3 along the river until just after Schallemmersdorf (and just before Emmersdorf), where a bridge leads across the river to Melk. In Melk, signs to *Stift Melk* lead to the Benediktinerstift (Benedictine Abbey).

From Melk, it's a speedy 60 minutes to Mauthausen via the autobahn, but the curvy and scenic Route 3 along the river is worth the nausea. At Mauthausen, follow *Ehemaliges KZ-Gedenkstätte Lager* signs to the concentration camp memorial. Leaving Mauthausen, cross the Danube and follow signs to Enns (5 min from Mauthausen town), and join the autobahn there (heading west). Leave the autobahn at exit #224 and follow scenic Route 145 past Gmunden to Stambach, then to the 166, which leads to Hallstatt.

Hallstatt to Vienna, via Mauthausen, Melk, and Wachau Valley: Leave Hallstatt early. Follow the scenic Route 145 through Gmunden to the autobahn and head east. After Linz, take exit #155 at Enns, and follow the signs for *Mauthausen* (5 miles from freeway). Go through Mauthausen town and follow the *Ehemaliges KZ-Gedenkstätte Lager* signs. When leaving Mauthausen for Melk, enjoy the riverside drive along scenic Route 3 (or take the autobahn if you're in a hurry or prone to carsickness). At Melk, signs to *Stift Melk* lead to the abbey. Other *Melk* signs lead into the town.

From Melk (get a Vienna map at the TI), cross the river again (signs to *Donaubrücke*) and stay on Route 3. After Krems, the riverside route (now the S-5) hits the autobahn (A-22), and you'll barrel right into Vienna's traffic. (See "By Car—Route Tips for Drivers" in the Vienna's Transportation Connections chapter for details, page 174.)

MAUTHAUSEN

BRATISLAVA, SLOVAKIA

Bratislava, long a drab lesson in the failings of the communist system, is turning things around...fast. A decade ago, the city center was grim, deserted, and dangerous—a place where only thieves and fools dared to tread. Today it's a downright charming people zone, bursting with colorfully restored facades, lively outdoor cafés, swanky boutiques, in-love-with-life locals, and (on sunny days) an almost Mediterranean ambience.

The rejuvenation doesn't end in the Old Town. The ramshackle quarter to the east is gradually being flattened and redeveloped into a new forest of skyscrapers. Bratislava is working together with its neighbor Vienna to forge a new super-capital for trade and commerce, bridging the former Western Europe and the former Eastern Europe. The hilltop castle is getting a facelift. And even the glum commie suburb of Petržalka is getting a Technicolor makeover. Before our eyes, Bratislava is becoming the quintessential post-communist Central European city...what can happen when government and business leaders make a concerted effort to jump-start a failing city.

You get the feeling that workaday Bratislavans—who strike some visitors as gruff—are being pulled to the cutting edge of the 21st century kicking and screaming. But many Slovaks embrace the changes, and fancy themselves as the yang to Vienna's yin: If Vienna is a staid, elderly aristocrat sipping coffee, then Bratislava is a vivacious young professional jet-setting around Europe.

Bratislava is not worth going far out of your way for. But its priceless location—on the Danube (and the tourist circuit) smack-dab between Vienna and Budapest—makes it worth considering as an illuminating "on the way" destination. Frankly, the city used to leave me cold. But all the new changes are positively inspiring. See Bratislava now...in a few years, it'll be a different city.

Planning Your Time

A few hours is enough to get the gist of Bratislava. Head straight for the Old Town and follow my self-guided walk, dropping into your choice of museums. With more time, ascend to the "UFO" observation deck atop the funky suspension bridge. Or hike up to the castle, which offers great views over town (even though its interior is closed for renovation). Spend the night if you like, but I find hotel values and evening fun better in Vienna and Budapest.

ORIENTATION

(area code: 02)

Bratislava, with nearly half a million residents, is Slovakia's capital and biggest city. It has a small, colorful Old Town (Staré Mesto), with the castle on the hill above it. This small area is surrounded by a vast construction zone of new buildings and a few colorized communist suburbs (including Petržalka, across the river). The north and west of the city is hilly and cool (these "Little Carpathians" are draped with vineyards), while the south and east is flat and warmer.

Tourist Information

The TI has two branches in the heart of the city. There's a small window in the **train station** (June–Oct Mon–Fri 8:00–19:00, Sat–Sun 9:00–17:00; Nov–May Mon–Fri 9:00–17:00, Sat–Sun 9:00–14:00; tel. 02/5249-5906), and a main branch on **Primate's Square** behind the Old Town Hall (June–Sept Mon–Fri 8:30–19:00, Sat 9:00–17:00, Sun 10:00–17:00; Oct–May Mon–Fri 8:30–18:00, Sat 9:00–16:00, Sun 10:00–15:00; Klobučnícka 2, tel. 02/5443-3715, www.bkis.sk and www.bratislava.sk). There are also TI windows at the airport and passenger boat terminals.

At any TI, pick up the free *Bratislava Guide* (with map) and browse their brochures. They can help you find a room for a modest fee. The **Bratislava City Card,** which includes free transit and sightseeing discounts, is worthwhile only if you're doing the Old Town walking tour (see "Tours," later in this section; €10/day, includes walking tour April–Oct, 50 percent discount on tour Nov–March, sold at TI).

Arrival in Bratislava

By Train: Bratislava's Main Train Station, called Bratislava Hlavná Stanica, is about a half-mile north of the Old Town. The city plans to tear down most of the station and start from scratch in the next few years (to accommodate, among other things, a new high-speed rail line connecting Bratislava to Paris). Therefore, these arrival

Welcome to Slovakia

In many ways, Slovakia is the "West Virginia of Europe"—poor and relatively undeveloped, but spectacularly beautiful in its own rustic way. Sitting quietly in the very center of Central Europe, wedged between bigger and stronger nations (Hungary, Austria, the Czech Republic, and Poland), Slovakia was brutally disfigured by the communists, then overshadowed by the Czechs. But in recent years, this fledgling republic has begun to find its wings.

With about 5.4 million people in a country of 19,000 square miles (similar to Massachusetts and New Hampshire combined), Slovakia is one of Europe's smallest nations. Recent economic reforms are causing two very different Slovakias to emerge: the modern, industrialized, flat, affluent west, centered on the capital of Bratislava; and the remote, poorer, mountainous, "backwards" east, with high unemployment and traditional lifestyles. Slovakia is quite ethnically diverse: In addition to the Slavic Slovaks, there are  Hungarians (about 10 percent of the population, "stranded" here when Hungary lost this land after World War I) and Roma (Gypsies, also about 10 percent). Slovakia has struggled to incorporate both of these large and often-mistreated minority groups.

Slovakia has spent most of its history as someone else's backyard. For centuries, Slovakia was ruled from Budapest and known as "Upper Hungary." At other times, it was an important chunk of the Habsburg Empire, ruled from nearby Vienna. But most people think first of another era: the 75 years that Slovakia was joined with the Czech Republic as the country of "Czechoslovakia." From its start in the aftermath of World War I, this union of the Czechs and Slovaks was troubled; some Slovaks

instructions are likely to change; just look for signs or ask the TI for help.

As you emerge from the tracks, the TI is down the hall to your left, and the left-luggage desk is to your right (€1–2, depending on size; look for *ú schovňa batožín;* there are no lockers, and the check desk usually closes for 30-min lunch and dinner breaks—try to confirm that they'll be there when you get back if you'll be rushing to catch a train).

It's an easy 15-minute **walk** to the town center. Leave straight ahead and walk to the busy cross street. Take the overpass across the street, and continue straight on Štefánikova. This formerly chafed at being ruled from Prague, while many Czechs resented the financial burden of their poorer neighbors to the east.

After they gained their freedom from the communists during 1989's peaceful "Velvet Revolution," the Czechs and Slovaks began to think of the future. The Slovaks wanted to rename the country Czecho-Slovakia, and to redistribute powers to give themselves more autonomy within the union. The Czechs balked, relations gradually deteriorated, and the Slovak nationalist candidate Vladimír Mečiar fared surprisingly well in the 1992 elections. Taking it as a sign that the two peoples wanted to part ways, politicians pushed through (in just three months) the peaceful separation of the now-independent Czech and Slovak Republics. (The people in both countries never actually voted on the change, and most opposed it.) The "Velvet Divorce" became official on January 1, 1993.

At first the Slovaks struggled. Communist rule had been particularly unkind to them, and their economy was in a shambles. Visionary leaders set forth bold solutions, including the 2003 implementation of a Steve Forbes–style flat tax (19 percent), followed by EU membership in 2004. And before long, a funny thing started happening...major international corporations began to notice the same thing the communists had: This is a great place to build stuff, thanks to a magnificent location, low labor costs, and a well-trained workforce. Multiple foreign automakers have built plants here, making the country the world's biggest car producer (per capita) and leading the *New York Times* to dub Slovakia "the European Detroit."

While the flat tax is not without its critics—especially in the very impoverished eastern half of the country, where poor people feel they're becoming even poorer—there's no doubt it has been a boon for middle-class areas in the west. In 2007, Slovakia had Europe's fastest-growing economy (10.4 percent). And in 2009, Slovakia became the first former Warsaw Pact country to adopt the euro currency.

elegant old boulevard is lined with rotting facades from Bratislava's high-on-the-hog Habsburg era. After about 10 minutes, you'll pass the nicely manicured presidential gardens on your left, then the Grassalkovich Palace, Slovakia's "White House." Continue straight through the busy intersection onto Súche Mýho, and head for the green onion-domed steeple (get there by taking the narrow street next to the mod, green, white-capped Alizé restaurant). This is St. Michael's Gate, at the start of the Old Town (and my self-guided walk, described later in this chapter).

If you want to shave a few minutes off the trip, you can go part of the way by **tram** (from train station's main hall, with tracks at

BRATISLAVA

1. Hotel Marrol's
2. Hotel Michalská Brána
3. Hotel Corso
4. Penzion Chez David
5. Hotel Ibis
6. Downtown Backpackers Hostel
7. Prazdroj Beer Hall
8. 1. Slovak Pub
9. Erdody Palace Eateries
10. Kaffee Mayer

ULICA PALISÁDY

GODROVA

ŠTETINOVA

PANENSKÁ

LÝCEJNÁ

KOZIA ULICA

KONVENTNÁ

PARTIZÁNSKA

ZOCHOVA

PODJAVOR.

STAROMESTSKÁ

Župné Nám.

SVORADOVA

DANKOVSKÉHO

ŠKARNÍCLOVA

ULICA PALISÁDY

ZÁMOCKÁ ULICA

4

2

BAŠTOVÁ

KORENIČOVA

5

Zochova

B

3

Fashion Courtyard

TVAROŽKOVA

ZIDOVSKÁ

KLARISKÁ

KRÁTKA

KAPITULSKÁ

PREPOŠTSKÁ

STRELECKÁ

CASTLE

SUMMER RIDING SCHOOL

STAROMESTSKÁ

VENTÚRSKA

9

VODNÝ

PARLIAMENT

ST. MARTIN'S CATHEDRAL

ZÁM. SCHODY

WALK ENDS

SCHODY PRI STAREJ VODÁRNI

NÁBR. ARMÁDNEHO GENERÁLA L. SVOBODU

B Nový Most

RÁZUSOVO NÁBR.

N

NEW BRIDGE

"UFO" OBSERVATION DECK

100 Meters
100 Yards

To Petržalka

To Main Train Station

TOLSTÉHO

SLADKOVIČOVA

ŠTEFAN.

Presidential Gardens

GRASSALKOVICH PALACE

Hodžovo Nám.

NÁM. 1 MÁJA

Kollárovo Nám.

❻

BIG FOUNTAIN

VYSOKÁ

MARIÁNSKA

POŠTOVÁ

DREVENÁ

SUCHÉ MÝTO

OBCHODNÁ

❽

Ⓣ Poštová

HOLLÉHO

HEYDUKOVA

Hurbanovo Nám.

🚶 **WALK BEGINS**

Nám. SNP

KOLÁRSKA

ŠPITÁLSKA

ST. MICHAEL'S GATE

ZÁMOČNÍCKA

FRANTIŠK.

NEDBALOVA

TESCO DEP'T. STORE

MICHALSKÁ

CHOCOLATE SHOP

BIELA

OLD TOWN HALL & CITY HISTORY MUSEUM

KLOBUČNÍKA

Kamenné Nám.

Františkánske Nám.

Primate's Square ℹ

DUNAJSKÁ

SEDLÁRSKA

NAPOLEONIC SOLDIER STATUE

Main Square

APPONYI PALACE

PRIMATE'S PALACE

❿

LAURINSKÁ

GORKÉHO

GRÖSSLINGOVÁ

SCHÖNER NÁCI STATUE

PAPARAZZO STATUE

JESENSKÉHO

PANSKÁ

ČUMIL STATUE

RYBÁRSKA

DISPLAY CASE

ŠTÚROVA

HVIEZDOSLAVOVO NÁM.

FOUNTAIN

NATIONAL THEATER

MEDENÁ

TALLEROVA

U.S. EMBASSY

❼

PHILHARMONIC

❶

SLOVAK NATIONAL GALLERY

Nám. Ľ. Štúra

VAJANSKÉHO NÁBR.

HYDROFOIL TERMINAL

Danube River

your back, look for signs to *električky* on left; take escalator down, buy a €0.60/30-minute ticket from the machine, hop on tram #13, and ride it five stops).

The Main Train Station described above is the most convenient place to arrive. But if you wind up instead at Bratislava's other major train station (called "ŽST Petržalka"), in the **Petržalka** suburb, you can take bus #80, #93, #94, or #N93 to the Zochova stop (near St. Michael's Gate), or bus #91 or #191 to the Nový Most stop (at the Old Town end of the New Bridge). Buses #93 (by day) and #N93 (by night) also connect the two stations.

By Boat or Plane: For information on Bratislava's riverboats and airport, see "Transportation Connections," at the end of this chapter.

Helpful Hints

Money: Slovakia officially adopted the euro currency in January of 2009 (€1 = about $1.40). You'll find ATMs at the train stations and airport. You might still see references to the old currency, the Slovak *koruna* (30 Sk = about €1).

Language: While many people in Bratislava speak English, the official language is Slovak (closely related to Czech and Polish). The local "ciao"—used informally for both "hi" and "bye"—is easy to remember: *ahoj* (pronounced AH-hoy, like a pirate). "Please" is *prosím* (PROH-seem), "thank you" is *ďakujem* (DYAH-koo-yehm), and "Cheers!" is *Na zdravie!* (nah ZDRAH-vyeh).

Phone Tips: Slovakia's phone system works like Austria's. When calling locally (such as within Bratislava), dial the number without the area code. To make a long-distance call within Slovakia, start with the area code (which begins with 0). Slovakia's country code is 421. To call from Austria to Slovakia, you'd dial 00-421, then the area code minus the initial zero, then the number (from the US, dial 011-421-area code minus zero, then the number). To call from Slovakia to Austria, you'd dial 00-43, then the area code minus the initial zero and the number.

Internet Access: You'll see signs advertising Internet cafés around the Old Town. If you have a laptop with Wi-Fi, you can get online free at the three main squares in the Old Town (Old Town Square, Primate's Square, and Hviezdoslav Square).

Local Guidebook: For in-depth suggestions on Bratislava sightseeing, dining, and more, look for the excellent and eye-pleasing *Bratislava Active* guidebook by Martin Sloboda (see "Tours," next; around €10, sold at every postcard rack).

TOURS

Walking Tour—The TI offers a one-hour Old Town walking tour in English every day in the summer at 14:00 (€12.50, free or discounted with Bratislava City Card—see page 197; runs sporadically based on demand Nov–March—call ahead to confirm, tel. 02/5443-4059, guides@bkis.sk).

Local Guide—MS Agency, run by **Martin Sloboda** (a can-do entrepreneur and tireless Bratislava booster, and author of the great local guidebook described under "Helpful Hints," earlier in this chapter), can set you up with a good local guide (€120/3 hrs, €150/4 hrs), and can help you track down your Slovak roots (tel. 02/5464-1467, www.msagency.sk, info@msagency.sk).

SELF-GUIDED WALK

Bratislava's Old Town

This orientation walk through the heart of delightfully traffic-free old Bratislava takes about an hour (not including stops). If you're coming from the station, make your way toward the green onion-domed steeple of St. Michael's Gate (explained in "Arrival in Bratislava," earlier in this chapter). Before going through the passage into the Old Town, peek over the railing on your left to the inviting garden below—once part of the city moat.

• *Step through the first gate, walk along the passageway, and pause as you come through the onion-domed...*

St. Michael's Gate (Michalská Brána)

This is the last surviving tower of the city wall. Just below the gate, notice the "kilometer zero" plaque in the ground, marking the point from which distances in Slovakia are measured.

• *You're at the head of...*

Michalská Street

Pretty as it is now, the Old Town was a decrepit ghost town during the communist era. Locals avoided this desolate corner of the city, preferring to spend time in the Petržalka suburb across the river. But after the fall of communism, city leaders decided to revitalize this zone. They replaced all of the cobbles, spruced up the public buildings, and encouraged the new private owners of other

City of Three Cultures: Pressburg, Pozsony, Bratislava

Historically an Austrian and Hungarian city as much a Slovak one, Bratislava has always been a Central European melting pot. The Hungarians used Pozsony (as they called it) as their capital during the century and a half that Buda and Pest were occupied by Ottoman invaders. Later, the city was a favorite retreat of Habsburg Empress Maria Theresa (who used its German name, Pressburg). Everyone from Hans Christian Andersen to Casanova sang the wonders of this bustling burg on the Danube.

By its late-19th-century glory days, the city was a rich intersection of cultures. Shop clerks had to be able to greet customers in German, Hungarian, and Slovak. It was said that the mornings belonged to the Slovaks (farmers who came into the city to sell their wares at market), the afternoons to the Hungarians (diplomats and office-workers filling the cafés), and the evenings to the Austrians (wine-producers who ran convivial neighborhood wine pubs where all three groups would gather). In those wine pubs, the vintner would listen to which language his customers used, then automatically bring them the correct size glass: 0.3 liters for Hungarians, 0.25 liters for Austrians, and 0.2 liters for Slovaks (a distinction that still exists today). Jews (one-tenth of the population), Romanians, and Roma (Gypsies) rounded out the city's ethnic brew.

When the new nation of Czechoslovakia was formed from the rubble of World War I, the city shed its German and Hungarian names, proudly taking the new Slavic name Bratislava. The Slovak population—which had been at only about 10 percent—was on the rise, but the city remained tri-cultural.

World War II changed all of that. With the dissolution of Czechoslovakia, Slovakia became an "independent" country under the thumb of the Nazis—who decimated the Jewish popu-

buildings to invest in careful restoration. It worked: Today the Old Town is gleaming, and packed with locals and tourists alike.

The cafés and restaurants that line this street are inviting, especially in summer. But if you don't look beyond the facades and outdoor tables, you'll miss much of Bratislava's charm. Courtyards and galleries—most of them open to the public—burrow through the city's buildings. For example, a half-block down on the right, the gallery at #7 is home to several fashion designers.

Speaking of fashion...are you noticing a lot of skin? Tight jeans? Low-cut tops? Slovak women are known for their provocative dress. When pressed for a reason for this, local men smirk and say, "That's just the way it is."

On the left (at #6), the **Čokoládovňa pod Michalom** chocolate shop is highly regarded among locals for its delicious, creamy lation. Then, at the end of the war, in retribution for Hitler's mis-deeds, a reunited Czechoslovakia expelled people of Germanic descent (including all of those Austrians). And finally, a "mutual exchange of populations" sent the city's Hungarians back to Hungary.

Bratislava suffered terribly under the communists. It became the textbook example of a historic city whose multilayered charm and delicate cultural fabric were ripped apart, then shrouded in gray by the communist regime. For example, the communists were more proud of their ultramodern New Bridge than of the historic Jewish quarter they razed to make way for it. Now the bridge and its highway slice through the center of the Old Town, and the heavy traffic rattles the stained-glass windows of St. Martin's Cathedral.

But Bratislava's most recent chapter is one of great success. Over the last decade, the city has gone from gloomy victim of communism to thriving economic center and social hub. Its population of 450,000 includes some 70,000 students (at the city's six universities), creating an atmosphere of youthful energy and optimism. Its remarkable position on the Danube, a short commute from Vienna, is prompting its redevelopment as one of Europe's most up-and-coming cities.

Bratislava and Vienna have realized it's in both cities' interest to work together to bring the Slovak capital up to snuff. They're cooperating as a new "twin city" commerce super-zone...and things are happening at an astonishing pace. In the coming years, foreign investors plan to erect a skyline of 600-foot-tall skyscrapers and a clutch of glittering new mega-malls. You'd never have guessed it a few years ago, but today calling Bratislava "the next Berlin on a smaller scale" is only a bit of a stretch.

truffles (Mon–Fri 9:00–21:00, Sat–Sun 10:00–21:00, tel. 02/5443-3945).

Look over the shop's entrance and find the **cannonball** embedded in the wall above the seal. This commemorates Napoleon's two sieges of Bratislava, which together caused massive devastation—even worse than the city suffered during World War II. Keep an eye out for these cannonballs all over town...somber reminders of one of Bratislava's darkest times.

• *Two blocks down from St. Michael's Gate, the name of this main drag changes to Ventúrska, the street jogs to the right, and the café scene continues. At the jog, detour left (along Sedlárska) and head for the...*

Main Square (Hlavné Námestie)

This is the bustling centerpiece of Old World Bratislava. Virtually

every building around this square dates from a different architectural period, from Gothic (the yellow tower) to Art Nouveau (the fancy facade facing it from across the square). When these buildings were restored a few years ago, great pains were taken to achieve authenticity—each one matches the color most likely used when it was originally built. Extremely atmospheric cafés line the bottom of the square. **Kaffee Mayer** is the classic choice (described on page 216), but you can't miss along here. Choose the ambience you like best (indoors or out) and nurse a drink with arguably Slovakia's best urban view.

Peering over one of the benches is a cartoonish statue of a **Napoleonic officer** (notice the French flag marking the embassy right behind him). With bare feet and a hat pulled over his eyes, it's hardly a flattering portrait—you could call it the Slovaks' revenge for the difficulties they faced at Napoleon's hands.

At the top of the Main Square is the impressive **Old Town Hall** (Stará Radnica), marked by a bold yellow tower. Near the bottom of the tower (to the left of the window), notice the cannonball embedded in the facade— yet another reminder of Napoleon's impact on Bratislava. Over time, the Old Town Hall gradually grew, annexing the buildings next to it—creating a mishmash of architectural styles along this side of the square. (A few steps down the street to the right are the historic apartments and wine museum at the Apponyi House—see "Sights" on page 210.)

Step through the passageway into the Old Town Hall's gorgeously restored **courtyard,** with its Renaissance arcades. (If the City History Museum is open, its entrance is here—see "Sights.")

Then, to see another fine old square, continue through the other end of the courtyard into **Primate's Square** (Primaciálne Námestie). The pink mansion on the right is the Primate's Palace, with a fine interior decorated with six English tapestries (see "Sights"). Do you see a lot of people using laptops? In a progressive move befitting its status as an emerging business center of Europe, Bratislava provides free Wi-Fi on three squares in the Old Town. The huge student population (not to mention tourists) happily surfs in this beautiful setting. At the far end of this square is the main branch of the TI.

• *Backtrack to the Main Square. With your back to the Old Town Hall, go to the end of the square and follow the street to the left (Rybárska Brána). Soon you'll pass a pair of…*

Whimsical Statues

Several playful statues (such as the Napoleonic officer we met earlier) dot Bratislava's Old Town. Most of these date from the late 1990s, when city leaders wanted to entice locals back into the newly prettied-up Old Town.

A half-block down this street (on the left), you'll come to a jovial chap doffing his top hat. This is a statue of **Schöner Náci,**

who lived in Bratislava until the 1960s. This eccentric old man, a poor carpet cleaner, would dress up in his one black suit and top hat, and go strolling through the city, offering gifts to the women he fancied. (He'd often whisper *"schön"*—German for "pretty"—to the women, which is how he got his nickname.) After spending his life cheering up the gloomy streets of communist Bratislava, Schöner Náci now gets to spend eternity greeting visitors in front of his favorite café, Kaffee Mayer.

As a sad epilogue, Schöner Náci's arm was broken off recently by a bunch of drunks. As Prague gets more expensive, Bratislava is becoming the cheaper alternative for weekend "stag parties," popular with Brits lured here by cheap flights and cheap beer. Locals hope this is a short-lived trend, and that those rowdy louts will move farther east before long.

• *Continue down Rybárska.*

At the end of this block, at the intersection with Panská, watch out on the right for **Čumil** ("the Peeper"), grinning at passersby from a manhole. This was the first and is still the favorite Bratislava statue. There's no story behind this one—the artist simply wanted to create a fun icon, and let the townspeople make up their own tales. Čumil has survived being driven over by a truck—twice—and he's still grinning.

For a peek at a third statue—a nosy
Paparazzo—you can turn left up Panská and
go one block, watching the corner on the left.
• *Continuing straight past Čumil, you'll reach the
long, skinny square called...*

Hviezdoslav Square (Hviezdoslavovo Námestie)

This square, named for a beloved Slovak
poet, is yet another part of Bratislava that has
undergone a much-needed sprucing-up. The
landscaped park in the center is particularly

inviting. At this end of the square
is the impressive, silver-topped
Slovak National Theater (Slovenské
Národné Divadlo). Beyond that, the
opulent yellow building that seems
to be melting is the Philharmonic.
The prominence of these two venues is evidence of Bratislava's strong
performing arts tradition.

Right in front of the theater
(by the McDonald's), look down
into the glass **display case** to see
the foundation of the one-time Fishermen's Gate into the city.
Surrounding the base of the gate is water. This entire square was
once a tributary of the Danube, and the Carlton Hotel across the
way was a series of inns on different islands. The buildings along
the Old Town side of the square mark where the city wall once
stood.

• *From here, it's just a block to the Danube—passing the **Slovak
National Gallery,** for those curious about local art (lime-green building on the corner with a modern annex). Once at the Danube, cross the
street and belly up to the railing.*

The Danube (Dunaj)

Here you get a good look at the communists' pride and joy, the
New Bridge (Nový Most, a.k.a.
Most SNP). As with most Soviet-
era landmarks in former communist countries, locals aren't
crazy about this structure—not
only for the questionable starship
Enterprise design, but also because
of the oppressive regime it represents. However, the restaurant

and observation deck up top—long a stale holdover from communist times—was recently renovated into a posh eatery called (appropriately enough) "UFO." You can visit for the views, a drink, or a full meal (see page 212).

• *Backtrack to the silver-topped National Theater at Hviezdoslav Square. Follow this square to the left, passing some fun public art: a statue of the square's namesake; the heavily fortified US Embassy (on the left); a glass pavilion (popular venue for summer concerts); and, on the right near the end, a statue of Hans Christian Andersen (the Danish storyteller, who enjoyed his visit to Bratislava).*

    Reaching the end of the square (at the column with the big highway behind it), jog right and head for the big...

St. Martin's Cathedral (Dóm Sv. Martina)

This historic church isn't looking too sharp these days—and the highway thundering a few feet in front of its door (courtesy of the Soviets) doesn't help matters. If it were any closer, the off-ramp would go through the nave. Sad as it is now, the cathedral has been party to some pretty important history. While Buda and Pest were occupied by Ottomans for a century and a half, Bratislava was the capital of Hungary. A total of 19 Hungarian kings and queens were crowned in this church—more than have been crowned anywhere in Hungary. A replica of the Hungarian crown still tops the steeple.

• *Our tour is finished. From here, you have some sightseeing options (described in detail under "Sights," next). To reach the **castle**, take the underpass beneath the highway, go up the stairs on the right (marked by* Hrad/Castle *sign), then turn left up the stepped lane marked* Zámocké Schody. *Or, to get to the **New Bridge's** "UFO" view platform, turn left, walk toward the Danube, then walk the length of the bridge (pedestrian walkway on lower level) to reach the tower's entrance at the far end.*

SIGHTS

It seems that all of Bratislava's sights have just reopened after a renovation...or are about to undergo one. In any event, most of Bratislava's charm is in its streets, not its museums. But these sights are fine for a rainy day or for "extra credit."

On or near the Old Town's Main Square

These three museums cluster within a few steps of the Main Square.

City History Museum (Mestské Múzeum)—This museum, in the Old Town Hall, will likely be closed through 2010 for a long-overdue renovation. When open, it offers an exhibit on town history (including torture equipment, or "feudal justice") and a chance to climb the Old Town Hall tower for a view of the square (if open, likely €3, Tue–Fri 10:00–17:00, Sat–Sun 11:00–18:00, closed Mon, enter through courtyard of Old Town Hall, tel. 02/5920-5130, www.muzeum.bratislava.sk).

▲**Apponyi House (Apponyiho Palác)**—This brand-new museum, which reopened in 2008 in the gorgeously restored mansion of a Hungarian aristocrat, comes in two parts. The cellar holds an interesting exhibit on the vineyards of the nearby "Little Carpathian" hills, with historic presses and barrels, and a replica of an old-time wine-pub table. Upstairs are two floors of urban apartments from old Bratislava: The first floor up shows off the 18th-century Rococo-style rooms of the nobility, while the second floor up (with lower ceilings and simpler wall decorations) illustrates 19th-century bourgeois/middle-class lifestyles, including some fine Empire-style furniture (€7, Tue–Fri 10:00–17:00, Sat–Sun 11:00–18:00, closed Mon, Radničná ulica 1, tel. 02/5920-5135).

▲**Primate's Palace (Primaciálny Palác)**—Probably Bratislava's most interesting museum, this tastefully restored French-Neoclassical mansion (formerly the residence of the archbishop, or "primate") dates from 1781. The smaller rooms were the archbishop's private quarters, now decorated with Dutch, Flemish, German, and Italian paintings. You'll peer from a bay window down into the archbishop's own, private marble chapel. When the  archbishop became too ill to walk down to Mass, this window was built for him to take part in the service. The larger rooms were public...designed to impress. Among these is the Mirror Hall, used for concerts, city council meetings, and other important events.

But the museum's highlight is its series of six English tapestries, illustrating the ancient Greek myth of the tragic love between Hero and Leander. The tapestries—the only complete cycle of their kind in existence—were woven in England by Flemish weavers for the court of King Charles I (in the 1630s). After the king was deposed and beheaded, the tapestries disappeared. Centuries later, in 1903, restorers broke through a false wall in this mansion and discovered the six tapestries, neatly folded and perfectly preserved. Nobody knows how they got there (perhaps they were squirreled away during the Napoleonic invasion, and whoever hid them didn't survive). The archbishop—who had just sold the palace to the city, but emptied it of furniture before he left—cried foul and tried to get the tapestries back...but the city said, a deal's a deal (€2, Tue–Fri 10:00–17:00, Sat–Sun 11:00–18:00, closed Mon, Primaciálne Námestie 3, tel. 02/5935-6394).

Bratislava Castle (Bratislavský Hrad)

This imposing fortress, nicknamed the "upside-down table," is the city's most prominent landmark. There has surely been a castle

on this spot for centuries, but the oldest surviving chunk is the 13th-century Romanesque watchtower (the one slightly taller than the other three). When Habsburg Empress Maria Theresa took a liking to Bratislava in the 18th century, she transformed the castle from a military fortress to a royal residence suitable for holding

court. She added a summer riding school (the U-shaped complex next to the castle), an enclosed winter riding school out back, and lots more...and painted the whole thing yellow. Maria Theresa's favorite daughter, Maria Christina, lived here with her husband Albert when they were newlyweds. Locals nicknamed the place "little Schönbrunn," in reference to the Habsburgs' summer palace on the outskirts of Vienna.

But M.T.'s castle burned to the ground in an 1811 fire, and it was left as a ruin for a century and a half—not reconstructed until 1953. Unfortunately, the communist rebuild was drab and uninviting; the inner courtyard felt like a prison exercise yard.

The good news is that the city is in the midst of a five-year renovation project to rehabilitate the castle from top to bottom. They've already reconstructed the summer riding school, and plan

to rebuild the winter riding school and terraced French gardens out back...as well as paint the whole thing that pretty "Habsburg yellow" once again. The bad news is that during the restoration, the castle interior is closed to visitors. But more good news: The interior was never

appealing anyway, so the main reason to visit—for up-close views of the castle, over the rooftops of the Old Town, and across the Danube to Petržalka—remains the same (and free).

For details on the best way to hike up to the castle, see the end of my self-guided walk on page 209.

The "UFO" at New Bridge (Nový Most)

The bizarre, flying-saucer-capped bridge near the Old Town—

completed in 1972 in heavy-handed communist style—has been reclaimed by capitalists. It's been spruced up and turned into an overpriced café/restaurant, with an observation deck that allows visitors sweeping 360-degree views of Bratislava from about 300 feet above the Danube. Think of it as the "Slovak Space Needle."

Cost and Hours: €7, daily 10:00–23:00, elevator free if you have a meal reservation—main courses steeply priced at €25–30, tel. 02/6252-0300, www.u-f-o.sk/en.

Getting There: Just walk across the New Bridge from the Old Town—the elevator entrance is underneath the tower on the Petržalka side.

❷ Self-Guided Tour: The "**elevator**" that takes you up is actually a funicular—you'll notice you're moving at an angle. At the top, walk up the stairs to the observation deck.

Begin by viewing the **castle** and **Old Town.** Notice, to the right of the Old Town, the massive construction zone. If you set up a time-lapse camera here over the next few years, you'd watch skyscrapers pop up like dandelions. International investors are throwing many billions of euros at Bratislava, before rents skyrocket. (Imagine having so much prime, undeveloped real estate available downtown in

the capital of an emerging European economic power…just an hour down the road from Vienna, no less.) Most of the development is taking place along the banks of the Danube. In a decade, this will be a futuristic city.

The huge, pointy monument back toward the train station (behind the Old Town) is **Slavín,** where more than 6,800 Soviet soldiers who fought to liberate Bratislava from the Nazis are buried. A nearby church had to take down its steeple so as not to draw atten-

tion away from the huge Soviet soldier on top of the monument.

Now turn 180 degrees to face **Petržalka,** a planned communist suburb that sprouted here in the 1970s. The site was once occupied by a village, and the various districts of modern Petržalka still carry their original names (which now seem ironic): "Meadows" *(Háje),* "Woods" *(Lúky),* and "Courtyards" *(Dvory).* The ambitious Soviet planners envisioned a city laced with Venetian-style canals to help drain the marshy land, but the plans were abandoned after the harsh crackdown on the 1968 Prague Spring uprising. Today, one in four Bratislavans lives in Petržalka. A few years ago, this was a grim and decaying sea of miserable communist apartment *panelák* ("panel buildings," so called because they're made of huge prefab concrete panels that were built elsewhere, then brought here to assemble on-site). But things are changing fast. Many of the *panelák* are being retrofitted with new layers of insulation, and the apartments inside are being updated. And, like Dorothy opening the door to Oz, the formerly drab buildings are being splashed with bright new colors. Far from being a slum, Petržalka is a popular neighborhood for Bratislavan yuppies who can't yet afford to build their dream house. Locals read the Czech-language home-improvement magazine *Panel Plus* for ideas on how to give their *panelák* apartments some style (www.panelplus.cz).

Still facing Petržalka, notice that new construction is also happening along this riverbank (such as the supermall down below). But there's still history here. The **park** called Sad Janka Kráľa, a.k.a. "Aupark"—just downriver from the bridge—was technically the first public park in Europe, and is still a popular place for locals to relax and court.

Scanning the **horizon** beyond Petržalka, two things stick out: on the left, the old communist refinery (which has been fully updated); and on the right, a sea of modern windmills. These are just over the border, in Austria...and Bratislava is sure to grow in that direction quickly.

Before you leave, consider nursing a drink at the café (€3 coffee or beer, €5–15 cocktails). If nothing else, be sure to use the memorable WCs.

BRATISLAVA, SLOVAKIA

Sleep Code

(€1 = about $1.40, country code: 421, area code: 02)
S = Single, **D** = Double/Twin, **T** = Triple, **Q** = Quad, **b** = bathroom, **s** = shower only. English is spoken at each place. Unless otherwise noted, breakfast is included and you can pay by credit card.

To help you sort easily through these listings, I've divided the rooms into three categories, based on the price for a standard double room with bath:

$$$ Higher Priced—Most rooms €100 or more.
$$ Moderately Priced—Most rooms between €50-100.
$ Lower Priced—Most rooms €50 or less.

SLEEPING

A few years ago, there were no sleepable hotels near Bratislava's Old Town. But new accommodations open every year, so the scene is rapidly improving. Hotel values here still aren't great. I'd rather sleep in Vienna or Budapest. But if the city entices you to stay longer than a day trip, these options are all inside or within a short walk of the Old Town. Business-oriented places charge more on weekdays (Mon–Thu) than on weekends (Fri–Sun).

$$$ Hotel Marrol's is the town's most enticing splurge. Although it's in a drab urban neighborhood, it's a five-minute walk from the Old Town, and the 54 rooms are luxurious and tastefully appointed Old World country-style. While pricey, the rates drop to temping lows on weekends (Mon–Thu: Sb-€227, Db-€255; Fri–Sun: Sb-€134, Db-€153; air-con, non-smoking, free cable Internet, gorgeous lounge, Tobrucká ulica 4, tel. 02/5778-4600, www.hotelmarrols.sk, rec@hotelmarrols.sk).

$$$ Hotel Michalská Brána is a charming boutique hotel hiding down a tight, atmospheric little lane just inside St. Michael's Gate in the Old Town. The 14 rooms are sleek, mod, and classy (Mon–Thu: Sb-€150, Db-€160; Fri–Sun: Sb-€125, Db-€135; pricier suites also available, air-con, non-smoking, free cable Internet, elevator, Baštová 4, tel. 02/5930-7200, www.michalskabrana.com, michalskabrana@gmail.com).

$$ Hotel Corso has four rooms at the top floor of an office building right on the edge of the Old Town (Sb-€69, Db-€81, Tb-€104, cash only, elevator and some stairs, free Wi-Fi, some tram noise, Kapucínska 7, tel. 02/5441-6450, www.bratislava hotel.sk).

$$ Penzion Chez David is a simple, Jewish-themed hotel with 10 budget rooms just outside the Old Town (Mon–Thu:

Sb-€64, Db-€88; Fri–Sun: Sb-€54, Db-€78; fee for Wi-Fi, some street noise from busy road and tram—request quieter room, Zámocká 13, tel. 02/5441-3824, www.chezdavid.sk, recepcia @chezdavid.sk).

$$ Hotel Ibis, part of the cookie-cutter chain, offers 120 rooms overlooking a busy tram junction across the street from Penzion Chez David (Mon–Thu: Sb/Db-€94; Fri–Sun: Sb/Db-€79; rates flex with demand, optional breakfast-€10 per person, Zámocká 38, tel. 02/5929-2000, fax 02/5929-2111, www.ibishotel.com, h3566@accor.com).

$ Downtown Backpackers Hostel is Bratislava's best hostel option. Funky but well-run, it's near the Grassalkovich (presidential) Palace about a five-minute walk from the Old Town (61 beds in 12 rooms, Db-€70, D-€55, bunk in Qb-€25, bunk in 7–8-bed dorm-€20, bunk in 10-bed dorm-€18, Panenská 31, tel. 02/5464-1191, www.backpackers.sk, info@backpackers.sk).

EATING

Slovak cuisine shows some Austrian and Hungarian influences, but it's closer to Czech cuisine—with lots of starches and gravy, and plenty of pork, cabbage, and potatoes. Keep an eye out for Slovakia's national dish, *bryndzové halušky* (small potato dumplings with sheep's cheese and bits of bacon). Like the Czechs, the Slovaks produce excellent beer (*pivo*, PEE-voh). One of the top brands is Zlatý Bažant ("Golden Pheasant"). Bratislava is packed with inviting new eateries. In addition to the heavy Slovak staples, you'll find trendy new bars and bistros, and a wide range of ethnic offerings. The best plan may be to stroll the Old Town and keep your eyes open for  the setting and cuisine that appeals to you most. Or consider one of these options.

Prazdroj ("Urquell") is a Czech-style beer hall with lively ambience and good traditional food. It sprawls through several rooms of a building just off Hviezdoslav Square at the edge of the Old Town (€7–10 main dishes, Mon–Fri 10:00–24:00, Sat–Sun 11:00–24:00, Mostová 8, tel. 02/5441-1108).

1. Slovak Pub (as in "the first") is the Slovak equivalent of Prazdroj, attracting a younger crowd. Enter from a bustling modern shopping street just outside the Old Town, and climb the stairs into a vast warren of rustic old countryside-style pub rooms.

While enjoying the lively, loud, almost chaotic ambience, you'll dine on affordable and truly authentic Slovak fare, made with products from the pub's own farm. This is a good place to try the Slovak specialty, *bryndzové halušky* (described above; €6–9 main dishes, Mon–Sat 10:00–24:00, Sun 12:00–24:00, Obchodná 62, tel. 02/5292-6367).

Erdody Palace, a newly renovated mansion in the center of the Old Town at Ventúrska 1, is a great place to splurge at one of two eateries with an Andy Warhol theme (after all, he was Slovak). As the owner is a huge Warhol fan, original Warhols hang in each restaurant, named for the theme of the works: **Flowers** dishes up Mediterranean fare in a bright, covered courtyard (€7–14 pastas, €15–25 main dishes, daily 11:30–1:00 in the morning, tel. 02/2092-2733); the stuffier **Camouflage** features nouvelle cuisine in a somewhat snooty white-minimalist setting (€15–30 main dishes, Mon–Sat 11:30–1:00 in the morning, closed Sun, reservations smart, tel. 02/2092-2711). Even if you're not eating here, peek in the window at Camouflage to see Warhol enjoying the place.

Fast and Cheap: A local chain called **Coffee & Co,** with branches throughout the Old Town and beyond, serves up good €3–4 sandwiches—ideal for a bite on the run (various locations, all open long hours daily).

Classic Coffeehouse: The venerable **Kaffee Mayer,** at the corner of the main square, is an institution—they've been selling coffee and cakes to a genteel clientele since 1873. You can enjoy your pick-me-up in the swanky old interior, or out on the square (€2–3 cakes, Mon–Fri 9:30–22:00, Sat–Sun 9:30–23:00, Hlavné Námestie 4, tel. 02/5441-1741).

TRANSPORTATION CONNECTIONS

By Train

Bratislava has two major train stations. The Main Train Station (Hlavná Stanica, abbreviated "Bratislava hl. st." on schedules) is closer to the Old Town, while the Petržalka station (ŽST Petržalka), in the suburb across the river, can be more convenient for some connections. When checking schedules (http://bahn .hafas.de/bin/query.exe/en is helpful), pay attention to which station your train uses. Bus #93 connects these two Bratislava stations (5–12/hr, 10 min; or use bus #N93 at night).

From Bratislava by Train to: Vienna (2–3/hr, 1 hr), **Budapest** (5/day direct, 2.5 hrs; more with transfers), **Prague** (3/day direct, 4.25–5.5 hrs). For Austrian destinations such as **Salzburg** or **Innsbruck,** you'll connect through Vienna.

By Boat

Riverboats connect Bratislava to the nearby capitals of Vienna and Budapest. Conveniently, these boats dock right along the Danube in front of Bratislava's Old Town. While they are more expensive, less frequent, and slower than the train, some travelers enjoy getting out on the Danube.

To Vienna: The Vienna-based DDSG line offers several daily boat trips between Bratislava and Vienna's Schwedenplatz (where Vienna's town center hits the canal; €28 each way, €17 at less convenient times, €2 more on weekends, 1.25-hr trip; daily April–Oct only, Austrian tel. 01/58880, www.ddsg-blue-danube.at). The Budapest-based Mahart boat connects Bratislava to Vienna's Reichsbrücke dock once daily (€29 one-way, €39 round-trip, 1.5–2 hrs, daily late April–early Oct only; Hungarian tel. 1/484-4010, www.mahartpassnave.hu).

To Budapest: Mahart links Bratislava and Budapest once daily (€79 one-way, €99 round-trip, 4–4.5 hrs, daily late April–early Oct only, see above for contact info).

Bratislava Airport (Letisko Bratislava)

Bratislava Airport (airport code: BTS, www.letiskobratislava .sk) is six miles northeast of downtown Bratislava. The low-cost carriers who fly here (including SkyEurope) sometimes market it as "Vienna-Bratislava," thanks to its proximity to both capitals. The airport is officially named for Milan Rastislav Štefánik, who worked toward the creation of Czechoslovakia at the end of World War I. It's compact and manageable, with all the usual amenities (including ATMs).

To Downtown Bratislava: The airport has easy **public bus** connections to Bratislava's Main Train Station (€0.60, plus €0.30 ticket for each big bag, bus #61, 6/hr in peak times, 3/hr in slow times, trip takes 30 min). To reach the bus stop, exit straight out of the arrivals hall, cross the street, buy a ticket at the kiosk, and look for the bus stop on your right. For directions from the train station into the Old Town, see "Arrival in Bratislava," page 197. A **taxi** from the airport into central Bratislava should cost less than €20.

To Vienna: A slow option is to connect through Bratislava's train station (described above). More direct and still affordable, you can take a Eurolines bus from Bratislava Airport to the Erdberg stop of Vienna's U-3 subway line (9/day, trip takes about an hour, €10, book in advance, www.gratislava.at). A taxi from Bratislava Airport directly to Vienna costs €60–90 (depending on whether you use a cheaper Slovak or more expensive Austrian cab).

SALZBURG

SALZBURG

Salzburg is forever smiling to the tunes of Mozart and *The Sound of Music*. Thanks to its charmingly preserved old town, splendid gardens, Baroque churches, and Europe's largest intact medieval fortress, Salzburg feels made for tourism. It's a museum city with class. Vagabonds wish they had nicer clothes.

Even without Mozart and the von Trapps, Salzburg is steeped in history. In about A.D. 700, Bavaria gave Salzburg to Bishop Rupert in return for his promise to Christianize the area. Salzburg remained an independent city (belonging to no state) until Napoleon came in the early 1800s. Thanks in part to its formidable fortress, Salzburg managed to avoid the ravages of war for 1,200 years...until World War II. Much of the city was destroyed by WWII bombs (mostly around the train station), but the historic old town survived.

Eight million tourists crawl its cobbles each year. That's a lot of Mozart balls—and all that popularity has led to a glut of businesses hoping to catch the tourist dollar. Still, Salzburg is both a must and a joy.

Planning Your Time

While Salzburg's sights are rather mediocre, the town itself is a Baroque museum of cobbled streets and elegant buildings—simply a touristy stroller's delight. Even if your time is short, consider allowing half a day for the *Sound of Music* tour. The *S.O.M.* tour kills a nest of sightseeing birds with one ticket (city overview, *S.O.M.* sights, and a fine drive through the lakes).

You'd probably enjoy at least two nights in Salzburg—nights are important for swilling beer in atmospheric local gardens and attending concerts in Baroque halls and chapels. Seriously consider one of Salzburg's many evening musical events (a few are free, some are as cheap as €12, and most average €30–40).

To get away from it all, bike down the river or hike across the Mönchsberg. Or consider swinging by Berchtesgaden, an alpine town enjoyed by Hitler and nature-lovers, just 12 miles away in Germany. A direct bus gets you there in 45 minutes (see next chapter).

A day trip from Salzburg to Hallstatt (the small-town highlight of the Salzkammergut Lake District—see page 277) is doable, but involves about five hours for the round-trip transportation alone and makes for a very long day. An overnight in Hallstatt is better.

ORIENTATION

(area code: 0662)

Salzburg, a city of 150,000 (Austria's fourth-largest), is divided into old and new. The old town, sitting between the Salzach River and its mini-mountain (Mönchsberg), holds nearly all the charm and most of the tourists. The new town, across the river, has its own share of sights and museums, plus some good accommodations.

Tourist Information

Salzburg has three helpful TIs (main tel. 0662/889-870, www.salzburg.info): at the **train station** (daily June–Aug 8:15–20:00, April–May and Sept–Oct 8:45–19:00, Nov–March 8:45–18:00, tel. 0662/8898-7340); on **Mozartplatz** in the old center (daily 9:00–18:00, July–mid-Sept until 19:00, closed Sun mid-Jan–Easter and Oct–mid-Nov, tel. 0662/889-870); and at the **Salzburg Süd park-and-ride** (generally open daily July–Aug 10:00–16:30 but sometimes longer hours, May–June Thu–Sat 10:00–16:30, Sept Mon–Sat 10:00–16:30, closed in winter, tel. 0662/8898-7360).

At any TI, you can pick up a free city-center map (the €0.70 map has a broader coverage and more information on sights, but probably isn't necessary), the Salzburg Card brochure (listing sights with current hours and prices), and a bimonthly schedule of events. Book a concert upon arrival. The TIs also book rooms for a €2.20 fee.

Salzburg Card: The TIs sell the Salzburg Card, which covers all your public transportation (including elevator and funicular) and admission to all the city sights (including Hellbrunn Castle and a river cruise). The card is pricey (€24/24 hrs, €32/48 hrs, €37/72 hrs, €2 cheaper Oct–April), but if you'd like to pop into all the sights, it can save money and enhance your experience. To analyze your potential savings, here are the major sights and what you'd pay without the card: Hohensalzburg Fortress and funicular-€10.50; Mozart's Birthplace and Residence-€10; Hellbrunn Castle-€8.50; Salzburg Panorama 1829-€2; Salzach River cruise-€13; 24-hour transit pass-€4.20. Busy sightseers can save plenty. Get this card, feel the financial pain once, and the city will be all yours.

Arrival in Salzburg

By Train: The Salzburg station is user-friendly. The TI is at track 2A. Downstairs at street level, you can store your luggage, buy tickets, and get train information. Bike rental is nearby (see "Getting Around Salzburg," later in this chapter). City buses depart from the lot facing the station (monitors clearly show each bus' destination— any bus heading for *Zentrum* stops near the main bridge in the old town, including buses #1, #3, #5,

#6, and #25; get off at the first stop after you cross the river for most sights and city-center hotels, or just before the bridge for Linzergasse hotels). Figure €7 for a taxi to the center.

To walk downtown (15 min), leave the station ticket hall to the left, and walk straight down Rainerstrasse, which leads under the tracks past Mirabellplatz, turning into Dreifaltigkeitsgasse. From here, you can turn left onto Linzergasse for many of my recommended hotels, or cross the Staatsbrücke bridge for the old town (and more hotels). For a more dramatic approach, leave the station the same way but follow the tracks to the river, turn left, and walk the riverside path toward the fortress.

By Car: Coming on the A-1 from Vienna or Munich, take the A-10 toward Hallein and then take the next exit (Salzburg Süd) in the direction of Anif. First, you'll pass Hellbrunn Castle (and zoo), then the Salzburg Süd TI and a park-and-ride service—a smart place to park while visiting Salzburg. Park your car (€5), get sightseeing information and transit tickets from the TI (see above), and catch the shuttle bus into town (€1.80 for a single ticket, or covered by €4.20 *Tageskarte* day pass, both sold at the TI, more expensive if you buy tickets on board, every 5 min, bus #3, #8, or #28).

Mozart never drove in the old town, and neither should you. If you don't believe in park-and-rides, the easiest, cheapest, most central parking lot is the 1,500-car Altstadt lot in the tunnel under the Mönchsberg (€14/day, note your slot number and which of the twin lots you're in, tel. 0662/846-434). Your hotel may provide discounted parking passes.

Helpful Hints

Recommendations Skewed by Kickbacks: Salzburg is addicted to the tourist dollar, and it can never get enough. Virtually all hotels are on the take when it comes to concert and tour recommendations, influenced more by their potential kickback than by what's best for you. Take their advice with a grain of salt.

Internet Access: The Internet kiosk a few doors down from the Mozartplatz TI is well-located, but too expensive (€2/10 min). Cheaper places around the old town aren't hard to find. Two Internet cafés at the bottom of the cliff, between Getreidegasse and the Mönchsberg lift, have good prices and hours (€2/hr, daily 10:00–22:00). Across the river, there's a big, handy Internet café on Theatergasse (near Mozart's Residence, €2/hr, daily 9:00–23:00), and plenty more near the station (including **Bubblepoint,** a modern launderette—see "Laundry" below). Readers of this book can get online free at the Panorama Tours terminal on Mirabellplatz (daily 8:00–18:00).

Post Office: A full-service post office is located in the heart of town, in the new Residenz (Mon–Fri 7:00–18:30, Sat 8:00–10:00, closed Sun).

Laundry: The launderette at the corner of Paris-Lodron-Strasse and Wolf-Dietrich-Strasse, near my recommended Linzergasse hotels, is handy (€10 self-service, €15 same-day full-service, Mon–Fri 7:30–18:00, Sat 8:00–12:00, closed Sun, tel. 0662/876-381). To do your laundry and email at the same time, head to **Bubblepoint** (wash and dry for €6, 6 Internet terminals, daily 7:00–23:00; with your back to the train station, take the first left for one block, then head right to Karl-Wurmb-Strasse 2; tel. 0664/471-1484).

Getting Around Salzburg

By Bus: Single-ride tickets for central Salzburg *(Einzelkarte–Kernzone)* are sold on the bus for €2. At machines and *Tabak/Trafik* shops, you can buy €1.80 single-ride tickets or a €4.20 day pass *(Tageskarte,* good for 24 hours, €5 if you buy it on the bus). To signal the driver that you want to get off, press the buzzer on the

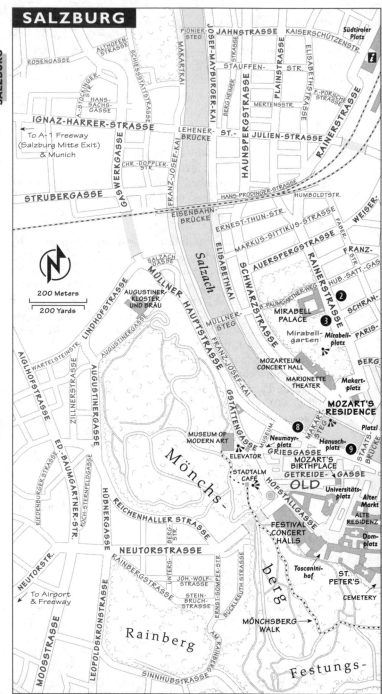

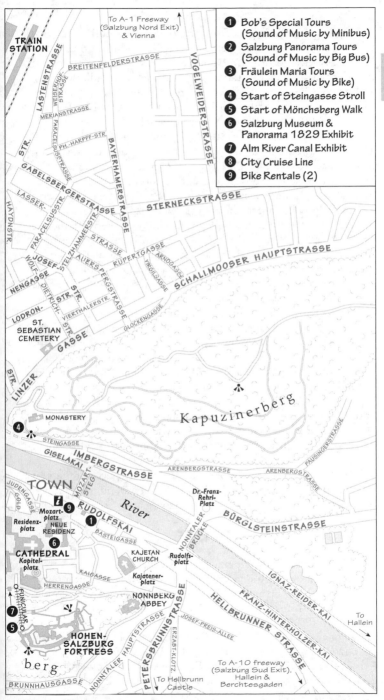

1. Bob's Special Tours (Sound of Music by Minibus)
2. Salzburg Panorama Tours (Sound of Music by Big Bus)
3. Fräulein Maria Tours (Sound of Music by Bike)
4. Start of Steingasse Stroll
5. Start of Mönchsberg Walk
6. Salzburg Museum & Panorama 1829 Exhibit
7. Alm River Canal Exhibit
8. City Cruise Line
9. Bike Rentals (2)

pole. Bus info: tel. 800-660-660.

By Bike: Salzburg is fun for cyclists. The following two bike-rental shops offer 20 percent off with a valid train ticket or Eurailpass—ask for it. **Top Bike** rents bikes from two outlets: at the river side of the train station (exit to the left and walk 50 yards), and on the river next to the Staatsbrücke (€6/2 hrs, €10/4 hrs, €15/24 hrs, usually daily April–June and Sept–Oct 10:00–17:00, July–Aug 9:00–19:00, closed Nov–March, tel. 06272/4656, mobile 0676-476-7259 and 0676-720-0047, www.topbike.at, Sabine). **Velo-Active** rents bikes in the old town, just outside the TI on Mozartplatz (€4.50/1 hr, €7/2 hrs, €15/24 hrs; mountain bikes-€6/hr, €18/24 hrs; daily 9:00–18:00, until 19:00 July–Aug, but hours unreliable—you may have to call or let the Panorama Tours man nearby help you, shorter hours off-season and in bad weather, passport number for security deposit, tel. 0662/435-5950, mobile 0676-435-5950). Some of my recommended hotels and pensions also rent bikes, and several of the B&Bs on Moosstrasse let guests use them for free.

By Funicular and Elevator: The old town is connected to the top of the Mönchsberg mountain (and great views) via funicular and elevator. The **funicular** *(Festungsbahn)* whisks you up to the imposing Hohensalzburg Fortress (included in castle admission, goes every few minutes—for details, see page 240). The **elevator** *(MönchsbergAufzug)* on the east side of the old town propels you to the recommended Gasthaus Stadtalm café and hostel, the Museum of Modern Art, wooded paths, and more great views (€2 one-way, €3 round-trip, daily 8:30–19:00, Wed until 21:00; July–Aug daily until 1:00 in the morning, May–Sept starts running at 8:00).

By Taxi: Meters start at about €3 (from train station to your hotel, allow about €7). As always, small groups can taxi for about the same price as riding the bus.

By Buggy: The horse buggies *(Fiaker)* that congregate at Residenzplatz charge €36 for a 25-minute trot around the old town (German-only website: www.fiaker-salzburg.at).

TOURS

Walking Tours—On any day of the week, you can take a two-language, one-hour guided walk of the old town without a reservation—just show up at the TI on Mozartplatz and pay the guide. The tours are informative, but you'll be listening to a half-hour of German (€8, daily at 12:15 and 14:00, tel. 0662/8898-7330). To save money (and avoid all that German), you can easily do it on your own using my self-guided walk (see page 230).

Private Guides—**Christiana Schneeweiss** ("Snow White"), a hardworking young guide and art historian with a passion for fitting local history into the big picture, gives spirited private tours (€80/1 hr, €129/2 hrs, €150/3 hrs, tel. 0664/340-1757, www .kultur-tourismus.com, info@kultur-tourismus.com). Check her website for bike tours, private minibus tours, and more. **Bärbel Schalber,** one of Salzburg's senior guides, offers a two-hour walk packed with information and spicy opinions (€75 per family, €108 for a group of adults, tel. 0662/632-225, mobile 0664-412-3708, schalber.salzburg@aon.at). Salzburg has many other good guides (to book, call 0662/840-406).

▲▲*Sound of Music* **Tour**—I took this tour skeptically (as part of my research)—and liked it. It includes a quick but good gen-

eral city tour, hits the *S.O.M.* spots (including the stately home, flirtatious gazebo, and grand wedding church), and shows you a lovely stretch of the Salzkammergut Lake District. This is worthwhile for *S.O.M.* fans and those who won't otherwise be going into the Salzkammergut. Warning: Many think rolling through the Austrian countryside with 30 Americans singing "Doe, a Deer" is pretty schmaltzy. Local Austrians don't understand all the commotion, and the audience is mostly native English speakers. For more on *S.O.M.*, see the "*Sound of Music* Debunked" sidebar on page 252.

Of the many companies doing the tour, consider Bob's Special Tours (usually uses a minibus) and Panorama Tours (more typical and professional, big 50-seat bus). Each one provides essentially the same tour (in English with a live guide, 4 hrs, free hotel pickup) for essentially the same price: €37 for Panorama, €40 for Bob's. You'll get a €5 discount from either if you book direct, mention Rick Steves, bring this book along, and pay cash. Getting a spot is simple—just call and make a reservation (calling Bob's a week or two in advance is smart). Note: Your hotel will be eager to call to reserve for you—to get their commission—but if you let them do it, you're unlikely to get the discount I've negotiated.

Minibus Option: Most of **Bob's Special Tours** use an eight-seat minibus and therefore have good access to old-town sights, promote a more casual feel, and spend less time waiting to load and unload. Calling well in advance increases your chances of getting a seat (€40 for adults, €5 discount with this book if you pay cash and book direct, €35 for kids and students with ID, €30 for kids in car seats, daily at 9:00 and 14:00 year-round, buses leave from Bob's office along the river just east of Mozartplatz at Rudolfskai 38—or they'll pick you up at your hotel for the morning tour,

Salzburg at a Glance

▲▲▲**Salzburg's Old Town Walk** Old town's best sights in handy orientation walk. **Hours:** Always open. See page 230.

▲▲**Salzburg Cathedral** Glorious, harmonious, Baroque main church of Salzburg. **Hours:** Easter–Oct Mon–Sat 9:00–18:00, Sun 13:00–18:00; Nov–Easter Mon–Sat 10:00–17:00, Sun 13:00–17:00. See page 233.

▲▲**Getreidegasse** Picturesque old shopping lane with characteristic wrought-iron signs. **Hours:** Always open. See page 238.

▲▲**Hohensalzburg Fortress** Imposing castle capping the Mönchsberg mountain overlooking town, with tourable grounds, impressive interior, commanding views, and good evening concerts. **Hours:** Daily May–Sept 9:00–19:00, Oct–April 9:30–17:00. Concerts nearly nightly. See page 240.

▲▲**Mozart's Residence** Restored house where the composer lived, with the best Mozart exhibit in town. **Hours:** Daily 9:00–17:00, July–Aug until 20:00. See page 245.

▲▲**Sound of Music Tour** Cheesy but fun tour through the *S.O.M.* sights of Salzburg and the surrounding Salzkammergut Lake District, by minibus or big bus. **Hours:** Various options daily at 9:00, 9:30, 14:00, and 16:30. See page 227.

▲**Salzburg Panorama 1829** A vivid peek at the city in 1829. **Hours:** Daily 9:00–17:00, Thu until 20:00. See page 232.

▲**Mozart's Birthplace** House where Mozart was born in 1756, featuring his instruments and other exhibits. **Hours:** Daily 9:00–17:00, July–Aug until 20:00. See page 239.

tel. 0662/849-511, mobile 0664-541-7492, www.bobstours.com). Nearly all of Bob's tours stop for the luge ride when the weather is dry (mountain bobsled–€4 extra, generally April–Oct, confirm beforehand). Some travelers looking for Bob's tours at Mozartplatz have been hijacked by other companies...have Bob's pick you up at your hotel (morning only) or meet the bus at their office (see map on page 230). If you're unable to book with Bob's, and still want a minibus tour, try **Kultur Tourismus** (€50, tel. 0664/340-1757, www.kultur-tourismus.com, info@kultur-tourismus.com).

Big-Bus Option: Salzburg Panorama Tours depart from their smart kiosk at Mirabellplatz daily at 9:30 and 14:00 year-round (€37, €5 discount with this book if you book direct and pay

▲Mönchsberg Walk "The hills are alive" stroll you can enjoy right in downtown Salzburg. **Hours:** Doable anytime during daylight hours. See page 243.

▲Mirabell Gardens and Palace Beautiful palace complex with fine views, Salzburg's best concert venue, and *Sound of Music* memories. **Hours:** Gardens—always open; concerts—free in the park May–Aug Sun at 10:30 and Wed at 20:30, in the palace nearly nightly. See page 245.

▲Steingasse Historic cobbled lane with trendy pubs—a tranquil, tourist-free section of old Salzburg. **Hours:** Always open. See page 246.

▲St. Sebastian Cemetery Baroque cemetery with graves of Mozart's wife and father, and other Salzburg VIPs. **Hours:** Daily April–Oct 9:00–18:30, Nov–March 9:00–16:00. See page 247.

▲Hellbrunn Castle Palace on the outskirts of town featuring gardens with trick fountains. **Hours:** Daily May–Sept 9:00–17:30, July–Aug until 21:00, mid-March–April and Oct 9:00–16:30, closed Nov–mid-March. See page 248.

St. Peter's Cemetery Atmospheric old cemetery with mini-gardens overlooked by cliff face with monks' caves. **Hours:** Cemetery—daily April–Sept 6:30–19:00, Oct–March 6:30–18:00; caves—May–Sept Tue–Sun 10:30–17:00, closed Mon, shorter hours Oct–April. See page 235.

St. Peter's Church Romanesque church with Rococo decor. **Hours:** Open long hours daily. See page 236.

cash, book by calling 0662/874-029 or online at www.panorama tours.com). Many travelers appreciate their more businesslike feel, roomier buses, and slightly higher vantage point.

Bike Option: For some exercise with your tour, you can meet **Fräulein Maria** at the Mirabell Gardens (at Mirabellplatz 4, 50 yards to the left of palace entry) for a *S.O.M.* bike tour. The main attractions that you'll pass during the seven-mile pedal include the Mirabell Gardens, the horse pond, St. Peter's Cemetery, Nonnberg Abbey, Leopoldskron Palace and, of course, the gazebo (€24 includes bike, €2 discount with this book, €15 for kids 6–15, €10 for kids under 6, daily May–Sept at 9:30, June–Aug also at 16:30, allow 3.5 hrs, family-friendly, reservations required only for afternoon tours, tel. 0650/342-6297, www.mariasbicycle tours.com).

More Tours—Both Bob's and Panorama Tours also offer an extensive array of other day trips from Salzburg (Berchtesgaden/ Eagle's Nest, salt mines, and Salzkammergut lakes and mountains are the most popular, with the same discount—€5 off with this book if you book direct and pay cash). The tours are explained in their brochures, which litter hotel lobbies all over town.

City Cruise Line (a.k.a. Stadt Schiff-Fahrt) runs a basic 40-minute round-trip river cruise with recorded commentary (€13, 9/day July–Aug, 7/day in June, fewer Sept–Oct and April–May, no boats Nov–March). For a longer cruise, ride to Hellbrunn and return by bus (€16, 1–2/day April–Oct). Boats leave from the old-town side of the river just downstream of the Makartsteg bridge (tel. 0662/8257-6912). While views can be cramped, passengers are treated to a fun finale just before docking, when the captain twirls a fun "waltz."

SELF-GUIDED WALK

▲▲▲Salzburg's Old Town

I've linked the best sights in the old town into this handy self-guided orientation walk.

• *Begin in the heart of town, just up from the river, near the TI on...*

❶ Mozartplatz

All the happy tourists around you probably wouldn't be here if not for the man honored by this statue—Wolfgang Amadeus Mozart (erected in 1842). Mozart spent much of his first 25 years (1756–1777) in Salzburg, the greatest Baroque city north of the Alps. But the city itself is much older: The Mozart statue sits on bits of Roman Salzburg, and the pink Church of St. Michael that overlooks the square dates from A.D. 800. The first Salzburgers settled right around here. Near you is the TI (with a concert box office), and just around the downhill corner is a pedestrian bridge leading over the Salzach River to the quiet and most medieval street in town, Steingasse (described on page 246).

• *Walk toward the cathedral and into the big square with the huge fountain.*

❷ Residenzplatz

Important buildings ringed this square when it was the ancient Roman forum...and they still do. Salzburg's energetic Prince-Archbishop Wolf Dietrich (who ruled 1587–1612) was raised in Rome, counted the Medicis as his buddies, and had grandiose Italian ambitions for Salzburg. After a convenient fire destroyed

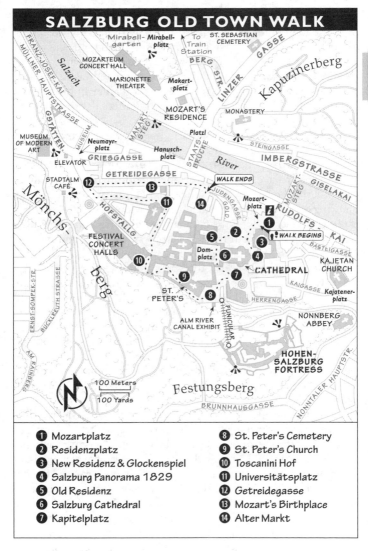

SALZBURG OLD TOWN WALK

1. Mozartplatz
2. Residenzplatz
3. New Residenz & Glockenspiel
4. Salzburg Panorama 1829
5. Old Residenz
6. Salzburg Cathedral
7. Kapitelplatz
8. St. Peter's Cemetery
9. St. Peter's Church
10. Toscanini Hof
11. Universitätsplatz
12. Getreidegasse
13. Mozart's Birthplace
14. Alter Markt

the cathedral, he set about building the "Rome of the North." This square, with his new cathedral and palace, was the centerpiece of his Baroque dream city. A series of interconnecting squares—like you'll see nowhere else—make a grand processional way, leading from here through the old town.

For centuries, Salzburg's leaders were both important church officials *and* princes of the Holy Roman Empire, hence the title "prince-archbishop"—mixing sacred and secular authority. But Wolf Dietrich misplayed his hand, losing power and spending his last five years imprisoned in the Salzburg castle.

The fountain is as Italian as can be, with a Triton matching Bernini's famous Triton Fountain in Rome. Lying on a busy trade route to the south, Salzburg was well-aware of the exciting things going on in Italy. Things Italian were respected (as in colonial America, when a bumpkin would "stick a feather in his cap and call it macaroni"). Local artists even Italianized their names in order to raise their rates.

• *Along the left side of Residenzplatz (as you face the cathedral) is the...*

❸ New (Neue) Residenz & Glockenspiel

This former palace, long a government administration building, now houses the central post office, the Heimatwerk (a fine shop showing off all the best local handicrafts, Mon–Fri 9:00–18:00, Sat 9:00–17:00, closed Sun), the fascinating **Salzburg Panorama 1829** exhibit (definitely worth the €2 and described later), and the new **Salzburg Museum.** The first floor of this museum shows off various influential Salzburgers. The second floor explores Salzburg's history, particularly its longstanding reputation as a fairy-tale "Alpine Arcadia." While it's impressively well-done and described in English, the museum is only enjoyable to the extent that you're fascinated with the city—so most will find this merely a good rainy-day option (€7, €8 combo-ticket with Salzburg Panorama, both tickets about €2 cheaper on Sun, includes audioguide, Tue–Sun 9:00–17:00, Thu until 20:00, closed Mon except July–Aug and Dec—when it's open Mon 9:00–17:00, tel. 0662/620-808-700, www.smca.at).

The famous **glockenspiel** rings atop the new Residenz. This bell tower has a carillon of 35 17th-century bells (cast in Antwerp) that chimes throughout the day and plays tunes (appropriate to the month) at 7:00, 11:00, and 18:00. There was a time when Salzburg could afford to take tourists to the top of the tower to see the big barrel with adjustable tabs turn (like a giant music-box mechanism)...pulling the right bells in the right rhythm. Notice the ornamental top: an upside-down heart in flames surrounding the solar system (symbolizing that God loves all of creation).

Look back, past Mozart's statue, to the 4,220-foot-high Gaisberg—the forested hill with the television tower. A road leads to the top for a commanding view. Its summit is a favorite destination for local nature-lovers and kids learning to ski.

• *Before continuing our walk, round the corner toward the back of the cathedral and drop into the...*

❹ Salzburg Panorama 1829

In the early 19th century, 360-degree "panorama" paintings of great cities or events were popular. These creations were even taken on extended road trips. Salzburg, at a stagnant stage in its development, had this circular view painted by Johann Michael Sattler: the city as seen from the top of its castle. When complete, it spent 10 years touring the great cities of Europe, showing off Salzburg's breathtaking setting. Today, the exquisitely restored painting, rated ▲, offers a fascinating look at the city in 1829. The river was slower and had beaches. The old town looks essentially as it does today, and Moosstrasse still leads into idyllic farm country. Paintings from that era of other great cities around the world are hung around the outside wall with numbers but without labels, as a kind of quiz game. A flier gives the cities' names on one side, and keys them to the numbers. See how many 19th-century cities you can identify (€2, €8 combo-ticket with Salzburg Museum, combo-ticket is about €2 cheaper on Sun, open daily 9:00–17:00, Thu until 20:00, Residenzplatz 9).

• *Backtrack into Residenzplatz and head to the opposite end from the new Residenz. This building is the...*

❺ Old (Alte) Residenz

Opposite the new Residenz is Wolf Dietrich's skippable palace, the old Residenz, which is connected to the cathedral by a sky-way. A series of ornately decorated rooms and an art gallery are open to visitors with time to kill (€8, €5 without gallery, Tue–Sun 10:00–17:00, closed Mon, tel. 0662/840-4510).

• *Walk under the prince-archbishop's skyway and step into Domplatz (Cathedral Square), where you'll find the...*

❻ Salzburg Cathedral (Salzburger Dom)

This cathedral, rated ▲▲, was one of the first Baroque buildings north of the Alps. It was consecrated in 1628, during the Thirty Years' War. (Pitting Roman Catholics against Protestants, this war devastated much of Europe and brought most grand construction projects to a halt.) Experts differ on what motivated the builders: to emphasize Salzburg's commit-ment to the Roman Catholic cause and the power of the Church here, or to show that there could be a peaceful alternative to the religious strife that was racking Europe at the time. Salzburg's archbishop was technically the top papal offi-cial north of the Alps, but the city managed to steer clear of the war. With its rich salt production, it had enough money to stay out of the conflict and carefully maintain its

independence from the warring sides.

The dates on the iron gates refer to milestones in the church's history: In 774, the previous church (long since destroyed) was founded by St. Virgil, to be replaced in 1628 by the church you see today. In 1959, a partial reconstruction was completed, made necessary by a WWII bomb that had blown through the dome.

Domplatz is surrounded by the prince-archbishop's secular administration buildings. The **statue of Mary** (1771) is looking away from the church, welcoming visitors. If you stand in the rear of the square, immediately under the middle arch, you'll see that she's positioned to be crowned by the two angels on the church facade.

Step inside the cathedral (donation requested; Easter–Oct Mon–Sat 9:00–18:00, Sun 13:00–18:00; Nov–Easter Mon–Sat 10:00–17:00, Sun 13:00–17:00). Enter the cathedral as if part of a festival procession—drawn toward the resurrected Christ by the brightly lit area under the dome, and cheered on by ceiling paintings of the Passion. The stucco, by a Milanese artist, is exceptional. Sit under the dome—surrounded by the tombs of 10 archbishops from the 17th century—and imagine all four organs playing, each balcony filled with musicians...glorious surround-sound. Mozart, who was the organist here for two years, would advise you that the acoustics

are best in pews immediately under the dome. Study the symbolism of the decor all around you—intellectual, complex, and cohesive. Think of the altar in Baroque terms, as the center of a stage, with sunrays as spotlights in this dramatic and sacred theater. In the left transept, stairs lead down into the crypt *(Krypta),* where you can see foundations of the earlier church, more tombs, and a tourist-free chapel (reserved for prayer) directly under the dome.

Built in just 14 years (1614–1628), the church boasts harmonious architecture. When Pope John Paul II visited in 1998, some 5,000 people filled the cathedral (330 feet long and 230 feet tall). The baptismal font (dark bronze, left of the entry) is from the previous cathedral (basin from about 1320, although the lid is modern). Mozart was baptized here (Amadeus means "beloved by God"). Concert and Mass schedules are posted at the entrance; the Sunday Mass at 10:00 is famous for its music.

The **Cathedral Museum** (Dom Museum) has a rich collection of church art (entry at portico, €5, mid-May–Oct Mon–Sat 10:00–17:00, Sun 11:00–18:00, closed Nov–mid-May except during Advent, tel. 0662/8047-1870).

• *From the cathedral, exit left and walk toward the fortress into the next square.*

❼ Kapitelplatz

Head past the underground public WCs (free, but small tip expected) to the giant **chessboard.** It's just under the golden orb topped by a man gazing up at the castle, trying to decide whether to walk up or shell out €10 for the funicular. Every year since 2002, a foundation has commissioned a different artist to create a new work of public art somewhere in the city; this is the piece from 2008. A small road leads uphill to the fortress (and fortress funicular; see arrow pointing to the *Steigkeller*).

Keep going across the square to the pond. This was a **horse bath,** the 18th-century equivalent of a car wash. Notice the puzzle above it—the artist wove the date of the structure into a phrase. It says, "Leopold the Prince Built Me," using the letters LLDVICMXVXI, which total 1732 (add it up...it works)—the year it was built. With your back to the cathedral, leave the square through a gate in the right corner that reads *zum Peterskeller.* It leads to a waterfall and St. Peter's Cemetery.

The **waterwheel** is part of a canal system that has brought water into Salzburg from Berchtesgaden, 16 miles away, since the 13th century. Climb uphill a few steps to feel the medieval water power. The stream, divided from here into smaller canals, was channeled through town to provide fire protection, to flush out the streets (Saturday morning was flood-the-streets day), and to power factories (there were more than 100 watermill-powered firms as late as the 19th century). Drop into the fragrant and traditional **bakery** at the waterfall. It's hard to beat their rocklike *Roggenbrot* (various fresh rolls for less than €1, Thu–Tue 7:00–17:30, Sat until 13:00, closed Wed). There's a good view of the funicular climbing up to the castle from here. For more on the canal system, check out the free **Alm River Canal exhibit** nearby (described on page 243).

• *Now find the* Katakomben *sign and step into...*

❽ St. Peter's Cemetery

This collection of lovingly tended mini-gardens abuts the Mönchberg's rock wall (free, silence is requested, daily April–Sept 6:30–19:00, Oct–March 6:30–18:00). Walk in about 50 yards to the intersection of lanes at the base of the cliff marked by a stone ball. (It's seemingly made-to-order for a little back-stretching break. Go ahead...I'll wait.) You're surrounded by three churches, each founded in the sixth century atop a pagan Celtic holy site. St. Peter's Church is closest to the stone ball. Notice the fine Romanesque stonework on the chapel nearest you, and the fancy rich guys' Renaissance-style tombs decorating its walls.

Wealthy as those guys were, they ran out of caring relatives. The graves surrounding you are tended by descendants of the deceased. In Austria, gravesites are rented, not owned. Rent bills are sent out every 10 years. If no one cares enough to make the payment, your remains are chucked. Iron crosses were much cheaper than tombstones. While the cemetery where the von Trapp family hid out in *The Sound of Music* was a Hollywood set, it was inspired by this one.

Look up the cliff. Legendary medieval hermit monks are said to have lived in the hillside—but "catacombs" they're not. For €1, you can climb lots of steps to see a few old caves, a chapel, and some fine views (May–Sept Tue–Sun 10:30–17:00, closed Mon; Oct–April Wed–Thu 10:30–15:30, Fri–Sun 10:30–16:00, closed Mon–Tue).

• *Continue downhill through the cemetery and out the opposite end. Just outside, hook right and drop into...*

❾ St. Peter's Church

Just inside, enjoy a carved Romanesque welcome. Over the inner doorway, a fine tympanum shows Jesus on a rainbow flanked by Peter and Paul over a stylized Tree of Life and under a Latin inscription reading, "I am the door to life, and only through me can you find eternal life." Enter the nave and notice how the once purely Romanesque vaulting has since been iced with a sugary Rococo finish. Salzburg's only Rococo interior feels Bavarian (because it is—the fancy stucco work was done by Bavarian artists). Up the right side aisle is the tomb of St. Rupert, with a painting showing Salzburg in 1750 (one bridge, salt ships sailing the river, and angels hoisting barrels of salt to heaven as St. Rupert prays for his city). If you're here during the town's Ruperti-Kirtag festival in late September, you'll see candles and fresh flowers, honoring the city's not-forgotten saint. On pillars farther up the aisle are faded bits of 13th-century Romanesque frescos. Similar frescoes hide under Rococo whitewash throughout the church.

Leaving the church, notice the Stiftskeller St. Peter restaurant (on the left—described under "Eating," page 263, and known for its Mozart Dinner Concert, page 251). Charlemagne ate here in A.D. 803—allowing locals to claim that it's the oldest restaurant in Europe. Opposite where you entered the square (look through the arch), you'll see St. Rupert waving you into the next square (early-20th-century Bauhaus-style dorms for student monks), with a modern crucifix (1926) on the far wall.

• *Walk through the archway next to the crucifix into...*

⑩ Toscanini Hof

This square faces the 1925 **Festival Hall.** The hall's three theaters seat 5,000. This is where Captain von Trapp nervously waited before walking onstage (in the movie, he sang "Edelweiss"), just before he escaped with his family. On the left is the city's 1,500-space, inside-the-mountain parking lot; ahead, behind the *Felsenkeller* sign, is a tunnel (generally closed) leading to the actual concert hall; and to the right is the backstage of a smaller hall where carpenters are often building stage sets (door open on hot days). The stairway leads to the top of the cliff and eventually to the Stadtalm Café and hostel (see page 259).

• *Walk downhill through Max-Reinhardt-Platz, to the right of the church and past the public WC, into...*

⑪ Universitätsplatz

This square hosts an **open-air produce market**—Salzburg's liveliest (mornings Mon–Sat, best on Sat). Locals are happy to pay more here for the reliably fresh and top-quality produce. (These days, half of Austria's produce is grown organically.) The market really bustles on Saturday mornings, when the farmers are in town. Public marketplaces have fountains for washing fruit and vegetables. The fountain here—a part of the medieval water system—plummets down a hole and to the river. The sundial (over the water hole) is accurate (except for the daylight savings hour) and two-dimensional, showing  both the time (obvious) and the date (less obvious). The fanciest facade overlooking the square (the yellow one) is the backside of Mozart's Birthplace (described on the next page).

• *Continue past the fountain to the end of the square, passing several characteristic and nicely arcaded medieval tunnels (on right) that connect the square to Getreidegasse. Cross the big road for a look at the giant horse troughs, adjacent to the prince's stables. Paintings show the various breeds and temperaments of horses in his stable. Like Vienna, Salzburg had a passion for the equestrian arts.*

Take two right turns and you're at the start of...

20 + C + M + B + 09

All over Austria and Germany (and much of Catholic Europe), you'll likely see written on doorways a mysterious message: "20 + C + M + B + 09." This is marked in chalk on Epiphany (Jan 6), the Christian holiday celebrating the arrival of the Magi to adore the newborn Baby Jesus. In addition to being the initials of the three wise men (Caspar, Melchior, and Balthazar), the letters also stand for the Latin phrase *Christus*

mansionem benedicat—"May Christ bless the house." The little crosses separating the letters remind all who enter that the house has been blessed in this year (20+09 or 20+10). Epiphany is a bigger deal in Catholic Europe than in the US. The holiday includes gift-giving, feasting, and caroling door to door—often collecting for a charity organization. Those who donate get their doors chalked up as in thanks, and these marks are left on the door through the year.

⑫ Getreidegasse

This street, rated ▲▲, was old Salzburg's busy, colorful main drag. It's lined with *Schmuck* (jewelry) shops. Famous for its old wrought-

iron signs (best viewed from this end), the architecture on the street still looks much as it did in Mozart's day—though its former elegance is now mostly gone, replaced by chain outlets.

On the right at #39, **Sporer** serves up homemade spirits (€1.40 per shot). This has been a family-run show for a century—fun-loving, proud, and English-speaking. *Nuss* is nut, *Marille* is apricot (typical of this region), the *Kletzen* cocktail is like a super-thick Baileys with pear, and *Edle Brande* are the stronger schnapps. The many homemade firewaters are in jugs at the end of the bar.

Continue down Getreidegasse, noticing the old doorbells—one per floor. At #40, **Eisgrotte** serves good ice cream. Across from Eisgrotte, a tunnel leads to the **Balkan Grill** (signed as *Bosna Grill*), the local choice for the very best sausage in town (see page 267). Farther along, you'll pass McDonald's (while required to keep its arches Baroque and low-key, it just couldn't hang anything less than the biggest sign on the street).

The knot of excited tourists and salesmen hawking goofy gimmicks marks the home of Salzburg's most famous resident. **Mozart's Birthplace** (Geburtshaus, ⓫ on map)—the house where Mozart was born, and where he composed many of his early works—is worth a visit for his true fans (described next). But for most, his Residence, across the river, is more interesting (described on page 245).

• *Continue on, past City Hall (Rathaus) and its clock tower, and turn right into...*

⓮ Alter Markt

Here in Salzburg's old marketplace you'll find a sausage stand, the recommended **Café Tomaselli** (see page 266), a fun **candy shop** at #7 (Mon–Fri 9:00–18:00, Sat 10:00–18:00, closed Sun), and, next door, the beautifully old-fashioned **Alte F.E. Hofapotheke** pharmacy—duck in discreetly to peek at the Baroque shelves and containers (be polite—the people in line are here for medicine, Mon–Fri 8:00–18:00, Sat 8:00–12:00, closed Sun, no photography).

• *Our walk is finished. From here, you can head up to the Hohensalzburg Fortress on the cliffs over the old town (see page 240); or continue to some of the sights across the river. To reach those sights, head for the river, jog left (past the fast-food fish restaurant and free WCs), climb to the top of the Makartsteg pedestrian bridge, and turn to page 244.*

SIGHTS AND ACTIVITIES

▲Mozart's Birthplace (Geburtshaus)

Mozart was born here in 1756. It was in this building—the most popular Mozart sight in town—that he composed most of his boy-

genius works. For fans, it's almost a pilgrimage. American artist Robert Wilson was recently hired to spiff up the exhibit, to make it feel more conceptual and less like a museum. But I was unimpressed. If you're tackling just one Mozart sight, skip this one. Instead, walk 10 minutes from here to Mozart's Residence (described on page 245), which provides a more informative visit. But if you want to max out on Mozart, a visit here is worthwhile.

Cost, Hours, Location: €6.50, or €10 for combo-ticket that includes Mozart's Residence, daily 9:00–17:00, July–Aug until 20:00, last entry 30 min before closing, Getreidegasse 9, tel. 0662/844-313.

⊙ Self-Guided Tour: Here's what you'll see as you shuffle through with the herd:

Room 1: Around a baby crib showing an infant both old and young (Mozart's music is timeless...get it?) are walls heavy with historic etchings, portraits, and documents. Most important: an engraving of the family (lower right) and a fine "portrait with a bird's nest" of Mozart, painted from life when he was nine years old (upper left).

Room 2: The living room shows off authentic family portraits: Wolfgang's mom, dad, sister, and wife. Wolfgang composed his first pieces as a child on a clavichord (like the one in this room). A predecessor of the piano, it hit the strings with simple teeter-totter keys that played very softly...ideal for composers living in tight apartment quarters.

Room 3: The nursery is decorated like Mozart's music: light and free as a bird (hence the flying birds). Embedded in the walls are Mozart's personal possessions—his ring, silk wallet, and violin. He was born in this room, and the entire family slept here until Wolfgang was 14.

Room 4: Exactly what Mozart looked like is a bit of a mystery. Various portraits in this room give us something to go on.

Corridor: The neon phrase shows Mozart's juvenile sense of humor. It's a rhyme: *Madame Mutter, ich esse gerne Butter.* (Dear mother, I love to eat butter.) The next room is wallpapered with reproductions of circa-1840 photos of Mozart's wife and son (as an old man). More strange Wilson-designed rooms follow: Mozart loved to turn things upside-down—so the Salzburg cityscapes are that way, with stars on the floor. Downstairs, just before the shop, rooms dedicated to Mozart's operas play various video clips continuously.

Atop the Cliffs Above the Old Town

The main "sight" above town is the Hohensalzburg Fortress. But if you just want to enjoy the sweeping views over Salzburg, you have a couple of cheap options: Head up to the castle grounds on foot, take the elevator up the cliffs of Mönchsberg (explained under "Getting Around Salzburg," page 223), or visit the castle in the evening on a night when they're hosting a concert (about 300 nights a year). This is the only time you can buy a funicular ticket without paying for the castle entrance—since the castle museum is closed, but the funicular is still running to bring up concertgoers.

▲▲Hohensalzburg Fortress (Festung)—Built on a rock (called Festungsberg) 400 feet above the Salzach River, this fortress was never really used. That's the idea. It was a good investment—so foreboding, nobody attacked the town for a thousand

years. The city was never taken by force, but when Napoleon stopped by, Salzburg wisely surrendered. After a stint as a military barracks, the fortress was opened to the public in the 1860s by Emperor Franz Josef. Today, it remains one of Europe's mightiest castles, dominating Salzburg's skyline and offering incredible views.

Cost: Your daytime funicular ticket includes admission to the fortress grounds and all the museums inside—whether you want to see them or not (€10.50, €24.50 family ticket). Save money by walking up—the climb is much easier than it looks, and the views are fantastic. From the top you can opt to see the museums for €7, but many visitors are content to simply take in the grounds and views (free if you've walked up). If you'd rather take the funicular but want to skip the museums, head up the hill in the evening (within one hour of the museum's closing time, it's €6 one-way/€7.50 round-trip for funicular and entry to castle grounds; after closing time, the funicular is €3.60 round-trip).

Hours: The complex is open daily year-round (May–Sept 9:00–19:00, Oct–April 9:30–17:00, last entry 30 min before closing, tel. 0662/8424-3011). On nights when there's a concert, the castle grounds are free and open after the museum closes until 21:30.

Concerts: The fortress also serves as a venue for evening concerts (Festungskonzerte). For details, see the "Entertainment" section on page 250.

Café: The café between the funicular station and the castle entry is a great place to nibble on apple strudel while taking in the jaw-dropping view.

Orientation: The fortress visit has three parts: a relatively dull courtyard with some fine views from its various ramparts; the fortress itself (with a required and escorted 45-min audiotour); and the palace museum (by far the best exhibit of the lot). At the bottom of the funicular, you'll pass through an interesting little exhibit on the town's canal system (free, described on page 244).

○ Self-Guided Tour: From the top of the funicular, head to your right and down the stairs to bask in the view, either from the café or the view terrace a little farther along. Once you're done snapping photos, walk through to the castle grounds and go left, following the path up and around to reach the inner courtyard (labeled *Inneres Schloß*). Immediately inside, circling to the right (clockwise), you'll encounter cannons (still poised to defend Salzburg against an Ottoman invasion), the marionette exhibit, the palace museum, the Kuenburg bastion, scant ruins of a Romanesque church, the courtyard (with path down for those walking), toilets, shops, a restaurant, and the fortress tour.

• *Begin at the...*

Marionette Exhibit: Several fun rooms show off this local tradition, with three videos playing continuously: two with peeks at Salzburg's ever-enchanting Marionette Theater performances of Mozart classics (see listing, page 251), and one with a behind-the-scenes look at the action. Give the hands-on marionette a whirl.

• *Hiking through the former palace, you'll find the sight's best exhibits at the...*

Palace Museum (Festungsmuseum Carolino Augusteum): The second floor has exhibits on castle life, from music to torture. The top floor shows off fancy royal apartments, a sneak preview of the room used for the nightly fortress concerts, and the Rainier military museum, dedicated to the Salzburg regiments that fought in both World Wars.

Castle Courtyard: The courtyard was the main square of the castle residents, a community of a thousand—which could be self-sufficient when necessary. The square was ringed by the shops of craftsmen, blacksmiths, bakers, and so on. The well dipped into a rain-fed cistern. The church is dedicated to St. George, the protector of horses (logical for an army church) and decorated by fine red marble reliefs (c. 1502). Behind the church is the top of the old lift that helped supply the fortress. (From near here, steps lead back into the city, or to the mountaintop "Mönchsberg Walk," described later in this section.) You'll also see the remains of a Romanesque chapel, which are well-described.

• *Near the chapel, turn left into the Kuenburg Bastion (once a garden) for fine city and castle views.*

Kuenburg Bastion: Notice how the castle has three parts: the original castle inside the courtyard, the vast white-washed walls (built when the castle was a residence), and the lower, beefed-up fortifications (added for extra defense against the expected Ottoman invasion). Survey Salzburg from here and think about fortifying an important city by

using nature. Mönchsberg (the cliffs to the left) and Festungsberg (the little mountain you're on) naturally cradle the old town, with just a small gate between the ridge and the river needed to bottle up the place. The new town across the river needed a bit of a wall arcing from the river to its hill. Back then, only one bridge crossed the Salzach into town, and it had a fortified gate.

• *Back inside the castle courtyard, continue your circle. The Round Tower (1497) helps you visualize the inner original castle.*

Fortress Interior: Tourists are allowed in this part of the fortified palace only with an escort. (They say that's for security, though while touring it, you wonder what they're protecting.) A crowd assembles at the turnstile, and every quarter-hour 40 people are issued their audioguides and let in for the escorted walk. You'll go one room at a time, listening to a 45-minute commentary. While the interior furnishings are mostly gone—taken by Napoleon—the rooms survived as well as they did because no one wanted to live here after 1500, so the building was never modernized. Your tour includes a room dedicated to the art of "excruciating questioning" ("softening up" prisoners, in current American jargon)— filled with tools of that gruesome trade. The highlight is the commanding city view from the top of a tower.

• *After seeing the fortress, consider hiking down to the old town, or along the top of Mönchsberg (see "Mönchsberg Walk"). If you take the funicular down, keep an eye out for the...*

Alm River Canal Exhibit: At the base of the funicular, below the castle, is this fine little exhibit on how the river was broken into five smaller streams—powering the city until steam took up the energy-supply baton. Pretend it's the year 1200 and follow (by video) the flow of the water from the river through the canals, into the mills, and as it's finally dumped into the Salzach River (free, access from the bottom of the lift as you're leaving, or through amber shop next door if you're not riding the funicular).

▲**Mönchsberg Walk**—For a great 30-minute hike, exit the fortress by taking the steep lane down from the castle courtyard. At the first intersection, right leads into the old town, and left leads across the Mönchsberg. The lane leads 20 minutes through the woods high above the city (stick to the high lanes, or you'll end up back in town), taking you to the Gasthaus Stadtalm café (light meals, cheap beds—see page 259 in "Sleeping" and page 267 in "Eating"). From the Stadtalm, pass under the medieval wall and walk left along the wall to a tableau showing how it once looked. Take the switchback to the right and follow the lane downhill to the Museum of Modern Art (described next), where the elevator zips you back into town (€2 one-way, €3 round-trip, daily 8:30–19:00, Wed until 21:00, July–Aug daily until 1:00 in the morning, May–Sept starts running at 8:00). If you stay on the lane past the elevator, you eventually pass the Augustine church that marks the rollicking Augustiner Bräustübl (see page 268).

In 1669, a huge Mönchsberg landslide killed more than 200 townspeople. Since then the cliffs have been carefully checked each spring and fall. Even today, you might see crews on the cliff, monitoring its stability.

Museum of Modern Art on Mönchsberg—The modern-art museum on top of Mönchsberg, built in 2004, houses Salzburg's Rupertinum Gallery, plus special exhibitions. While the collection is not worth climbing a mountain for, the M32 restaurant has some of the best views in town (€8, €9.70 including elevator ticket, Tue–Sun 10:00–18:00, Wed until 20:00, closed Mon except during festival; restaurant open Tue–Sat 9:00–24:00, Sun 9:00–18:00, closed Mon except during festival; both at top of Mönchsberg elevator, tel. 0662/842-220, www.museumdermoderne.at).

In the New Town, North of the River

The following sights are across the river from the old town. I've connected them with walking instructions.

• *Begin at the Makartsteg pedestrian bridge, where you can survey the...*

Salzach River—Salzburg's river is called "salt river" not because it's salty, but because of the precious cargo it once carried—the salt mines of Hallein are just nine miles upstream. Salt could be transported from here all the way to the Danube, and on to the Mediterranean via the Black Sea. The riverbanks and roads were built when the river was regulated in the 1850s. Before that, the Salzach was much wider and slower-moving. Houses opposite the old town fronted the river with docks and "garages" for boats. The grand buildings just past the bridge (with their elegant promenades and cafés) were built on reclaimed land in the late 19th century, in the historicist style of Vienna's Ringstrasse (see "Historicism" sidebar on page 106).

Scan the cityscape. Notice all the churches. Salzburg, nicknamed the "Rome of the North," has 38 Catholic churches (plus two Protestant churches and a synagogue). Find the five streams gushing into the river. These date from the 13th century, when the river was split into five canals running through the town to power its mills. The Stein Hotel (upstream, just left of next bridge), described on page 247, has a popular roof-terrace café. Downstream, notice the Museum of Modern Art atop Mönchsberg, with a view restaurant and a faux castle (actually a water reservoir). The Romanesque bell tower with the green copper dome in the distance is the Augustine church, site of the best beer hall in town (the Augustiner Bräustübl—see page 268).

• *Cross the bridge, pass the Café Bazar (a fine place for a drink—see page 269), walk two blocks inland, and take a left past the heroic statues into...*

▲**Mirabell Gardens and Palace (Schloss)**—The bubbly gardens laid out in 1730 for the prince-archbishop have been open

to the public since 1850 (thanks to Emperor Franz Josef, who was rattled by the popular revolutions of 1848). The gardens are free and open until dusk. The palace is open only as a concert venue (explained later). The statues and the arbor (far left) were featured in *The Sound of Music*. Walk through the gardens to the palace. Look back, enjoy the garden/cathedral/castle view, and imagine how the prince-archbishop must have reveled in a vista that reminded him of all his secular and religious power. Then go around to the river side of the palace and find the horse.

The rearing **Pegasus statue** (rare and very well-balanced) is the site of a famous *Sound of Music* scene where the kids all danced before lining up on the stairs (with Maria 30 yards farther along). The steps lead to a small mound in the park (made of rubble from a former theatre, and today a rendezvous point for Salzburg's gay community).

Nearest the horse, stairs lead between two lions to a pair of tough dwarfs (early volleyball players with spiked mittens) welcoming you to Salzburg's **Dwarf Park.** Cross the elevated walk (noticing the city's fortified walls) to meet statues of a dozen dwarfs who served the prince-archbishop—modeled after real people with real fashions in about 1600. This was Mannerist art, from the hyper-realistic age that followed the Renaissance.

There's plenty of **music,** both in the park and in the palace. A brass band plays free park concerts (May–Aug Sun at 10:30 and Wed with lighted fountains at 20:30, unless it's raining). To properly enjoy the lavish Mirabell Palace—once the prince-archbishop's summer palace, and now the seat of the mayor—get a ticket to a Schlosskonzerte (my favorite venue for a classical concert—see page 251).

• *To visit Salzburg's best Mozart sight, go a long block southeast to Makartplatz, where you'll find...*

▲▲**Mozart's Residence (Wohnhaus)**—This reconstruction of Mozart's second home (his family moved here when he was 17) is the most informative Mozart sight in town. The English-language audioguide (included with admission, 90 min) provides fascinating insight into Mozart's life and music, with the usual scores, old pianos, and an interesting 30-minute film (#17 on your audioguide for soundtrack) that runs continuously (€6.50, or €10 for combo-ticket that includes Mozart's Birthplace in the old town, daily 9:00–17:00, July–Aug until 20:00, last entry 30 min before closing, allow at least one hour for visit, Makartplatz 8, tel. 0662/8742-2740).

In the main hall—used by the Mozarts to entertain Salzburg's high society—you can hear original instruments from Mozart's time. Mozart was proud to be the first in his family to compose a duet. Notice the family portrait (circa 1780) on the wall, showing Mozart with his sister Nannerl, their father, and their mother—who'd died two years earlier in Paris. Mozart also had silly crude bull's-eyes made for the pop-gun game popular at the time (licking an "arse," Wolfgang showed his disdain for the rigors of high society). Later rooms feature real artifacts that explore his loves, his intellectual pursuits, his travels, and more.

• *From here, you can walk a few blocks back to the main bridge (Staatsbrücke), where you'll find the Platzl, a square once used as a hay market. Pause to enjoy the kid-pleasing little fountain. Near the fountain (with your back to the river), Steingasse leads darkly to the right.*

▲**Steingasse Stroll**—This street, a block in from the river, was the only road in the Middle Ages going south over the Alps to Venice (this was the first stop north of the Alps). Today, it's wonderfully tranquil and free of Salzburg's touristy crush.

At #9, a plaque (of questionable veracity) shows where Joseph Mohr, who wrote the words to "Silent Night," was born—poor and illegitimate—in 1792. There is no doubt, however, that the popular Christmas carol was composed and first sung in the village of Oberndorf, just outside of Salzburg, in 1818. Stairs lead from near here up to a 17th-century Capuchin monastery.

On the next corner, the wall is gouged out. This scar was left even after the building was restored, to remind locals of the American GI who tried to get a tank down this road during a visit to the town brothel—two blocks farther up Steingasse. Inviting cocktail bars along here come alive at night (see "Steingasse Pub Crawl" on page 269).

At #19, find the carvings on the old door. Some say these are notices from beggars to the begging community (more numerous after post-Reformation religious wars, which forced many people out of their homes and towns)—a kind of "hobo code" indicating whether the residents would give or not. Trace the wires of the old-fashioned doorbells to the highest floors.

Farther on, you'll find a commanding Salzburg view across the river. Notice the red dome marking the oldest nunnery in the German-speaking world (established in 712) under the fortress and to the left. The real Maria from *The Sound of Music* taught in this nunnery's school. In 1927, she and Captain von Trapp were married in the church you see here (not the church filmed in the movie). He was 47. She was 22. Hmmmm.

From here look back, above the arch you just passed through, at part of the town's medieval fortification. The coat of arms on the arch is of the prince-archbishop who paid Bavaria a huge ransom to stay out of the Thirty Years' War (smart move). He then built this fortification (in 1634) in anticipation of rampaging armies from both sides.

Today, this street is for making love, not war. The Maison de Plaisir (a few doors down, at #24) has for centuries been a Salzburg brothel. But the climax of this walk is more touristic.

• *For a grand view, head back to the Platzl and the bridge, enter the Stein Hotel (left corner, overlooking the river), and ride the elevator to...*

Stein Terrasse—This café offers perhaps the best views in town (aside from the castle). Hidden from the tourist crush, it's a trendy, professional, local scene. You can discretely peek at the view, or enjoy a drink or light meal (small snacks, indoor/outdoor seating, Sun–Thu 9:00–24:00, Fri–Sat 9:00–1:00 in the morning).

• *Back at the Platzl and the bridge, you can head straight up Linzergasse (away from the river) into a neighborhood packed with recommended accommodations, as well as our final new-town sight...*

▲**St. Sebastian Cemetery**—Wander through this quiet place, so Baroque and so Italian (free, daily April–Oct 9:00–18:30,

Nov–March 9:00–16:00, entry at Linzergasse 43 in summer; in winter go around the corner to the right, through the arch at #37, and around the building to the doorway under the blue seal). Mozart is buried in Vienna, his mom's in Paris, and his sister is in Salzburg's old town (St. Peter's)—but Wolfgang's wife Constanze ("Constantia") and his father Leopold are buried here (from the black iron gate entrance on Linzergasse, walk 17 paces and look left). When Prince-Archbishop Wolf Dietrich had the cemetery moved from around the cathedral and put here, across the river, people didn't like it. To help popularize it, he had his own mausoleum built as its centerpiece. Continue straight past the Mozart tomb to this circular building (English description at door).

Near Salzburg

For information on Berchtesgaden—also near Salzburg—see the next chapter.

▲**Hellbrunn Castle**—About the year 1610, Prince-Archbishop Sittikus (after meditating on stewardship and Christ-like values) decided he needed a lavish palace with a vast and ornate garden
purely for pleasure. He built this
and just loved inviting his VIP
guests out for fun with his trick
fountains. Today, the visit is
worthwhile for the garden full of
clever fountains...and the sadis-
tic joy the tour guide gets from
soaking tourists. (Hint: When

you see a wet place, cover your camera.) After buying your ticket, you must wait for the English tour, laugh and scramble through the entertaining 40-minute trick-water-toy tour, and are then free to tour the forgettable palace with an included audioguide (€8.50, daily May–Sept 9:00–17:30, July–Aug until 21:00—but tours from 18:00 on don't include the castle, mid-March–April and Oct 9:00–16:30, these are last tour times, closed Nov–mid-March, tel. 0662/820-3720, www.hellbrunn.at).

Hellbrunn is nearly four miles south of Salzburg (bus #25 from station or from Staatsbrücke bridge, 2–3/hr, 20 min). While it can be fun—especially on a hot day or with kids—for many, it's a lot of trouble for a few water tricks. The Hellbrunn Baroque gar-den, one of the oldest in Europe, now features *S.O.M.*'s "Sixteen Going on Seventeen" gazebo.

Hellbrunn makes a good 30-minute bike excursion along the riverbank from Salzburg (described next).

▲▲**Riverside or Meadow Bike Ride**—The Salzach River has smooth, flat, and scenic bike lanes along each side (thanks to medieval tow paths—cargo boats would float downstream and be dragged back up by horses). On a sunny day, I can think of no more shout-worthy escape from the city. The nearly four-mile path upstream to Hellbrunn Castle is easy, with a worthy destina-tion (leave Salzburg on castle side). For a nine-mile ride, continue on to Hallein (where you can tour a salt mine—see next listing; the north, or new town, side of river is most scenic). Perhaps the most pristine, meadow-filled farm-country route is the four-mile Hellbrunner Allee from Akademiestrasse. Even a quickie ride across town is a great Salzburg experience. In the evening, the riv-erbanks are a world of floodlit spires.

▲**Hallein Bad Dürrnberg Salt Mine (Salzbergwerke)**—This salt-mine tour (above the town of Hallein, nine miles from

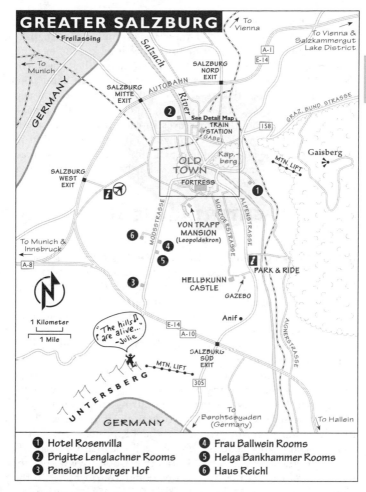

GREATER SALZBURG

To Vienna
To Vienna &
Salzkammergut
Lake District
A-1
E-14
Freilassing
To Munich
GERMANY
Salzach River
AUTOBAHN
SALZBURG NORD EXIT
SALZBURG MITTE EXIT
GRAZ. BUND. STRASSE
158
See Detail Map
TRAIN STATION
GABEL
Gaisberg
MTN. LIFT
OLD TOWN
Kap-berg
SALZBURG WEST EXIT
FORTRESS
①
ALPENSTRASSE
MÖRZGERSTRASSE
MOOSSTRASSE
VON TRAPP MANSION (Leopoldskron)
⑥
④
⑤
PARK & RIDE
To Munich & Innsbruck
A-8
HELLBRUNN CASTLE
③
GAZEBO
Anif
AIGNERSTRASSE
N
1 Kilometer
1 Mile
"The hills are alive... ~Julie"
E-14
A-10
SALZBURG SÜD EXIT
MTN. LIFT
UNTERSBERG
305
GERMANY
To Berchtesgaden (Germany)
To Hallein

① Hotel Rosenvilla	④ Frau Ballwein Rooms
② Brigitte Lenglachner Rooms	⑤ Helga Bankhammer Rooms
③ Pension Bloberger Hof	⑥ Haus Reichl

Salzburg) is a popular excursion from Salzburg. Wearing white overalls and sliding down the sleek wooden chutes, you'll cross

underground from Austria into Germany while learning about the old-time salt-mining process. The tour entails lots of time on your feet as you walk from cavern to cavern, learning the history of the mine by watching a series of video skits with an actor channeling Prince-Archbishop Wolf Dietrich. The visit also includes a "Celtic Village" open-air museum (€17, allow 2.5 hrs for the visit, daily April–Oct 9:00–17:00, Nov–March 10:00–15:00, these are last tour times, English-speaking guides—but let your linguistic needs be known loud and clear, tel. 06132/200-2400, www.salzwelten.at). The convenient *Salz Erlebnis* ticket from Salzburg's train station covers admission, train, and shuttle bus tickets, all in one money-saving round-trip ticket (€22, buy ticket at train station, no discount with railpass; 40-min trip with hourly departures in each direction at about :15 after the hour, with synchronized train-bus connection in Hallein—schedule posted in flier). Salt mine tours cost substantial time and money. One's plenty. This one is better than Hallstatt's (described on page 286).

ENTERTAINMENT

Music

▲▲**Salzburg Festival (Salzburger Festspiele)**—Each summer, from late July to the end of August, Salzburg hosts its famous Salzburg Festival, founded in 1920 to employ Vienna's musicians in the summer. This fun and festive time is crowded, but there are plenty of beds (except for a few August weekends). There are three big halls: the Opera and Orchestra venues in the Festival House, and the Landes Theater, where German-language plays are performed. Tickets for the big festival events are generally expensive (€50–600) and sell out well in advance (bookable from Jan). Most tourists think they're "going to the Salzburg Festival" by seeing smaller non-festival events that go on during the festival weeks. For these lesser events, same-day tickets are normally available (the ticket office on Mozartplatz, in the TI, prints a daily list of concerts and charges a 30 percent fee to book them). For specifics on this year's festival schedule and tickets, visit www.salzburg festival.at, or contact the Austrian National Tourist Office in the United States (tel. 212/944-6880, fax 212/730-4568, www.austria .info, travel@austria.info).

▲▲**Musical Events Year-Round**—Salzburg is busy throughout the year, with 2,000 classical performances in its palaces and churches annually. Pick up the events calendar at the TI (free, bimonthly). I've never planned in advance, and I've enjoyed great concerts with every visit. Whenever you visit, you'll have a number of concerts (generally small chamber groups) to choose from. Here are some of the more accessible events:

Concerts at Hohensalzburg Fortress (Festungskonzerte): Nearly nightly concerts—Mozart's greatest hits for beginners—are held atop Festungsberg, in the "prince's chamber" of the fortress, featuring small chamber groups (open seating after the first six more expensive rows, €31 or €38 plus €3.40 for the funicular; at

19:30, 20:00, or 20:30; doors open 30 min early, tel. 0662/825-858 to reserve, pick up tickets at the door). The medieval-feeling chamber has windows overlooking the city, and the concert gives you a chance to enjoy the grand city view and a stroll through the castle courtyard. (The funicular ticket costs €3.40 within an hour of the show—ideal for people who just want to ascend for the view.) For €51, you can combine the concert with a four-course dinner (starts 2 hrs before concert).

Concerts at the Mirabell Palace (Schlosskonzerte): The nearly nightly chamber music concerts at the Mirabell Palace are performed in a lavish Baroque setting. They come with more sophisticated programs and better musicians than the fortress concerts. Baroque music flying around a Baroque hall is a happy bird in the right cage (open seating after the first five pricier rows, €29, usually at 20:00—but check flyer for times, doors open 1 hr ahead, tel. 0662/848-586, www.salzburger-schlosskonzerte.at).

"Five O'Clock Concerts" (5-Uhr-Konzerte): These concerts—next to St. Peter's in the old town—are cheaper, since they feature young artists (€12, July–Sept Thu–Tue at 17:00, no concerts Wed or Oct–June, 45–60 min, tel. 0662/8445-7619, www.5-uhr-konzerte.com). While the series is formally named after the brother of Joseph Haydn, it offers music from various masters.

Mozart Piano Sonatas: St. Peter's Abbey hosts these concerts each weekend (€18, €9 for children, €45 for a family of four, Fri and Sat at 19:00 year-round, in the abbey's Romanesque Hall—a.k.a. Romanischer Saal, tel. 0664/423-5645). This short and inexpensive concert is ideal for families.

Marionette Theater: Salzburg's much-loved marionette theater offers operas with spellbinding marionettes and recorded music. Music-lovers are mesmerized by the little people on stage (€18–35, nearly nightly at 17:00 or 19:30 June–Sept except Sun, also 3–4/week in May, some 14:00 matinees, box office open Mon–Sat 9:00–13:00 and 2 hrs before shows, near the Mirabell Gardens and Mozart's Residence at Schwarzstrasse 24, tel. 0662/872-406, www.marionetten.at). For a sneak preview, check out the videos playing at the marionette exhibit up in the fortress.

Mozart Dinner Concert: For those who'd like some classical music but would rather not sit through a concert, Stiftskeller St. Peter offers a traditional candlelit meal with Mozart's greatest hits performed by a string quartet and singers in historic costumes gavotting among the tables. In this elegant Baroque setting, tourists clap between movements and get three courses of food (from Mozart-era recipes) mixed with three 20-minute courses of crowd-pleasing music (€48, Mozart-lovers with this guidebook pay €39 when booking direct, almost nightly at 20:00, dress is "smart casual," call to reserve at 0662/828-695,

Sound of Music Debunked

Rather than visit the real-life sights from the life of Maria von Trapp and family, most tourists want to see the places where Hollywood chose to film this fanciful story. Local guides are happy not to burst any *S.O.M.* pilgrim's bubble, but keep these points in mind:

- "Edelweiss" is not a cherished Austrian folk tune or national anthem. Like all the "Austrian" music in *The S.O.M.*, it was composed for Broadway by Rodgers and Hammerstein. It was, however, the last composition that the famed team wrote together, as Hammerstein died in 1960—nine months after the musical opened.
- *The S.O.M.* implies that Maria was devoutly religious throughout her life, but Maria's foster parents raised her as a socialist and atheist. Maria discovered her religious calling while studying to be a teacher. After completing school, she joined the convent not as a nun, but as a novitiate (that is, she hadn't taken her vows yet).
- Maria's position was not as governess to all the children, as portrayed in the musical, but specifically as governess and teacher for the Captain's second-oldest daughter, Maria, who was bedridden with rheumatic fever.
- The Captain didn't run a tight domestic ship. In fact, his seven children were as unruly as most. But he did use a whistle to call them—each kid was trained to respond to a certain pitch.
- Though the von Trapp family did have seven children, the show changed all their names and even their genders. Rupert, the eldest child, responded to the often-asked question, "Which one are you?" with a simple, "I'm Liesl!"
- The family didn't escape by hiking to Switzerland (which is a 5-hr drive away). Rather, they pretended to go on one of their frequent mountain hikes. With only the possessions in their backpacks, they "hiked" all the way to the train station

www.mozartdinnerconcert.com). When they run out of space, they book a second quartet to perform in the adjacent Haydn Zimmer. I find the ambience much nicer in the main Baroque Hall—when making the booking, get a promise that that's where you'll be seated. For more details, see page 263.

Sound of Salzburg Dinner Show: The show at the Sternbräu Inn (see page 266) is Broadway in a dirndl with tired food. But it's a good show, and *Sound of Music* fans leave with hands red from clapping. A piano player and a hardworking quartet of singers wearing historical costumes perform an entertaining mix of *S.O.M.* hits and traditional folk songs (€46 for dinner, begins at 19:30). You can also come by at 20:30, pay €32, skip the dinner, (it was at the edge of their estate) and took a train to Italy. The movie scene showing them climbing into Switzerland was actually filmed near Berchtesgaden, Germany...home to Hitler's Eagle's Nest, and certainly not a smart place to flee to.

- The actual von Trapp family house exists...but it's not the one in the film. The mansion in the movie is actually two different buildings—one used for the front, the other for the back. The interiors were all filmed on Hollywood sets.

- For the film, Boris Levin designed a reproduction of the Nonnberg Abbey courtyard so faithful to the original (down to its cobblestones and stained-glass windows) that many still believe the cloister scenes were really shot at the abbey. And no matter what you hear in Salzburg, the graveyard scene (in which the von Trapps hide from the Nazis) was also filmed on the Fox lot.

- In 1956, a German film producer offered Maria $10,000 for the rights to her book. She asked for royalties, too, and a share of the profits. The agent explained that German law forbids film companies from paying royalties to foreigners (Maria had by then become a US citizen). She agreed to the contract and unknowingly signed away all film rights to her story. Only a few weeks later, he offered to pay immediately if she would accept $9,000 in cash. Because it was more money than the family had seen in all of their years of singing, she accepted the deal. Later, she discovered the agent had swindled them—no such law existed.

  Rodgers, Hammerstein, and other producers gave the von Trapps a percentage of the royalties, even though they weren't required to—but it was a fraction of what they otherwise would have earned. Maria was not bitter. "The great good the film and the play are doing to individual lives is far beyond money," she said.

and get the show. Those who book direct (not through a hotel) and pay cash get a 10 percent discount with this book (nightly mid-May–mid-Oct, Griesgasse 23, tel. 0662/826-617, www.soundof salzburgshow.com).

Music at Mass: Each Sunday morning, two great churches offer a Mass generally with glorious music. The Salzburg Cathedral is likely your best bet for fine music to worship by (10:00). The Franciscan church (9:00) is enthusiastic about its musical Masses, and St. Peter's Church also has music (10:30). See the Salzburg events guide for details.

Free Brass Band Concert: A traditional brass band plays in the Mirabell Gardens (May–Aug Sun at 10:30 and Wed at 20:30).

SLEEPING

Finding a room in Salzburg, even during its music festival (mid-July–Aug), is usually easy. Rates rise significantly (20–30 percent) during the music festival, and sometimes around Easter and Christmas; these higher prices do not appear in the ranges I've listed. Many places charge 10 percent extra for a one-night stay.

In the New Town, North of the River

These listings, clustering around Linzergasse, are in a pleasant neighborhood (with easy parking) a 15-minute walk from the train station (for directions, see "Arrival in Salzburg," earlier in this chapter) and a 10-minute walk to the old town. If you're coming from the old town, simply cross the main bridge (Staatsbrücke) to the mostly traffic-free Linzergasse. If driving, exit the highway at Salzburg-Nord, follow Vogelweiderstrasse straight to its end, and turn right.

$$$ Altstadthotel Wolf-Dietrich, around the corner from Linzergasse on pedestrians-only Wolf-Dietrich-Strasse, is well-located (with half its rooms overlooking St. Sebastian Cemetery). With 27 tastefully plush rooms, it's the best value I could find for a big, stylish hotel (Sb-€85–105, Db-€140–190, price depends on size, family deals, €20–40 more during festival, complex pricing but readers of this book get a 10 percent discount on prevailing price—insist on this discount deducted from whatever price is offered that day, elevator, pool with loaner swimsuits, sauna, free DVD library, Wolf-Dietrich-Strasse 7, tel. 0662/871-275, fax 0662/871-2759, www.salzburg-hotel.at, office@salzburg-hotel.at). Their annex across the street has 14 equally comfortable rooms (but no elevator, and therefore slightly cheaper prices).

$$$ Hotel Trumer Stube, three blocks from the river just off Linzergasse, has 20 clean, cozy rooms and a friendly, can-do owner (Sb-€65, Db-€105, Tb-€128, Qb-€147, about €30 more during music festival, top-floor rooms have lower ceilings and are €7 less expensive, 10 percent discount if you book direct with this book and pay cash—except during festival, non-smoking, elevator, free Wi-Fi except in top-floor rooms, free Internet access, Bergstrasse 6, tel. 0662/874-776, fax 0662/874-326, www.trumer-stube.at, info@trumer-stube.at, Marianne and Hermann).

$$$ Hotel Goldene Krone, about five blocks from the river, is plain and basic, with 25 big, quiet, creaky, and well-kept

---

Sleep Code

(€1 = about $1.40, country code: 43, area code: 0662)
S = Single, **D** = Double/Twin, **T** = Triple, **Q** = Quad, **b** = bathroom,
s = shower only. Unless otherwise noted, credit cards are accepted and breakfast is included. All of these places speak English.

To help you sort easily through these listings, I've divided the rooms into three categories, based on the price for a standard double room with bath:

$$$ Higher Priced—Most rooms €90 or more.
$$ Moderately Priced—Most rooms between €60-90.
$ Lower Priced—Most rooms €60 or less.

---

rooms. Stay a while in their pleasant cliffside garden (Sb-€69, Db-€119, Tb-€159, Qb-€189, claim your 10 percent discount off these prices with this book, dim lights, elevator, parking-€12/day, Linzergasse 48, tel. 0662/872-300, fax 0662/8723-0066, www.hotel-goldenekrone.com, office@hotel-goldenekrone.com, Claudia and Günther Hausknost). Günther offers tours (€10/person, 2 hrs, 5 people minimum) and a "Rick Steves Two Nights in Salzburg" deal, which covers your room, a 24-hr Salzburg Card, a concert in Mirabell Palace, and a tour with Günther (Sb-€171, Db-€304, Tb-€429, Qb-€532).

$$ Institute St. Sebastian is in a somewhat sterile but very clean historic building next to St. Sebastian Cemetery. From October through June, the institute houses female students from various Salzburg colleges, and also rents 40 beds for travelers (men and women). From July through September, the students are gone and they rent all 100 beds (including 20 doubles) to travelers. The building has spacious public areas, a roof garden, a piano that guests are welcome to play, and some of the best rooms and dorm beds in town for the money. The immaculate doubles come with modern baths and head-to-toe twin beds (S-€33.50, Sb-€41.50, D-€53.50, Db-€67, Tb-€81, Qb-€96, €2.50/person extra for 1-night stay, includes very basic breakfast, elevator, self-service laundry-€4/load; reception open daily July–Sept 7:30–12:00 & 13:00–21:30, Oct–June 8:00–12:00 & 16:00–21:00; Linzergasse 41, enter through arch at #37, tel. 0662/871-386, fax 0662/8713-8685, www.st-sebastian-salzburg.at, office@st-sebastian-salzburg.at). Students like the €21 bunks in 4- to 10-bed dorms (€2 less if you have sheets, no lockout time, free lockers, free showers). You'll find self-service kitchens on each floor (fridge space is free; request a key). If you need parking, request it well in advance.

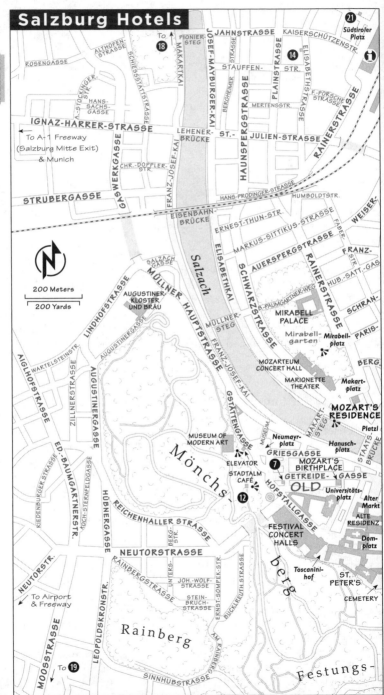

Salzburg Hotels

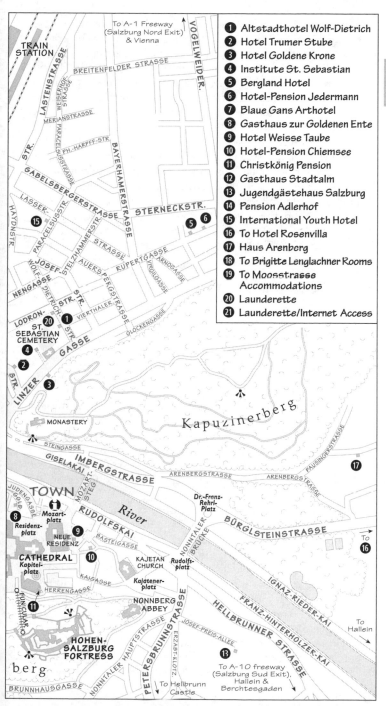

1 Altstadthotel Wolf-Dietrich
2 Hotel Trumer Stube
3 Hotel Goldene Krone
4 Institute St. Sebastian
5 Bergland Hotel
6 Hotel-Pension Jedermann
7 Blaue Gans Arthotel
8 Gasthaus zur Goldenen Ente
9 Hotel Weisse Taube
10 Hotel-Pension Chiemsee
11 Christkönig Pension
12 Gasthaus Stadtalm
13 Jugendgästehaus Salzburg
14 Pension Adlerhof
15 International Youth Hotel
16 To Hotel Rosenvilla
17 Haus Arenberg
18 To Brigitte Lenglachner Rooms
19 To Moosstrasse Accommodations
20 Launderette
21 Launderette/Internet Access

Pensions on Rupertgasse: These two hotels are about five blocks farther from the river on Rupertgasse, a breeze for drivers but with more street noise than the places on Linzergasse. They're both modern and well-run—good values if you don't mind being a bit away from the old town. **$$$ Bergland Hotel** is charming and classy, with comfortable, neo-rustic rooms. It's a modern building, and therefore spacious and solid (Sb-€65, Db-€95, Tb-€117, Qb-€140, elevator, Internet access, English library, bike rental-€6/day, Rupertgasse 15, tel. 0662/872-318, fax 0662/872-3188, www.berglandhotel.at, kuhn@berglandhotel.at, Kuhn family). The similar, boutique-like **$$$ Hotel-Pension Jedermann,** a few doors down, is tastefully done and comfortable, with an artsy painted-concrete ambience and a backyard garden (Sb-€65–85, Db-€90–130, Tb-€120–160, Qb-€160–200, much more during festival, elevator, Internet access, Rupertgasse 25, tel. 0662/873-2410, fax 0662/873-2419, www.hotel-jedermann.com, office @hotel-jedermann.com, Herr und Frau Gmachl).

In or Above the Old Town

Most of these hotels are near Residenzplatz. While this area is car-restricted, you're allowed to drive your car in to unload, pick up a map and parking instructions, and head for the €14-per-day garage in the mountain.

$$$ Blaue Gans Arthotel is ultra-modern and in the old town, beautifully located at the far end of Getreidegasse. Its public spaces feature contemporary Austrian art, and the 40 sleek, thoughtfully designed rooms are decorated with local materials (Sb-€115–125, standard Db-€135–160, bigger superior Db-€185–195, fancier suites, extra bed-€35–40; prices €20–25 higher per person during festival, around Christmas, and on holiday weekends; elevator, free Internet access and Wi-Fi, Getreidegasse 41, tel. 0662/842-4910, fax 0662/8424-9175, www.blauegans.at, office@blauegans.at).

$$$ Gasthaus zur Goldenen Ente is in a 600-year-old building with medieval stone arches and narrow stairs. Located above a good, smoke-free restaurant, it's as central as you can be on a pedestrian street in old Salzburg. The 17 rooms are modern and newly renovated, and include classy amenities. While this hotel's advertised rates are too high, travelers with this book get 10 percent off—and prices may dip lower according to demand. Ulrike, Franziska, and Anita run a tight ship for the absentee owners (most of the year: Sb-€85, Db-€140; late July–Aug and Dec: Sb-€95, Db-€160; extra person-€29, firm mattresses, non-smoking, elevator, free Internet access, Goldgasse 10, tel. 0662/845-622, fax 0662/845-6229, www.ente.at, hotel@ente.at).

SALZBURG

$$$ Hotel Weisse Taube has 30 comfortable rooms in a quiet, dark-wood, 14th-century building, well-located about a block off Mozartplatz (Sb-€67–85, Db with shower-€98–138, bigger Db with bath-€119–162, 10 percent discount with this book if you reserve direct and pay cash, elevator, Internet access, tel. 0662/842-404, fax 0662/841-783, Kaigasse 9, www.weissetaube.at, hotel@weissetaube.at).

$$$ Hotel-Pension Chiemsee is a stony dollhouse nestled in a quiet lane just behind the cathedral. Hardworking Frau Höllbacher rents 10 big, beautifully renovated rooms and three suites (Sb-€48–58, Db-€88–98, Tb-€110–120; suite-€110 for 2 people, €28/person extra up to 5; during festival and Dec: Sb-€68, Db-€98–116, Tb-€120–130; these special Rick Steves prices available if you book direct and pay cash, Chiemseegasse 5, tel. 0662/844-208, fax 0662/8442-0870, www.hotel-ami.de/hotel /chiemsee, hotel-chiemsee@aon.at).

$$ Christkönig Pension makes you feel like a guest of the bishop because, in a sense...you are. With 20 rooms in a 14th-century church building just under the castle and behind the cathedral, this is where the bishop's visitors stay. It's a charming, quiet, convenient, and unique way to sleep well and affordably in the old center. Heavenly Frau Anna Huemer will take excellent care of you (S-€35, Ss-€41, Sb-€46, Ds-€68, Db-€80, suite for 2–4 people roughly €45/person, twin beds only, €3/person extra for 1-night stays, usually booked up during festival, cash only, Kapitelplatz 2a, tel. 0662/842-627, www.christkoenig-kolleg.at, christkoenig -pension@salzburg.co.at).

Hostels

For another hostel (on the other side of the river), see "International Youth Hotel," next page.

$ Gasthaus Stadtalm (a.k.a. the *Naturfreundehaus*) is a local version of a mountaineer's hut and a great budget alternative. Snuggled in a forest on the remains of a 15th-century castle wall atop the little mountain overlooking Salzburg, it has magnificent town and mountain views. While the 26 beds are designed-for-backpackers basic, the price and view are the best in town—with the right attitude, it's a fine experience (€18.50/person in 2-, 4-, and 6-bed dorms, same price for room with double bed; includes breakfast, sheets, and shower; lockers, 2 min from top of €2 Mönchsberg elevator, Mönchsberg 19C, tel. & fax 0662/841-729, www.diestadtalm.com—German only, info@diestadtalm.com, Peter). Once you've dropped your bags here, it's a five-minute walk down the cliffside stairs into Toscanini Hof, in the middle of the old town (path always lit).

$ **Jugendgästehaus Salzburg,** just steps from the old town center, is nevertheless removed from the bustle. While its dorm rooms are the standard crammed-with-beds variety—and the hallways will bring back high-school memories—the doubles and family rooms are modern, roomy, and bright, and a recent renovation has made the public spaces quite pleasant (bed in 8-person dorm-€20–22, Db-€65–68, Qs-€98–104, higher prices are for May–Sept, non-members pay €1.50 extra, includes breakfast and sheets, pay Internet access, free Wi-Fi, *The Sound of Music* plays daily; bike rental-€10/day, €6/half-day; free parking, just around the east side of the castle hill at Josef-Preis-Allee 18; from train station take bus #5 or #25 to the Justizgebäude stop, then head left one block along the bushy wall, cross Petersbrunnstrasse, find shady Josefs-Preis-Alle, and walk a few minutes to the end—the hostel is the big orange/green building on the right; tel. 0662/842-670, fax 0662/841-101, www.jfgh.at/salzburg.php, salzburg@jfgh.at). The new hotel at the back of the hostel isn't as cheap, but does offer more standard hotel amenities, such as TVs (Db-€82–96 depending on season, includes breakfast).

Near the Train Station

$$ **Pension Adlerhof,** a plain and decent old pension, is two blocks in front of the train station (left off Kaiserschutzenstrasse), but a 15-minute walk from the sightseeing action. It has a quirky staff, a boring location, and 30 stodgy-but-spacious rooms (Sb-€49–68, Db-€69–108, Tb-€93–123, Qb-€108–156, price depends on season and size of room, cash only, elevator, free Wi-Fi, limited free parking, Elisabethstrasse 25, tel. 0662/875-236, fax 0662/873-663, www.gosalzburg.com, adlerhof@pension-adlerhof.at).

$ **International Youth Hotel,** a.k.a. the "Yo-Ho," is the most lively, handy, and American of Salzburg's hostels. This easygoing place speaks English first; has cheap meals, 180 beds, lockers, tour discounts, and no curfew; plays *The Sound of Music* free daily at 10:30; runs a lively bar; and welcomes anyone of any age. The noisy atmosphere and lack of a curfew can make it hard to sleep (€18–19 in 4- to 8-bed dorms, €21–22 in dorms with bathrooms, D-€44, Ds-€56, Q-€76, Qs-€88, includes sheets, cheap breakfast, fee for Internet access and Wi-Fi, laundry-€4 wash and dry, 6 blocks from station toward Linzergasse and 6 blocks from river at Paracelsusstrasse 9, tel. 0662/879-649, fax 0662/878-810, www.yoho.at, office@yoho.at).

Four-Star Hotels in Residential Neighborhoods away from the Center

If you want plush furnishings, spacious public spaces, generous balconies, gardens, and free parking, consider the following places. These two modern hotels in nondescript residential neighborhoods are a fine value if you don't mind the 15-minute walk from the old town. While not ideal for train travelers, drivers in need of no-stress comfort for a home base should consider these (see map on pages 256-257).

$$$ Hotel Rosenvilla, close to the river, offers 14 rooms with bright furnishings, surrounded by a leafy garden (Sb-€79, Db-€128, bigger Db-€142, Db suite-€188, at least €30 more during festival, free Wi-Fi, Höfelgasse 4, tel. 0662/621-765, fax 0662/625-2308, www.rosenvilla.com, hotel@rosenvilla.com).

$$$ Haus Arenberg, higher up opposite the old town, rents 17 big, breezy rooms—most with generous balconies—in a quiet garden setting (Sb-€79–88, Db-€125–142, Tb-€148–158, Qb-€158–165, €25 more during music festival, Blumensteinstrasse 8, tel. 0662/640-097, fax 0662/640-0973, www.arenberg-salzburg.at, info@arenberg-salzburg.at, family Leobacher).

Private Rooms

These are generally roomy and comfortable, and come with a good breakfast, easy parking, and tourist information. Off-season, competition softens prices. While they are a bus ride from town, with a €4.20 transit day pass *(Tageskarte)* and the frequent service, this shouldn't keep you away (see map page 249). In fact, most homeowners will happily pick you up at the train station if you simply telephone them and ask. Most will also do laundry for a small fee for those staying at least two nights. I've listed prices for two nights or more—if staying only one night, expect a 10 percent surcharge. Most push tours and concerts to make money on the side. As they are earning a commission, if you go through them, you'll probably lose the discount I've negotiated for my readers who go direct.

Beyond the Train Station

$ Brigitte Lenglachner rents eight basic, well-cared-for rooms in her home in a quiet, suburban-feeling neighborhood that's a 25-minute walk, 10-minute bike ride, or easy bus ride away from the center. Frau Lenglachner serves breakfast in the garden (in good weather) and happily provides plenty of local information and advice (S-€25, D-€40, Db-€48, T-€53, Qb-€96, 5b-€113; apartment with kitchen-€56 for Db, €90 for Tb, €110 for Qb; easy and free parking, Scheibenweg 8, tel. & fax 0662/438-044, bedandbreakfast4u@yahoo.de). It's a 10-minute walk from station: Head for the river, cross the pedestrian Pioneer Bridge

(Pioniersteg), turn right, and walk along the river to the third street (Scheibenweg). Turn left, and it's halfway down on the right.

On Moosstrasse

The busy street called Moosstrasse, which runs southwest of Mönchsberg (behind the mountain and away from the old town center), is lined with farmhouses offering rooms. To locate these places, see the map on page 249. Handy bus #21 connects Moosstrasse to the center frequently (Mon–Fri 4/hr until 19:00, Sat 4/hr until 17:00, evenings and Sun 2/hr, 20 min). To get to these pensions from the train station, take bus #1, #5, #6, or #25 to Makartplatz, where you'll change to #21. If you're coming from the old town, catch bus #21 from Hanuschplatz, just downstream of the Staatsbrücke bridge near the *Tabak* kiosk. Buy a €1.80 *Einzelkarte–Kernzone* ticket (for 1 trip) or a €4.20 *Tageskarte* (day pass, good for 24 hrs) from the streetside machine and punch it when you board the bus. The bus stop you use for each place is included in the following listings. If you're driving from the center, go through the tunnel, continue straight on Neutorstrasse, and take the fourth left onto Moosstrasse. Drivers exit the autobahn at *Süd* and then head in the direction of *Grodig*.

$$ Pension Bloberger Hof, while more a hotel than a pension, is comfortable and friendly, with a peaceful, rural location and 20 farmer-plush, good-value rooms. It's the farthest out, but reached by the same bus #21 from the center. Inge and her daughter Sylvia offer a 10 percent discount to those who have this book, reserve direct, and pay cash (Sb-€50–60, Db-€70, big new Db with balcony-€90, Db suite-€120, extra bed-€20, family apartment with kitchen, non-smoking, free Internet access and Wi-Fi, restaurant for guests, free loaner bikes, free station pick-up if staying 3 nights, Hammerauer Strasse 4, bus stop: Hammerauer Strasse, tel. 0662/830-227, fax 0662/827-061, www.blobergerhof .at, office@blobergerhof.at).

$ Frau Ballwein offers four cozy, charming, and fresh rooms in two buildings, some with intoxicating view balconies (Sb-€35–40, Db-€55–65, Tb-€78–85, Qb-€80–90, prices depend on season, family deals, cash only, farm-fresh breakfasts amid her hanging teapot collection, non-smoking, small pool, 2 free loaner bikes, free parking, Moosstrasse 69-A, bus stop: Gsengerweg, tel. & fax 0662/824-029, www.haus-ballwein.at, haus.ballwein@gmx.net).

$ Helga Bankhammer rents four nondescript rooms in a farmhouse, with a real dairy farm out back (D-€46, Db-€52, no surcharge for 1-night stays, family deals, non-smoking, laundry about €6 per load, Moosstrasse 77, bus stop: Marienbad, tel. & fax 0662/830-067, www.privatzimmer.at/helga.bankhammer, bank hammer@aon.at).

$ Haus Reichl, with three good rooms at the end of a long lane, feels the most remote. Franziska offers free loaner bike (20-min pedal to the center) and bakes fresh cakes most days (Db-€58–65, Tb-€75–85, Qb-€94–104, cash preferred, doubles and triples have balcony and view, all have tea/coffee in room, non-smoking, between Ballwein and Bankhammer B&Bs, 200 yards down Reiterweg to #52, bus stop: Gsengerweg, tel. & fax 0662/826-248, www.privatzimmer.at/haus-reichl, haus.reichl@telering.at).

EATING

In the Old Town

Salzburg boasts many inexpensive, fun, and atmospheric eateries. I'm a sucker for big cellars with their smoky, Old World atmosphere, heavy medieval arches, time-darkened paintings, antlers, hearty meals, and plump patrons. Most of these restaurants are centrally located in the old town, famous with visitors, but also enjoyed by the locals.

Gasthaus zum Wilden Mann is *the* place if the weather's bad and you're in the mood for *Hofbräu* atmosphere and a hearty, cheap meal at a shared table in one small, smoky, well-antlered room. Notice the 1899 flood photo on the wall. For a quick lunch, get the *Bauernschmaus,* a mountain of dumplings, kraut, and peasant's meats (€10.50). Owner Robert—who runs the restaurant with Schwarzenegger-like energy—enjoys fostering a convivial ambience (you'll share tables with strangers) and serving fresh traditional cuisine at great prices. I simply love this place (€7–12 daily specials, Mon–Sat 11:00–21:00, closed Sun, 2 min from Mozart's Birthplace, enter from Getreidegasse 22 or from Griesgasse 17, tel. 0662/841-787).

Stiftskeller St. Peter has been in business for more than 1,000 years—it was mentioned in the biography of Charlemagne. It's classy and central as can be, serving uninspired traditional Austrian cuisine (€10–25 meals, daily 11:30–22:30, indoor/outdoor seating, next to St. Peter's Church at foot of Mönchsberg, restaurant tel. 0662/841-268). They host the Mozart Dinner Concert described on page 251 (€48, nearly nightly at 20:00, call 0662/828-6950 to reserve, ask about a discount if you book direct with this guidebook). Through the centuries, they've learned to charge for each piece of bread and don't serve free tap water.

St. Paul's Stub'n Beer Garden is tucked secretly away under the castle with a decidedly untouristy atmosphere. The food is better than a beer hall, and a young, Bohemian-chic clientele fills its two smoky, troll-like rooms and its idyllic, tree-shaded garden. *Kasnock'n* is a tasty mountaineers' pasta with cheese served in an iron pan with a side salad for €9—it's enough for two (€6–12 daily

SALZBURG

SALZBURG RESTAURANTS

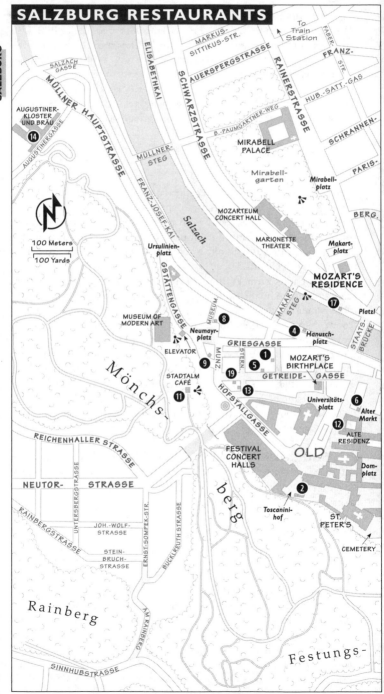

To Train Station

SALZACH GASSE

ELISABETHKAI

MARKUS-SITTIKUS-STR.

AUERSPERGSTRASSE

SCHWARZSTRASSE

RAINERSTRASSE

FRANZ-STR.

FABER-STR.

HUB.-SATT.-GAS.

SCHRANNEN-

B.-PAUMGARTNER-WEG

MIRABELL PALACE

Mirabell-garten

Mirabell-platz

PARIS-

BERG.

MÜLLNER HAUPTSTRASSE

AUGUSTINER-KLOSTER UND BRÄU

AUGUSTINERGASSE

14

MÜLLNER-STEG

FRANZ-JOSEF-KAI

Salzach

MOZARTEUM CONCERT HALL

MARIONETTE THEATER

Makart-platz

MOZART'S RESIDENCE

N

100 Meters
100 Yards

Ursulinen-platz

GSTÄTTENGASSE

MAKART-STEG

17

Platzl

STAATS-BRÜCKE

MUSEUM OF MODERN ART

ELEVATOR

Neumayr-platz

MUSEUMS-PLATZ

8

GRIESGASSE

4   Hanusch-platz

STERN.

9

MUNZ.

STADTALM CAFÉ

11

19

5

1

MOZART'S BIRTHPLACE

GETREIDE- GASSE

6

Alter Markt

Mönchs-

HOFSTALLGASSE

13

Universitäts-platz

12

ALTE RESIDENZ

REICHENHALLER STRASSE

NEUTOR- STRASSE

berg

FESTIVAL CONCERT HALLS

OLD

Dom-platz

RAINBERGSTRASSE

UNTERSBERGSTRASSE

ERNST-SOMPEK-STR.

BUCKLREUTH STRASSE

JOH.-WOLF-STRASSE

STEIN-BRUCH-STRASSE

2

Toscanini-hof

ST. PETER'S

CEMETERY

AM RAINBERG

Rainberg

SINNHUBSTRASSE

Festungs-

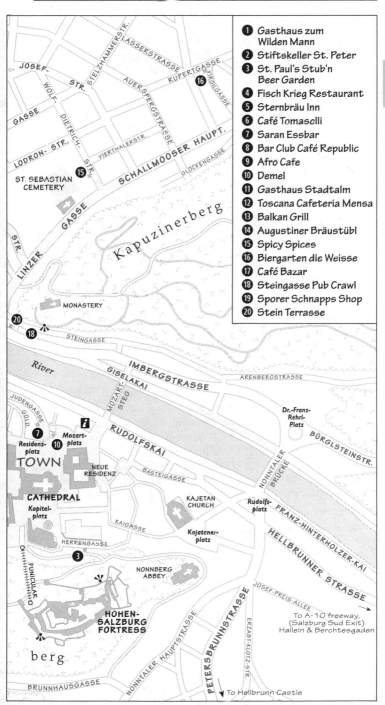

1 Gasthaus zum Wilden Mann
2 Stiftskeller St. Peter
3 St. Paul's Stub'n Beer Garden
4 Fisch Krieg Restaurant
5 Sternbräu Inn
6 Café Tomaselli
7 Saran Essbar
8 Bar Club Café Republic
9 Afro Cafe
10 Demel
11 Gasthaus Stadtalm
12 Toscana Cafeteria Mensa
13 Balkan Grill
14 Augustiner Bräustübl
15 Spicy Spices
16 Biergarten die Weisse
17 Café Bazar
18 Steingasse Pub Crawl
19 Sporer Schnapps Shop
20 Stein Terrasse

specials, €7–15 plates, Mon–Sat 17:00–22:30, open later for drinks only, closed Sun, Herrengasse 16, tel. 0662/843-220).

Fisch Krieg Restaurant, on the river where the fishermen used to sell their catch, is a great value. They serve fast, fresh, and inexpensive fish in a casual dining room—where trees grow through the ceiling—as well as great riverside seating (€2 fishwiches to go, self-serve €7 meals, salad bar, Mon–Fri 8:30–18:30, Sat 8:30–13:00 except July–Aug until 14:00, closed Sun, Hanuschplatz 4, tel. 0662/843-732).

Sternbräu Inn, a sloppy, touristy Austrian food circus, is a sprawling complex of popular eateries (traditional, Italian, self-serve, and vegetarian) in a cheery garden setting. Explore both courtyards before choosing a seat (Bürgerstube is classic, most restaurants open daily 9:00–24:00, enter from Getreidegasse 34, tel. 0662/842-140). One fancy, air-conditioned room hosts the Sound of Salzburg dinner show (see description on page 252).

Café Tomaselli (with its Kiosk annex across the way) has long been Salzburg's top place to see and be seen. While overpriced and often overcrowded, it is good for lingering and people-watching. Tomaselli serves light meals and lots of drinks, keeps long hours daily, and has fine seating on the square, a view terrace upstairs, and indoor tables. Despite its fancy inlaid wood paneling, 19th-century portraits, and chandeliers, it is surprisingly low-key (€3–7 entrées, daily 7:00–21:00, until 24:00 during music festival, Alter Markt 9, tel. 0662/844-488).

Saran Essbar is the product of hardworking Mr. Saran (from the Punjab), who cooks and serves with his heart. This delightful little eatery casts a rich orange glow under medieval vaults. Its fun menu is small (Mr. Saran is committed to both freshness and value), mixing Austrian (great schnitzel and strudel), Italian, Asian vegetarian, and salads (€9–12 meals, daily 11:00–22:00, often open later, a block off Mozartplatz at Judengasse 10, tel. 0662/846-628).

Bar Club Café Republic, a hip hangout for local young people near the end of Getreidegasse, feels like a theater lobby during intermission. It serves good food with smoky indoor and outdoor seating. It's ideal if you want something mod, untouristy, and un-wursty (trendy breakfasts 8:00–18:00, Asian and international menu, €7–12 plates, lots of hard drinks, daily until late, music with a DJ Fri and Sat from 23:00, salsa music on Tue night, no cover, Anton Neumayr Platz 2, tel. 0662/841-613).

Afro Cafe, between Getreidegasse and the Mönchsberg lift, is understandably popular with its student clientele. They serve tea, coffee, cocktails, and tasty food with a dose of '70s funk and a healthy sense of humor. The menu includes pan-African specialties—try the spicy chicken couscous—as well as standard soups and salads (€9–13 main dishes, Mon–Fri 10:00–24:00, Sat 9:00–24:00, closed Sun, between Getreidegasse and cliff face at Bürgerspitalplatz 5, tel. 0662/844-888).

Demel, the only outpost of Vienna's famed chocolatier (see page 87), is a wonderland of desserts that are as beautiful as they are delectable. Sink into the pink couches upstairs, or have them box up a treat for later (daily 9:00–19:00, near TI and cathedral at Mozartplatz 2, tel. 0662/840-358).

On the Cliffs Above the Old Town: **Gasthaus Stadtalm,** Salzburg's mountaineers' hut, sits high above the old town on the edge of the cliff with cheap prices, good food, and great views. If hiking across Mönchsberg, make this your goal (traditional food, salads, cliffside garden seating or cozy-mountain-hut indoor seating—one indoor view table is booked for a decade of New Year's celebrations, daily 10:00–19:00, July–Aug until 24:00, 2 min from top of €3 round-trip Mönchsberg elevator, also reachable by stairs from Toscanini Hof, Mönchsberg 19C, tel. 0662/841-729, Peter).

Eating Cheaply in the Old Town

Toscana Cafeteria Mensa is the students' lunch canteen, fast and cheap—with indoor seating and a great courtyard for sitting outside with students and teachers instead of tourists. They serve a daily soup-and-main course special for €5 (Mon–Fri 9:00–15:00, hot meals served 11:00–13:30 only, closed Sat–Sun, behind the Residenz, in the courtyard opposite Sigmund-Haffnergasse 16).

Sausage stands *(Würstelstände)* serve the town's favorite "fast food." The best stands (like those on Universitätsplatz) use the same boiling water all day, which gives the weenies more flavor. (For more words on *Wurst,* see page 22.) The Salzburgers' favorite spicy sausage is sold at the 60-year-old **Balkan Grill,** run by chatty Frau Ebner (€2.80; survey the five spicy options—described in English—and choose a number; take-away only, steady and sturdy local crowd, Mon–Fri 11:00–19:00, Feb–Dec also Sat 11:00–17:00, May–Dec also Sun 16:00–20:00, hours vary with  demand, hiding down the tunnel at Getreidegasse 33 across from Eisgrotte).

Picnickers will appreciate the bustling morning **produce market** (daily except Sun) on Universitätsplatz, behind Mozart's house (see page 237).

Away from the Center

Augustiner Bräustübl, a huge 1,000-seat beer garden within a monk-run brewery in the Kloster Mülln, is rustic and raw. On busy nights, it's like a Munich beer hall with no music but the volume turned up. When it's cool outside, you'll enjoy a historic setting inside beer-sloshed and smoke-stained halls. On balmy evenings, it's like a Renoir painting—but with beer breath—under chestnut trees. Local students mix with tourists eating hearty

slabs of schnitzel with their fingers or cold meals from the self-serve picnic counter, while children frolic on the playground kegs. For your beer: Pick up a half-liter or full-liter mug, pay the lady (*schank* means self-serve price, *bedienung* is the price with waiter service), wash your mug, give Mr. Keg your receipt and empty mug, and you will be made happy. Waiters only bring beer; they don't bring food—instead, go up the stairs, survey the hallway of deli counters, and assemble your own meal (or, as long as you buy a drink, you can bring in a picnic). Classic pretzels from the bakery and spiraled, salty radishes make great beer even better. For dessert—after a visit to the strudel kiosk—enjoy the incomparable floodlit view of old Salzburg from the nearby Müllnersteg pedestrian bridge and a riverside stroll home (open daily 15:00–23:00, closed for lunch, Augustinergasse 4, tel. 0662/431-246). It's about a 15-minute walk along the river (with the river on your right) from the Staatsbrücke bridge. After passing the pedestrian Müllnersteg bridge, just after Café am Kai, follow the stairs up to a busy street, and cross it. From here, either continue up more stairs into the trees and around the small church (for a scenic approach to the monastery), or stick to the sidewalk as it curves around to Augustinergasse. Either way, your goal is the huge yellow building. Don't be fooled by second-rate gardens serving the same beer nearby.

North of the River, near Recommended Linzergasse Hotels

Spicy Spices is a trippy vegetarian-Indian restaurant where Suresh Syad serves tasty take-out curry and rice, samosas, organic salads, vegan soups, and fresh juices (€6.50 specials, Mon–Fri 10:30–21:30, Sat–Sun 12:00–21:30, Wolf-Dietrich-Strasse 1, tel. 0662/870-712).

Biergarten die Weisse, close to the hotels on Rupertgasse and away from the tourists, is a longtime hit with the natives. If a beer hall can be happening, this one—modern yet with antlers—is it. Their famously good beer is made right there; favorites include their fizzy wheat beer *(Weisse)* and their seasonal beers (on request). Enjoy the beer with their good, cheap traditional food in the great garden seating, or in the wide variety of indoor rooms—sports bar, young and noisy, or older and more elegant (daily specials, Mon–Sat 10:00–24:00, closed Sun, Rupertgasse 10, east of Bayerhamerstrasse, tel. 0662/872-246).

Café Bazar, overlooking the river between Mirabell Gardens and the Staatsbrücke bridge, is as close as you'll get to a Vienna coffee house in Salzburg. It's *the* venerable spot for a classy drink with an old-town-and-castle view (light meals, Mon–Sat 7:30–23:00, Sun 9:00–18:00, Schwarzstrasse 3, tel. 0662/874-278).

Steingasse Pub Crawl

For a fun post-concert activity, crawl through medieval Steingasse's trendy pubs (all open until the wee hours). This is a local and hip scene, but accessible to older tourists: dark bars filled with well-dressed Salzburgers lazily smoking cigarettes and talking philosophy as avant-garde Euro-pop throbs on the soundtrack. Most of the pubs are in cellar-like caves...extremely atmospheric. (For more on Steingasse, see page 246.) These four pubs are all within about 100 yards of each other. Start at the Linzergasse end of Steingasse.

Pepe Cocktail Bar, with Mexican decor and Latin music, serves Mexican snacks *con* cocktails (nightly 19:00–3:00 in the morning, live DJs Fri–Sat from 19:00, Steingasse 3, tel. 0662/873-662).

Shrimps, next door and less claustrophobic, is more a restaurant than a bar, serving creative international dishes (spicy shrimp sandwiches and salads, Tue–Sun 18:00–24:00, closed Mon, Steingasse 5, tel. 0662/874-484).

Saiten Sprung wins the "Best Atmosphere" award. The door is kept closed to keep out the crude and rowdy. Ring the bell and enter its hellish interior—lots of stone and red decor, with mountains of melted wax beneath age-old candlesticks and a classic soul music ambience. Stelios, who speaks English with Greek charm, serves cocktails, fine wine, and wine-friendly Italian antipasti (nightly 21:00–4:00 in the morning, Steingasse 11, tel. 0662/881-377).

Fridrich, a tiny place next door with lots of mirrors and a silver ceiling fan, specializes in wine. Bernd Fridrich is famous for his martinis, and passionate about Austrian wines and food (€5–12 small entrées, nightly from 18:00 in summer or 17:00 in winter, Steingasse 15, tel. 0662/876-218).

SALZBURG

TRANSPORTATION CONNECTIONS

Salzburg's station, located so close to the German border, is covered not just by Austrian railpasses, but German ones as well—including the Bayern-Ticket (see page 321).

From Salzburg by Train to: Berchtesgaden (hourly, 45–60 min; bus #840 is easier—hourly, 45 min, buses leave across from Salzburg train station and also stop in Mirabellplatz and near Mozartplatz), **Innsbruck** (direct every 2 hrs, 2 hrs), **Vienna** (2/hr, 2.5–3 hrs), **Hallstatt** (hourly, 50 min to Attnang Puchheim, 20-min wait, then 90 min to Hallstatt), **Mauthausen** (hourly, 2 hrs, change in St. Valentin, allow extra 20 min to get from station to camp memorial), **Melk** (at least hourly, 2.5 hrs, transfer in Amstetten or St. Pölten), **Reutte** (hourly, 5 hrs, change either in Munich and Kempten, or in Innsbruck and Garmisch), **Munich** (2/hr, 1.5–2 hrs), **Nürnberg** (hourly with change in Munich, 3 hrs). Train info: tel. 051-717 (to get an operator, dial 2, then 2).

Route Tips for Drivers

From Salzburg to Innsbruck: To leave town driving west, go through the Mönchsberg tunnel and follow blue *A-1* signs for Munich. It's 90 minutes from Salzburg to Innsbruck.

From Salzburg to Hallstatt: Get on the Munich–Wien autobahn (follow blue *A-1* signs), head for Vienna, exit at Thalgau (#274), and follow signs to *Hof, Fuschl,* and *St. Gilgen.* The Salzburg–Hallstatt road passes two luge rides (see Hallstatt chapter), St. Gilgen (pleasant but touristy), and Bad Ischl (the center of the Salzkammergut, with a spa, the emperor's villa if you need a Habsburg history fix, and a good **TI**—Mon–Fri 8:00–18:00, Sat 9:00–15:00, Sun 10:00–13:00, tel. 06132/277-570).

BERCHTESGADEN, GERMANY

This alpine ski town in the region of the same name (just across the border in Germany's southeastern tip, 12 miles south of Salzburg) is famous for its fjord-like lake and its mountaintop Nazi retreat. Long before its association with Hitler, it was one of the classic Romantic corners of Germany. In fact, Hitler's propagandists capitalized on the Führer's love of this region to establish the notion that the native Austrian was truly German at heart.

Getting There
From Salzburg, bus #840 is more scenic and direct than the train (bus runs hourly, 45 min, €8.50 round-trip, bus station across street from Salzburg's train station, bus also stops on Mirabellplatz, and in Salzburg's old town—on Rudolfskai, near Mozartplatz).

Planning Your Time
Berchtesgaden's attractions include the **town** (a touristy mess); **salt mines** (similar to the Hallein salt mine tour—see the next page); the romantic, pristine lake called **Königsee** (extremely popular with less-adventurous Germans); and Obersalzberg with **Hitler's Eagle's Nest** (fascinating if you're into Nazi history, and stunningly scenic from the top).

ORIENTATION

Berchtesgaden can be inundated with Germans on vacation. During peak season, you may find yourself in a traffic jam of tourists desperately trying to turn their money into fun. Still, its sights are impressive, connections from Salzburg (and Munich) are excellent, and its various attractions are quite handy by local bus from the train station.

Tourist Information: The TI is across from the train station, in the yellow building with green shutters (Mon–Fri 9:00–18:00, Sat 9:00–17:00, Sun 9:00–15:00, German tel. 08652/656-500, from Austria call 00-49-8652-656-500, www.berchtesgadener-land .com).

Getting Around: From the train station, bus #840 goes to the salt mines (a 20-min walk otherwise), bus #838 goes to the Nazi Documentation Center (roughly hourly, Obersalzberg stop, plus a 5-min walk), and bus #841 goes to the Königsee (roughly hourly).

TOURS

Eagle's Nest Historical Tours—For 20 years, David and Christine Harper—who rightly consider this visit more an educational opportunity than simple sightseeing—have organized thoughtful tours of the Hitler-related sites of Berchtesgaden. Their bus tours, always led by native English speakers, depart from the TI opposite the train station (€48, €1 discount with this book, English only, daily at 13:15 mid-May–Oct, 4 hrs, 25 people maximum, reservation required, German tel. 08652/64971, from Austria call 00-49-8652-64971, www.eagles-nest-tours.com). While the price is €48, your actual cost for the guiding is only about €23, as the tour includes the (otherwise obligatory) bus connections and admissions. They also arrange private guides and *Sound of Music* excursions to Salzburg (see their website for details).

SIGHTS

▲Salt Mines

At the Berchtesgaden salt mines, you put on traditional miners' outfits, get on funny little trains, and zip deep into the mountain. For two hours, you'll cruise subterranean lakes; slide speedily down two long, slick, wooden banisters; and learn how they mined salt so long ago. Call for crowd-avoidance advice. When the weather gets bad, this place is mobbed. You can buy a ticket early and browse through the town until your appointed tour time. Tours are in German, while English-speakers get audioguides (€14, daily May–Oct 9:00–17:00, Nov–April 11:30–15:00, German tel. 08652/60020, from Austria tel. 00-49-8652-60020, www .salzzeitreise.de).

▲Königsee

The idyllic Königsee stretches like a fjord through pristine mountain scenery from Berchtesgaden to the dramatically situated Church of St. Bartholomew, and beyond. Most visitors simply

NEAR BERCHTESGADEN

To Vienna

To Vienna

AUTOBAHN A-1

To Munich

Freilassing

TRAIN STATION

158

Salzburg

To Salzkammergut & Hallstatt

AUSTRIA

A-8

SALZBURG SUD EXIT

Untersberg

Hallein

SALT MINE

GERMANY

305

Unterau

SALT MINES

NAZI DOCUMENTATION CENTER

Ober-salzberg

A-10

Berchtesgaden

Kehlstein

HITLER'S EAGLE'S NEST

2 Kilometers

2 Miles

Königsee

ROAD OPEN TO SHUTTLE BUS ONLY

Königsee

To Villach, Italy & Slovenia

St. Bartholomew

glide scenically for 35 minutes on the silent, electronically propelled boat to the church, enjoy that peaceful setting, then glide back. Boats, going at a sedate Bavarian speed and filled with Germans chuckling at the captain's commentary, leave with demand—usually three per hour (€12 round-trip, bus #841 runs about hourly from train station to boat dock, parking-€3). At a rock cliff midway through the journey, your captain stops, and the first mate pulls out a trumpet to demonstrate the fine echo.

The remote, red-onion–domed **Church of St. Bartholomew** (once home of a monastery, then a hunting lodge of the Bavarian royal family) is surrounded by a fine beer garden, rustic fishermen's pub, and inviting lakeside trails. The family next to St. Bartholomew's lives in the middle of this national park and has a license to fish—so very fresh trout is the lunchtime favorite.

▲▲▲Obersalzberg and Hitler's Eagle's Nest (Kehlsteinhaus)

Early in his career as a wannabe tyrant, Adolf Hitler was inspired by this dramatic corner of Bavaria, so steeped in legend and close to the soul of the German people.
This place, partly Austrian and partly Bavarian, held a special appeal to the Austrian-German Hitler. In the 1920s, just out of prison, he checked into an alpine hotel here to finish up work on his memoir and Nazi primer, *Mein Kampf.* Because it was here that he claimed to be inspired and laid out his vision, some call Obersalzberg the "cradle of the Third Reich."

In the 1930s, as the German Führer, Hitler chose this place for his mountain retreat (and later, had it prepared for his last stand). His handlers crafted Hitler's image here—surrounded by nature, gently receiving alpine flowers from adoring little children, lounging around with farmers in lederhosen...no modern arms industry, no big-time industrialists, no ugly extermination camps. In reality, rather than an alpine chalet, it was a huge compound of 80 buildings—closed to the public after 1936—where the major decisions leading up to World War II were hatched. It was here that Hitler hosted world leaders, wowing them with the aesthetics and engineering of his mountain palace, the adoration of his people...and National Socialism.

Orientation: Your visit has three parts: the Obersalzberg complex and its small, modern **Nazi Documentation Center museum** (a short bus ride from Berchtesgaden, with free parking; also the terminus for the shuttle bus providing the only access to the Eagle's Nest high above); the vast and tourable remains of the **bunker system** (below the museum and included in that ticket); and the actual **Eagle's Nest** (a small yet mighty stone chalet capping the mountain high above).

Between 1945 and 1952, almost everything was destroyed by the victorious Allies (wanting to leave nothing as a magnet for future neo-Nazi pilgrims). If looking for pre-1945 artifacts, you'll only see this: the foundations of the Documentation Center (now mostly a modern building); the stripped-bare yet still evocative bunkers under it; the dramatic road to the Eagle's Nest; the stone-work, elevator, and fireplace of the Eagle's Nest itself; and a very few papers and memorabilia in glass cases in the Documentation Center.

Nazi Documentation Center: This exhibit is built upon the remains of what was the second seat of Nazi administration. It's

small—three floors of exhibits—with almost no actual artifacts, but evocative for the setting. This center, with only German descriptions (rent the €2 English audioguide), is designed primarily for Germans to learn and understand their recent history. Only since the late 1990s has interest in Nazi history been considered healthy rather than

taboo. Non-Germans, too, can learn from a thoughtful visit (€3; April–Oct daily 9:00–17:00; Nov–March Tue–Sun 10:00–15:00, closed Mon; last entry one hour before closing, allow 90 min for visit, German tel. 08652/947-960, from Austria tel. 00-49-8652-947-960, www.obersalzberg.de). Buses depart from here to the Eagle's Nest.

Bunkers: From the Documentation Center, stairs lead into a complex and vast bunker system (same ticket and hours as Documentation Center). Construction began in 1943, after the Battle of Stalingrad ended the Nazi aura of invincibility. This is an incredibly engineered underground town with meeting rooms, offices, archives for the government, and lavish living quarters for Hitler—all connected by four miles of tunnels cut by slave labor through solid rock. It was stripped bare after the war. Today, you can wander among the concrete and marvel at megalomania gone mad.

Eagle's Nest: Many call the entire area "Hitler's Eagle's

Nest," but that name actually belongs only to the mountaintop chalet, given to the Führer for his 50th birthday in 1939. While a fortune was spent to build this perch, Hitler made only 14 official visits. Today, the chalet is basi-cally a restaurant with a scenic terrace 100 yards below the summit of a mountain. The views are magnificent. From the bus stop, a finely crafted tunnel (which will have you humming the *Get Smart* TV theme song) leads to a polished brass elevator—one of the rare original elements of the complex. Wander into the fancy back dining room (the best-preserved from Hitler's time) where you can see the once-sleek marble fireplace chipped up by souvenir-seeking troops in 1945.

The site is open to visitors from mid-May through October (in snowy conditions, however, the shuttle bus may stop running). Catch the bus at the parking lot at the Documentation Center. It costs €15 for the round-trip bus ride up the private road and the lift to the top (a 2,000-foot altitude gain, leaves twice hourly).

HALLSTATT
and the
SALZKAMMERGUT

Commune with nature in Austria's Salzkammergut Lake District. "The hills are alive," and you're surrounded by the loveliness that has turned on everyone from Emperor Franz Josef to Julie Andrews. This is *Sound of Music* country. Idyllic and majestic, but not rugged, it's a gentle land of lakes, forested mountains, and storybook villages, rich in hiking opportunities and inexpensive lodging. Settle down in the postcard-pretty, lake-cuddling town of Hallstatt.

Planning Your Time

While there are plenty of lakes and charming villages in the Salzkammergut, Hallstatt is really the only one that matters. One night and a few hours to browse are all you'll need to fall in love. To relax or take a hike in the surroundings, give it two nights and a day. It's a relaxing break between Vienna and Salzburg.

ORIENTATION

(area code: 06134)
Lovable Hallstatt is a tiny town bullied onto a ledge between a selfish mountain and a swan-ruled lake, with a waterfall ripping furiously through its middle. It can be toured on foot in about 15 minutes. The town is one of Europe's oldest, going back centuries before Christ. The symbol of Hallstatt, which you'll see all over town, consists of two adjacent spirals—a design based on jewelry found in Bronze Age Celtic graves high in the nearby mountains.

The charms of Hallstatt are the village and its lakeside setting. Go there to relax, nibble, wander, and paddle. While tourist crowds can trample much of Hallstatt's charm in August, the place is almost dead in the off-season. The lake is famous for its good fishing and pure water.

Two tiny boat docks serve town: The "main" dock, where boats from the train station arrive, is in the center of town; the Lahn boat dock is on the south end of town, near a small grocery store (see page 296) and the town's bus stop.

Tourist Information

At the helpful TI, located on the main drag above the "Post Partner," Claudia and her staff can explain hikes and excursions, and find you a room (July–Aug Mon–Fri 9:00–17:00, Sat 10:00–14:00, closed Sun; Sept–June Mon–Fri 9:00–12:00 & 14:00–17:00, closed Sat–Sun; one block from Market Square, across from museum at Seestrasse 169, tel. 06134/8208, www.inneres -salzkammergut.at, hallstatt@inneres-salzkammergut.at).

In the summer, the TI offers 90-minute **walking tours** of the town in English and German (€4, May–Sept Sat at 10:00, July–Aug also Wed at 10:00, confirm schedule at TI). They can arrange private tours for €75.

Arrival in Hallstatt

By Train: If you're coming on the main train line that runs between Salzburg and Vienna, you'll change trains at Attnang-Puchheim to get to Hallstatt (you won't see Hallstatt on the schedules, but trains to Ebensee and Bad Ischl stop here). Day-trippers can check their bags at the Attnang-Puchheim station (follow signs for *Schliessfächer*, coin-op lockers are at the street,  curbside near track 1, €2.50/24 hrs, a ticket serves as your key). Note: Connections can be fast—check the TV monitor.

Hallstatt's train station is a wide spot on the tracks across the lake from town. *Stefanie* (a boat) meets you at the station and glides scenically across the lake into town (€2.20, meets each train until about 18:30—don't arrive after that). The last departing boat-train connection leaves Hallstatt at about 18:00, and the first boat goes in the morning at 6:50 (9:20 on Sun). Once in Hallstatt, walk left from the boat dock for the TI and most hotels. Since there's no train station in town, the TI can help you find schedule information, or check www.oebb.at.

By Car: The main road skirts Hallstatt via a long tunnel above the town. Hallstatt has several numbered parking areas outside the town center. Parking lot #1 is in the tunnel above the town (often full mid-June–mid-Oct; swing through to check for a spot). If it's full, try lot #2, just after the tunnel, a lovely 10- to 20-minute lakeside walk from the town center. More lots are available away from town.

If you have a hotel reservation, the guard will let you drive into town to drop your bags; ask your hotel if it has any in-town parking when you book. Parking is free with a guest card (available from your hotel), and it's a laid-back system—just show your card later. Without a guest card, per-day parking is still quite reasonable (lot #1: €4.20/day, lot #2: €6/day; less after 14:00). Off-season (Nov–April), parking in town is easy and free.

Helpful Hints

Internet Access: Try **Hallstatt Umbrella Bar** (€4/hr, summers only, weather permitting—since it's literally under a big umbrella, halfway between Lahn boat dock and Museum Square at Seestrasse 145). You can get online all year at the **Lakeside Lounge** (€4/hr, daily 10:00–22:00, between Museum Square and Market Square at Badergraben 188).

Laundry: A small full-service **launderette** is at the campground up from the town's man-made island, Bade-Insel, just off the main road (about €8/load, mid-April–mid-Oct daily 8:00–12:00 & 14:00–20:00, closed off-season, tel. 06134/83224). In the center, **Hotel Grüner Baum** does laundry for non-guests (€13/load, on Market Square, see "Sleeping").

Bike Rental: See page 288.

Boat Rental: Two places rent electric boats; both rent from two locations in high season. **Riedler** is next to the main boat dock, and 75 yards past Bräugasthof (€14/hr, tel. 06134/8320). **Hemetsberger** is near Gasthof Simony, and the Lahn boat dock (€12/hr, tel. 06134/8228). Both are open daily until 19:00 in peak season and in good weather. Boats have two speeds: slow and stop (spend an extra €3/hr for faster 500-watt boats). Both places also rent rowboats and paddleboats.

Parks and Swimming: Green and peaceful lakeside parks line the south end of Lake Hallstatt. If you walk 10 minutes south of town to Hallstatt-Lahn, you'll find a grassy public park, playground, mini-golf, and swimming area *(Badestrand)* with the fun Bade-Insel play-island.

Views: For a great view over Hallstatt, hike above Helga Lenz's B&B as far as you like (see page 295), or climb any path leading up the hill. The 40-minute steep hike down from the salt-mine tour gives the best views (see page 286). While most visitors stroll the lakeside drag between the old and new parts of town, make a point to do the trip once by taking the more higgledy-piggledy high lane called Dr.-Morton-Weg.

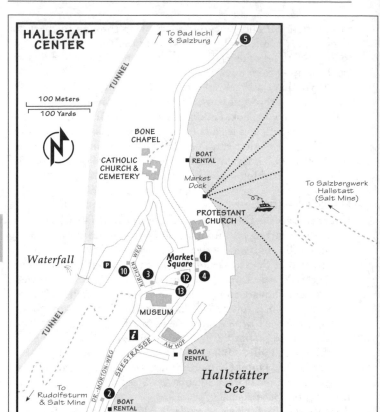

HALLSTATT

HALLSTATT CENTER

100 Meters
100 Yards

To Bad Ischl & Salzburg

BONE CHAPEL

CATHOLIC CHURCH & CEMETERY

BOAT RENTAL

Market Dock

To Salzbergwerk Hallstatt (Salt Mine)

PROTESTANT CHURCH

Waterfall

KIRCHEN WEG

Market Square

MUSEUM

AM HOF

BOAT RENTAL

Hallstätter See

TUNNEL

TUNNEL

SEESTRASSE

DR. MORTON-WEG

To Rudolfsturm & Salt Mine

BOAT RENTAL

ECHERNTAL

ECHERNTALWEG

① Hotel/Rest. Grüner Baum
② Bräugasthof Hallstatt
③ Gasthof Zauner
④ Gasthof Simony
⑤ Pension Sarstein
⑥ Gasthof Pension Grüner Anger
⑦ Helga Lenz Rooms
⑧ Haus Trausner
⑨ Herta Höll Rooms
⑩ Gasthaus zur Mühle Hostel & Pizza
⑪ Strand Café
⑫ Ruth Zimmerman Pub
⑬ Internet Access (2)
⑭ Launderette/Campgrounds

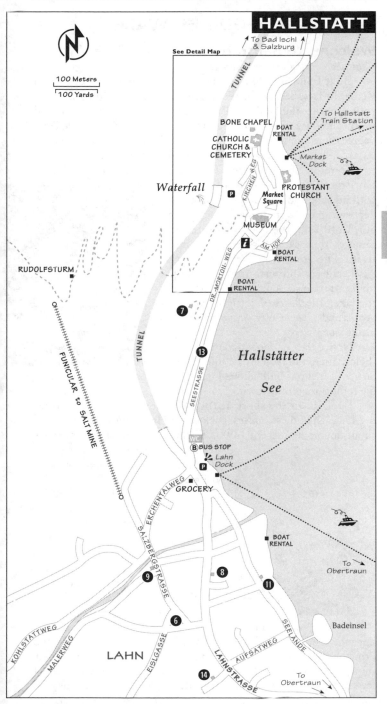

HALLSTATT

100 Meters
100 Yards

To Bad Ischl & Salzburg

See Detail Map

TUNNEL

BONE CHAPEL

BOAT RENTAL

CATHOLIC CHURCH & CEMETERY

To Hallstatt Train Station

Market Dock

KIRCHEN WEG

Waterfall

Market Square

PROTESTANT CHURCH

MUSEUM

AM HOF

RUDOLFSTURM

DR. MORTON-WEG

BOAT RENTAL

BOAT RENTAL

TUNNEL

7

FUNICULAR to SALT MINE

13

SEESTRASSE

Hallstätter

See

WC

B BUS STOP

Lahn Dock

ERCHENTALWEG

GROCERY

SALZBERGSTRASSE

BOAT RENTAL

To Obertraun

9

8

11

6

KOHLSTATTWEG

MALERWEG

EISLGASSE

LAHN

AUFSATWEG

SEELÄNDE

Badeinsel

14

LAHNSTRASSE

To Obertraun

HALLSTATT

SELF-GUIDED WALK

Welcome to Hallstatt

• *This short walk starts at the dock.*

Boat Landing: There was a Hallstatt before there was a Rome. In fact, because of the importance of salt mining here, an entire epoch—the Hallstatt Era, from 800 to 400 B.C.—is named for this important spot. Through the centuries, salt was traded and people came and went by boat. You'll still see the traditional *Fuhr* boats, designed to carry heavy loads in shallow water.

Towering above the town is the Catholic church. Its faded St. Christopher—patron saint of travelers, with his cane and baby Jesus on his shoulder—watched over those sailing in and out. Until 1875, the town was extremely remote...then came a real road and the train. The good ship *Stefanie* shuttles travelers back and forth from here to the Hallstatt train station, immediately across the lake. The *Bootverleih* sign advertises boat rentals. By the way, *Schmuck* is not an insult...it's jewelry.

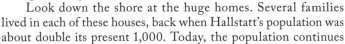

Notice the one-lane road out of town (below the church). Until 1966, when a bigger tunnel was built above Hallstatt, all the traffic crept single-file right through the town.

Look down the shore at the huge homes. Several families lived in each of these houses, back when Hallstatt's population was about double its present 1,000. Today, the population continues

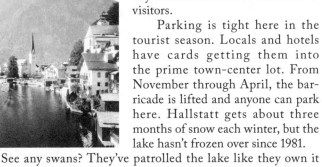

to shrink, and many of these generally underused houses rent rooms to visitors.

Parking is tight here in the tourist season. Locals and hotels have cards getting them into the prime town-center lot. From November through April, the barricade is lifted and anyone can park here. Hallstatt gets about three months of snow each winter, but the lake hasn't frozen over since 1981.

See any swans? They've patrolled the lake like they own it since the 1860s, when Emperor Franz Josef and Empress Sisi—the Princess Diana of her day (see page 112)—made this region their annual holiday retreat. Sisi loved swans, so locals made sure she'd see them here. During this period, the Romantics discovered

Hallstatt, many top painters worked here, and the town got its first hotel. Today, that hotel (the big, derelict Haus Kranz facing the square) has an absentee owner and a floor plan so tangled that it's too expensive to renovate, so it just sits, looking ugly in the heart of Hallstatt.

Tiny Hallstatt has two big churches—Protestant (bordering the square on the left, with a grassy lakeside playground) and Catholic up above (with its fascinating bone chapel—described under "Sights and Activities," page 285).

• *Walk over the town's stream, and pop into the...*

Protestant Church: In 1860, Emperor Franz Josef allowed non-Catholic Christians to build churches. Before that, they were allowed only to worship in low-key "houses of prayer." Back then, the Catholic Church was the church of royalty and the wealthy. The working class was more likely to be Protestant. As this was a mining town, it was quite Protestant. In 1863, the miners pooled their humble resources and built this fine church. Step inside (free and often open). It's very plain, emphasizing the pulpit and organ rather than fancy art and saints. Check out the portraits: Martin Luther (left of altar), the town in about 1865 with its new church (left wall), and a century of pastors.

• *Continue past the church to the...*

Market Square (Marktplatz): In 1750, a fire leveled this part of town. The buildings you see now are all late 18th-century and built of stone rather than flammable wood. The three big buildings on the left are government-subsidized housing (mostly for seniors and people with health problems). Take a close look at the two-dimensional, up-against-the-wall pear tree (it likes the sun-warmed wall). The statue features the Holy Trinity.

• *Continue a block past Gasthof Simony. At the first corner, just before the Gemeindeamt (City Hall), jog left across the little square and then right down the tiny lane marked* Am Hof, *which leads through an intimate bit of domestic town architecture, boat houses, lots of firewood, and maybe a couple of swans hanging out. The lane circles back to the main drag and the...*

Museum Square: Because 20th-century Hallstatt was of no industrial importance, it was untouched by World War II. But once upon a time, its salt was worth defending. High above, peeking out of the trees, is Rudolfsturm (Rudolf's Tower). Originally a 13th-century watchtower protecting the salt mines, and later the mansion of a salt-mine boss, it's now a restaurant with a great view. A zigzag trail connects the town with Rudolfsturm and the salt mines just beyond. The big, white houses by the waterfall were water-powered mills that once ground Hallstatt's grain. (If you hike up a few blocks, you'll see the river raging through town.)

Around you are the town's TI, post office, museum, City Hall, and Dachstein Sport Shop (described later). A statue recalls the mine manager who excavated prehistoric graves in about 1850. Much of the *Schmuck* sold locally is inspired by the jewelry found in the area's Bronze Age tombs.

The memorial wooden stairs in front of the museum are a copy of those found in Hallstatt's prehistoric mine—the original stairs are more than 2,500 years old. For thousands of years, people have been leaching salt out of this mountain. A brine spring sprung here, attracting Bronze Age people in about 1600 B.C. Later, they dug tunnels to mine the rock (which was 70 percent salt), dissolved it into a brine, and distilled out the salt—precious for preserving meat. For a look at early salt-mining implements and the town's story, visit the museum (described under "Sights and Activities").

Across from the TI, Pension Hallberg has a quirky hallway full of Nazi paraphernalia and other stuff found on the lake bed (€1). Only recently did local divers realize that, for centuries, the lake had been Hallstatt's garbage can. If something was *kaput,* locals would just toss it into the lake. In 1945, Nazi medals decorating German and Austrian war heroes suddenly became dangerous to own. Throughout the former Third Reich, hard-earned medals floated down to lonely lake beds, including Hallstatt's.

Under the TI is the "Post Partner"—a government-funded attempt to turn inefficient post offices into something more viable (selling souvenirs, renting bikes, and employing people with disabilities who otherwise wouldn't work). The *Fischerei* provides the town with its cherished fresh lake fish. The county allows two commercial fishermen on the lake. They spread their nets each morning and sell their catch here to town restaurants, or to any locals cooking up a special dinner (Mon–Fri 9:00–12:00, closed Sat–Sun).

• *Nearby, still on Museum Square, find the...*

Dachstein Sport Shop: During a renovation project, the builders dug down and hit a Celtic and ancient Roman settlement. Peek through the glass pavement on the covered porch to see where the Roman street level was. If the shop is open, pop in and go downstairs (free). You'll walk on Roman flagstones and see the small gutter that channeled water to power an ancient hammer mill (used to pound iron into usable shapes). In prehistoric times, people lived near the mines. Romans were the first Hallstatt lakeside settlers. The store's owners are committed to sharing Hallstatt's fascinating history, and often display old town paintings and folk art.

• *From this square, the first right (after the bank) leads up a few stairs to...*

Dr.-Morton-Weg: House #26A dates from 1597. Follow the lane uphill to the left past more old houses. Until 1890, this was the town's main drag, and the lake lapped at the lower doors of these houses. Therefore, many main entrances were via the attic, from this level. Enjoy this back-street view of town. Just after the arch, near #133, check out the old tools hanging outside the workshop, and the piece of wooden piping. It's a section taken from the 25-mile wooden pipeline that carried salt brine from Hallstatt to Ebensee. This was in place from 1595 until the last generation, when the last stretch of wood was replaced by plastic piping. At the pipe, enjoy the lake view and climb down the stairs. From lake level, look back up at the striking traditional architecture (the fine woodwork on the left was recently rebuilt after a fire; parts of the old house on the right date to medieval times).

• *Your tour is finished. From here, you have boat rentals, the salt-mine tour, the town museum, and the Catholic church (with its bone chapel) all within a few minutes' walk.*

SIGHTS AND ACTIVITIES

▲▲Catholic Church and Bone Chapel—Hallstatt's Catholic church overlooks the town from above. From near the main boat dock, hike up the covered wooden stairway and follow the *Kath. Kirche* signs. The lovely church has twin altars. The one on the left was made by town artists in 1897. The one on the right is more historic—dedicated in 1515 to Mary, who's flanked by St. Barbara (on right, patron of miners) and St. Catherine (on left, patron of foresters—a lot of wood was needed to fortify the many miles of tunnels, and to boil the brine to distill out the salt).

Behind the church, in the well-tended graveyard, is the 12th-century Chapel of St. Michael (even older than the church). Its bone chapel—or charnel house *(Beinhaus)*—contains more than 600 painted skulls. Each skull has been lovingly named, dated, and decorated (skulls with dark, thick garlands are oldest—18th century; those with flowers are more recent—19th century). Space was so limited in this cemetery that bones had only 12 peaceful, buried years here before making way for the freshly dead. Many of the dug-up bones and skulls ended up in this chapel. They stopped this practice in the 1960s, about the same time the Catholic

Church began permitting cremation. But one woman (who died in 1983) managed to sneak her skull in later (dated 1995, under the cross, with the gold tooth). The skulls on the books are those of priests (€1, free English flier, daily May–Sept 10:00–18:00, Oct 10:00–16:00, closed Nov–April, tel. 06134/8279).

▲**Hallstatt Museum**—This pricey little museum tells the story of Hallstatt. It focuses on the Hallstatt Era (800–400 B.C.), when this village was the salt-mining hub of a culture that spread from France to the Balkans. Back then, Celtic tribes dug for precious salt, and Hallstatt was, as its name means, the "place of salt." While its treasures are the countless artifacts excavated from prehistoric gravesites around the mine, you'll get the whole gamut—with displays on everything from the region's flora and fauna to local artists and the surge in Hallstatt tourism during the Romantic Age. Since the museum recently posted English explanations, the skimpy €3 English guide is not worth buying (€7.50, May–Sept daily 9:00–18:00, shorter hours off-season, closed Mon–Tue Nov–March, adjacent to TI at Seestrasse 56, tel. 06134/828-015). On summer Tuesdays, when candlelit boats run, the museum stays open until 20:00 (see "candlelit boat rides" under "Nightlife," page 292).

▲**Lake Trip**—For a quick boat trip, you can ride the *Stefanie* across the lake and back for €4.40. It stops at the tiny Hallstatt train station for 30 minutes (note return time in the boat's window), giving you time to walk to a hanging bridge (ask the captain to point you to the *Hängebrücke*—HENG-eh-brick-eh—a 10-minute lakeside stroll to the left). Longer lake tours are also available (€8/50 min, €9.50/75 min, sporadic schedules—especially off-season—so check chalkboards by boat docks for today's times). Those into relaxation can rent a sleepy electric motorboat to enjoy town views from the water (see page 279).

▲**Salt-Mine Tour**—If you have yet to tour a salt mine, consider visiting Hallstatt's, which claims to be the oldest in the world. First, you'll ride a steep funicular high above the town (€10 round-trip, €6 one-way, 4/hr, daily May–mid-Sept 9:00–18:00, mid-Sept–Oct 9:00–16:30, closed Nov–April). Then you'll hike 10 minutes to the mine (past excavation sites of many prehistoric tombs and

a glass case with 2,500-year-old bones—but there's little to actually see). Report back 10 minutes before the tour time on your ticket, check your bag, and put on old miners' clothes. Then hike 200 yards higher in your funny outfit to meet your guide, who escorts your group down a tunnel dug in 1719. Inside the mountain, you'll watch a slide show, follow your guide through several caverns as you learn about mining techniques over the last 7,000 years, see a silly laser show on a glassy subterranean lake, peek at a few waxy cavemen with pickaxes, and ride the train out. The highlight for most is sliding down two banisters (the second one is longer and ends with a flash for an automatic souvenir photo that clocks your speed—see how you did compared to the rest of your group after the tour).

The presentation is very low-tech, as the mining company owns all three mine tours in the area and sees little reason to invest in the experience when they can simply mine the tourists. While the tour is mostly in German, the guide is required to speak English if you ask...so ask (salt-mine tour–€16, €22 combo-ticket for mine and funicular round-trip saves about €4, you can buy mine tickets at cable-car station—note the time and tour number on your ticket, daily May–mid-Sept 9:00–16:30, mid-Sept–Oct 9:00–15:00, closed Nov–April, the 16:00 funicular departure catches the last tour at 16:30, no children under age 4, arrive early or late to avoid summer crowds, dress for the constant 47-degree temperature, tel. 06132/200-2400). If you skip the funicular, the scenic 40-minute hike back into town is (with strong knees) a joy.

At the base of the funicular, notice train tracks leading to the Erbstollen tunnel entrance. This lowest of the salt tunnels goes many miles into the mountain, where a shaft connects it to the tunnels you just explored. Today, the salty brine from these tunnels flows 25 miles through the world's oldest pipeline—made of wood until quite recently—to the huge modern salt works (next to the highway) at Ebensee.

▲**Local Hikes**—Mountain-lovers, hikers, and spelunkers who use Hallstatt as their home base keep busy for days (ask the TI for ideas). A good, short, and easy walk is the two-hour round-trip up the Echern Valley to the Waldbachstrub waterfall and back: From the parking lot, follow signs to the salt mines, then follow the little wooden signs marked *Echerntalweg*. With a car, consider hiking around nearby Altaussee (flat, 3-hr hike) or along Grundlsee to Toplitzsee. Regular buses connect Hallstatt with

(side tab) HALLSTATT

Gosausee for a pleasant hour-long walk around that lake. Or consider walking nine miles halfway around Lake Hallstatt via the town of Steeg (boat to train station, walk left along lake and past idyllic farmsteads, returning to Hallstatt along the old salt trail, *Soleleitungsweg*); for a shorter hike, walk to Steeg along either side of the lake, and catch the train from Steeg back to Hallstatt's station. The TI can also recommend a great two-day hike with an overnight in a nearby mountain hut.

Biking—The best two bike rides take nearly the same routes as the hikes listed previously: up the Echern Valley, and around the lake (bikers do better going via Obertraun along the new lakeside bike path—start with a ride on the *Stefanie*). Two places in town rent bikes: **Post Partner** (the stamp-selling place formerly known as the post office; €5/2 hrs, €9/half-day, €13/day, €30/weekend rental—Fri–Mon, open Mon–Fri 8:00–12:00 & 14:30–16:00, closed Sat–Sun, on Museum Square, tel. 06134/8201) and **Hotel Grüner Baum** (€2.50/hr, €9/half-day, €16/day, on Market Square, see "Sleeping").

Near Hallstatt

▲▲**Dachstein Mountain Cable Car and Caves**—For a refreshing activity, ride a scenic cable car up a mountain to visit huge, chilly caves.

Dachstein Cable Car: From Obertraun, three miles beyond Hallstatt on the main road (or directly across the lake as the crow flies), a mighty gondola goes in three stages high up the Dachstein Plateau—crowned by Dachstein, the highest mountain in the Salzkammergut (9,800 ft). The first segment stops at Schönbergalm (4,500 ft, runs May–Oct), which has a mountain restaurant and two huge caves (described next). The second segment goes to the summit of Krippenstein (6,600 ft, runs mid-May–Oct). The third segment descends to Gjaidalm (5,800 ft, runs mid-June–Oct), where several hikes begin. For a quick high-country experience, Krippenstein is better than Gjaidalm. From Krippenstein, you'll survey a scrubby, limestone, karstic landscape (which absorbs, through its many cracks, the rainfall that ultimately carves all those caves) with 360-degree views of the surrounding mountains (round-trip cable-car ride to Schönbergalm and the caves-€15, to Krippenstein-€22, to Gjaidalm-€24; combo-ticket covering ride to Gjaidalm and entry to both caves-€35; cheaper family rates available, last cable car back down usually at about 17:00, tel. 06131/51310, www.dachsteinwelterbe.at).

Giant Ice Caves (Riesen-Eishöhle, 4,500 ft): These were discovered in 1910. Today, guides lead tours in German and English on an hour-long, half-mile hike through an eerie, icy, subterranean world, passing limestone canyons the size of subway stations. The limestone caverns, carved by rushing water, are named for scenes from Wagner's operas—the favorite of the mountaineers who first came here. If you're nervous, note that the iron oxide covering the ceiling takes 5,000 years to form. Things are very stable.

At the lift station, report to the ticket window to get your cave appointment. The temperature is just above freezing, and although the 700 steps help keep you warm, you'll want to bring a sweater. Allow 90 minutes, including the 10-minute hike up from the station (€10, €15 combo-ticket with Mammoth Caves, €35 combo-ticket covers the cable car up to Gjaidalm and entry to both caves, open May–Oct, hour-long tours start at 9:00, last tour at 15:30, stay in front and assert yourself to get English information, tel. 06131/51310).

Drop by the little free museum near the lift station—in a local-style wood cabin designed to support 200 tons of snow—to see the cave-system model, exhibits about its exploration, and info about life in the caves.

Mammoth Caves (Mammuthöhle): While huge and well-promoted, these are much less interesting than the ice caves and—for most—not worth the time. Of the 30-mile limestone labyrinth excavated so far, you'll walk a half-mile with a German-speaking guide (€10, €15 combo-ticket with ice caves, €35 combo-ticket covers the cable car up to Gjaidalm and entry to both caves, open May–Oct, hour-long tours in English and German 10:00–15:00, entrance a 10-min hike from lift station).

Combo-Ticket Tips: The several combo-tickets available generally won't save you any money over buying individual tickets. But if you're gung-ho enough to want to visit one or both caves, and plan to ride the cable car farther up the mountain, the €35 same-day combo-ticket makes sense (covers the cable car all the way to Gjaidalm and back, as well as entry to both caves; it's slightly cheaper to buy separate tickets if you're riding only to Krippenstein and skipping one of the caves).

Getting to Obertraun: The cable car to Dachstein leaves from the outskirts of Obertraun, across the lake from Hallstatt. To reach the Obertraun cable car from Hallstatt, the handiest and cheapest option is the bus (€1.70, 5–6/day, leaves from Lahn boat dock, drops you directly at cable-car station). Romantics can take the boat to Obertraun (€5, 5/day July–Aug, 4/day Sept–June, 15 min)—but it's a 40-minute hike from there to the lift station. The impatient can consider hitching a ride—virtually all cars leaving Hallstatt to the south will pass through Obertraun in a few minutes.

SALZKAMMERGUT

Returning to Hallstatt: Plan to leave by mid-afternoon. The last bus from the cable-car station back to Hallstatt (at 17:05 in summer) inconveniently leaves before the last cable car down—if you miss the bus, try getting a ride from a fellow cable-car passenger. Otherwise, you can either call a taxi (€13, ask cable-car staff for help), or simply walk back along the lakefront (about one hour).

Luge Rides *(Sommerrodelbahnen)* **on the Hallstatt-Salzburg Road**—If you're driving between Salzburg and Hallstatt, you'll pass two luge rides. Each is a ski lift that drags you backward up the hill as you sit on your go-cart. At the top, you ride the cart down the winding metal course. It's easy: Push to go, pull to stop, take your hands off your stick and you get hurt. For more details, see "Luge Lesson" on page 359.

Each course is just off the road with easy parking. The ride up and down takes about 15 minutes. The one near Fuschlsee (closest to Salzburg, look for *Sommerrodelbahn* sign) is half as long and cheaper (€4.30/ride, 1,970 ft, tel. 06235/7297). The one near Wolfgangsee (look for *Riesenschutzbahn* sign) is a double course, more scenic with grand lake views (€6.40/ride, €43/10 rides, 4,265 ft, each track is the same speed, tel. 06137/7085). Courses are open May (or earlier) through October from 10:00 to 18:00 (Wolfgangsee luge also open July–Aug 9:30–20:00)—but generally close in bad weather. These are fun, but the concrete courses near Reutte are better (see page 358).

NIGHTLIFE

Locals would laugh at the thought. But if you do want some action after dinner, you do have a few options: **Gasthaus zur Mühle** (youth hostel with a rustic sports-bar ambience in its restaurant when drinks replace the food, open late, closed Tue Sept–mid-May, run by Ferdinand). Or, for your late-night drink, savor the Market Square from the trendy little pub called **Ruth Zimmermann,** where locals congregate with soft music, a good selection of drinks, two small rooms, and tables on the square (daily May–Sept 10:00–2:00 in the morning, Oct–April 11:00–2:00, tel. 06134/8306). In July and August, **candlelit boat rides** leave at 20:30 on Tuesday evenings (€12.50, €16 combo-ticket with Hallstatt Museum).

SLEEPING

Hallstatt's TI can almost always find you a room (either in town or at B&Bs and small hotels outside of town—which are more likely to have rooms available and come with easy parking). Drivers, remember to ask if your hotel has in-town parking when you book your room.

Mid-July and August can be tight. Early August is worst. Hallstatt is not the place to splurge—some of the best rooms are *Privatzimmer,* just as nice and modern as rooms in bigger hotels, at half the cost. In summer, a double bed in a private home costs about €50 with breakfast. It's hard to get a one-night advance reservation (try calling the TI for help). But if you drop in and they have a spot, one-nighters are welcome. Prices include breakfast, lots of stairs, and a silent night. *"Zimmer mit Aussicht?"* (TSIM-mer mit OWS-zeekt) means "Room with view?"—worth asking for.

Sleep Code

(€1 = about $1.40, country code: 43, area code: 06134)
S = Single, **D** = Double/Twin, **T** = Triple, **Q** = Quad, **b** = bathroom,
s = shower only. Unless otherwise noted, credit cards are
accepted, English is spoken, and breakfast is included.

To help you sort easily through these listings, I've divided
the rooms into three categories, based on the price for a
standard double room with bath:

$$$ Higher Priced—Most rooms €90 or more.
$$ Moderately Priced—Most rooms between €50-90.
$ Lower Priced—Most rooms €50 or less.

Unlike many businesses in town, the cheaper places don't take
credit cards.

As most rooms here are in old buildings with well-cared-for
wooden interiors, dripping laundry is a no-no at Hallstatt pensions. Be especially considerate when hanging laundry over anything but tile—if you must wash larger clothing items here, ask
your host about using their clothesline.

$$$ Hotel Grüner Baum offers the priciest beds in town. Its
22 rooms are huge, each with a separate living area with modern

furnishings on ancient hard-
woods. The owner, Monika,
moved in from Vienna and
renovated this stately old hotel
with urban taste (suite-like
Db-€130–200, price depends
on view, 8 percent discount
with this book, family rooms,
Internet access, laundry ser-
vice, closed in Nov, 20 yards
from boat dock and overlooking the lake and Market Square, tel.
06134/82630, fax 06134/826-344, www.gruenerbaum.cc, contact
@gruenerbaum.cc).

$$$ Bräugasthof Hallstatt is
like a museum filled with antique
furniture and ancient family portraits. This creaky old place—a former brewery with eight clean, cozy
rooms—is run by Virena and her
daughter, Virena. Six of the rooms
have gorgeous little lakeview balconies (Sb-€50, Db-€90, Db with

balcony-€95, Tb-€130, free parking, just past TI on the main drag at Seestrasse 120, tel. 06134/8221, fax 06134/82214, www.brau haus-lobisser.com, info@brauhaus-lobisser.com, Lobisser family).

$$$ Gasthof Zauner is run by a friendly mountaineer, Herr Zauner, whose family has owned it since 1893. The 13 pricey, pine-flavored rooms on the inland side of the main square are decorated with sturdy alpine-inspired furniture (sealed not with lacquer but with wax, to let the wood breathe out its calming scent). Lederhosen-clad Herr Zauner recounts tales of local mountaineering lore, including his own impressive ascents (Sb-€58, Db-€100, Db with lakeview-€108, cheaper mid-Oct–April, closed mid-Nov–mid-Dec, Marktplatz 51, tel. 06134/8246, fax 06134/82468, www .zauner.hallstatt.net, zauner@hallstatt.at).

$$$ Gasthof Simony is a well-worn, grandmotherly place on the square, with a lake view, balconies, ancient beds, creaky wood floors, slippery rag rugs, antique furniture, a lakefront garden for swimming, and a huge breakfast. Reserve in advance, and call if arriving late (S-€35, D-€55, Ds-€65, Db-€95, third person-€30–35 extra, cash only, kayaks for guests, Marktplatz 105, tel. & fax 06134/8231, www.hallstatt.net/gasthof/simony, info@gasthof -simony.at, Susanna Scheutz and grandson Valentin).

$$ Pension Sarstein is a big, flower-bedecked house right on the water. Its recently renovated rooms are bright, and all have lakeview balconies. You can swim from its plush and inviting lakeside garden (D-€50, Db-€65, Tb-€85; apartments with kitchen: Db-€65, Tb-€75, Qb-€85, apartment prices don't include breakfast; €3 extra per person for 1-night stay, cash only, fee for Internet access, 200 yards to the right of boat dock at Gosaumühlstrasse 83, tel. 06134/8217, fax 06134/20635, www.pension-sarstein.at.tf, pension.sarstein@aon.at, helpful Isabelle and Klaus Fischer).

$$ Gasthof Pension Grüner Anger is practical and modern, but located away from the medieval town center (a few blocks from  the base of the salt-mine lift, and a 15-minute walk from the Market Square). It's big and quiet, with 11 rooms and no creaks or squeaks (Sb-€43–48, Db-€76–86, third person-€15, price depends on season, non-smoking, Internet access and Wi-Fi, free loaner bikes, free parking, Lahn 10, tel. 06134/8397, fax 06134/83974, www.anger.hallstatt.net, anger@aon.at, Sulzbacher family). If arriving by train, have the boat captain call Herr Sulzbacher, who will pick you up at the dock. They run a good-value restaurant, too.

$ Helga Lenz rents two fine *Zimmer* a steep five-minute climb above Dr.-Morton-Weg (look for the green *Zimmer* sign). This large, sprawling, woodsy house has a nifty garden perch, wins the "Best View" award, and is ideal for those who sleep well in tree houses and don't mind the ascent from town (Db-€50, Tb-€72, €2 more per person for one-night stay, cash only, family room, closed Nov–March, Hallberg 17, tel. & fax 06134/8508, www.hallstatt .net/privatzimmer/helga.lenz, haus-lenz@aon.at).

$ Two places with ***Privatzimmer*** are a few minutes' stroll south of the center, just past the bus stop/parking lot and over the bridge. **Haus Trausner** has four clean, bright, new-feeling rooms adjacent to the Trausner family home (Ds/Db-€50, 2-night minimum for reservations, cash only, breakfast comes to your room, free parking, Lahnstrasse 27, tel. 06134/8710, trausner1@utanet .at, charming Maria Trausner makes you want to settle right in). **Herta Höll** rents out three spacious, modern rooms on the ground floor of her modern riverside house crawling with kids (Db-€46, apartment for up to five-€60, €2 more per person for one-night stay, cash only, free parking, Malerweg 45, tel. 06134/8531, fax 06134/825-533, frank.hoell@aon.at).

$ *Hostel:* **Gasthaus zur Mühle Jugendherberge,** below the waterfall and along the gushing town stream, has 46 of the cheapest good beds in town (bed in 3- to 14-bed coed dorms-€14, D-€28, family quads, sheets-€4 extra, breakfast-€5, big lockers with a €15 deposit, closed Nov, reception closed Tue Sept–mid-May—so arrange in advance if arriving on Tue, below tunnel car park, Kirchenweg 36, tel. & fax 06134/8318, toeroe-f@hallstatt urlaub.at, Ferdinand Törö). It's also popular for its great, inexpensive pizza; see "Eating," next.

EATING

In this town, when someone is happy to see you, they'll often say, "Can I cook you a fish?" While everyone cooks the typical Austrian fare, your best bet here is trout. *Reinanke* trout is caught wild out of Lake Hallstatt and served the same day. You can enjoy good food inexpensively, with delightful lakeside settings. Restaurants

in Hallstatt tend to have unreliable hours and close early on slow nights, so don't wait too long to get dinner. Most of the eateries listed here are run by hotels recommended under "Sleeping."

Restaurant Bräugasthof has great lakeside tables. You can feed the swans while your trout is being

HALLSTATT

cooked. On a balmy evening, its lakeside dining offers the best ambience in town (€10–15 three-course meals, daily May–Oct 11:30–late, closed Nov–April, Seestrasse 120, tel. 06134/8221).

Hotel Grüner Baum is another lakefront option (Dec–Oct daily 8:00–22:00, closed Nov, at bottom of Market Square, tel. 06134/8263). Its **Restaurant zum Salzbaron** is an upscale place with tables overlooking the lake inside and out (elegant service, €15–20 plates). Its **Kaiserstüberl** is more casual and rustic, with a folksy feel, no lake views, and €10 meals.

Gasthof Zauner's classy restaurant lacks a lakeside setting, but it's well-respected for its grilled meat with "cracklings" and its fish. The service comes in lederhosen, the ivy is real, and most agree that the food is worth the few extra euros (daily 11:30–14:30 & 17:30–22:00, closed mid-Oct–mid-Dec, at top of Market Square).

Gasthof Simony's Restaurant am See serves Austrian cuisine on a gorgeous lakeside terrace, as well as indoors (€10 entrées, Thu–Tue 11:30–20:00, until 21:00 June–Sept and on winter weekends, closed Wed).

Gasthaus zur Mühle serves the best pizza in town. Chow down cheap and hearty here with fun-loving locals and the youth-hostel crowd (€7 pizza, lots of Italian, some Austrian, daily in summer 11:00–14:00 & 17:00–21:00, closed Tue and no lunch Sept–mid-May, Kirchenweg 36, Ferdinand).

Strand Café, a smoky local favorite, is a 10-minute lakeside hike away, near Bade-Insel, the town beach (€8–12 plates, plenty of alcohol, Tue–Sun April–mid-Sept 10:00–21:00, mid-Sept–Oct 11:30–14:00 & 16:30–20:00, closed Mon and Nov–March, great garden setting on the lake, Seelande 102, tel. 06134/8234).

Picnics and Cheap Eats: The **Zauner** bakery/butcher/grocer, great for picnickers, makes fresh sandwiches to go (Tue–Fri 7:00–12:00 & 15:00–18:00, Sat and Mon 7:00–12:00, closed Sun, uphill to the left from Market Square). The only **supermarket** is Konsum, in Lahn at the bus stop (Mon–Fri 7:30–12:00 & 15:00–18:00, Sat 7:30–12:00, closed Sun, July–Aug no midday break and until 17:00 on Sat, Sept–April closed Wed). The **snack stand** near the main boat dock sells *Döner Kebab* and so on for €3 (tables and fine lakeside picnic options nearby); another snack stand is near the Lahn boat/bus stop.

TRANSPORTATION CONNECTIONS

For tips for drivers coming here from Salzburg, see the end of the Salzburg chapter.

From Hallstatt by Train: Most travelers leaving Hallstatt are going to Salzburg or Vienna. In either case, you need to catch the shuttle boat (€2.20, departs 15 minutes before every train) to the

little station across the lake, and then ride 90 minutes to **Attnang-Puchheim** (hourly from about 7:00 to 18:00). Trains are synchronized, so after a short wait in Attnang-Puchheim, you'll catch your connection to **Salzburg** (50 min) or **Vienna** (2.5 hrs). Train info: tel. 051-717 (to get an operator, dial 2, then 2).

By Bus: Some consider the bus ride from Hallstatt to **Salzburg** more scenic than the train, and just as practical (6–8/day, allow 3 hrs, €11.20, leaves from Lahn boat dock, no bus in icy weather, easy changes in Gosaumühle—a few minutes up the lake from Hallstatt—and in Bad Ischl, where you'll catch bus #150). The Hallstatt TI has a schedule.

TIROL

INNSBRUCK AND HALL

Tirol—in Austria's panhandle, south of Bavaria—is a winter sports mecca known for its mountainous panoramas. In the region's capital, Innsbruck, the Golden Roof glitters—but you'll strike it rich in neighboring Hall, which has twice the charm and none of the tourist crowds.

Innsbruck

Innsbruck is world-famous as a resort for skiers and a haven for hikers...but when compared to Salzburg and Vienna, it's stale strudel. Still, a quick look is easy and interesting. Innsbruck was the Habsburgs' capital of the Tirol, and its medieval center—now a glitzy, tourist-filled pedestrian zone—still gives you the feel of a provincial medieval capital. The much-ogled Golden Roof is the centerpiece.

ORIENTATION

(area code: 0512)

Tourist Information

Innsbruck has two TIs: **downtown** (daily 9:00–18:00, Burggraben 3, three blocks in front of Golden Roof, tel. 0512/5356, www.innsbruck.info) and at the **train station** (daily 9:00–19:00, tel. 0512/583-766). At either one, you can pick up a free city map (the €1 map, with more information on sights, isn't necessary) or book a room (free).

Innsbruck Card: The €25, 24-hour Innsbruck Card pays for

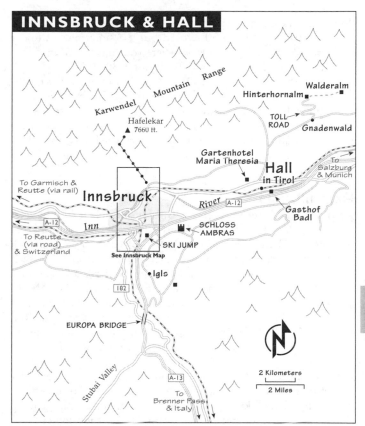

INNSBRUCK & HALL

Karwendel Mountain Range

Hafelekar
▲ 7660 ft.

Walderalm

Hinterhornalm

TOLL
ROAD

Gnadenwald

Gartenhotel
Maria Theresia

Hall
in Tirol

To
Salzburg
& Munich

To Garmisch &
Reutte (via rail)

Innsbruck

River A-12

Gasthof
Badl

A-12

Inn

To Reutte
(via road)
& Switzerland

SCHLOSS
AMBRAS

SKI JUMP

See Innsbruck Map

• Igls

102

EUROPA BRIDGE

2 Kilometers

2 Miles

Stubai Valley

A-13

To
Brenner Pass
& Italy

INNSBRUCK

itself if you take in four major sights and connect them with the bus or Sightseer minibus (easy to do, since the card is valid 24 hours and covers public transportation, including local funiculars, cable cars, and other lifts). You could validate it in the early afternoon, visit two sights, climb the Stadtturm tower, and do two more the next day before your 24 hours expire. If you see only one sight and ride the lifts to the top of the Hafelekar and back (see page 309), you'd still save money buying this pass. The Innsbruck Card is sold at the TI and most participating sights, and includes the Mint Museum in Hall (but not the Mint Museum Tower).

Walking Tours: The TI offers a basic one-hour city walk of Innsbruck (€8, €5 with Innsbruck Card, May–Oct daily at 14:00, July–Sept also daily at 11:00, Nov–April Fri–Sun at 14:00).

Arrival in Innsbruck

By Train: Some trains stop at Innsbruck's Westbahnhof, but stay on until you reach the main train station (Hauptbahnhof).

The main station has lockers (€2–3.50), a post office (Mon–Fri 7:00–19:00, Sat 8:00–13:00, closed Sun), a supermarket (daily 6:00–21:00), and a *Reisezentrum,* where you can get rail information and tickets (Mon–Sat 6:00–21:30, Sun 6:30–21:30).

From the station, it's a 10-minute walk to the old town center. Leave by veering right to Brixnerstrasse. Follow it past the fountain at Boznerplatz where it turns into Meranerstrasse and go straight until it dead-ends into Maria-Theresien-Strasse. Turn right and head 300 yards into the old town (you'll pass the TI on Burggraben on your right), where you'll see the Golden Roof and Hotel Weisses Kreuz.

Helpful Hints

Laundry and Internet Access: Bubblepoint is a handy self-service launderette (€4/load plus €1/10 min for dryer, Internet access-€3/hr, Mon–Fri 8:00–22:00, Sat–Sun 8:00–20:00, between train station and Golden Roof at Brixnerstrasse 1, tel. 0512/5650-0750, www.bubblepoint.com). You can also get online (but not wash your skivvies) at **Call On Me,** in the center of town (€3/hr, daily 12:00–23:00, at the end of Herzog-Friedrich-Strasse—between Golden Roof and river, tel. 0512/574-952). To save money, walk a few minutes more to Call On Me's second café (€2/hr, between Maria-Theresien-Strasse and the river at Innrain 20).

Bike Rental: Die Börse has a good range of bikes, from city cruisers (€15/day) to mountain bikes (€28/day). For €5, they'll drop off the bike at your hotel or, even better, pick you up at your hotel for free and take you to their shop to get fitted for the proper bike (May–Oct Mon–Fri 9:00–18:00, Sat–Sun 9:00–17:00—except May and Oct open Sun only by request; closed Nov–April; Leopoldstrasse 4, by the Triumphal Arch, tel. 0512/5817-4217, if you're staying at Hotel Weisses Kreuz they will phone for you). Die Börse is also a good contact for any adventure sports you might want to do (such as bungee jumping).

Getting Around Innsbruck

You won't need transportation if you're sticking to Innsbruck's compact medieval center. If you're headed beyond town (to the Bergisel ski jump, for example), the city's easy-to-use trams and buses are the cheapest way to go. A single ticket costs €1.70; a day ticket is €3.80. Buy tickets from the machine at the tram stop, train station, or the TI; single tickets can also be purchased from the driver (www.ivb.at).

A made-for-tourists minibus called the **Sightseer** follows two popular routes around town, connecting the key sights (€3 for any one-way trip, €6 for whole day, covered by Innsbruck Card, minimal headphone commentary in English, May–Oct 2/hr 9:00–17:30, Nov–April hourly 10:00–17:00, www.sightseer.at). If visiting several outlying sights, you can buy a €6 Sightseer day ticket (*Tagesticket*, includes transportation on the city bus system) and use the Sightseer as a hop-on, hop-off bus. It's pricey—nearly twice the cost of a day pass on public transit—and runs less frequently, but some find it more convenient (for information and tickets, visit the TI, or buy directly from driver).

SIGHTS AND ACTIVITIES

Innsbruck's Old Town

▲▲The Golden Roof (Goldenes Dachl) and Herzog-Friedrich-Strasse—The three-block pedestrian street (Herzog-Friedrich-Strasse) in front of the Golden Roof is Innsbruck's tourism central.

Stand in front of the Roof to get oriented. Emperor Maximilian I loved Innsbruck, and built a palace here—including the balcony topped with 2,657 gilded copper tiles. The Golden Roof (1494) offered Maximilian an impressive spot from which to view his medieval spectacles.

Most buildings along this street are Gothic (notice the entry arches), but across the street from the Golden Roof (to the left as you face the Roof) is the frilly Baroque-style **Helblinghaus** facade.

Above you is the bulbous **city tower** (*Stadtturm*), with 148 steps you can climb for a great view (€3, daily June–Sept 10:00–20:00, Oct–May 10:00–17:00, tel. 0512/561-500). This was the old town watchtower. A prison was on the second floor. Like many Austrian buildings (including the nearby Hofkirche), the tower originally had a pointy Gothic spire—replaced with this onion-shaped one when Baroque was in vogue.

A block in front of the Golden Roof—next to the McDonald's—is the historic **Hotel Weisses Kreuz**. It's built on Roman foundations, but has only been hosting guests for the last 500 years. The white cross (*weisses Kreuz*) is the symbol of the Order of Malta—knights who opened up guest houses for Holy Land–bound pilgrims during the Crusades. In 1769, a 13-year-old Wolfgang Amadeus Mozart and his father stayed here on their way to Italy. A generation later, this hotel was one of the centers of resistance against Napoleon, and later still, against the Nazis

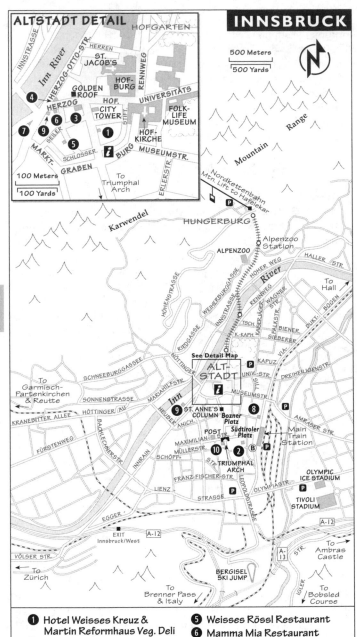

ALTSTADT DETAIL

INNSBRUCK

500 Meters

500 Yards

HOFGARTEN

HERREN

ST. JACOB'S

HOFBURG

RENNWEG

GOLDEN ROOF

HOF. CITY TOWER

UNIVERSITÄTS

FOLK-LIFE MUSEUM

HOF-KIRCHE

BURG

MUSEUMSTR.

GRABEN

SCHLOSSER.

SEILER

MARKT.

HERZOG

HERZOG-OTTO-STR.

STIFT

ERLERSTR.

INNSTRASSE

Inn River

To Triumphal Arch

100 Meters

100 Yards

Mountain Range

Nordkettenbahn Mtn. Lift to Hafelekar

HUNGERBURG

ALPENZOO

Alpenzoo Station

HOHER WEG

HALLER STR.

To Hall

Karwendel

HÖHENSTRASSE

WEIHERBURGGASSE

INNSTRASSE

RENNWEG

KAISERJÄGER

WAGNER STR.

TSCH.

FALKSTR.

BIENER.

VIA.

DUKT.-BOGEN

K.-KAPH.

SIEBERER

RIEDGASSE

HÖTTINGER

SCHNEEBURGGASSEE

To Garmisch-Partenkirchen & Reutte

SONNENSTRASSE

HÖTTINGER AU

KRANEBITTER ALLEE

MARIAHILFSTR.

HEUBER.

ANICH.

See Detail Map

ALT-STADT

UNIV.-STR.

MUSEUMSTR.

SILL

KAPUZ

DREIHEILIGENSTR.

AMRASER STR.

Inn

St. Anne's Column

Bozner Platz

POST

MAXIMILIAN

MÜLLERSTR.

SCHÖPF-

STR.

Südtiroler Platz

TRIUMPHAL ARCH

FRANZ-FISCHER-STR.

LIENZ

STRASSE

Main Train Station

LEOPOLDSTRASSE

OLYMPIA STR.

OLYMPIC ICE STADIUM

TIVOLI STADIUM

To Ambras Castle

A-12

A-13

IGLER STR.

To Bobsled Course

FÜRSTENWEG

BACHLECHNERSTR.

INNRAIN

EGGER

EXIT Innsbruck/West

A-12

VÖLSER STR.

To Zürich

BERGISEL SKI JUMP

To Brenner Pass & Italy

●	Hotel Weisses Kreuz & Martin Reformhaus Veg. Deli
●	Pension Stoi
●	Weinhaus Happ & Helblinghaus
●	Ottoburg Restaurant
●	Weisses Rössl Restaurant
●	Mamma Mia Restaurant
●	Cammerlander Restaurant
●	Launderette/Internet Access
●	Internet Café (2)
●	Bike Rental

INNSBRUCK

(giving shelter to Jewish refugees). When the American soldiers moved in from Italy, they made the hotel their headquarters. Today, it's still a functioning hotel (see "Sleeping and Eating," page 316). It recently hosted Otto von Habsburg, the Man Who Would Be Emperor, if his great-great-uncle hadn't started—and lost—World War I. Though Otto could have stayed in the fanciest place in town, he chose this historic, comfortable inn instead.

If you walk down the shop-lined Hofgasse (facing the Golden Roof, go right), you'll reach the Hofburg palace, Hofkirche, and Tirolean Folklife Museum (all described next).

Hofburg—This 18th-century Baroque palace, built by Maria Theresa, is only worth a visit if you aren't going to the much bigger and better palaces in Vienna or near Füssen, Germany. (What's more, the palace is undergoing an extensive renovation, so the empress' private apartments may be closed during your visit.) The lone advantage is that, unlike those more famous palaces, you'll have this one virtually to yourself (€5.50, daily 9:00–17:00, last entry at 16:30; helpful €1.80 English booklet, tel. 0512/5871-8612, www.hofburg-innsbruck.at). Your admission also includes a somewhat peculiar exhibit put on by the Austrian Alpine Club, exploring humanity's fascination with mountains and evoking the sensations and emotions of mountaineering (explanations in English, located in palace).

Should you need a **Sacher torte** fix, opposite the Hofburg entrance you'll find the local outpost of the venerable Viennese institution (Café Sacher, daily 8:30–24:00).

▲▲Hofkirche—Emperor Maximilian I liked Innsbruck so much, he wanted to be buried here, surrounded by 28 larger-than-life  cast-bronze statues of his ancestors, relatives, in-laws...and his favorite heroes of the dying Middle Ages (such as King Arthur). They stand like giant chess pieces on the black-and-white checked-marble floor. The good €1 English book tells you who everyone is. Don't miss King Arthur (as you face the altar, he's the fifth from the front on the right, next to the heavy-metal dude) and Mary of Burgundy, Maximilian's first—and favorite—wife (third from the front on the left). Some of these sculptures, including that of König Artur, were designed by German Renaissance painter Albrecht Dürer.

That's Maximilian himself, kneeling on top of the huge sarcophagus. Sadly, the real Max isn't inside. By the time he died, Maximilian had become notorious for running up debts, and his men weren't allowed to bring his body here. Just inside the door to the church, you'll find the tomb of the popular Tirolean soldier

Emperor Maximilian I
(1459–1519)

The big name in Innsbruck is Emperor Maximilian I, who made this city a regional capital and built the Golden Roof. This Habsburg emperor was a dynamic, larger-than-life Renaissance man—soldier, sculptor, and statesman (though not very good at any of these). At the same time, he clung to the last romantic fantasies of the Middle Ages; for example, he was the last Habsburg who personally led his troops into battle. (To see where he fits in among other Habsburgs, see the family tree on page 367.)

Most people associate the Habsburg Empire with Vienna, which was the capital of the empire's Eastern European holdings during its peak in the 17th and 18th centuries. But during Maximilian's time, two centuries earlier, the focus was on Italy—he took the "Roman" part of "Holy Roman Emperor" very seriously. This made Innsbruck very important, since it was the capital of Tirol (which then included much of today's northern Italy, and was on the Italian frontier).

This visionary emperor hoped that once all of Italy was his, Innsbruck would become the permanent capital of his empire. In reality, he was unlucky at war and ran up huge debts. But his strategic marriage to Mary of Burgundy set the stage for the large-scale expansion of the empire. Though he wanted to be a war hero, as with most Habsburgs, his biggest victory came with a trip to the altar.

Andreas Hofer, who fought against Napoleon (€4, €8 combo-ticket with Tirolean Folklife Museum, Mon–Sat 9:00–17:00, Sun 12:30–17:00, until 17:30 in July–Aug, Universitätsstrasse 2).

▲▲**Tirolean Folklife Museum (Tiroler Volkskunst Museum)**—This recently renovated museum, next door to the Hofkirche, offers the best look anywhere at traditional Tirolean lifestyles. Fascinating exhibits range from wedding dresses and gaily painted cribs and nativity scenes, to maternity clothes and babies' trousers. My favorite part is the carefully reconstructed interiors of several Tirolean homes through the ages (€8, includes admission to Hofkirche; daily 9:00–18:00; Universitätsstrasse 2, tel. 0512/5948-9513).

Maria-Theresien-Strasse—The fine, Baroque Maria-Theresien-Strasse stretches south from the medieval center. **St. Anne's Column** (Annasäule) marks the middle of the old marketplace. This was erected in the 18th century by townspeople thankful that their army had defeated an invading Bavarian army and saved the town (it's the same idea as the plague columns throughout Central Europe).

At the far end of the street, the **Triumphal Arch** is a gate Maria Theresa built to commemorate a happy and a sad occasion.

The happy: Her son Leopold II, archduke of Tuscany, met and married a Spanish princess here in Innsbruck—and Maria Theresa and her husband Franz came for the ceremony. But Franz partied a little too hard, and died the day after the wedding. (Maria Theresa wore black for the rest of her life.) The south-facing side of the arch—what you see as you approach the center—shows the interlocked rings of the happy couple. But the flipside, visible as you leave town, features mournful statuary.

▲**Slap-Dancing (Tyrolerabend)**—For your Tirolean folk fun, Innsbruck hotels offer an entertaining evening of slap-dancing and yodeling nearly nightly at 20:30 from April through October (€20 includes a drink with 2-hr show, tickets and info at TI). Every summer Thursday, the town puts on a free outdoor folk show under the Golden Roof (July–Sept, weather permitting).

St. James' Cathedral (Dom zu St. Jakob)—Innsbruck's own cathedral is your typical Baroque pastry: pink, frilly, and lots of gold. What makes it unique is that the high altar houses one of Lucas Cranach's best-known Madonna-and-Childs, the *Mariahilf* (free, Mon–Sat 10:15–19:30, Sun 12:30–18:30, Domplatz 6, tel. 0512/583-902).

▲**Ambras Castle (Schloss Ambras)**—Just southeast of town is the Renaissance palace Archduke Ferdinand II (1529–1595) reno-vated for his wife (it was originally a medieval castle). Its extensive grounds are replete with manicured gardens, a 17th-century fake waterfall, and resident peacocks. Visit the armory and the "curi-osities" collection, containing the archduke's assortment of the beautiful and bizarre (*Kunst- und Wunderkammer*, ranging from stuffed sharks to ancient Portuguese frocks). The beautiful Spanish Hall (built 1569–1572) is clearly the prize of the whole complex. Its intricate wooden ceiling and 27 life-size portraits of Tirolean princes make this a popular venue for classical music concerts (€8, daily 10:00–17:00, Aug until 19:00, closed Nov, audioguide-€2, Schlossstrasse 20; take tram #3 to last stop and then walk 15 min, or go direct on the Sightseer; tel. 0152/525-244-802, www.khm .at/ambras).

▲**Ski Jump Stadium (Bergisel)**—A new, modern ski jump stands in the same location as the original one that was used for the 1964 and 1976 Olympics (demolished in 2000). With a car, it's an inviting side-trip with a superb view, overlooking the city just off the Brenner Pass road on the south side of town (follow signs to *Bergisel*). Using public transportation, it's an easy tram ride from the center (tram #1, 6/hr) and then a 10-minute uphill walk; near the top of the woodsy path, take the right fork (or avoid the walk altogether by taking the pricier Sightseer bus, which drops you near the parking lot). The jump is interesting—but for mountain thrills, you're better off riding up to the ridge on the other side of the valley (see "Nordkettenbahn up to Hafelekar," opposite page).

For the best view of the jump itself, climb the steps to the Olympic rings under the dishes that held the Olympic flame,

where Dorothy Hamill and a host of others who brought home the gold are honored. Note the thoughtfully placed cemetery just below the jump. To get to the top of the ski jump, you can zip up in a funicular (2-min ride), then an elevator—or walk up the 455 steps—for a great view and a panorama café. As you ride the funicular down alongside the jump, imagine yourself speeding down the ramp and flying into the air...gulp (€8.30 whether you take funicular or not, may include Kaiserjäger Museum—described next, daily 9:00–17:00, until 18:00 in summer, last entrance 30 min before closing, funicular back down runs until 15 min after closing, tel. 0512/589-259, www.bergisel.info).

Near the ski jump parking lot is the **Kaiserjäger Museum** and a memorial to Andreas Hofer, the hero of the Tirolean battles against Napoleon. The museum, closed for renovation until mid-2010, is dedicated to the Habsburg emperor's infantry division, active from 1816 until 1918. If it's open and included in your Bergisel ticket—or if you're a military-history buff—it's worth popping in. Apart from two rooms honoring Hofer, the museum features paintings of important battles and officers, maps, battle plans, flags, uniforms, and weapons. Most interesting are the two upper floors, which contain black-and-white photographs and WWI weapons (closed until mid-2010, then likely €4, may be included in ski-jump entrance, likely open daily 9:00–17:00, tel. 0512/582-312, www.kaiserjaegermuseum.org). Hofer's 1809 victory at Bergisel is depicted in a huge panorama painting

(Riesenrundgemälde)—well-loved by locals but ignored by most tourists, as it's long been inconveniently located clear across town. It may, however, be moved to Bergisel by the time the museum reopens, making a stop here even more worthwhile (check with TI for details).

Into the Mountains

A popular mountain-sports center and home of the 1964 and 1976 Winter Olympics, Innsbruck is surrounded by 150 mountain lifts, 1,250 miles of trails, and 250 hikers' huts. Ask your hotel or hostel for a free Innsbruck Club card (different from the Innsbruck Card sold by TI), which offers overnight guests various discounts, bike tours, and free guided hikes in summer. Hikers meet in front of Congress Innsbruck daily at 8:45; each day, it's a different hike in the surrounding mountains and valleys (bring only lunch and water; boots, rucksack, and transport are provided; confirm with TI).

▲▲▲**Nordkettenbahn up to Hafelekar**—From the center of town, three lifts—collectively called the Nordkettenbahn—whisk you above the tree line to the ridge perched directly over, and thou-

sands of feet above, the Golden Roof. This is the fastest and easiest way to get your Tirolean mountain high. It's not cheap, but on a clear day, the trip is worth every euro. If you're going to the top (€24.50 round-trip), it makes sense to get the Innsbruck Card for €25, which covers your trip, the Alpenzoo (described next), and much more; see page 300.

The first stage, the Hungerburg-bahn **funicular,** leaves from the *Star Trek*–esque station outside Congress Innsbruck, right behind the Hofburg, and stops at the Alpenzoo before reaching the Hungerburg hillside viewpoint (€5.60 round-trip, €9 combo-ticket with Alpenzoo, prices slightly higher in winter, Mon–Fri 7:00–19:30, Sat–Sun 8:00–19:30, every 15 min).

From the Hungerburg viewpoint, you'll catch the first of two **cable cars** that lead up into the mountains. The first one gets you to the Seegrube perch (with a self-serve café—no picnicking allowed); you'll change there for the highest station, Hafelekar, which also has a café (round-trip: €24.50 from Innsbruck, €21 from Hungerburg, zoo not included; last lift down from Hafelekar at 17:00, from Seegrube at 17:30; both run every 15 min, cable-car tickets cover parking in Innsbruck's Congress garage).

If you've lucked out on weather, you'll see Innsbruck stretching across the valley to the Bergisel ski jump and, just to its right, the graceful Europa Bridge that leads up the Brenner Pass to Italy, beyond the peaks. Looking down the valley to the left, see if you can spot the town of Hall and its Mint Tower. Hike the 10-minute trail up to the Hafelekar peak (7,657 feet, no hiking boots needed), or choose from a range of longer hiking/walking options (well-explained in lift brochures). Serious mountain bikers will thrill at the steep trails—some of Europe's toughest (see page 302 for bike-rental information). At a minimum, walk the short path behind the lift station to peer over the ridge into the Karwendel Alps, jutting up between you and the German border. Take time to relax and soak in the view before returning to earth.

Alpenzoo—This zoo is one of Innsbruck's most popular attractions (understandable when the competition is the Golden Roof). You'll see all of the animals that hide out in the Alps, including bears, wolves, wildcats, elk, marmots, and at least one gigantic vulture (€7, €9 combo-ticket with Hungerburgbahn funicular, daily April–Oct 9:00–18:00, Nov–March 9:00–17:00, Weiherburggasse 37, tel. 0512/292-323, www.alpenzoo.at). The

easiest way up is with the funicular (described previously; it's okay to stop off on a round-trip ticket to Hungerburg and continue up or down). Or you could take the Sightseer or local #W buses, or just walk (following *Fussweg Alpenzoo* signs from the river).

Olympic Bobsled—For those who envy Olympics bobsled teams whooshing down curvy chutes (who doesn't?), Innsbruck offers the chance to ride an actual Olympic course. In the summer, you'll ride with a pilot and three others down the 4,000-foot-long course in a sled-on-wheels; in the winter it's the real thing on ice (summer: €25, July–Aug only, Wed–Fri 16:00–18:00; winter: €30, Jan–March only, Tue at 10:00 and 19:00, Thu at 19:00; in both seasons call ahead, no kids under 12, tel. 05275/5386, mobile 0664/357-8607, www.knauseder-event.at—select "Events" and "Guest bob" or "Summerbobsled"). To get there from the city center, take bus #J from Marktgraben (near Maria-Theresien-Strasse and the TI) to the Olympiaexpress stop (2/hr, 25 min)—it's a short walk along Römerstrasse to the building with the silver *Zielhaus* sign. Drivers coming from the A-12 autobahn should take the Innsbruck Mitte exit, and follow signs to *Igls* and then to *Olympia Bobbahn*.

Near Innsbruck

▲▲**Alpine Side-Trip by Car to Hinterhornalm**—In Gnaden-wald, a village sandwiched between Hall and its Alps, pay a €5 toll, pick up a brochure, then corkscrew your way up the mountain.

Sleep Code

(€1 = about $1.40, country code: 43, area code: 0512)
S = Single, **D** = Double/Twin, **T** = Triple, **Q** = Quad, **b** = bathroom,
s = shower only. Unless otherwise noted, credit cards are
accepted, English is spoken, and breakfast is included.

To help you sort easily through these listings, I've divided
the rooms into two categories, based on the price for a
standard double room with bath:

$$ Higher Priced—Most rooms €75 or more.
$ Lower Priced—Most rooms less than €75.

Marveling at the crazy amount of energy put into such a remote
road project, you'll finally end up at the rustic Hinterhornalm Berg
restaurant (generally daily mid-May–Oct 11:00–18:00, open later
in summer—but entirely weather-dependent and often closed,
closed Nov–mid-May, mobile 0664-211-2745). Hinterhornalm is a
hang-gliding springboard. On good days, it's a butterfly nest. From
there, it's a level 20-minute walk to Walderalm, a cluster of three
dairy farms with 70 cows that share their meadow with the clouds.
The cows ramble along ridge-top lanes surrounded by cut-glass
peaks. The ladies of the farms serve soup, sandwiches, and drinks
(very fresh milk in the afternoon) on rough plank tables. Below
you spreads the Inn River Valley and, in the distance, tourist-filled
Innsbruck.

SLEEPING

$$ Hotel Weisses Kreuz, near the Golden Roof, has been housing visitors for 500 years (see page 303). While its common spaces
still have an old-inn feel—with an airy atrium stairway, antique
Tirolean furniture, and big wood beams—its 40 rooms are newly
renovated and comfortable (S-€41, Sb-€66, D-€68, small Db-€103,
big Db at €114–122 is a better value, about €2 less per person
Oct–May, extra bed-€17–25, non-smoking rooms, elevator, fee for
Internet access, free Wi-Fi in lobby, parking €10.50/day—reserve
ahead, 50 yards in front of Golden Roof, as central as can be in the
old town at Herzog-Friedrich-Strasse 31, tel. 0512/594-790, fax
0512/594-7990, www.weisseskreuz.at, hotel@weisseskreuz.at).

$ Pension Stoi rents 17 pleasant, basic rooms 200 yards
from the train station and a 10-minute walk from the old town
center (S-€35–38, Sb-€40–44, D-€56–58, Db-€64–68, T-€68–74,
Tb-€78–84, Q-€80–86, Qb-€90–96, cash only, no breakfast,
reception open daily 8:00–21:00; walk left as you leave the station

to Salurnerstrasse, take first left on Adamgasse, then watch for signs in the courtyard on the right, Salurnerstrasse 7; tel. 0512/585-434, pensionstoi@aon.at, Stoi family).

EATING

You'll find plenty of expensive places in the pedestrian zone around the Golden Roof. Locals favor **Weinhaus Happ,** offering standards like Wiener Schnitzel, but also game, fish, and salads, all consumed in a labyrinth of cozy, traditional *Stuben* (€9–23 plates, daily 11:00–22:45, on the left as you face the Roof at Herzog-Friedrich-Strasse 14, tel. 0512/582-980). For a more elegant splurge, try **Ottoburg** (€15–24 main dishes, Tue–Sun 11:30–14:00 & 18:00–22:00, closed Mon, jog left down street in front of Roof to Herzog-Friedrich-Strasse 1—it's the gray mini-castle with the red and white shutters, tel. 0512/584-338).

Weisses Rössl is a little off the tourist track and, for culinary adventurers, features traditional Tirolean treats such as oven-roasted liver and calf's head. Fear not: Schnitzels and steaks abound, as do the tasty *Grillteller* (an assortment of grilled meats) and *Pfandl*—meat, potatoes, and veggies served up in a cast-iron skillet (€9–24 plates, Mon–Sat 11:30–14:30 & 17:00–22:00, closed Sun; facing the Roof, go one block left to Kiebachgasse 8; tel. 0512/583-057).

Cammerlander is *the* place if you need a steak, and has a varied menu full of reliably tasty international and Austrian dishes. Sit in their sleek, candlelit dining room, on the glassed-in veranda, or riverside with a mountain view (€4.60 salad bar, €8–22 entrées, lots of good vegetarian options, daily 11:30–23:30, Innrain 2, tel. 0512/586-398).

Mamma Mia, a cheaper escape from traditional fare, dishes up hearty portions of pizza and pasta (€7 main dishes, pizza also available by the slice–€3, daily 10:30–24:00, indoor/outdoor seating, Kiebachgasse 2, tel. 0512/562-902).

Martin Reformhaus, a health-food store with an eat-in or take-out deli, is where vegetarians can feast on tasty organic meals (daily soups and salads, €6 lunch specials on Mon–Thu; open Mon–Fri 8:30–18:30, Sat 8:30–18:00, closed Sun; Herzog-Friedrich-Strasse 29).

TRANSPORTATION CONNECTIONS

From Innsbruck by Train to: Hall (hourly trains, 10 min, Hall is the second stop and is not always announced; also 2 buses/hr, 25 min, take bus #4—leaves from area A, right in front of train station), **Salzburg** (direct every 2 hrs, 2 hrs), **Vienna** (every 2 hrs, 5 hrs), **Reutte** (every 2 hrs, 2.5 hrs, change in Garmisch), **Füssen** (5/day, 4.25 hrs, change in Munich), **Bregenz** (nearly hourly, some with transfer in Feldkirch, 2.5 hrs), **Zürich** (3/day direct, every 1–2 hours with changes, 3.75 hrs), **Munich** (every 2 hrs, 2 hrs), **Paris** (4/day, none direct, 8–10 hrs, change in Stuttgart or Zürich), **Milan** (6/day, 5.5 hrs, 1 direct, most with change in Verona, fastest connections require seat reservation), **Venice** (1/day direct, 5 hrs; 7/day, 5–6 hours with changes). Night trains run to Vienna, Venice, and Rome. Train info: tel. 051-717 (to get an operator, dial 2, then 2).

For driving directions to Reutte, Switzerland, and Italy, see page 317.

Hall

Hall was a rich salt-mining center when Innsbruck was just a

humble bridge *(Brücke)* town on the Inn River, and has a larger old town than does its sprawling neighbor. Hall hosts a colorful morning scene before the daily tour buses arrive, closes down tight for its daily siesta, and sleeps on Sunday. There's a brisk farmers market on Saturday mornings. (For drivers, Hall is a convenient overnight stop on the long drive from Vienna to Switzerland.)

ORIENTATION

Tourist Information
Hall's helpful TI offers lots of town information and brochures on a wide range of topics. If it's not too busy, they can also help you find a room (Mon–Fri 8:30–18:00, Sat 9:00–13:00, closed Sun, just off main square at Wallpachgasse 5, tel. 05223/455-440, regional info: www.regionhall.at, office@regionhall.at).

The TI organizes one-hour town **walking tours** in English (€6, includes admissions, €8 also includes tour of Mining Museum, see page 315; generally Mon–Tue and Thu–Sat at 10:00). The TI can also put you in touch with an English-speaking private guide (about €80/hr).

Arrival in Hall

For directions to my two recommended hotels in Hall, see page 316.

By Bus: Coming from Innsbruck, get off at the Unterer Stadtplatz stop, just below downtown Hall. From the Unterer Stadtplatz bus stop, you're a five-minute uphill walk from the town square and TI.

By Train: Hall's train station is a 10-minute walk from the town center (exit straight ahead up Bahnhofstrasse, turn right at the busy road, and you'll soon reach the fountain that marks the bottom of town).

By Car: Drivers approaching on the autobahn take the Hall-Mitte exit. You'll cross a big bridge, then you'll see two convenient parking lots (each one a 5-min walk from old town center). Find parking immediately after the bridge in P5 (€1/hr, maximum 3 hrs, Mon–Fri 8:30–18:00, free 12:00–14:00, Sat 8:30–12:00, free on Sun), or go through the light to find P2 on the left (first hour free, €1.40/hr after that, free after 18:30).

On Foot or by Bike: Hall and Innsbruck are connected by a pleasant bike path along the Inn River and through some parks. From Innsbruck, cross the Inn River, then simply follow the river downstream along the *Inntal Radweg*, minding signs to *Hall*. A comfortable 30-minute pedal will get you there.

SIGHTS AND ACTIVITIES

Main Square (Oberer Stadtplatz)— Hall's quaint main square at the top of town is worth a visit (TI just up the street). In the adjacent square (Pfarrplatz) is the Town Hall (Rathaus) and St. Nicholas Parish Church (Pfarrkirche St. Nikolaus). This much-appended Gothic church is decorated Baroque, with fine altars, a twisted apse, and a north wall lined with bony relics.

Hall Mint in Hasegg Castle (Münze Hall in Burg Hasegg)—Beginning in the 15th century, Hall began minting coins—most notably the *Taler* (which eventually became "dollar" in English). The former town mint, housed in Hasegg Castle, is between the river and the center at the south end of town. The Hall Mint Museum was renovated and expanded in 2003 to show off the town's proud minting heritage. The centerpiece is a huge, fully functioning replica of a 16th-century minting press—powered by water and made almost entirely of wood. The newly renovated tower *(Münzerturm)* provides a workout (185 steps, or 202 if you go medieval and take the narrow original stairs) and a great view. On your way out, check out the world's largest silver coin, worth roughly $20,000 (and weighing 44 pounds—suddenly the change in my pocket doesn't feel so heavy). It was made in 2008 to commemorate the 500th anniversary of Maximilian I's coronation,

and another event, apparently equally momentous: Austria's co-hosting of the 2008 European soccer championships (€6 for Mint Museum, includes excellent audioguide, €4 for tower, €8 combo-ticket for both; April–Oct Tue–Sun 10:00–17:00, closed Mon; Nov–March Tue–Sat 10:00–17:00, closed Sun–Mon; last entry one hour before closing, tel. 05223/585-5165, www.muenze -hall.at). The bus from Innsbruck drops you off right by the castle (stop: Unterer Stadtplatz, go through door marked #17 and *Burg Hasegg*); from Gasthof Badl, it's the first big building you'll see after crossing the old wooden pedestrian bridge.

Mining Museum (Bergbaumuseum)—Back when salt was money, Hall was loaded. Try catching a tour at this museum, where the town has reconstructed one of its original salt mines, complete with pits, shafts, drills, tools, and a tiny-but-slippery wooden slide (€3.50, €8 town walk includes museum, English tours May–Sept Mon and Thu–Sat at 11:30, no need to reserve—but punctuality is crucial, tel. 05223/455-440). The museum is a block south of the main square at Eugenstrasse.

Biking—If you're here for a few days, consider enjoying the valley on two wheels. The riverside bike path (7 miles from Hall to Volders) is a treat. Rent bikes at **Die Bike-Box** (€15/half-day, €20/ day, Mon–Fri 9:00–14:00 & 15:00–19:00, Sat 9:00–15:00, closed Sun, across street and 75 yards down from Unterer Stadtplatz bus stop at Unterer Stadtplatz 10, 05223/55944).

Swimming—To really make a splash, check out Hall's magnificent *Freischwimmbad*, a huge outdoor pool complex with four diving boards, giant lap pool, big slide, and kiddies' pool, all surrounded by a lush garden, sauna, mini-golf, and lounging locals (€3.50, mid-May–mid-Sept daily 9:00–19:00, closed mid-Sept–mid-May, at campground northwest of Hall, follow *Schwimmbad* signs from downtown to Scheidensteinstrasse 24, tel. 05223/454-647).

HALL

SLEEPING AND EATING

(€1 = about $1.40, country code: 43, area code: 05223)

Lovable towns that specialize in lowering the pulse of local vacationers line the Inn River Valley. Hall, the best town, has the shortest list of accommodations. Up the hill on either side of the river are more towns strewn with fine farmhouse hotels and pensions. Most *Zimmer* in private homes cost about €25 per person.

$$ Gartenhotel Maria Theresia, just a 15-minute walk from Hall's center, makes you feel a little bit like landed Tirolean gentry. This spacious, elegantly comfortable, family-run place is a fine splurge and makes a great hub from which to explore the Inn Valley (Sb-€70, Db-€110–130, Tb-€165, beautiful garden patio, restaurant, fine-dining room in wine cellar, free parking, ask about mountain-bike tours, Reimmichlstrasse 25, tel. 05223/56313, fax 05223/563-1366, www.gartenhotel.at, info@gartenhotel.at).

Getting to Gartenhotel Maria Theresia: If you arrive by **car** from Innsbruck, take the Hall-Mitte exit, go over the bridge, and through the light. At the roundabout, veer left (you'll already see signs) onto Speckbacherstrasse. Go left on Scheidensteinstrasse, right on Badgasse, and left on Reimmichelstrasse. If you arrive by **bus** or **train,** it's a long walk (especially from the train station)—consider taking a taxi (about €10 from station or main bus stop). To shorten the walk, ride the bus three stops past the Unterer Stadtplatz stop to the Kurhaus stop, then follow Stadtgraben (with the town on your left) until it turns downhill, and go right onto Kathreinstrasse, which feeds into Scheidensteinstrasse (20-min walk from Kurhaus stop to hotel).

$ Gasthof Badl is a big, comfortable, friendly place with 26 rooms run by sunny Frau Steiner and her daughter, Sonja, with help from Max, their enormous, easygoing dog. I like its convenience, peace, big breakfast, easy telephone reservations, and warm welcome (Sb-€41–43, Db-€68–72, Tb-€96, Qb-€120, family rates, elevator, laundry-€7, Innbrücke 4, tel. 05223/56784, fax 05223/567-843, www.badl.at, info@badl.at). Hall's kitchens close early, but Gasthof Badl's **restaurant** serves excellent dinners until 21:30 (€7–11 entrées, closed Tue). They stock the essential TI brochures and maps of Hall and Innsbruck in English.

Getting to Gasthof Badl: It's easy for **drivers** to find: From the east, it's immediately off the Hall-Mitte freeway exit; you'll see the orange-lit *Bed* sign. From Innsbruck, take the Hall-Mitte exit and, rather than turning left over the big bridge into town, go straight. To reach Gasthof Badl from the Unterer Stadtplatz **bus stop,** go through the door next to the bus stop (marked #17 and *Burg Hasegg*), cut through a couple of courtyards until you're under the castle tower, then follow Münzergasse (marked by red-and-blue no-parking signs) across the creek. Go straight until you hit the train tracks, then go left to use the railroad underpass, which is about 10 yards away. Coming out of the underpass, go right up the ramp and, from there, cross the old wooden bridge to the hotel. From the **train station,** leave the station to the right, follow the tracks straight ahead, and as the street curves left, veer right on the footpath that follows the tracks to access the railroad underpass, then head straight across the old wooden bridge.

TRANSPORTATION CONNECTIONS

Innsbruck is the nearest major train station. Hall and Innsbruck are connected by train and bus. Trains do the trip faster but leave only hourly; bus #4 takes a bit longer (25 min, €2.80 each way) but leaves twice an hour and drops you closer to town (see "Arrival in Hall," earlier in this chapter). Buses go to and from the Innsbruck train station, a 10-minute walk from the old town center. Drivers staying in freeway-handy Hall can side-trip into Innsbruck on the bus.

Route Tips for Drivers

From Hall into Innsbruck: For old Innsbruck, take the autobahn from Hall to the Innsbruck Ost exit and follow the signs to *Zentrum,* then *Kongresshaus,* and park as close as you can to the old center on the river *(Hofgarten).* If you'll be riding up the cable-car section of the Nordkettenbahn (see page 309), you can park for free at the Congress garage (8:00–18:00).

Just south of Innsbruck is the ski jump (see page 307; from the autobahn take the Innsbruck Süd exit and follow signs to *Bergisel).* Park at the end of the road near the Andreas Hofer Memorial, and climb to the empty, grassy stands for a picnic.

From Hall or Innsbruck to Reutte: Head west (direction Bregenz/Switzerland) and leave the freeway at Telfs, where signs direct you to Reutte (a 90-min drive).

From Innsbruck to Switzerland: Head west on the autobahn, as above. (If you're coming directly from Innsbruck's ski jump, go down into town along the huge cemetery and follow blue *A-12/ Garmisch/Arlberg* signs). The eight-mile-long Arlberg tunnel saves you 30 minutes on your way to Switzerland, but costs you lots of scenery and €8.50 (Swiss francs and credit cards accepted). For a joyride and to save a few bucks, skip the tunnel, exit at St. Anton, and go via Stuben.

After the speedy Arlberg tunnel, you're 30 minutes from Switzerland. Bludenz, with its characteristic medieval quarter, makes a good rest stop. Pass Feldkirch (and another long tunnel) and exit the autobahn at Rankweil/Feldkirch Nord, following signs for *Altstätten* and *Meiningen (CH).* Crossing the baby Rhine

River, you've left Austria.

Side-Trip over Brenner Pass into Italy: A short swing into Italy is fast and easy from Innsbruck or Hall (45-min drive, easy border crossing). To get to Italy, take the A-13/E-45 highway, which heads across the great Europa Bridge over Brenner Pass. It costs €8, but in 30 minutes you'll be at the border. (Note: Traffic can be heavy on summer weekends.)

In Italy, drive to the colorful market town of Vipiteno/ Sterzing. **Reifenstein Castle** is a unique and wonderfully preserved medieval castle, just south of town on the west side of the valley, down a small road next to the autobahn. Frau Blanc leads several tours a day in Italian and German, squeezing in whatever English she can (€5, open Easter–Oct; tours Sat–Thu at 10:30, 14:00, and 15:00; mid-July–mid-Sept also at 16:00, closed Fri; picnic spot at drawbridge; from Austria tel. 00-39-0472-765-879, from Italy tel. 0472-765-879).

HALL

BAVARIA
and WESTERN TIROL

Germany: Füssen • King's Castles • Wieskirche • Oberammergau • Linderhof Castle • Ettal Monastery • Zugspitze • Austria: Reutte

In Germany's Bavaria and Austria's Tirol (2.5 hours west of Innsbruck), you'll find a timeless land of fairy-tale castles, painted buildings shared by cows and farmers, and locals who still yodel when they're happy.

In Bavaria, tour "Mad" King Ludwig II's ornate Neuschwanstein Castle, Europe's most spectacular. Stop by the Wieskirche, a textbook example of Bavarian Rococo bursting with curly curlicues, and browse through Oberammergau, Germany's woodcarving capital and home of the famous Passion Play. Just over the border, in Tirol, explore the ruined Ehrenberg Castle and scream down the mountain on a luge (similar to a bobsled with wheels).

This region—which has long spanned two nations—is best seen from one of two home-base towns, on either side of the border. Choose between Füssen, Germany (it's bigger, touristy-but-charming, handy to Munich, and closer to the castles) and Reutte, Austria (it's sleepy, handy to Innsbruck, and oh-so-Austrian).

Stay in Füssen if you're coming by train from Munich or using Munich's airport. If convenience is a factor, Füssen has better public transportation connections to most of the major sights in the region. Reutte can be a better home base if you're traveling by train from Innsbruck or by car. Keep in mind that there are no weekend buses between Füssen and Reutte. In this chapter, I'll cover Bavaria first (because it has many more sights), then Tirol.

Planning Your Time

While Austrians and Germans vacation here for a week or two at a time, the typical speedy American traveler will find two days' worth of sightseeing. With a car and more time, you could enjoy three or four days, but the basic visit ranges anywhere from a long day trip from Innsbruck or Munich to a three-night, two-day visit.

By Car: Here's a good, one-day circular drive from Reutte (or from Füssen, starting a half-hour later): 7:30—Breakfast; 8:00—Depart hotel; 8:30—Arrive at Neuschwanstein to pick up tickets for the two castles (Neuschwanstein and Hohenschwangau); 9:00—Tour Hohenschwangau; 11:00—Tour Neuschwanstein; 13:00—Drive to Oberammergau, and spend an hour there to browse the carving shops; 15:00—Drive to Ettal Monastery for a half-hour stop (if you're not otherwise seeing the Wieskirche), then on to Linderhof Castle; 16:00—Tour Linderhof; 18:00—Drive along scenic Plansee lake back into Austria (or return to Füssen); 19:00—Back at hotel; 20:00—Dinner at hotel. Off-season (Oct–March), start your day an hour later, since Neuschwanstein and Hohenschwangau don't open until 10:00; and skip Linderhof, as it closes an hour early.

The next morning, you could stroll through Reutte, hike to the Ehrenberg ruins, and ride the luge on your way to Innsbruck, Vienna, Munich, Switzerland, Venice, or wherever.

By Public Transportation: Train travelers from Munich can use Füssen as a base and bus or bike the three miles to Neuschwanstein. Reutte is connected by bus with Füssen (except Sat–Sun; taxi €30 one-way). If you're based in Reutte, you can bike to the Ehrenberg ruins (just outside Reutte) and to Neuschwanstein Castle/Tegelberg luge (90 min). A one-way taxi from Reutte to Neuschwanstein costs about €35. Or, if you stay at the recommended Gutshof zum Schluxen hotel (in Pinswang, Austria—see page 363), it's a pleasant one-hour hike through the woods to Neuschwanstein.

Getting Around Bavaria and Tirol
By Car: This region is ideal by car. All the sights are within an easy 60-mile loop from Füssen or Reutte. Even if you're doing the rest of your trip by train, consider renting a car in Füssen (see page 323) or in Reutte (see page 352).

By Public Transportation: Local bus service in the region is spotty for sightseeing. If you're rushed and without wheels, Reutte, the Wieskirche, Linderhof, Ettal Monastery, and the Biberwier luge ride are probably not worth the trouble (speed freaks should instead consider the less exciting but more convenient Tegelberg luge near Neuschwanstein, which is within walking distance of the castle and served regularly by bus). I've listed connections below for each of the possible home bases in the region: Füssen (best overall base for non-drivers, especially for Ludwig's castles,

also decent for Oberammergau and Reutte); Oberammergau (good base for Linderhof, Ettal Monastery, and Garmisch/Zugspitze); and Reutte (most challenging home base for non-drivers). Note that the bus connections listed below are for summer weekdays; on weekends and out of season, frequency plummets. Confirm all bus schedules locally: Check the big board at the bus stop across from the Füssen train station, buy the indispensable bus timetable (€0.30, *OVG Fahrpläne der Linienbusse*) at the TI or train station, check online at www.rva-bus.de, or call 08362/939-0505. For longer-distance bus trips (such as side-tripping from Füssen to Oberammergau), you'll likely save money if you buy a *Tagesticket* (day pass). If you'll be taking a lot of trains in Bavaria (for example, day-tripping to Munich), consider the **Bayern-Ticket** (covers up to five people from anywhere in Bavaria to Munich and back for only €27/day, not valid Mon-Fri before 9:00).

From Füssen: Füssen is connected by hourly train with **Munich** (2-hr trip, some with transfer in Buchloe). Füssen is three miles from Ludwig's castles (Neuschwanstein and Hohen-schwangau), easily reachable by bus (or by bike—see next page).

From Füssen, handy buses connect to **Ludwig's castles** and the **Tegelberg luge** (buses #73 and #78, 2/hr, 10 min). There's also a bus connection to **Oberammergau** (bus #73 to Echelsbacher Brücke, change there to bus #9622—often marked *Garmisch*, confirm with driver that bus will stop in Oberammergau; 4–6/day in summer, 1.5 hrs total); the same bus continues to **Garmisch,** where you can ascend the **Zugspitze.** (From Oberammergau, you can also connect to **Linderhof Castle** and **Ettal Monastery**—see "From Oberammergau," next—but sparse buses make these sights challenging to do in a day from Füssen; rent a car instead.) To reach **Reutte,** you can take the bus (#74, Mon–Fri 6/day—but only 4 return buses/day, no buses at all Sat–Sun, less off-season, 35 min, €3.40) or a taxi (€30). You can reach the **Wieskirche** relatively easily (various buses, 4–5/day, 40–50 min each way, more frequently with a transfer in Steingaden; however, return connections from the Wieskirche to Füssen are infrequent, likely leaving you with more time at the church than you want.

From Oberammergau: Oberammergau is a fine home base for seeing Linderhof Castle, Ettal Monastery, and the Zugspitze. Bus #9622 heads from Oberammergau to **Linderhof** (nearly hourly, 25–40 min); some also stop at **Ettal Monastery** en route. Buses also go to **Garmisch** (nearly hourly, 40 min; also possible by train with a transfer in Murnau, 1.5 hrs), where you can head up to the **Zugspitze.** Oberammergau is also reasonably well-connected to **Füssen** by bus (4–6/day in summer, transfer at Echelsbacher Brücke, 1.5 hrs total). The trip between Oberammergau and **Munich** is better directly by train (nearly hourly, 1.75 hrs, change in Murnau or Oberau) than via Füssen by bus.

From Reutte: Reutte is the most challenging home base for non-drivers. It's a 35-minute bus ride from Füssen (Mon–Fri 6/day, none Sat–Sun, less off-season, €3.40; taxis from Reutte to Ludwig's castles are €35 one-way; to Füssen, €30). There are only four return buses (from Reutte back to Füssen), but Reutte is planning a more regular bus service to Füssen and the sights across the border—ask your hotel for the latest information. In Füssen, you can connect to **Ludwig's castles, Oberammergau,** and other sights (see "From Füssen," earlier in this section). From Reutte, a train departs every two hours to **Ehrwald** (30 min) and then **Garmisch** (1 hr), each of which has connections up to the **Zugspitze;** in Garmisch, you can also connect to **Oberammergau** and **Innsbruck.**

By Bike: This is great biking country. Shops in or near train stations rent bikes for €8–15 per day. The ride from Reutte to Neuschwanstein and the Tegelberg luge (90 min) is a natural.

By Thumb: Hitchhiking, always risky, is a slow-but-possible way to connect the public-transportation gaps. For example, even reluctant hitchhikers can catch a ride from Linderhof back to Oberammergau, as virtually everyone leaving there is a tourist like you and heading that way.

Füssen

Dramatically situated under a renovated castle on the lively Lech River, Füssen is a handy home base for exploring the region.

Füssen has been a strategic stop since ancient times. Its main street sits on the Via Claudia Augusta, which crossed the Alps (over the Brenner Pass) in Roman times. The town was the southern terminus of a medieval trade route, now known among modern tourists as the "Romantic Road." Today, while Füssen is overrun by tourists in the summer, few venture to the back streets...where you'll find the real charm. Apart from my self-guided walk (see the next page) and the City Museum, there's little to do here. It's just a pleasant small town with a big history and lots of hardworking people in the tourist business.

Halfway between Füssen and the border (as you drive, or a woodsy walk from the town) is the **Lechfall,** a thunderous waterfall (with a handy WC).

ORIENTATION

(Germany country code: 49; area code: 08362)
Füssen's train station is a few blocks from the TI, the town center (a cobbled shopping mall), and all my hotel listings (see "Sleeping").

Tourist Information
The TI is in the center of town (June–mid-Sept Mon–Fri 9:00–18:00, until 17:00 off-season, Sat 10:00–14:00, Sun 10:00–12:00, one free Internet terminal, 3 blocks down Bahnhofstrasse from station, tel. 08362/93850, www.fuessen.de). If necessary, the TI can help you find a room. After hours, the little self-service info pavilion near the front of the TI features an automated room-finding service (7:00–24:30).

Arrival in Füssen

From the train station (lockers available, €2–3), exit to the left and walk a few straight blocks to the center of town and the TI. Buses leave from the station to Neuschwanstein (2/hr) and Reutte (6/day Mon–Fri in summer).

Helpful Hints

Phone Tips and More: Remember, Füssen is in a different country. While Germans use the same currency as Austrians, postage stamps and phone cards only work in the country where you buy them. To call from Austria to Germany, dial 00-49 and then the number listed in this section (omitting the initial zero). To telephone from Germany to Austria, dial 00-43 and then the number (again, omitting the initial zero).

Internet Access: Beans & Bytes is the best place to get online, with fast terminals and good drink service (€1/30 min, Wi-Fi, Skype, disc-burning for your photos, daily 10:00–22:00, down the pedestrian alley off the main drag at Reichenstrasse 33, tel. 08362/926-8960).

Bike Rental: Bike Station, sitting right where the train tracks end, outfits sightseers with good bikes and tips on two-wheeled fun in the area (€8/24 hrs, April–Sept Mon–Fri 9:00–18:00, Sat 10:00–14:00, Sun 9:00–12:00 in good weather, closed Oct–March, mobile 0176-2205-3080). For a strenuous but enjoyable 20-mile loop trip, see page 340.

Car Rental: Peter Schlichtling, in the town center, rents cars for reasonable prices (€62/day, includes insurance, Mon–Fri 8:00–18:00, Sat 9:00–12:00, closed Sun, Kemptener Strasse 26, tel. 08362/922-122, www.schlichtling.de). **Auto Osterried/Europcar** rents at similar prices, but is an €8 taxi ride away from the train station. Their cheapest car is a fun-to-try SmartCar going for about €40 per day (daily 8:00–19:00, across river from Füssen at Tiroler Strasse 65, tel. 08362/6381).

Local Guide: Silvia Beyer speaks English and knows the region very well (silliby@web.de, mobile 0160-901-13431).

SELF-GUIDED WALK

Welcome to Füssen

For most, Füssen is just a touristy home base for visiting Ludwig's famous castles. But the town has a rich history and hides some evocative corners, as you'll see when you follow this short orientation walk. Throughout the town, "City Tour" information plaques explain points of interest in English. Use them to supplement the information I've provided.

• *Begin at the square in front of the TI, three blocks from the train station.*

Kaiser-Maximilian-Platz: The entertaining "Seven Stones" fountain on this square (in front of the TI) was built in 1995 to celebrate Füssen's 700th birthday. The stones symbolize community, groups of people gathering, conviviality...each is different, with "heads" nodding and talking. It's granite on granite. The moving heads are not connected, and nod only with waterpower. While frozen in winter, it's a popular and splashy play zone for kids on hot summer days.

• *Just half a block down the busy street stands...*

Hotel Hirsch and Medieval Wall: Hotel Hirsch, one of the first hotels in town, dates from the 19th century, when aristocratic tourists started coming to appreciate the castles and natural wonders of the Alps. Across the busy street stands one of two surviving towers from Füssen's medieval town wall (c. 1515). Farther down the street (50 yards, just before the second tower), a gate leads into the old town (see information plaque).

• *Step through the gate (onto today's Klosterstrasse), and immediately turn left into the old cemetery.*

Historic Cemetery of St. Sebastian (Alter Friedhof): This peaceful oasis of Füssen history, established in the 16th century, fills a corner between the town wall and the Franciscan monastery. It's technically full, and only members of great and venerable Füssen families (who already own a plot here) can join those who are buried (free, daily 7:30–19:00).

Just inside the gate (on right) is the tomb of Dominic Quaglio, who painted the Romantic scenes decorating the walls of Hohenschwangau Castle in 1835. Over on the old city wall is the World War I memorial, listing all the names of men from this small town killed in that devastating conflict (along with each one's rank and place of death). A bit to the right, also along the old wall, is a statue of the hand of God holding a fetus—a place to remember babies who died before being born. And in the corner, farther to the right, are the simple wooden crosses of Franciscans who lived just over the wall in the monastery. Note the fine tomb art from many ages collected here, and the loving care this community gives its cemetery.

• *Exit on the far side, just past the dead Franciscans, and continue toward the big church.*

Town View from Franciscan Monastery (Franziskaner-kloster): From the Franciscan Monastery (which still has big

1 Hotel/Rest. Kurcafe
2 Hotel Hirsch
3 Hotel Sonne
4 Altstadthotel zum Hechten & Rest. Ritterstub'n
5 Suzanne's B&B
6 Hotel Bräustüberl
7 Gasthof Krone
8 House LA
9 Allgäuer Gästehaus
10 To Magdalena Höbel
11 Haus Peters
12 Youth Hostel
13 Aquila das Rest.
14 Markthalle Food Court
15 Bike Rental
16 Car Rental
17 To Car Rental
18 Internet Café

FÜSSEN

YOUTH HOSTEL 12

5

Ziegelberg

OBLISBERGSTRASSE
MARIAHILFER R.
STRASSE
ZIEGELANGERWEG

PRÖBSTLSTRASSE
KREUZSTRASSE
PAPPENHEIMSTRASSE
VON-FREYBERG-STRASSE
VON-

BAUMEISTER-FISCHER-STRASSE
KNÖRINGENSTRASSE

RIEBEL-BRAND-STRASSE
HOHENSTAUFENSTRASSE
HERKOMERSTRASSE
FRÜHLINGSTRASSE

BAURSTRASSE
MAURERSTRASSE
GOSSENBRODSTR.
RUDOLFSTRASSE

KAROLINGERSTRASSE
FURTENBACHWEG
SONNENSTRASSE
KIRCHSTRASSE
GLÜCKSTRASSE

KELTENSTEINSTRASSE

16

FLORIAN-STRASSE
KEMPTENER STRASSE

AM RIESENANGER

KOBELSTRASSE
MORISSE

Baumgarten

AM ANGER
AM KAPELLENBERG
MÜHLENWEG
LANDEWEG

SCHWÄRZERWEG

SELF-GUIDED WALK

A Kaiser-Maximilian-Platz
B Medieval Wall
C Cemetery of St. Sebastian
D Town View
E Lech Riverbank
F Church of the Holy Ghost, Bread Market & Lute-Makers
G Benedictine Monastery
H City Museum
I St. Magnus Basilica
J High Castle

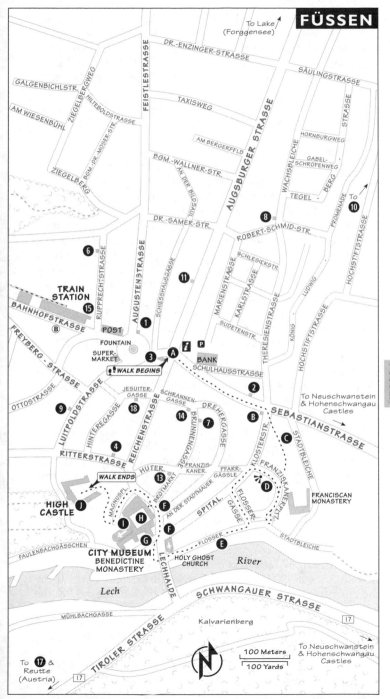

FÜSSEN

To Lake
(Forggensee)

DR.-ENZINGER-STRASSE

SÄULINGSTRASSE

GALGENBICHLSTR.

ZIEGELBERGWEG

HILTEBOLDSTRASSE

FEISTLESTRASSE

TAXISWEG

AM WIESENBÜHL

HORNBURGWEG

GABEL-
SCHROFENWEG

BGM.-DR.-MOSER-STR.

AM BERGERFFLD

AUGSBURGER STRASSE

WACHSBLEICHE

ZIEGELBERG

BGM.-WALLNER-STR.

AN DER BILDSAUL

TEGEL - BERG

DR.-SAMER-STR.

ROBERT-SCHMID-STR.

8

To
10

PROMENADE

HOCHSTIFTSTRASSE

6

RUPPRECHTSTRASSE

SCHIESSHAUSGASSE

11

MARIENSTRASSE

SCHLESIEKSTR.

KARLSTRASSE

THERESIENSTRASSE

LUDWIG

KÖNIG

HOCHSTIFTSTRASSE

**TRAIN
STATION**

15

BAHNHOFSTRASSE

(B)

AUGUSTENSTRASSE

1

SUDETENSTR.

FREYBERG - STRASSE

POST

FOUNTAIN

SUPER-
MARKET

3 **A**

🛈 **P**

BANK

SCHULHAUSSTRASSE

2

To Neuschwanstein
& Hohenschwangau
Castles

WALK BEGINS

OTTOSTRASSE

JESUITER-
GASSE

SCHRANNEN-
GASSE

DREHERGASSE

B

SEBASTIANSTRASSE

9

LUITPOLDSTRASSE

HINTEREGASSE

18

REICHENSTRASSE

14

BRUNNENGASSE

7

KLOSTERSTR.

C

STADTBLEICHE

4

RITTERSTRASSE

FRANZIS-
KANER.

FRANZISKANERPLTZ

FRANCISCAN
MONASTERY

WALK ENDS

HUTER.

13

BROTMARKT

PFARR-
GÄSSLE

D

FLOSSER-
GASSE

**HIGH
CASTLE**

J

MAGNUSPL.

I **H**

AN DER STADTMAUER

F

SPITAL

STADTBLEICHE

FAULENBACHGÄSSCHEN

G

F

FLOSSER-

E

**CITY MUSEUM
BENEDICTINE
MONASTERY**

LECHHALDE

HOLY GHOST
CHURCH

River

Lech

SCHWANGAUER STRASSE

MÜHLBACHGASSE

TIROLER STRASSE

Kalvarienberg

17

100 Meters
100 Yards

To **17** &
Reutte
(Austria)

17

To Neuschwanstein
& Hohenschwangau
Castles

FÜSSEN

responsibilities, but only a handful of monks in residence), there's a fine view over the medieval town. The Church of St. Magnus and the High Castle (the summer residence of the Bishops of Augsburg) break the horizon. The chimney (c. 1886) on the left is a reminder that when Ludwig built Neuschwanstein, the textile industry (linen and flax) was very big here.

• *Go down the steps into the flood zone, and stay left, following the roar of the charging river, through the medieval "Bleachers' Gate," to the riverbank.*

Lech Riverbank: This low end of town, the flood zone, was the home of those whose work depended on the river—bleachers, rafters, and fishermen. The Lech River was—in its day—an expressway to Augsburg (about 70 miles to the north). Around the year 1500, the rafters established the first professional guild in Füssen. As Füssen was on the Via Claudia, cargo from Italy passed here en route to big German cities farther north. Rafters would assemble rafts, and pile them high with goods—or with people needing a lift. If the water was high, they could float all the way to Augsburg in as little as one day. There they'd disassemble their raft and sell off the lumber along with the goods they'd carried, then make their way home to raft again. Today you'll see no water sports here, as there's a hydroelectric plant just downstream.

• *Walk upstream a bit, and head inland immediately after crossing under the bridge.*

Church of the Holy Ghost, Bread Market, and Lute-Makers: Climbing uphill, you pass the colorful Church of the Holy Ghost (Heilig-Geist-Spitalkirche) on the left. As this was the church of the rafters, their patron, St. Christopher, is prominent on the facade. Today it's the church of Füssen's old folks' home (it's adjacent—notice the easy-access skyway).

Farther up the lane (opposite the entry to the big monastery) is Bread Market Square (Brotmarkt), with its fountain honoring the famous 16th-century lute-making family, the Tieffenbruckers. In its day, Füssen was a huge center of violin- and lute-making, with about 200 workshops. Today only two survive.

• *Backtrack and enter the courtyard in the huge monastery just across the street.*

Benedictine Monastery (Kloster St. Mang): From 1717 until secularization in 1802, this was the powerful center of town. Today the courtyard is popular for concerts, and the building houses the City Hall and City Museum (and a public WC).

City Museum: This is Füssen's one must-see sight (€2.50, €3 includes castle gallery; April–Oct Tue–Sun 11:00–17:00, closed Mon; Nov–March Fri–Sun 13:00–16:00, closed Mon–Thu; tel. 08362/903-146). Pick up the loaner English translations and follow the one-way route. In the St. Anna Chapel, you'll see the famous

Dance of Death. This was painted shortly after a plague devastated the community in 1590. It shows 20 social classes, each dancing with the Grim Reaper—starting with the pope and the emperor. The words above say, essentially, "You can say yes or you can say no, but you must ultimately dance with death." Leaving the chapel, you walk over the metal lid of the crypt. Farther on, exhibits illustrate the rafting trade and violin- and lute-making (with a complete workshop). The museum also includes an exquisite *Festsaal* (main festival hall), an old library, a textile factory, and a Ludwig's "castle dream room."

• *Leaving the courtyard, hook left around the monastery and uphill. The square tower marks...*

St. Magnus Basilica (Basilika St. Mang): St. Mang (or Magnus) is Füssen's favorite saint. In the eighth century, he worked miracles all over the area with his holy rod. For centuries, pilgrims came from far and wide to enjoy art depicting the great works of St. Magnus. Above the altar dangles a glass cross containing his relics (including that holy stick). Just inside the door is a chapel remembering a much more modern saint—Franz Seelos (1819–1867), the local boy who went to America (Pittsburg and New Orleans) and lived such a saintly life that in 2000 he was made a saint. If you're in need of a miracle, there are cards to fill out next to the candles.

• *From the church, a lane leads high above, into the castle courtyard.*

High Castle (Hohes Schloss): This castle, long the summer residence of the Bishop of Augsburg, houses a painting gallery. Its courtyard is interesting for the striking perspective tricks painted onto its flat walls. From below the castle, the city's main drag (once the Roman Via Claudia and now Reichenstrasse) leads from a grand statue of St. Magnus past lots of shops, cafés, and strolling people to Kaiser-Maximilian-Platz and the TI...where you began.

SLEEPING

(Germany country code: 49, area code: 08362)
Though I prefer sleeping in Reutte (see page 352), convenient Füssen is just three miles from Ludwig's castles and offers a cobbled, riverside retreat. It's very touristy, but it has plenty of rooms. All recommended accommodations are within a few blocks of the train station and the town center. Parking is easy at the station. Prices listed are for one-night stays. Most hotels give about 5–10 percent off for two-night stays—always request this discount. Competition is fierce, and off-season prices are soft. High season is mid-June through September. Rooms are generally about 12 percent less in shoulder season and much cheaper in off-season. To locate these hotels, see the map on pages 326-327. Remember, to

Sleep Code

(€1 = about $1.40, Germany country code: 49, Austria country code: 43)

S = Single, **D** = Double/Twin, **T** = Triple, **Q** = Quad, **b** = bathroom, **s** = shower only. Unless otherwise noted, credit cards are accepted, English is spoken, and breakfast is included. Germany's "tourist tax" of €1.35 per person per night is not included in these rates.

To help you sort easily through these listings, I've divided the rooms into three categories, based on the price for a standard double room with bath:

$$$ Higher Priced—Most rooms €100 or more.

$$ Moderately Priced—Most rooms between €60–100.

$ Lower Priced—Most rooms €60 or less.

call Füssen from Austria, dial 00-49 and then the number (minus the initial zero).

$$$ Hotel Kurcafe is deluxe, with 30 spacious rooms and all of the amenities. The standard rooms are comfortable, and the newer, bigger rooms have elegant touches and fun decor—such as canopy drapes and cherubic frescoes over the bed (Sb-€89, standard Db-€109–125, bigger Db-€135–149 depending on size, Tb-€135, Qb-€149, 4-person suite-€179–209, high prices are for July–Aug, €10 more for weekends and holidays, you'll likely save money by booking via their website, elevator, Internet access, parking-€5/day, a block from station at Bahnhofstrasse 4, tel. 08362/930-180, fax 08362/930-1850, www.kurcafe.com, info@kurcafe.com, Norbert and the Schöll family).

$$$ Hotel Hirsch is a big, romantic, old tourist-class hotel with 53 rooms on the main street in the center of town. Their standard rooms are fine, and their theme rooms are a fun splurge (Sb-€65–85, standard Db-€110–140, theme Db-€140–170, price depends on room size and demand, cheaper Nov–March and during slow times, family rooms, elevator, free parking, Kaiser-Maximilian-Platz 7, tel. 08362/93980, fax 08362/939-877, www.hotelhirsch.de, info@hotelhirsch.de).

$$$ Hotel Sonne, in the heart of town, rents 51 stylish and spacious rooms (Sb-€93–109, Db-€93–159, Tb-€118–148, Qb-164–200, higher prices are for huge rooms in the new wing, cheaper Oct–mid-May, elevator, Internet access, free sauna, parking-€4/day, kitty-corner from TI at Prinzregentenplatz 1, tel. 08362/9080, fax 08362/908-100, www.hotel-sonne.de, info@hotel-sonne.de).

$$ Altstadthotel zum Hechten, with 35 rooms, offers all the modern comforts in a friendly, traditional building right under

FÜSSEN

Füssen Castle in the old-town pedestrian zone (Sb-€57, Db-€90, Tb-€117, Qb-€140, request Rick Steves discount, beds can be short, fun miniature bowling alley in basement, free parking with this book; from TI, walk down pedestrian street and take second right to Ritterstrasse 6; tel. 08362/91600, fax 08362/916-099, www.hotel-hechten.com, hotel.hechten@t-online.de, Pfeiffer and Tramp families).

$$ Suzanne's B&B is run by a plainspoken, no-nonsense American woman who strikes some travelers as a brusque drill sergeant. Suzanne runs a tight ship, offering travel advice, local cheese, a children's yard, garden, and bright, woody, spacious rooms (Db-€90, huge Db with waterbed and balcony-€110, Tb-€120, Qb-€156, suite sleeps up to 10, cash only, non-smoking, €8/day bike rental; exit station right and backtrack 2 blocks along tracks, cross tracks at Venetianerwinkel to #3; tel. 08362/38485, fax 08362/921-396, www.suzannes.de, svorbrugg@t-online.de).

$$ Hotel Bräustüberl has 17 decent rooms at fair rates attached to a gruff, musty, old beer hall. Don't expect much service (Db-€84, cash only, Rupprechtstrasse 5, 1 block from station, tel. 08362/7843, fax 08362/923-951, www.brauereigasthof-braeu stueberl.de, brauereigasthof-fuessen@t-online.de).

Füssen's Budget Beds

$ Gasthof Krone, a rare bit of pre-glitz Füssen in the pedestrian zone, has dumpy halls and stairs and 12 big, worn time-warp rooms (S-€31, D-€58, extra bed-€26, extra bed for kids under 12-€20, €3 more per person for 1-night stays, closed Nov–June; from TI, head down pedestrian street and take first left to Schrannengasse 17; tel. 08362/7824, fax 08362/37505, www.krone-fuessen.de, info @krone-fuessen.de).

$ House LA offers nine basic, clean rooms at rock-bottom prices near the town center (4-bed dorms-€18/bed, Db-€42, Wachsbleichstrasse 2, mobile 0170-624-8610, www.housela.de, info @housela.de). They also rent four very basic rooms and one apartment at Welfenstrasse 39 (D-€40, light breakfast served in room).

$ Allgäuer Gästehaus has four cheap and slightly run-down rooms on a busy street near the center of town (Db-€54, Luitpoldstrasse 10, tel. 08362/926-8425, hdnet@web.de).

$ Magdalena Höbel, your quintessential German grand-mother, rents two double rooms in a quiet neighborhood about a 10-minute walk from the train station. Magdalena speaks some English (D-€36, Frauensteinweg 42c, tel. 08362/2950).

$ At Haus Peters, Frau Peters rents great rooms in a clean and homey setting with an inviting garden that's a five-minute stroll from the train station (Db-€52, Augustenstrasse 5-1/2, tel. 08362/7171). Frau Peters may retire in 2010, so call ahead.

$ Füssen Youth Hostel, a fine, German-run place, welcomes travelers, especially younger ones (bed in 2- to 6-bed dorm rooms-€20, D-€56, €3 more for non-members, includes breakfast and sheets, guests over age 26 pay €4 penalty for being so old, laundry-€3.20/load, cheap dinners, office open 7:00–12:00 & 17:00–23:00, until 22:00 off-season, from station backtrack 10 min along tracks, Mariahilfer Strasse 5, tel. 08362/7754, fax 08362/2770, www.fuessen.jugendherberge.de, jhfuessen@djh-bayern.de).

EATING

Aquila das Restaurant serves modern international dishes in a simple, traditional *Gasthaus* setting with great seating outside on the delightful little Brotmarkt square (€10 plates, serious salads, daily from 11:30 and 17:00, Brotmarkt 9, tel. 08362/6253).

Restaurant Ritterstub'n offers delicious, reasonably priced fish, salads, veggie plates, and a fun kids' menu. They have three eating zones: dressy in front, casual in back, and courtyard. Demure Gabi serves while her husband cooks standard Bavarian fare (€5 lunch specials, €6–12 plates, Tue–Sun 11:30–14:30 & 17:30–23:00, Ritterstrasse 4, tel. 08362/7759).

Schenke & Wirtshaus (inside the Altstadthotel zum Hechten) dishes up hearty, traditional Bavarian fare. They specialize in pike *(Hecht)* pulled from the Lech River, served with a tasty, fresh herb sauce (€8–13 plates, salad bar, cafeteria ambience, daily 10:00–22:00, Ritterstrasse 6, tel. 0836/91600).

Hotel Kurcafe's fine restaurant, right on Füssen's main traffic circle, has good weekly specials. Choose between a traditional dining room and a pastel winter garden, and enjoy the live Bavarian zither music most Fridays and Saturdays during dinner (open daily 11:30–14:30 & 17:30–21:30, Bahnhofstrasse 4, tel. 08362/930-180).

Markthalle, just across the street from Gasthof Krone, is a fun food court offering a wide selection of reasonably priced, wurst-free food. Located in an old warehouse from 1483, it's now home to a fishmonger; Chinese, Turkish, and Italian delis; a fruit stand; a bakery; and a wine bar. Buy your food from one of the vendors, park yourself at any one of the tables, then look up and admire the Renaissance ceiling (Mon–Fri 7:30–18:30, Sat 7:30–14:00, closed Sun, corner of Schrannengasse and Brunnengasse).

Gelato: **Hohes Schloss Italian Ice Cream** is a good gelateria on the main drag, with cheap ice cream to go and an inviting perch for a coffee or dessert while people-watching (Reichenstrasse 14).

Picnic Supplies: Bakeries and *Metzgers* (butcher shops) abound and frequently have ready-made sandwiches. For groceries, try the **Plus** supermarket at the roundabout on your way into town from the train station (Mon–Sat 8:30–20:00, closed Sun).

TRANSPORTATION CONNECTIONS

From Füssen to: Neuschwanstein (bus #73 or #78, departs from train station, continues to Tegelberg lift station after castles, 2/hr, 10 min, €2 one-way, €3.50 round-trip; taxis cost €10 one-way); **Oberammergau** (bus #73 to Echelsbacher Brücke, change there to bus #9622—often marked *Garmisch,* confirm with driver that bus will stop in Oberammergau; 4–6/day in summer, 1.5 hrs total; from Oberammergau you can connect to **Linderhof Castle, Ettal Monastery,** and **Garmisch/Zugspitze**); **Wieskirche** (4–5 buses/day, 40–50 min each way, more frequent with transfer in Steingaden); **Munich** (hourly trains, 2 hrs, some change in Buchloe); **Reutte** (bus #74, Mon–Fri 6 buses/day, none Sat–Sun, 35 min, €3.40 one-way; taxis cost €30 one-way); **Innsbruck** (5 trains/day, 4.25 hrs, change in Munich). Train info: tel. 11861 (€0.60/min).

The Best of Bavaria

Within a short drive of Füssen or Reutte, you'll find some of the most enjoyable—and most tourist-filled—sights in Germany. The otherworldly "King's Castles" of Neuschwanstein and Hohenschwangau capture romantics' imaginations, the ornately decorated Wieskirche puts the faithful in a heavenly mood, and the little town of Oberammergau overwhelms visitors with cuteness. Yet another impressive castle (Linderhof), another fancy church (Ettal), and a sky-high viewpoint (the Zugspitze) round out Bavaria's top attractions.

THE BEST OF BAVARIA

The King's Castles

The most popular tourist destinations in Bavaria are the "King's Castles" *(Königsschlösser)*. The older Hohenschwangau, King Ludwig's boyhood home, is less touristy but more historic. The more dramatic Neuschwanstein, which inspired Walt Disney, is the one everyone visits. I'd recommend visiting both,

and planning some time to hike above Neuschwanstein to Mary's Bridge—and if you enjoy romantic hikes, down through the gorge below. With fairy-tale turrets in a fairy-tale alpine setting built by a fairy-tale king, these castles are understandably a huge hit.

Getting There

If arriving by **car,** note that road signs in the region refer to the sight as *Königsschlösser,* not Neuschwanstein. There's plenty of parking (all lots–€4.50). The first lots require more walking. Drive right through Touristville and past the ticket center, and park in lot #4 by the lake for the same price.

From **Füssen,** those without cars can catch the twice hourly **bus** #73 or #78 (€2 one-way, €3.50 round-trip, 10 min, catch bus at train station), take a **taxi** (€10 one-way), or ride a rental **bike** (two level miles).

From **Reutte,** take bus #74 to the Füssen train station (Mon–Fri 6/day, none Sat–Sun, €3.40, 35 min), then hop bus #73 or #78 to the castle.

For a romantic twist, hike or mountain-bike from the trailhead at the recommended hotel **Gutshof zum Schluxen** in Pinswang, Austria (see page 363, they rent bikes). When the dirt road forks at the top of the hill, go right (downhill), cross the Austria-Germany border (marked by a sign and deserted hut), and follow the narrow paved road to the castles. It's a 60- to 90-minute hike or a great circular bike trip (allow 30 min; cyclists can return to Schluxen from the castles on a different 30-min bike route via Füssen).

SIGHTS

For all the logistics, see "Visiting the Castles" on page 337.

▲▲▲Hohenschwangau Castle

Standing quietly below Neuschwanstein, the big, yellow Hohenschwangau (hoh-en-SHVAHN-gow) Castle was Ludwig's boyhood home. Originally built in the 12th century, it was ruined by Napoleon. Ludwig's father, King Maximilian II, rebuilt it in 1830. Hohenschwangau ("High Land of the Swans") was used by the royal family as a summer hunting lodge until 1912. This was Ludwig's boyhood escape.

The interior decor is harmonious, cohesive, and original—all done in 1835, with paintings inspired by Romantic themes. The

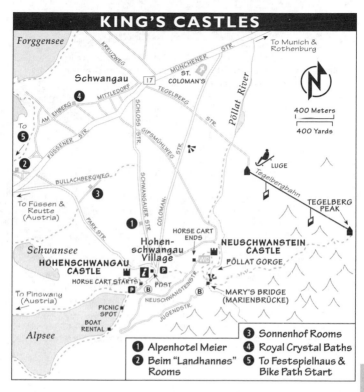

KING'S CASTLES

- ① Alpenhotel Meier
- ② Beim "Landhannes" Rooms
- ③ Sonnenhof Rooms
- ④ Royal Crystal Baths
- ⑤ To Festspielhaus & Bike Path Start

Wittelsbach family (which ruled Bavaria for nearly seven centuries) still owns the place (and lived in the annex—today's shop—until the 1970s). As you tour the castle, imagine how the paintings must have inspired young Ludwig. For 17 years, he followed the construction of his dream castle from his dad's place—you'll see the telescope still set up and directed at Neuschwanstein.

The excellent 30-minute tours give a better glimpse of Ludwig's life than the more-visited and famous Neuschwanstein Castle tour. Tours here are smaller (35 people rather than 60) and more relaxed.

▲▲▲Neuschwanstein Castle

Imagine "Mad" King Ludwig as a boy, climbing the hills above his dad's castle, Hohenschwangau, dreaming up the ultimate fairy-tale castle. Inheriting the throne at the young age of 18, he had the power to make his dream concrete and stucco. Neuschwanstein (noy-SHVAHN-shtine) was designed by a theater set designer first...and then by an architect. It looks medieval, but it's modern iron-and-brick construction with a sandstone veneer—only about as old as the Eiffel Tower. It feels like something you'd see at a

"Mad" King Ludwig

A tragic figure, Ludwig II (a.k.a. "Mad" King Ludwig) ruled Bavaria for 22 years until his death in 1886 at the age of 40. Bavaria was weak. Politically, Ludwig's reality was to "rule" either as a pawn of Prussia or a pawn of Austria. Rather than deal with politics in Bavaria's capital, Munich, Ludwig frittered away most of his time at his family's hunting palace, Hohenschwangau. He spent much of his adult life constructing his fanciful Neuschwanstein Castle—like a kid builds a tree house—on a neighboring hill upon the scant ruins of a medieval castle. Although Ludwig spent 17 years building Neuschwanstein, he lived in it only 172 days.

Ludwig was a true romantic living in a Romantic age. His best friends were artists, poets, and composers, such as Richard Wagner. His palaces are wallpapered with misty medieval themes—especially those from Wagnerian operas. Eventually he was declared mentally unfit to rule Bavaria and taken away from Neuschwanstein. Two days after this eviction, Ludwig was found dead in a lake. To this day, people debate whether the king was murdered or committed suicide.

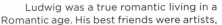

THE BEST OF BAVARIA

home show for 19th-century royalty. Built from 1869 to 1886, it's the epitome of the Romanticism popular in 19th-century Europe. Construction stopped with Ludwig's death (only a third of the interior was finished), and within six weeks, tourists were paying to go through it.

Today, guides herd groups of 60 through the castle, giving an interesting—if rushed—30-minute tour. You'll go up and down more than 300 steps, through lavish rooms based on Wagnerian opera themes, the king's gilded-lily bedroom, and his extravagant throne room. You'll visit 15 rooms with their original furnishings and fanciful wall paintings. After the tour, before you descend to the king's kitchen, see the 20-minute video about the king's life and passions accompanied by Wagner's music (next to the café, alternates between English and German, schedule board at the entry says what's playing and what's on deck). After the kitchen (state of the art for this high-tech king in its day), you'll see a room lined with fascinating drawings (described in English) of the castle plans, construction, and drawings from 1883 of Falkenstein—a whimsical, over-the-top, never-built castle that makes Neuschwanstein look stubby. Falkenstein occupied Ludwig's fantasies the year he died.

Visiting the Castles

Cost: Each castle costs €9, a *Königsticket* for both castles costs €17, and children under 18 (accompafnied by an adult) are admitted free.

Hours: Both castles are open April–Sept daily from 9:00 with last tour departing at 18:00, Oct–March daily from 10:00 with last tour at 16:00.

Getting Tickets for the Castles: Every tour bus in Bavaria converges on Neuschwanstein, and tourists flush in each morning from Munich. A handy reservation system (described below) sorts out the chaos for smart travelers. Tickets come with admission times. To tour both castles, you must do Hohenschwangau first (logical, since this gives a better introduction to Ludwig's short life). You'll get two tour times: Hohenschwangau and then, two hours later, Neuschwanstein. If you miss your appointed tour time, you can't get in.

A **ticket center** for both castles is located at street level between the two (daily April–Sept 8:00–17:00, Oct–March

9:00–15:00; last tickets sold for Neuschwanstein one hour before closing, for Hohenschwangau 30 min before closing). Arrive by 8:00 in summer, and you'll likely be touring by 9:00. During August, tickets for English tours can run out by 16:00.

Reservations: While chaotic crowd scenes are largely a thing of the past, it's smart to reserve in peak season (July–Sept, especially Aug). Reservations cost €2 per person per castle, and you should make them a minimum of 24 hours in advance by phone (tel. 08362/930-830), email (info @ticket-center-hohenschwangau.de), or online (www.ticket-center -hohenschwangau.de).

Tour Procedure: You must pick up tickets well before the appointed entry time (30 min before your Hohenschwangau tour, 1 hr before your Neuschwanstein tour). Why the long wait? Many of the businesses serving tourists are owned by the old royal family...so they require more waiting time than necessary in the hope that you'll spend more money. The same applies to the minimum

THE BEST OF BAVARIA

allowable time between the two castle tours: two hours. After completing the Hohenschwangau tour, this leaves you with about 45 minutes to kill. Ask for the minimum between tours. If they give you a longer gap, request less downtime.

For each castle, tourists jumble at the entry, waiting for their ticket number to light up on the board. When it does, power through the mob (most waiting there are holding higher numbers) and go to the turnstile. Warning: You must use your ticket while your number is still on the board. If you space out while waiting for a polite welcome, you'll miss your entry window and never get in.

Getting to the Castles: From the ticket booth, Hohenschwangau is an easy 10-minute climb, and Neuschwanstein is a steep 30-minute hike. To minimize hiking to Neuschwanstein, you can take a shuttle bus (leaves every few minutes from in front of Hotel Lisl, just above ticket office and to the left) or a horse-drawn carriage (in front of Hotel Müller, just above ticket office and to the right), but neither gets you to the castle doorstep. The shuttle bus drops you off near Mary's Bridge, leaving you a steep, 10-minute downhill walk to the castle—be sure to see the view from Mary's Bridge before hiking down (€1.80 one-way, the €2.60 round-trip is not worth it since you have to hike uphill to the bus stop for your return trip). Carriages (€5 up, €2.50 down) are slower than walking and stop below Neuschwanstein, leaving you a five-minute uphill hike. Here's the most economic and least strenuous plan: Ride the bus to Mary's Bridge for the view, hike down to Neuschwanstein, and then catch the horse carriage from the castle back down to the parking lot.

Services: The helpful TI, bus stop, ATM, WC (€0.50), and telephones cluster around the main intersection (**TI** open daily May–Sept 11:00–19:00, Oct–April 11:00–17:00, tel. 08362/819-765, www.schwangau.de).

Eating: The "village" at the foot of Europe's Disney castle feeds off the droves of hungry, shop-happy tourists. The Bräustüberl cafeteria serves the cheapest grub (€4 gut-bomb meals, often with live folk music, from 11:30). The Alpsee lake is ideal for a picnic, but there are no grocery shops nearby. Your best bet is to get food to go from one of the many bratwurst stands (between the ticket center and TI) or a sandwich at the shop adjacent the ticket booth. Take a lazy lunch at the lakeside park or in one of the old-fashioned rowboats (rented by the hour in summer).

Near the Castles

Mary's Bridge (Marienbrücke)—Before or after the Neuschwanstein tour, climb up to Mary's Bridge to marvel at Ludwig's castle, just as Ludwig did. This bridge was quite an engineering accomplishment 100 years ago. From the bridge, the frisky can hike even higher to the *Beware—Danger of Death* signs and an even more glorious castle view. (Access to the bridge is closed in bad winter weather, but many travelers walk around the barriers to get there—at their own risk, of course.) For the most interesting descent from Neuschwanstein (15 min longer but worth it, especially with new steel walkways and railings that make the slippery area safer), follow signs to the Pöllat Gorge (Pöllatschlucht).

▲**Tegelberg Gondola**—Just north of Neuschwanstein is a fun play zone around the mighty Tegelberg Gondola. For €16 round-trip (€10 one-way), you can ride the lift to the 5,500-foot summit (daily 9:00–17:00, closed Nov, 4/hr, last ride at 16:30, in bad weather call first to confirm, from Füssen buses #73 and #78 continue from the castles to Tegelberg, tel. 08362/98360). On a clear day, you get great views of the Alps and Bavaria and the vicarious thrill of watching hang gliders and paragliders leap into airborne ecstasy. Weather permitting, scores of adventurous Germans line up and leap from the launch ramp at the top of the lift. With someone leaving every two or three minutes, it's great for spectators. Thrill-seekers with exceptional social skills may talk themselves into a tandem ride with a paraglider. From the top of Tegelberg, it's a steep and demanding 2.5-hour hike down to Ludwig's castle. (Avoid the treacherous trail directly below the gondola.) At the base of the gondola, you'll find a playground, a cheery eatery, the stubby remains of an ancient Roman villa, and a luge ride (below).

▲**Tegelberg Luge**—Next to the Tegelberg Gondola is a luge course. A luge is like a bobsled on wheels (for more details, see "Luge Lesson" sidebar on page 359). This stainless-steel track is

heated, so it's often dry and open, even when drizzly weather shuts down the concrete luges. It's not as scenic as Austria's Biberwier luge (see page 358), but it's handy and half the price (€2.50/ride, 6-ride sharable card-€10, July–Sept daily 10:00–18:00, otherwise same hours as gondola, in winter sometimes opens late due to wet track, in bad weather call first to confirm, no children under 6, tel. 08362/98360). A funky cable system pulls riders (in their sleds) to the top without a ski lift.

▲**Royal Crystal Baths (Königliche Kristall-Therme)**—This pool/sauna complex just outside Füssen is the perfect way to relax on a rainy day, or to cool off on a hot one. The downstairs contains two heated indoor pools and a café; outside you'll find a shallow kiddie pool, a lap pool, a heated "Kristallbad" with massage jets and a whirlpool, and a salty mineral bath. The extensive saunas upstairs are well worth the few extra euros, as long as you're OK with nudity. (Swimsuits are required in the downstairs pools, but *verboten* in the upstairs saunas.) You'll see pool and sauna rules in German all over, but don't worry—just follow the locals' lead. To enter the baths, first choose the length of your visit and your focus (big outdoor pool only, all ground-floor pools but not the saunas, or the whole enchilada—a flyer explains all the prices in English). You'll get a wristband and a credit-card-sized ticket with a bar code. Insert that ticket into the entry gate, and keep it—you'll need it to get out. Enter through the yellow changing stalls— where you'll change into your bathing suit—then choose a storage locker (€1 coin deposit). When it's time to leave, reinsert your ticket in the gate—if you've gone over the time limit, feed extra euros into the machine (€8.50/2 hrs, €12.20/4 hrs, €15.80/day, saunas-€4, towel rental-€2, bathing suit rental-€3, daily 9:00–22:00, Fri–Sat until 23:00, nude swimming everywhere Tue and Fri after 19:00; from Füssen, drive, bike, or walk across the river, turn left toward Schwangau, and then, about a mile later, turn left at signs for *Kristall-Therme*, Am Ehberg 16; tel. 08362/819-630).

Bike Ride Around Forggensee—On a beautiful day, nothing beats a bike ride around the bright-turquoise Forggensee lake. This 20-mile ride is almost exclusively on bike paths, with just a few stretches on country roads. Locals swear that going clockwise is less work, but either way has a couple of strenuous uphill parts. Still, the amazing views of the surrounding Alps will distract you from your churning legs—so this is still a great way to spend the afternoon. Rent a bike (see page 324), pack a picnic lunch, and figure about a three-hour round-trip. From Füssen, follow *Festspielhaus* signs; once you reach the theater, follow *Forggensee Rundweg* signs. From the theater, you can also take a boat ride on the Forggensee (€7/50 min, 6/day; €9.50/2 hrs, 6/day; fewer departures Nov–May, confirm schedule at Füssen TI, tel. 08362/921-363).

SLEEPING

In Hohenschwangau, near Neuschwanstein Castle

(€1 = about $1.40, Germany country code: 49, area code: 08362)
Inexpensive farmhouse B&Bs abound in the Bavarian countryside around Neuschwanstein, offering drivers a decent value. Look for

Zimmer Frei signs ("room free," or vacancy). The going rate is about €50–65 for a double, including breakfast.

$$ Alpenhotel Meier is a small, family-run hotel with 18 rooms in a bucolic setting within walking distance of the castles, just beyond the lower parking lot (Sb-€48–58, perfectly fine older Db-€80, newer Db-€88, Tb-€110, these are book-direct prices, 5 percent discount with cash and this book, all rooms have porches or balconies—some with castle views, family rooms, elevator, sauna, free parking, just before tennis courts at Schwangauer Strasse 37, tel. 08362/81152, fax 08362/987-028, www.alpenhotel-allgaeu.de, info@alpenhotel-allgaeu.de, Frau Meier).

$ Beim "Landhannes," a 200-year-old working dairy farm run by Connie Schon, rents six creaky but sunny rooms, and keeps flowers on the balconies, big bells and antlers in the halls, and cows in the yard (Sb-€30, Db-€60, 20 percent discount for 3 or more nights, apartment with kitchen, cash only, poorly signed in the village of Horn on the Füssen side of Schwangau, look for the farm down a tiny lane through the grass 100 yards in front of Hotel Kleiner König, Am Lechrain 22, tel. 08362/8349, www.landhannes.de, mayr@landhannes.de).

$ Sonnenhof is a big, woody, old house with four spacious, traditionally decorated rooms (all with balconies) and a cheery garden. It's a 15-minute walk through the fields to the castles (S-€35, D-€50, Db-€60, cash only; at Pension Schwansee on the Füssen-Neuschwanstein road, follow the small lane 100 yards to Sonnenweg 11; they'll pick you up from the train station if you request ahead, tel. 08362/8420, Frau Görlich).

THE BEST OF BAVARIA

Wieskirche

Germany's greatest Rococo-style church, the "Church in the Meadow" (rated ▲▲) is newly restored and looking as brilliant

as the day it floated down from heaven. Overripe with decoration but bright and bursting with beauty, this church is a divine droplet, a curly curlicue, the final flowering of the Baroque movement.

Cost and Hours: Donation requested, daily in summer 8:00–19:00, in winter 8:00–17:00, tel. 08862/932-930, www.wieskirche.de.

Getting There: The Wieskirche is a 30-minute drive north of Neuschwanstein. For information on taking the bus from Füssen to the Wieskirche, see page 320 in "Getting Around Bavaria and

Tirol." By car, head north from Füssen, turn right at Steingaden, and follow the signs. Take a commune-with-nature-and-smell-the-farm detour back through the meadow to the parking lot (€1/hr).

○ **Self-Guided Tour:** This pilgrimage church is built around the much-venerated statue of a scourged (or whipped) Christ, which supposedly wept in 1738. The carving—too graphic to be accepted by that generation's church—was the focus of worship in a peasant's barn. Miraculously, it shed tears—empathizing with all those who suffer. Pilgrims came from all around. A tiny and humble chapel was built to house the statue in 1739. (You can see it where the lane to the church leaves the parking lot.) Bigger and bigger crowds came. Two of Bavaria's top Rococo architects, the Zimmermann brothers (Johann Baptist and Dominikus), were commissioned to build the Wieskirche that stands here today.

Follow the theological sweep from the altar to the ceiling: Jesus whipped, chained, and then killed (notice the pelican above

the altar—recalling a pre-Christian story of a bird that opened its breast to feed its young with its own blood); the painting of a baby Jesus posed as if on the cross; the sacrificial lamb; and finally, high on the ceiling, the resurrected Christ before the Last Judgment. This is the most positive depiction of the Last Judgment around. Jesus, rather than sitting on the throne to judge, rides high on a rainbow—a symbol of forgiveness—giving any sinner the feeling that there is still time to repent, with plenty of mercy on hand. In the back, above the pipe organ, notice the empty throne—waiting for Judgment Day—and the closed door to paradise.

Above the entrances to both side aisles are murky glass cases with 18th-century handkerchiefs. People wept, came here, were healed, and no longer needed their hankies. Walk up either aisle flanking the high altar to see votives—requests and thanks to God (for happy, healthy babies, and so on). Notice how the kneelers are positioned so that worshippers can meditate on scenes of biblical miracles painted high on the ceiling and visible through the ornate tunnel frames. A priest here once told me that faith, architecture, light, and music all combine to create the harmony of the Wieskirche.

Two paintings flank the door at the rear of the church. One shows the ceremonial parade in 1749 when the white-clad monks of Steingaden carried the carved statue of Christ from the tiny church to its new big one. The second painting, from 1757, is a votive from one of the Zimmermann brothers, the artists and architects who built this church. He is giving thanks for the successful construction of the new church.

If you can't visit the Wieskirche, visit one of the other churches that came out of the same heavenly spray can: Oberammergau's church (see below), the splendid Ettal Monastery (free and near Oberammergau, described below), and, on a lesser scale, Füssen's basilica.

Route Tips for Drivers: If you're driving from Wieskirche to Oberammergau (below), you'll cross the **Echelsbacher Bridge,** which arches 230 feet over the Pöllat Gorge. Thoughtful drivers let their passengers walk across (for the views) and meet them at the other side. Any kayakers? Notice the painting of the traditional village woodcarver (who used to walk from town to town with his art on his back) on the first big house on the Oberammergau side, a shop called Almdorf Ammertal. It has a huge selection of overpriced carvings and commission-hungry tour guides.

Oberammergau

The Shirley Temple of Bavarian villages, and exploited to the hilt by the tourist trade, Oberammergau wears way too much makeup. If you're passing through anyway, it's a ▲ sight—worth a wander among the half-timbered *Lüftlmalerei* houses frescoed (in a style popular throughout the town in the 18th century) with biblical scenes and famous fairy-tale characters. It's also a relatively convenient home base for visiting Linderhof Castle, Ettal Monastery, and the Zugspitze (via Garmisch).

Tourist Information: The TI is at Eugen-Papst-Strasse 9A (Mon–Fri 9:00–18:00, Sat 10:00–13:00, Sun 10:00–12:00; Nov–May closed Sun; tel. 08822/922-740, www.oberammergau.de).

Getting There

From Füssen to Oberammergau, four to six **buses** run daily (fewer in winter, 1.5 hrs). Buses connect Oberammergau, Ettal Monastery, and Linderhof Castle four times each day in the summer. All buses start at the train station and stop two minutes later near the TI closer to the center. **Trains** run from Reutte to Oberammergau (3/day, change in Garmisch and Murnau) and from Munich to Oberammergau (nearly hourly, 1.75 hrs, change in Murnau or Oberau). **Drivers** entering the town from the north should cross the bridge, take the second right, and park in the free lot a block beyond the TI. Leaving town (to Linderhof or Reutte), head out past the church and turn toward Ettal on Road 23. You're 20 miles from Reutte via the scenic Plansee.

OBERAMMERGAU

❶ Pilatus House
❷ Oberammergau Mus.
❸ To Sommerrodelbahn Steckenberg
❹ Gasthof zur Rose & Frau Magold Rooms
❺ Hotel Wittelsbach
❻ Hotel Garni Fux
❼ Anton Zwink Rooms
❽ Youth Hostel
❾ Hotel Maximilian (Beer Garden)

SIGHTS

Oberammergau Church—Visit the town church, a poor cousin of the one at Wies. Being in a woodcarving center, it's only logical that all the statues are made of wood, and then stuccoed and gilded to look like marble or gold. Saints Peter and Paul flank the altar, where the central painting can be raised to reveal a small stage decorated to celebrate special times during the church calendar. In the central dome, a touching painting shows Peter and Paul bidding each other farewell (with the city of Rome as a backdrop) on the day of their execution—the same day in the year A.D. 67. On the left, Peter is crucified upside-down. On the right, Paul is beheaded with a sword. (A fine little €3 booklet explains it all.) Wander through the lovingly maintained graveyard. A stone WWI and WWII memorial at the gate reads, "We honor and remember the victims of the violence that our land gave the world."

Passion Play—Back in 1633, in the midst of the bloody Thirty Years' War and with horrifying plagues devastating entire cities, the people of Oberammergau promised God that if they were spared from extinction, they'd "perform a play depicting the suffering, death, and resurrection of our Lord Jesus Christ" every

Woodcarving in Oberammergau

The Ammergau region is relatively poor, with no appreciable industry and no agriculture, save for some dairy farming. What they *do* have is wood. Carving religious and secular themes became a lucrative way for the locals to make some money, especially when confined to the house during the long, cold winter. Carvers from Oberammergau peddled their wares across Europe, carrying them on their back as far away as Rome. Today, the Oberammergau Carving School is a famous institution that takes only 20 students per year out of 450 applicants. Their graduates do important restorative work throughout Europe.

thereafter. The town survived and, heading into its 41st decade, the people of Oberammergau are still making good on the deal. For 100 days every 10 years (and 2010 is one of those years), about half of the town's population (a cast of 2,000) is involved in the production of this extravagant, five-hour Passion Play—telling the story of Jesus' entry into Jerusalem, Crucifixion, and Resurrection. After 2010, you'll have to settle for reading the book, seeing Nicodemus tool around town in his VW, or browsing through the theater's exhibition hall (€4, €6 combo-ticket includes Oberammergau Museum, German tours March–Oct daily 10:00–16:00, Dec–Feb weekends only except daily for a week before and after Christmas, no tours in Nov, tel. 08822/945-8833). English speakers get little respect here, with only two theater tours a day (April–Oct at 11:00 and 14:30).

Tickets for Oberammergau's 2010 Passion Play: Starting on May 15, 2010, about 5,000 people a day will watch the five-hour play. For the first time, rather than starting in the morning, the play will be shown in the afternoon and evening. Tickets are on sale for €50–165 (www.passionsspiele2010.de).

Local Arts and Crafts—The town's best sights are its woodcarving shops. Browse through these small art galleries filled with very expensive whittled works. The beautifully frescoed **Pilatus House** on Ludwig-Thomas-Strasse often has woodcarvers and painters at work (free; April–Oct Tue–Sat 13:00–18:00, closed Sun–Mon; open Dec weekends and two weeks after Christmas 13:00–17:00; closed rest of year). For folk art, see the **Oberammergau Museum** (€4, €6 combo-ticket includes Passion Play Theater, April–Oct and Dec–Jan Tue–Sun 10:00–17:00, closed Mon; closed Nov and Feb–March).

Sommerrodelbahn Steckenberg—This stainless-steel luge track (near Oberammergau) is faster than the Tegelberg luge, but not quite as wicked as the one in Biberwier (€2.50/ride, €11/6 rides, May–Oct daily 10:00–18:00, closed when wet, Liftweg 1 in Unterammergau, clearly marked and easy 2.5-mile bike ride to Unterammergau along Bahnhofstrasse/Rottenbucherstrasse, take the first left when entering Unterammergau, tel. 08822/4027).

SLEEPING

(€1 = about $1.40, Germany country code: 49, area code: 08822)
$$ Gasthof zur Rose is a big, central, family-run place with 21 rooms (Sb-€40, Db-€65, Tb-€75, Qb-€86, Internet access, Dedlerstrasse 9, tel. 08822/4706, fax 08822/6753, www.hotel-oberammergau.de, gasthof-rose@t-online.de, Frank family).

$$ Hotel Wittelsbach is a romantic, tourist-class hotel. Its creaky, 1970s-style public areas hide 40 deluxe, spacious rooms, many with geranium-clad balconies (Sb-€55–85, Db-€80–110, Tb-€100–140, Dorfstrasse 21, tel. 08822/92800, www.hotel wittelsbach.de, info@hotelwittelsbach.de).

$$ Hotel Garni Fux, quiet and romantic, rents six large rooms and eight apartments decorated in the Bavarian *Landhaus* style (Sb-€65, Db-€84, apartments €106–168, cheaper Nov–April, free Internet access and Wi-Fi, Mannagasse 2a, tel. 08822/93093, www.firmafux.de, info@firmafux.de).

$ Anton Zwink offers 10 small, quiet, no-frills rooms in a neighborhood adjacent to the town center (Sb-€30, Db-€50, behind Gasthof zur Rose at Daisenbergerstrasse 10, tel. 08822/6334, www.pension-zwink.de, info@pension-zwink.de).

$ Frau Magold's is a homey, grandmotherly place renting three bright and spacious rooms—twice as nice as the cheap hotel rooms, and for much less money (Db-€48, cash only, also has two family apartments, immediately behind Gasthof zur Rose at Kleppergasse 1, tel. & fax 08822/4340, Christine).

$ The **youth hostel,** on the river, is a short walk from the center (€18 beds, includes breakfast and sheets, Malensteinweg 10, tel. 08822/4114, fax 08822/1695, jhoberammergau@djh-bayern.de).

EATING

Locals won't be caught dead inside the chic **Hotel Maximilian.** But they fill its serene beer garden to enjoy the hotel's homemade beer and summertime grill, which cooks up delicious chicken, sausage, and spareribs for under €10 (daily 9:00–22:00, right behind the church, Ettaler Strasse 5, tel. 08822/948-740).

TRANSPORTATION CONNECTIONS

From Oberammergau to: Füssen (4–6 buses/day in summer, transfer at Echelsbacher Brücke, 1.5 hrs total), **Linderhof Castle** (bus #9622, nearly hourly, 25–40 min; some of these also stop at **Ettal Monastery**), **Garmisch** (nearly hourly buses, 40 min; also possible by train with a transfer in Murnau, 1.5 hrs; from Garmisch you can ascend the **Zugspitze**), **Munich** (nearly hourly trains, 1.75 hrs, change in Murnau or Oberau), **Reutte** (3/day, change in Murnau and Garmisch).

Linderhof Castle

This homiest of "Mad" King Ludwig's castles is small and comfortably exquisite—good enough for a minor god, and worth ▲▲. Set in the woods 15 minutes from Oberammergau and surrounded by fountains and sculpted, Italian-style gardens, it's the only palace I've toured that actually had me feeling envious.

Ludwig was king for 22 of his 40 years. He lived much of his last eight years here—the only one of his castles that was finished in his lifetime. Frustrated by the limits of being a "constitutional monarch," he retreated to Linderhof, inhabiting a private fantasy world where extravagant castles glorified his otherwise weakened kingship. He lived here as a royal hermit; his dinner table—set with dishes and food—rose from the kitchen below into his dining room, so he could eat alone.

Beyond the palace is Ludwig's **grotto.** Inspired by Wagner's *Tannhäuser* opera, this performance space is 300 feet long and 70 feet tall. Its rocky walls are made of cement poured over an iron frame. The grotto provided a private theater for the reclusive king to enjoy his beloved Wagnerian operas by himself. The first electricity in Bavaria was generated here, to change the colors of the stage lights and to power Ludwig's fountain and wave machine.

Cost and Hours: €7, daily April–Sept 9:00–18:00, Oct–March 10:00–16:00, last tour 30 min before closing, fountains often erupt on the half-hour, German tel. 08822/92030.

Getting There: Without a car, getting to (and from) Linderhof is a royal headache, unless you're staying in Oberammergau. From that village, bus #9622 goes nearly hourly in summer (less frequently off-season; see "Transportation Connections" for Oberammergau, above). If you're driving, park near the ticket office (€2.50).

Visiting the Castle: The complex sits isolated in natural splendor. Plan for lots of walking and a two-hour stop to fully enjoy this royal park. Your ticket comes with an entry time to tour the palace, which is a five-minute hike from the ticket office. At the palace entrance, wait in line for your number to take the required, 30-minute English tour. Afterwards, hike 10 minutes uphill to the grotto (take the brief but interesting free tour in English, no reservations necessary). Then see the other royal buildings dotting the king's playground if you like.

Crowd-Beating Tips: July and August crowds can cause delays at the palace of up to two hours. During this period, you're wise to arrive after 15:00. Any other time of year, you should get your palace tour time shortly after you arrive.

Ettal Monastery and Pilgrimage Church

In 1328, the Holy Roman Emperor was returning from Rome with what was considered a miraculous statue of Mary and Jesus. He was in political and financial trouble, so to please God, he founded a monastery with this statue as its centerpiece. The monastery was located here because it was suitably off the beaten path, but today Ettal is on one of the most-traveled tourist routes in Bavaria. Stopping here (free and easy for drivers) offers a convenient peek at a splendid Baroque church.

Cost and Hours: Free, daily 8:00–19:45 in summer, until 18:00 off-season.

Getting There: The Ettal Monastery is a few minutes' **drive** (or a delightful **bike** ride) from Oberammergau. Just park for free and wander in. Some Oberammergau-to-Linderhof **buses** stop here (see "Transportation Connections" for Oberammergau, on the previous page).

○ Self-Guided Tour: As you enter the more than 1,000-square-foot **courtyard,** imagine the 14th-century Benedictine abbey, an independent religious community. It produced everything it needed right here. In the late Middle Ages, abbeys like this had jurisdiction over the legal system, administration, and taxation of their district. Since then, the monastery has had its ups and downs. Secularized during the French Revolution and Napoleonic age, the Benedictines' property was confiscated by the state and sold. Religious life returned a century later. Today the abbey survives, with 50–60 monks. It remains a self-contained community, with living quarters for the monks, workshops, and guests' quarters. Along with their religious responsibilities, the brothers make their famous liqueur, brew beer, run a hotel, and educate 380 students in their private high school.

At the front of the church, you pass a **tympanum** over the door dating from 1350. It shows the founding couple, Emperor Louis the Bavarian and his wife Margaret, directing our attention to the crucified Lord and inviting us to enter the church contemplatively.

Stepping inside, the light draws our eyes to the **dome** (it's a double shell design 230 feet high) rather than to the high altar. Illusions—with the dome opening right to the sky—merge heaven and earth. The dome fresco shows hundreds of Benedictines worshipping the Holy Trinity...the glory of the Benedictine Order. This is classic "south German Baroque."

Statues of the **saints** on the altars are either engaged in a holy conversation with each other or singing the praises of God. Broken shell-style patterns seem to create constant movement, with cherubs adding to the energy. Side altars and confessionals seem to grow out of the architectural structure; its decorations and furnishings become part of an organic whole. Imagine how 18th-century farmers and woodcutters, who never traveled, would step in here on Sunday and be inspired to praise their God.

The origin of the monastery is shown over the **choir arch:** An angel wearing the robe of a Benedictine monk presents the emperor with a marble Madonna and commissions him to found this monastery. (In reality, the statue was made in Pisa, circa 1300, and given to the emperor in Italy.)

Dwarfed by all the magnificence and framed by a monumental tabernacle is that tiny, most precious statue of the abbey—the miraculous **statue of Mary and the baby Jesus.**

Zugspitze

The tallest peak in Germany, worth ▲▲, is also a border crossing. Lifts from both Austria and Germany meet at the 9,700-foot

summit of the Zugspitze. You can straddle the border between two great nations while enjoying an incredible view. Restaurants, shops, and telescopes await you at the summit.

Austrian Approach: The Tiroler Zugspitzbahn ascent is less crowded and cheaper than the German alternatives. Departing from above the village of Ehrwald (a 30-min train trip from Reutte, every 2 hrs), the tram zips you to the top in 10 minutes (€33 round-trip, departures in each direction at :00, :20, and :40 past the hour, daily 8:40–16:40 except closed April–mid-May and most of mid-Oct–Nov, drivers follow signs for *Tiroler Zugspitzbahn*, free parking, Austrian tel. 05673/2309, www.zugspitze.com). While the German ascent from Garmisch is easier for those without a car, buses connect the Ehrwald train station and the Austrian lift nearly every hour (or pay €8 for the 5-min taxi ride from Ehrwald train station).

German Approach: There are two ways to ascend the Zugspitze from Garmisch, Germany (which you can reach by bus from Füssen or Oberammergau—see "Getting Around Bavaria and Tirol," page 320): the whole way by cogwheel train (1.25 hrs one-way), or a faster cogwheel-train-plus-cable-car option (about 45 min one-way). Both cost the same (€47 round-trip). Although the train ride takes longer, many travelers enjoy the more involved cog-railway experience. The train departs from Garmisch, stops at Eibsee for the cable-car connection, and then continues up— and through—the mountain. The cable car simply zips you to the top in five minutes from the Eibsee station. Cable cars go up daily from 8:15–14:15. The last cable car down departs at about 16:30 (tel. 08821/7970, www.zugspitze.de). Allow plenty of time for afternoon descents: If bad weather hits in the late afternoon, cable cars can be delayed at the summit, causing tourists to miss their train connection from Eibsee back to Garmisch.

Drivers can park for €3 at the cable-car station at Eibsee. Hikers can enjoy the easy six-mile walk around the lovely Eibsee (start 5 min downhill from cable-car station).

◐ Self-Guided Tour: Whether you ascended from the Austrian or German side, you're high enough now to enjoy a little tour of the summit. The two terraces—Bavarian and Tirolean— are connected by a narrow walkway, which was the border station before Germany and Austria opened their borders. The Austrian (Tirolean) side was higher until the Germans blew its top off in World War II to make a flak tower, so let's start there.

Tirolean Terrace: Before you stretches the Zugspitzplatt glacier. Each summer, a 65,000-square-foot reflector is spread over the ice to try to slow the shrinking. Since metal ski lift towers collect heat, they, too, are wrapped to try to save the glacier. Many ski lifts fan out here, as if reaching for a ridge that defines the border between Germany and Austria. The circular metal building is the top of the cog-railway line that the Germans cut through the mountains in 1931. Just above that, find a small square building—the wedding chapel *(Hochzeitskapelle)* consecrated in 1981 by Cardinal Joseph Ratzinger (now Pope Benedict XVI).

Both Germany and Austria use this rocky pinnacle for communication purposes. The square box on the Tirolean Terrace provides the Innsbruck airport with air-traffic control, and a tower nearby is for the German *Katastrophenfunk* (civil defense network).

This highest point in Germany (there are many higher points in Austria) was first climbed in 1820. The Austrians built a cable car that nearly reached the  summit in 1926. (You can see it just over the ridge on the Austrian side—look for the ghostly abandoned concrete station.) In 1964, the final leg, a new lift, was built connecting that 1926 station to the actual summit, where you stand now. Before then, people needed to hike the last 650 feet to the top. Today's lift dates from 1980, but was renovated after a 2003 fire. It's really much nicer than the German station. The Austrian station has a fine little museum—free with Austrian ticket, €2 if you came up from Germany—which includes three interesting videos (6-min 3-D mountain show, 30-min making-of-the-lift documentary, and 45-min look at the nature, sport, and culture of the region).

Looking up the valley from the Tirolean Terrace, you can see the towns of Ehrwald and Lermoos in the distance, and the valley that leads to Reutte. Looking clockwise, you'll see the Eibsee lake below. Hell's Valley, stretching to the right of Eibsee, seems to merit its name.

Bavarian Terrace: The narrow passage connecting the two terraces used to be a big deal—you'd show your passport here at the little blue house, and shift from Austrian shillings to German marks. Notice the regional pride here: no German or Austrian banners, but regional ones instead—Freistaat Bayern and Land Tirol.

The German side features a golden cross marking the summit...the highest point in Germany. A priest and his friends hauled it up in 1851. The historic original was shot up by Americans soldiers using it for target practice in the late 1940s, so what you see today is a modern replacement. In the summer, it's easy to "summit" the Zugspitze, as there are steps and handholds all the way to the top. Or you can just stay behind and feed the birds. The yellow-beak ravens get chummy with those who share a little pretzel or bread.

The oldest building up here is the rustic, tin-and-wood weather tower, erected in 1900 by the *Deutscher Wetterdienst* (German weather service). The first mountaineers' hut was built in 1897, but didn't last. The existing one—entwined with mighty cables that cinch it down—dates from 1914. In 1985, observers clocked 200-mph winds up here—those cables were necessary. Step inside the restaurant to enjoy museum-quality photos and paintings on the wall (including a look at the team who hiked up with the golden cross in 1851).

Reutte

Reutte (ROY-teh, with a rolled *r*), a relaxed Austrian town of 5,700, is located 20 minutes across the border from Füssen. While

overlooked by the international tourist crowd, it's popular with Austrians and Germans for its climate. Doctors recommend its "grade 1" air. I like Reutte for the opportunity to simply be in a real community. Real estate can be sold only to those using it as a primary residence—an example of how much the town is committed to its character. (Many formerly vibrant alpine towns made a pile of money but lost their sense of community by becoming resorts. They allowed wealthy foreigners—who drop in for just a week or two a year—to buy up all the land, and are now shuttered up and dead most of the time.)

Reutte's one claim to fame with Americans: As Nazi Germany was falling in 1945, Hitler's top rocket scientist, Werner von Braun, joined the Americans (rather than the Russians) in Reutte. You could say the American space program began here.

ORIENTATION

(Austria country code: 43, area code: 05672)
Reutte isn't featured in any other American guidebook. While its generous sidewalks are filled with smart boutiques and lazy coffeehouses, its charms are subtle. It was never rich or important. Its castle is ruined, its buildings have painted-on "carvings," its churches are full, its men yodel for each other on birthdays, and its energy is spent soaking its Austrian and German guests in *Gemütlichkeit*. Most guests stay for a week, and the town's attractions are more time-consuming than thrilling.

Tourist Information

Reutte's TI is a block in front of the train station (Mon–Fri 8:00–12:00 & 14:00–17:00, no midday break July–Aug, Sat 8:30–12:00, closed Sun, tel. 05672/62336, www.reutte.com). Go over your sightseeing plans, ask about a folk evening, pick up city and biking maps and the *Sommerprogramm* events schedule (in German only), and ask about discounts with the hotel guest cards. Their free informational booklet has a good self-guided town walk.

Arrival in Reutte

If you're coming by **car** from Innsbruck, take the south *(Süd)* exit into town. If you are coming from Füssen or Munich, skip the north *(Nord)* exit and take the south *(Süd)* exit instead. For parking in town, blue lines denote pay-and-display spots. There's a free lot (P-1) near the train station on Muhlerstrasse.

Reutte's little **train** station is an easy, flat walk from my recommended hotels in central Reutte and Breitenwang (head left out of the station to reach the center of town). To reach hotels in Ehenbichl, take the bus from the station (get specifics from hotel), or consider asking your hosts to pick you up.

Helpful Hints

Internet Access: There's a **call shop** at Untermarkt 22 in the town center (Tue–Sun 11:00–22:00, closed Mon), and **Café Alte Post** at Untermarkt 15 has Internet access. Otherwise, rely on your hotel.

Laundry: There's no launderette in town, but the recommended hotels Maximilian and Ernberg let even non-guests use their self-service machines (see page 361).

Bike Rental: Try **Intersport** (€15/day, Mon–Fri 9:00–18:00, Sat 9:00–17:00, closed Sun, Lindenstrasse 25, tel. 05672/62352), or check at Hotel Maximilian (see page 361).

Car Rental: Autoreisen Köck rents cars at Muhlerstrasse 12 (€80/24 hrs, tel. 05672/62233).

"Nightlife": Reutte is pretty quiet. For any action at all, there's a strip of bars, dance clubs, and Italian restaurants on Lindenstrasse.

SIGHTS AND ACTIVITIES

▲▲Ehrenberg Castle Ensemble (Festungsensemble Ehrenberg)

If Neuschwanstein was the medieval castle dream, Ehrenburg is the medieval castle reality. Just a mile outside of Reutte are the brooding ruins of four castles that once made up the largest fort in Tirol. This impressive "castle ensemble" was built to defend

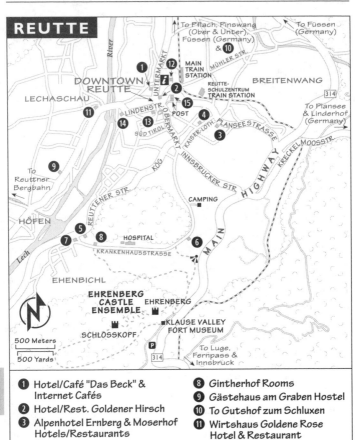

REUTTE

- ❶ Hotel/Café "Das Beck" & Internet Cafés
- ❷ Hotel/Rest. Goldener Hirsch
- ❸ Alpenhotel Ernberg & Moserhof Hotels/Restaurants
- ❹ Hosp Rooms
- ❺ Hotel/Rest. Maximilian
- ❻ Gasthof-Pension Waldrast
- ❼ Pension Hohenrainer
- ❽ Gintherhof Rooms
- ❾ Gästehaus am Graben Hostel
- ❿ To Gutshof zum Schluxen
- ⓫ Wirtshaus Goldene Rose Hotel & Restaurant
- ⓬ Storfwirt Restaurant
- ⓭ Non Solo Pasta
- ⓮ Bike Rental
- ⓯ Car Rental

against the Bavarians and to bottle up the strategic Via Claudia trade route, which cut through the Alps as it connected Italy and Germany. Today, these castles have become a European "castle museum," showing off 500 years of military architecture in one swoop. The European Union is helping fund the project (paying a third of its €9 million cost) because it promotes the heritage of a multinational region—Tirol—rather than a country.

The complex has four parts: the fortified Klause toll booth in the valley floor, the oldest castle on the first hill above (Ehrenberg), a mighty and more modern castle high above (Schlosskopf, built in the age when cannon positioned there made the original castle vulnerable), and a smaller fourth castle across the valley (Fort Claudia, an hour's hike away). All four were a fortified complex once connected by walls. Signs posted throughout the castle complex help visitors find their way and explain some background on the region's history, geology, geography, culture, flora, and fauna. (While the castles are free and open all the time, the museum and multimedia show at the fort's parking lot charge admission.)

Getting to the Castle Ensemble: The Klause, Ehrenberg, and Schlosskopf castles are on the road to Lermoos and Innsbruck. These are a pleasant walk or a short bike ride from Reutte; bikers can use the *Radwanderweg* along the Lech River (the TI has a good map).

▲**Klause Valley Fort Museum**— Historians estimate that about 10,000 tons of precious salt passed through this valley (along the route of Rome's Via Claudia) each year in medieval times, so it's no wonder the locals built this complex of fortresses and castles. Beginning in the 14th century, the fort controlled traffic and levied tolls on all who passed. Today, these scant remains hold a museum and a theater with a multimedia show (€8 for museum, €11 combo-ticket also includes multimedia show, €18 family pass for 2 adults and any number of kids, daily 10:00–17:00, closed Nov–mid-Dec, tel. 05672/62007, www.ehrenberg.at).

While there are no real artifacts here (other than the sword used in A.D. 2008 to make me the honorary First Knight of Ehrenberg), the clever, kid-friendly **museum** takes one 14th-century decade (1360–1370) and attempts to bring it to life. It's a hands-on experience, well-described in English. You can try on a set of armor (and then weigh yourself), see the limited vision knights had to put up with when wearing helmets, empathize with victims of the plague, and join a Crusade.

The **multimedia show** takes you on a 30-minute spin through the 2,000-year history of this valley's fortresses, with images projected on the old stone walls and modern screens (generally in German, in English at 13:00 and sometimes by request).

▲▲**Ehrenberg Ruins**—Ehrenberg, a 13th-century rock pile, provides a super opportunity to let your imagination off its leash. Hike up 30 minutes from the parking lot for a great view from your own private ruins. Ehrenberg ("Mountain of Honor") was the first castle here, built in 1296. Thirteenth-century castles were designed to stand boastfully tall. With the advent of gunpowder, castles dug in. (Notice the 18th-century **ramparts** around you.)

REUTTE

Approaching Ehrenberg Castle, look for the small **door** to the left. It's the night entrance (tight and awkward, and therefore safer  against a surprise attack). Entering this castle, you go through two doors. Castles allowed step-by-step retreat, giving defenders time to regroup and fight back against invading forces.

Before climbing to the top of the castle, follow the path around to the right to a big, grassy courtyard with commanding views and a fat, newly restored **turret.** This stored gunpowder and held a big cannon that enjoyed a clear view of the valley below. In medieval times, all the trees approaching the castle were cleared to keep an unobstructed view.

Look out over the valley. The pointy spire marks **Breitenwang,** which was a stop on the ancient Via Claudia and a Roman Camp in A.D. 46. In 1489, after the Reutte bridge crossed the Lech River, Reutte (marked by the onion-domed church) was made a market town and eclipsed Breitenwang in importance. Any gliders circling? They launch from just over the river in Höfen.

For centuries, this castle was the seat of government—ruling an area called the "judgment of Ehrenberg" (roughly the same as today's district of Reutte). When the emperor came by, he stayed here. In 1604, the ruler moved downtown into more comfortable quarters, and the castle was no longer a palace.

Now climb to the top of Ehrenberg Castle. Take the high ground. There was no water supply here—just kegs of wine, beer, and a cistern to collect rain.

Ehrenberg repelled 16,000 Swedish soldiers in the defense of Catholicism in 1632. Ehrenberg saw three or four other battles, but its end was not glorious. In the 1780s, a local businessman bought the castle in order to sell off its parts. Later, in the late 19th century, when vagabonds moved in, the roof was removed to make squatting miserable. With the roof gone, deterioration quickened, leaving only this evocative shell and a whiff of history.

▲**Schlosskopf**—From Ehrenberg, you can hike up another 30 minutes to the mighty Schlosskopf ("Castle Head"). When the Bavarians captured Ehrenberg in 1703, the Tiroleans climbed up to the bluff above it to rain cannonballs down on their former fortress. In 1740, a mighty new castle—designed to defend against modern artillery—was built on this sky-high strategic location. By the end of the 20th century, the castle was completely overgrown with trees—you literally couldn't see it from Reutte. But today the trees are shaved away, and the castle has been excavated. In 2008, the Castle Ensemble project, led by local architect Armin Walch, re-opened the site with English descriptions and view platforms. One spot gives spectacular views of the strategic valley. The other looks down on the older Ehrenberg Castle ruins, illustrating the strategic problems presented with the advent of cannon.

In Reutte

Reutte Museum (Museum Grünes Haus)—Reutte's city museum, offering a quick look at the local folk culture and the story of the castles, is more cute than impressive. Perhaps someday a little English will bring more meaning to the exhibits (€2, May–Oct Tue–Sun 10:00–16:00, closed Mon and Nov–April, in the bright-green building on Untermarkt, around corner from Hotel Goldener Hirsch, tel. 05672/72304, www.museum-reutte.at).

▲▲**Tirolean Folk Evening**—Ask the TI or your hotel if there's a Tirolean folk evening scheduled. During the summer (July–Aug), nearby towns (such as Höfen on Tuesdays) occasionally put on an evening of yodeling, slap dancing, and Tirolean frolic. These are generally free and worth the short drive. Off-season, you'll have to do your own yodeling. There are also weekly folk concerts featuring the local choir or brass band in Reutte's Zeiller Platz (free, July–Aug only, ask at TI). For listings of these and other local events, pick up a copy of the German-only *Sommerprogramm* schedule at the TI.

▲**Flying and Gliding**—For a major thrill on a sunny day, drop by the tiny airport in Höfen across the river and fly. A small, single-prop plane can buzz the Zugspitze and Ludwig's castles and give you a bird's-eye peek of Reutte's Ehrenberg ruins (2 people for 30 min–€110, 1 hr–€220, tel. 05672/63207, phone rarely answered and then not in English, so your best bet is to show up at the Höfen airport on good-weather afternoons). Or, for something more angelic, how about *Segelfliegen?* For €40, you get 30 minutes in a glider for two (you and the pilot, €60/1 hr) from Segelflugverein Ausserfern. Just watching the towrope launch the graceful glider like a giant, slow-motion rubber-band gun is exhilarating (May–mid-Sept 12:00–19:00, sometimes in April and Oct if not too snowy, in good but breezy weather only, find someone in the know at the "Thermik Ranch," tel. 05672/71550, mobile 0676-557-1085, www.segelflugverein-ausserfern.at).

Reuttener Bergbahn—This mountain lift swoops you high above the tree line to a starting point for several hikes and an alpine flower park, with special paths leading you past countless varieties of local flora. Unique to this lift is a barefoot hiking trail *(Barfusswanderweg)*, designed to be walked without shoes—no joke (€10 one-way, €14 round-trip, flowers best in late July, runs usually mid-June–Oct daily 9:00–12:00 & 13:00–17:00, weekends

REUTTE

only in spring and fall, across the river in Höfen, tel. 05672/62420, www.reuttener-seilbahnen.at).

Near Reutte

Bird Lookout Tower—Between Reutte and Füssen is a pristine (if you get past the small local industrial park) nature preserve with an impressive wooden tower from which to appreciate the vibrant birdlife in the wetlands along the Lech River. Look for *Vogel-Erlebnispfad* signs as you're driving through the village of Pflach (on the road between Reutte and Füssen). The EU gave half the money needed for the nature preserve—home to 110 different species of birds that nest here. The best action is early in the day. Be quiet—eggs are being laid.

▲▲Biberwier Luge Course—Near Lermoos, on the road from Reutte toward Innsbruck, you'll find the Biberwier *Sommerrodelbahn*. At 4,250 feet, it's the longest luge course in the Tirol (20 min from Reutte, stay on main road, Biberwier is the first exit after a long tunnel). The only drawbacks are its brief season, short hours, and a proclivity for shutting down sporadically—even at the slightest bit of rain (€6.60/ride, less for 3-, 5-, and 10-ride tickets, late May–mid-Oct daily 9:00–16:30, closed mid-Oct–late May, tel. 05673/2111, regional TI is more likely to have info in English—tel. 05673/20000). If you don't have a car, it's not worth the trouble; consider the luge near Neuschwanstein instead (see "Tegelberg Luge," page 339). Daredevils may want to rent the "monster roller" to literally skateboard down the mountain (€7 for the roller, €10/2 hrs lift usage). The ugly cube-shaped building marring the countryside near the luge course is a hotel for outdoor adventure enthusiasts. You can ride your mountain bike right into your room, or skip the elevator by using the indoor climbing wall.

▲Fallerschein—Easy for drivers and a special treat for those who may have been Kit Carson in a previous life, this extremely remote log-cabin village is a 4,000-foot-high, flower-speckled world of serene slopes and cowbells. Thunderstorms roll down the valley like it's God's bowling alley, but the pint-size church on the high ground, blissfully simple in a land of Baroque, seems to promise that this huddle of houses will survive, and the river and breeze will just keep flowing. The couples sitting on benches are mostly Austrian vacationers who've rented cabins here. Many of them, appreciating the remoteness of Fallerschein, are having affairs.

Sleeping in Fallerschein: **$ Lottes Fallerscheiner Stube** is a family-friendly mountain-hut restaurant with a low-ceilinged attic space that has basic beds for up to 17 sleepy hikers. The accommodations aren't fancy, but if you're looking for remote, this is it (dorm bed–€9, sheets–€4, open May–Oct only, closed Tue, wildlife

Luge Lesson

Taking a wild ride on a luge (pronounced "loozh") is a quintessential alpine experience. It's also called a *Sommerrodelbahn*, or "summer toboggan run." To try one of Europe's great accessible thrills (€3–6), take the lift up to the top of a mountain, grab a wheeled, sled-like go-cart, and scream back down the mountainside on a banked course. Then take the lift back up and start all over again.

Luge courses are highly weather-dependent, and can close at the least hint of rain. If the weather's questionable, call ahead to confirm that your preferred luge is open. Stainless-steel courses are more likely to stay open in drizzly weather than concrete ones.

Operating the sled is simple: Push the stick forward to go faster, pull back to apply brakes. Even a novice can go very, very fast. Most are cautious on their first run, speed demons on their second...and many end up bruised and bloody on their third. A woman once showed me her travel journal illustrated with her husband's dried, five-inch-long luge scab. He disobeyed the only essential rule of luging: Keep both hands on your stick. To avoid getting into a bumper-to-bumper traffic jam, let the person in front of you get way ahead before you start. You'll emerge from the course with a windblown hairdo and a smile-creased face.

viewing deck, tel. 05632/2140, www.alpe-fallerschein.at, Gapp family).

Getting to Fallerschein: From Reutte, it's a 45-minute drive. Take road 198 to Stanzach (passing Weisenbach am Loch, then Forchach), then turn left toward Namlos. Follow the L-21 Berwang road for about five miles to a parking lot. From there, it's a two-mile walk down a drivable but technically closed one-lane road. Those driving in do so at their own risk.

SLEEPING

In or near Reutte
(**€1 = about $1.40, Austria country code: 43, area code: 05672**)
Reutte is a mellow Füssen with fewer crowds and easygoing locals with a contagious love of life. Come here for a good dose of Austrian ambience and lower prices. While it's workable on public transit, staying here makes most sense for those with a car. Reutte

is popular with Austrians and Germans, who come here year after year for one- or two-week vacations. The hotels are big, elegant, and full of comfy, carved furnishings and creative ways to spend lots of time in one spot. They take great pride in their restaurants, and the owners send their children away to hotel-management schools. All include a great breakfast, but few accept credit cards. Most hotels give about a 5 percent discount for stays of two nights or longer.

The Reutte TI has a list of 50 private homes that rent out generally good rooms *(Zimmer)* with facilities down the hall, pleasant communal living rooms, and breakfast. Most charge €20 per person per night, and the owners speak little or no English. As these are family-run places, it is especially important to cancel in advance if your plans change. I've listed a few favorites below, but the TI can always find you a room when you arrive.

Reutte is surrounded by several distinct "villages" that basically feel like suburbs—many of them, such as Breitenwang, within easy walking distance of the Reutte town center. If you want to hike through the woods to Neuschwanstein Castle, stay at Gutshof zum Schluxen (listed on page 363). To locate the recommended accommodations, see the map on page 354.

In Central Reutte

$$ Hotel "Das Beck" offers 16 clean, sunny rooms (many with balconies) filling a modern building in the heart of town. It's a great value, and guests are personally taken care of by Hans, Inge, Tamara, and Pipi. Enjoy their homemade marmalade at breakfast in the open kitchen/coffee bar or on the pleasant patio. Their small café offers tasty snacks and specializes in Austrian and Italian wines. Expect good conversation overseen by Hans (Sb-€45, Db-€68, Tb suite-€89, Qb suite-€106, Internet access free for Rick Steves readers, free parking, they'll pick you up from the train station, Untermarkt 11, tel. 05672/62522, fax 05672/625-2235, www.hotel-das-beck.at, info@hotel-das-beck.at).

$$ Hotel Goldener Hirsch, located in the center of Reutte just two blocks from the station, is a grand old hotel with 56 rooms and one lonely set of antlers (Sb-€58–62, Db-€85–90, Db suite-€90–98, Tb-€125–135, Qb-€140–145, 2-night discounts, elevator, tel. 05672/62508, fax 05672/625-087, Mühler Strasse 1, www.goldener-hirsch.at, info@goldener-hirsch.at; Monika, Helmut, and daughters Vanessa and Nina).

In Breitenwang

Right next door to Reutte is the older and quieter village of Breitenwang (with good *Zimmer* and a fine bakery). It's a 20-minute

REUTTE

walk from the Reutte train station: At the post office roundabout, follow Planseestrasse past the onion-dome church to the pointy straight-dome church near the two hotels. The Hosps—as well as other B&Bs—are along unmarked Kaiser-Lothar-Strasse, the first right past this church. If your train stops at the tiny Reutte-Schulzentrum station, hop out here—you're just a five-minute walk from the hotels.

$$ Alpenhotel Ernberg is run with great care by friendly Hermann, who combines Old World elegance with modern touches. Nestle in for some serious coziness among the carved-wood eating nooks, tiled stoves, and family-friendly backyard (Sb-€45, Db-€84, less for longer stays, self-service laundry for €7—also available for non-guests, restaurant, Planseestrasse 50, tel. 05672/71912, fax 05672/191-240, www.ernberg.at, info @ernberg.at).

$$ Moserhof Hotel has 30 new-feeling rooms plus an elegant dining room (Sb-€52, Db-€88, for these special rates ask for the Rick Steves discount when you reserve, extra bed-€35, most rooms have balconies, elevator, restaurant, free parking, Planseestrasse 44, tel. 05672/62020, fax 05672/620-2040, www.hotel-moserhof .at, info@hotel-moserhof.at, Hosp family).

$ Walter and Emilie Hosp rent three rooms in a comfortable, quiet, and modern house two blocks from the Breitenwang church steeple. You'll feel like you're staying at Grandma's (D-€40, or €36 for 4 nights or more, T-€60, Q-€80, cash only, Kaiser-Lothar-Strasse 29, tel. 05672/65377).

In Ehenbichl, near the Ehrenberg Ruins

The next listings are a bit farther from central Reutte, a couple of miles upriver in the village of Ehenbichl (under the Ehrenberg ruins). From central Reutte, go south on Obermarkt and turn right on Kög, which becomes Reuttener Strasse, following signs to *Ehenbichl*.

$$ Hotel Maximilian is a great value. It includes free bicycles, table tennis, a children's playroom, a pool table, and the friendly service of Gabi, Monika, and the rest of the Koch family. They host many special events, and their hotel has lots of wonderful extras such as a sauna and a piano (Sb-€48–52, Db-€76–84, ask for these special Rick Steves prices when you reserve, family deals, elevator, free Internet access and Wi-Fi, laundry service for €12—or €16 for non-guests, good restaurant, tel. 05672/62585, fax 05672/625-8554, www.maxihotel.com, info@hotelmaximilian.at). They rent cars to guests only (one Renault, one VW van—€0.72/km, book in advance) and bikes to anyone (€6/half-day, €10/day).

$ Gasthof-Pension Waldrast, separating a forest and a meadow, is run by the farming Huter family. The place feels hauntingly quiet and has no restaurant, but it's inexpensive and offers 10 nice rooms with generous sitting areas and castle-view balconies (Sb-€37, Db-€60, Tb-€75, Qb-€95; discounts with this book: 5 percent for 2 nights, 10 percent for 3 nights or more; cash only, all rooms non-smoking, free parking; about a mile from Reutte, just off main drag toward Innsbruck, past campground and under castle ruins on Ehrenbergstrasse; tel. & fax 05672/62443, www.waldrasttirol.com, info@waldrasttirol.com, Gerd).

$ Pension Hohenrainer, a big, quiet, no-frills place, is a good value with 12 modern rooms and some castle-view balconies (Sb-€25–30, Db-€49–55, €3 per person extra for one-night stays, cheaper for longer stays and in April–June and Sept–Oct, cash only, family rooms, non-smoking rooms, free Internet access, restaurant across the street, follow signs up the road behind Hotel Maximilian into village of Ehenbichl, tel. 05672/62544 or 05672/63262, fax 05672/62052, www.hohenrainer.at, hohenrainer@aon.at).

$ Gintherhof is a working farm that provides its guests with fresh milk, butter, and bacon. Christl and Rudi Ginther offer geranium-covered balconies, six nice rooms with carved-wood ceilings, and a Madonna in every corner (Db-€46–50, Unterried 7, just up the road behind Hotel Maximilian, tel. 05672/67697, www .gintherhof.com, gintherhof@aon.at).

A Hostel Across the River

$ The homey **Gästehaus am Graben hostel** has two to six beds per room and includes breakfast and sheets. It's lovingly run by the Reyman family—Frau Reyman, Rudi, and Gabi keep the 50-bed place traditional, clean, and friendly, and they serve guests a great €7 dinner. This is a super value less than two miles from Reutte, and the castle views are fantastic. If you've never hosteled and are curious (and have a car or don't mind a bus ride), try it. If traveling with kids, this is a great choice. The double rooms are hotel-grade, and they accept non-members of any age (dorm bed-€22, bunk-bed D-€44, hotel-style Db-€56, cash only, non-smoking rooms, laundry service, no curfew, closed April and Nov–mid-Dec; from downtown Reutte, cross bridge and follow main road left along river, or take the bus—hourly until 19:30, ask for Graben stop, no buses Sun; Graben 1, tel. 05672/626-440, fax 05672/626-444, www.hoefen.at, info@hoefen.at).

In Pinswang

The village of Pinswang is closer to Füssen (and Ludwig's castles), but still in Austria.

$$ Gutshof zum Schluxen gets the "Remote Old Hotel in an Idyllic Setting" award. This family-friendly working farm offers rustic elegance draped in goose down and pastels, and a chance to feed the deer. Its picturesque meadow setting will turn you into a dandelion picker, and its proximity to Neusch-

wanstein will turn you into a hiker; the castle is just an hour's hike away—see page 335 (Sb-€45–50, Db-€80–92, extra person over age 15-€28, 5 percent discount for stays of 3 or more nights, self-service laundry, mountain-bike rental, restaurant, fun bar, between Reutte and Füssen in village of Pinswang, free pick-up from Reutte or Füssen, call ahead if you'll arrive after 18:00, tel. 05677/8903, fax 05677/890-323, www.schluxen.com, welcome @schluxen.com).

EATING

In Reutte
The hotels here take great pride in serving local cuisine at reasonable prices to their guests and the public. Rather than go to a cheap restaurant, eat at a hotel. Most offer €8–14 dinners from 18:00–21:00 and are closed one night a week. Reutte itself has plenty of inviting eateries, including traditional, ethnic, fast food, grocery stores, and delis.

Hotel Restaurants: Since hospitality is such a big part of the local scene, hotel restaurants are generally your best bet for a good meal. **Hotel Goldener Hirsch, Alpenhotel Ernberg, Moserhof Hotel,** and **Hotel Maximilian** all offer fine restaurants (see each listing under "Sleeping," page 359).

Storfwirt is *the* place for a quick and cheap lunch or light dinner. You can get the usual sausages here, as well as baked potatoes and salads (€5–8 daily meals, salad bar, always something for vegetarians, Mon–Fri 8:30–15:00, Sat 9:00–14:30, closed Sun, Schrettergasse 15, tel. 05672/62640).

Non Solo Pasta, just off the traffic circle, is a local favorite for Italian food (€7 pizzas, €7–10 entrées, Mon–Fri 11:30–14:00 & 18:00–23:00, Sat 18:00–23:00, closed Sun, Lindenstrasse 1, tel. 05672/72714).

Picnic Supplies: **Billa** supermarket has everything you'll need (across from TI, Mon–Fri 8:00–19:00, Sat 8:00–17:00, closed Sun).

TRANSPORTATION CONNECTIONS

From Reutte by Train to: Ehrwald (at base of Zugspitze lift, every 2 hrs, 30 min), **Garmisch** (every 2 hrs, 1 hr), **Innsbruck** (every 2 hrs, 2.5 hrs, change in Garmisch), **Munich** (every 2 hrs, 2.5 hrs, change in Garmisch).

By Bus to: Füssen (Mon–Fri 4/day, none Sat–Sun, 35 min, €3.40, buses depart from in front of the train station, pay driver). Taxis cost €30 one-way to Füssen, or €35 to the King's Castles.

AUSTRIAN HISTORY

TIMELINE

c. A.D. 1 The Romans occupy and defend the "crossroads of Europe," where the west–east Danube River crosses the north–south Brenner Pass through the Alps.

c. 800 Charlemagne designates Austria as one boundary of his European empire—the "Eastern Empire," or *Österreich*.

1273 An Austrian noble from the Habsburg family (Rudolf I) is elected Holy Roman Emperor, ruling Austria, Germany, and northern Italy. From 1438 until 1806, every emperor but one is a Habsburg. The Habsburgs arrange strategic marriages for their children with other prominent royalty around Europe, gaining power through international connections.

1493 Maximilian I is crowned emperor. His marriage to Mary of Burgundy weds two kingdoms together, and their grandson, Charles V, inherits a vast empire.

1519 Charles V (r. 1519–1556) is the most powerful man in Europe, ruling Austria, Germany, the Low Countries, parts of Italy, and Spain (with its New World possessions). Charles is responsible for trying to solve the problems of all those lands, including battling Ottomans in Vienna and Lutherans in Germany. While many lands north of the Danube turn Protestant, Austria remains Catholic.

1522 Charles V gives Austria (and the Ottoman problem) to his little brother, Ferdinand, who, four years later, marries into the Bohemian and Hungarian crowns.

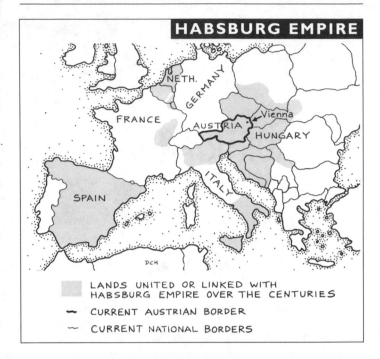

HABSBURG EMPIRE

LANDS UNITED OR LINKED WITH
HABSBURG EMPIRE OVER THE CENTURIES

~ CURRENT AUSTRIAN BORDER

~ CURRENT NATIONAL BORDERS

AUSTRIAN HISTORY

1529 Ottoman invaders from today's Turkey besiege Vienna, beginning almost two centuries of battles between Austria and the Ottoman Empire. In the course of the wars, Austria gains possession of Hungary and much of Eastern Europe.

1556 Charles V retires from the throne to enter a monastery, leaving his kingdom to his son (King Philip II of Spain), and the crown of Holy Roman Emperor to his brother, Ferdinand I of Austria. From now on, Austria's rulers would concentrate on ruling their eastern empire, which includes part or all of present-day Austria, Hungary, the Czech Republic, Slovakia, Romania, Slovenia, Croatia, Bosnia-Herzegovina, Serbia, northern Italy (Venice), and, later, parts of Poland and Ukraine.

1648 The Thirty Years' War ends, leaving the Holy Roman Empire an empire in name only; its figurehead emperor oversees a scattered group of German-speaking people, mainly in Austria and Germany.

1683 Almost 200,000 Muslims from Ottoman Turkey surround the city of Vienna once again. The Ottomans are driven off, leaving behind bags of coffee that help fuel a beverage craze around Europe.

HABSBURG FAMILY TREE

| **RUDOLF IV** (1339–1365) | Founded Habsburg dynasty—for the next six centuries, descendants ruled Austria; many were elected Holy Roman Emperors as well. |

Two ↓ *Generations*

| **MAXIMILLIAN I** (1459–1519) | By war and marriage, extended realm in all directions—making the Habsburgs a major European power. |

One ↓ *Generation*

| **CHARLES V** (1500–1558) | Ruled as the most powerful man in Europe, when Habsburg Empire reached its pinnacle, stretching from Bohemia to Bolivia. |

Five ↓ *Generations*

| **MARIA THERESA (& FRANZ I)** (1717–1780) | Defended Austria against France. Had 16 children, most of whom she married off to Europe's royalty, including Marie-Antoinette, who became Mrs. Louis XVI, the (last) Queen of France. |

↓ *Son*

| **JOSEF II** (1741–1790) | Enlightened rule abolished serfdom and brought about other democratic reforms. Patron of Mozart. |

↓ *Nephew*

| **FRANZ II** (1768–1835) | Demoted from HRE to Emperor of Austria after being defeated by (future son-in-law) Napoleon. |

One ↓ *Generation*

| **FRANZ JOSEF (& SISI)** (1830–1916) | The last Habsburg with any real power, his long reign saw the decline of his out-of-date empire. |

Great- ↓ *Nephew*   → *Nephew*

| **KARL I (& ZITA)** (1887–1922) | **FRANZ FERDINAND** (1863–1914) |

At the tail end of his ancestors' dynasty, ruled for two wartime years before renouncing political power.

Heir to the throne—until his assassination in 1914, which sparked World War I and the end of Habsburgs' rule...and Europe as they knew it.

Vienna's first coffeehouse opens.

1672–1714 Three wars with Louis XIV of France (including the War of the Spanish Succession) drain Austria.

1740 Maria Theresa (r. 1740–1780) has 16 children and still finds time to fight two wars in 25 years, defending her right to rule. Adored by her subjects for her down-to-earth personality, she brings Austria international prestige by marrying her daughters to Europe's royalty.

1781 Maria Theresa's son Josef II, who frees the serfs and takes piano lessons from Mozart, rules Austria as an "enlightened despot." Vienna becomes the world capital of symphonic music, home to Haydn (1732–1809), Mozart (1756–1791), and Beethoven (1770–1827).

1792 When Habsburg daughter Marie-Antoinette is imprisoned and (later) beheaded by revolutionaries in Paris, her nephew, Austria's Emperor Franz II, seeks revenge, beginning two decades of wars between revolutionary France and monarchist Austria.

1805 Napoleon defeats Austria at Austerlitz, his greatest triumph over the forces of monarchy. Napoleon forces Holy Roman Emperor Franz II to hand over the imperial crown (1806), ending a thousand years of empire, and he even marries Franz II's daughter, Marie-Louise.

1814–1815 After Napoleon is defeated once and for all, an Austrian, Chancellor Metternich, heads the Congress of Vienna—reinstalling kings and nobles recently deposed by Napoleon.

1848 Emperor Franz Josef (emperor of Austria and Hungary, not of the Holy Roman Empire) rules for the next 68 years, maintaining white-gloved tradition while overseeing great change—Austria's decline as an empire and entrance into the modern industrial world.

1849 Almost 100,000 Viennese attend the funeral of violinist Johann Strauss, responsible for the dance craze called the waltz. His son, Johann Strauss II (1825–1899), takes the baton of the Strauss Orchestra and waltzes on, writing "The Blue Danube."

1866 Prussia provokes war and defeats Austria, effectively freezing Austria out of any involvement in a modern German nation.

1867 To better suppress the huge Slavic population in its sprawling empire, and facing a low-morale moment after the war with Prussia, Austria gives partial control over its territories to Hungary. This creates the "Dual Monarchy" of the Austro-Hungarian Empire.

1899 Viennese psychiatrist Sigmund Freud publishes *The Interpretation of Dreams,* launching psychoanalysis and the 20th-century obsession with repressed sexual desires, the unconscious mind, and couches.

1914 Austria fires the opening shots of World War I to avenge the assassination of its heir to the throne, Archduke Franz Ferdinand.

1919 After its defeat in World War I, the Austro-Hungarian Empire is divided into separate democratic nations, with Austria assigned the small, landlocked borders that it has today.

1932 Mirroring events in Germany, a totalitarian government (of Engelbert Dollfuss) replaces a weak democracy floundering in economic depression.

1938 Nazi Germany—using the threat of force and riding a surge of Germanic nationalism—annexes Austria in the *Anschluss,* and leads it into World War II.

1945 Like Germany, a defeated Austria is divided by the victors into occupied zones, but Austria's occupation is short-lived.

1955 Modern Austria is born as a neutral nation, with the blessing of the international community.

1995 Austria joins the European Union.

2000 The European Union places sanctions on Austria (lifted a few months later) when the far-right Freedom Party—campaigning under the slogan *Überfremdung* ("Too many foreigners")—gains seats in Austria's parliament.

2002 The Freedom Party does badly in elections.

2004 Heinz Fischer, a center-left career politician, is elected president.

2008 In September, the revived far-right parties win 29 percent of the popular vote. But a month later, their leader Jörg Haider is killed in a car crash.

Today You arrive in Austria and make your own history.

AUSTRIAN HISTORY

NOTABLE AUSTRIANS

Charles V (1500-1558)

Through a series of marriages and unexpected deaths, Charles V inherited not only the Habsburg properties in Austria, but also the Netherlands and the Spanish Empire, including its colonies in the Americas. He said that he ruled an empire "upon which the sun never sets" (a phrase the British stole for their own dominions in the 19th century). But even the most powerful ruler on Earth couldn't stop the spread of Protestantism. Charles' vision of a unified, Catholic, European empire was thwarted by Martin Luther, German Protestant princes, and their allies, the French.

Maria Theresa (1717-1780)

The first and only female head of the Habsburg dynasty, Maria Theresa consolidated the power of the throne but also reformed Austria by banning torture, funding schools and universities, and allowing some religious freedom—for Protestants. Her changes, and those of her son, Josef II, allowed Austria to withstand the upheavals of the French Revolution. Her apartments at Vienna's Schönbrunn Palace are tourable today (see page 72, and for more on the empress, page 50).

Marie-Antoinette (1755-1793)

The youngest daughter of Maria Theresa, Marie-Antoinette's marriage to the heir to the French throne was supposed to cement the alliance between France and the Austrian empire. But she was not popular; even before the revolution, pamphleteers called her hopelessly stupid, accusing her of adultery, sexual deviance, and treason. During the Reign of Terror, she lost her head to the guillotine, inspiring countless romantic novels and two Hollywood movies.

Wolfgang Amadeus Mozart (1756-1791)

The ultimate child prodigy, Mozart started composing when he was five and performed for Empress Maria Theresa when he was eight. A giant of classical music, he wrote masterpieces in every genre he touched—operas, symphonies, chamber music, piano sonatas, and string quartets. Fans flock to visit his childhood homes in Salzburg (see page 239 and 245).

Johann Strauss II (1825-1899)

Vienna was the hometown of many great composers, such as Josef Haydn and Franz Schubert, but Johann Strauss II (the Younger) best captured its spirit. "The Waltz King" helped popularize this musical genre in the 19th century and wrote the most famous waltz of all, "The Blue Danube," as well as the operetta *Die Fledermaus*. These musical achievements came despite the objections of his father—also a famous composer—who wanted his son to be a banker.

Franz Josef (1831–1916)

At the age of 18, Franz Josef became emperor—beginning a 68-year reign surpassed in European history only by France's Louis XIV and a Lichtenstein prince. Franz Josef, a staunch conservative but a terrible general, presided over—and likely contributed to—the decline of the Austro-Hungarian Empire. His family life was similarly troubled; his estranged wife, Sisi, was assassinated by an Italian anarchist, and his only son, Crown Prince Rudolf, committed suicide in the arms of a mistress. The end of the Habsburg dynasty came two years after Franz Josef's death. His Hofburg Imperial Apartments in Vienna are open to the public (see page 109, and for more on the emperor, page 115).

Sigmund Freud (1856–1939)

The Austrian physician and psychoanalyst revolutionized the study of human behavior. According to Freud, repressed desires—sexual desires in particular—explained why humans behave the way we do. Although he was a world figure of immense influence, the Nazis despised his Jewish roots and burned his books. After they took over Austria in 1938, Freud left for London, where he died a year later. His office in Vienna has been turned into the Sigmund Freud Museum (see page 70).

Gustav Klimt (1862–1918)

Erotic, symbolic, Byzantine, radical—the turn-of-the-century paintings of Gustav Klimt shook Viennese society. A leader of the Vienna Secession movement, Klimt was criticized at one point for "pornographic" art—years before the gold-wrapped lovers of *The Kiss* became an art school icon. His portrait *The Golden Adele* set a record when American billionaire Ronald Lauder bought it in 2006 for $135 million—at that time the most expensive painting ever sold. Klimt's art is displayed in museums throughout Vienna; *The Kiss*, for example, is in Belvedere Palace (for more on the artist, see page 66).

Franz Ferdinand (1863–1914)

No one expected Archduke Franz Ferdinand to be the heir to the Habsburg dynasty. But when Crown Prince Rudolf killed himself in 1889—and Franz Ferdinand's father died in 1896—the young archduke suddenly became the hope of the Habsburgs. As inspector general of the army, he was invited to Sarajevo to review Austrian troops. On June 28, 1914, after his chauffeur took a wrong turn on the city's streets, Franz Ferdinand and his wife were assassinated by a Serbian nationalist, triggering World War I and the eventual end of the dynasty.

Adolf Loos (1870–1933)

The man who said "decoration is a crime" was one of the most influential architects of the modern era. Born in what is now the Czech Republic, he trained in Germany and even spent three years tramping around America as a dishwasher and a mason. But it was in Vienna where he made his name. Excessive ornamentation was criminal, he declared, because it wasted labor and materials; the modern era deserved stripped-down facades. Examples of Loos' architecture—a bookstore, bar, and even WCs—are in downtown Vienna (see page 84).

Ferdinand Porsche (1875–1951)

This Austrian automotive engineer is best known as the father of the Volkswagen Beetle. Hitler demanded that Germany build a cheap "people's car," so Porche began working on his world-famous design in 1934. Three years later, Hitler gave him one of Germany's highest awards. This automotive genius is also known for launching (with the help of his son) the Porsche sports car. But he was a century too soon with another one of his inventions: the world's first electric-gasoline hybrid car, the Mixte, created in 1901 in Vienna.

Adolf Hitler (1889–1945)

The future dictator—directly responsible for the deaths of more than 43 million people during World War II—was born in Braunau am Inn, north of Salzburg. After dropping out of high school at age 16, he spent eight years in pre-war Vienna trying to make his way as an artist. (He was rejected twice by Vienna's Academy of Fine Arts.) Although Hitler served in the German army during World War I, he didn't become a German citizen until 1932, just one year before becoming the nation's chancellor and *der Führer*.

Maria von Trapp (1905–1987)

An orphan by age seven, Maria Augusta Kitschier was raised in Tirol by an anti-Catholic socialist. When she mistakenly attended a religious lecture (she had thought it would be a Bach concert), she was so moved that she became a staunch Catholic. Her memoir of life as a novitiate at a Salzburg convent and later as governess for the von Trapp family was the basis for *The Sound of Music* (see page 252). Salzburg remains the epicenter for *S.O.M.* sights and tours.

Billy Wilder (1906-2002)

Born in Austria, Hollywood legend Billy Wilder won Oscars for directing *The Lost Weekend* and *The Apartment*. He also wrote and/or directed such Hollywood classics as *Some Like It Hot, The Seven Year Itch, Ball of Fire, Sunset Boulevard, Stalag 17, Sabrina,* and the dark and brooding *Double Indemnity*. He lost his mother in the Holocaust and was often bitter about his native country. "The Austrians are brilliant people," he once said. "They made the world believe that Hitler was a German and Beethoven an Austrian."

Otto Preminger (1906-1986)

Like Wilder, Otto Preminger grew up in Vienna's Jewish community. His success in Viennese theater eventually led to Hollywood, where Preminger hit the big time directing the 1944 mystery *Laura*. Twice nominated for a best-director Oscar (for *Laura* and *The Cardinal*), Preminger made films that challenged Hollywood taboos of the time, such as rape *(Anatomy of a Murder)*, drug addiction *(The Man with the Golden Arm)*, and homosexuality *(Advise and Consent)*.

Arnold Schwarzenegger (b. 1947)

Born in a village near Graz, Arnold Schwarzenegger was obsessed with bodybuilding even as a teenager. After winning international bodybuilding contests, Schwarzenegger got his big break as *Conan the Barbarian,* a role that spawned a string of blockbuster action movies, including the *Terminator* series. In 2003, Ah-nold switched careers and was elected the Republican governor of California. The "Governator" was re-elected in 2006.

AUSTRIAN HISTORY

APPENDIX

CONTENTS

RESOURCES

Tourist Offices

In the US

Austria's national tourist office in the US is a wealth of information. They have maps and information on festivals, hiking, the wine country, and more. Call 212/944-6880 or visit www.austria.info.

In Austria

The local tourist information office (abbreviated **TI** in this book) is your best first stop in any new town or city. Try to arrive, or at least telephone, before it closes. Throughout Austria, you'll find TIs are usually well-organized and have English-speaking staff.

As national budgets tighten, many TIs have been privatized. This means they have become sales agents for big tours and hotels, and their "information" becomes unavoidably colored. While TIs are eager to book you a room, you should use their room-finding service as a last resort. TIs can as easily book you a bad room as a good one—they are not allowed to promote one place over another. It's better to book direct, using the listings in this book.

More Resources from Rick Steves

Guidebooks and Online Updates

I've done my best to make sure that the information in this book is up-to-date, but things change. For the latest, visit www.rick steves.com/update. Also at my website, you'll find a valuable list of reports and experiences—good and bad—from fellow travelers (www.ricksteves.com/feedback).

This book is one of more than 30 titles in my series on European travel, which includes country guidebooks, city and regional

guidebooks, and my budget-travel skills handbook, *Rick Steves' Europe Through the Back Door*. My phrase books—for German, French, Italian, Spanish, and Portuguese—are practical and budget-oriented. My other books are *Europe 101* (a crash course on art and history, newly expanded and in full color), *European Christmas* (on traditional and modern-day celebrations, including Austria's), and *Postcards from Europe* (a fun memoir of my travels). For a complete list of my books, see the inside of the last page of this book.

Public Television and Radio Shows

My TV series, *Rick Steves' Europe*, covers European destinations in 80 shows, with three episodes on Austria. My weekly public radio show, *Travel with Rick Steves*, features interviews with travel experts from around the world, including several hours on Germanic culture. All the TV scripts and radio shows (which are easy and free to download to an iPod or other MP3 player) are at www.ricksteves.com.

Free Audiotours

If your travels take you beyond Austria to France or Italy, you could take advantage of free, self-guided audiotours we offer of the major sights in Paris, Florence, Rome, and Venice. The audiotours, produced by Rick Steves and Gene Openshaw (the co-author of seven books in the Rick Steves series) are available at www.ricksteves.com and through

Begin Your Trip at www.ricksteves.com

At our travel website, you'll find a wealth of free information on European destinations, including fresh monthly news and helpful tips from thousands of fellow travelers.

Our **online Travel Store** offers travel bags and accessories specially designed by Rick Steves to help you travel smarter and lighter. These include Rick's popular carry-on bags (wheeled and rucksack versions), money belts, totes, toiletries kits, adapters, other accessories, and a wide selection of guidebooks, planning maps, and DVDs.

Choosing the right **railpass** for your trip—amidst hundreds of options—can drive you nutty. We'll help you choose the best pass for your needs, plus give you a bunch of free extras.

Rick Steves' Europe Through the Back Door travel company offers **tours** with more than two dozen itineraries and about 450 departures reaching the best destinations in this book...and beyond. We offer a 14-day tour of Germany, Austria, and Switzerland, and a 12-day tour of Berlin, Prague, and Vienna. You'll enjoy great guides, a fun bunch of travel partners (with small groups of generally about 26), and plenty of room to spread out in a big, comfy bus. You'll find European adventures to fit every vacation length. For all the details, and to get our Tour Catalog and a free Rick Steves Tour Experience DVD (filmed on location during an actual tour), visit www.ricksteves.com or call the Tour Department at 425/608-4217.

iTunes. Simply download them onto your computer and transfer them to your iPod or other MP3 player. (Remember to bring a Y-jack and extra set of earbuds for your travel partner.)

Maps

The black-and-white maps in this book, designed by my well-traveled staff, are concise and simple. The maps are intended to help you locate recommended places and get to local TIs, where you can pick up a more in-depth map (usually free) of the city or region. Better maps are sold at newsstands—take a look before you buy to be sure the map has the level of detail you want.

European bookstores, especially in touristy areas, have good selections of maps. For drivers, I'd recommend a 1:200,000- or 1:300,000-scale map for each country. Train travelers usually manage fine with the freebies they get with the train pass and from the local tourist offices.

Other Guidebooks

For most travelers, this book is all you need. But if you're heading beyond my recommended destinations, you might want some supplemental information. Considering the improvements they'll make in your $4,000 vacation, $40 for extra maps and books is money well-spent. Note that none of the following guidebooks are updated annually; check the publication date before you buy.

Lonely Planet's guides to Vienna and Austria are thorough, well-researched, and packed with good maps and hotel recommendations for low- to moderate-budget travelers. The similar Rough Guides are written by insightful British researchers.

The skinny, green Michelin Guides are excellent, especially if you're driving. Michelin Guides are known for their city and sightseeing maps, dry but concise and helpful information on all major sights, and good cultural and historical background. English editions are sold in Europe at gas stations and tourist shops.

Recommended Books and Movies

To get a feel for Austria past and present, consider these books and films:

Non-Fiction

For an overview of Austrian history, try *The Austrians: A Thousand-Year Odyssey* (Brook-Shepherd), though most of its focus is on the 19th and 20th centuries. *Fin-de-Siecle Vienna: Politics and Culture* (Schorske) is a dense but comprehensive analysis of the birth of modernism through Klimt, Freud, and other Viennese luminaries. *The Spell of the Vienna Woods: Inspiration and Influence from Beethoven to Kafka* (Hofmann) blends personal anecdotes, history, tourist information, and stories about artists who found inspiration in the 540-square-mile area that serves as Vienna's playground. *Beethoven: The Music and the Life* (Lockwood) includes details about the musician's life in Vienna and his contributions to its culture.

Memoirs: *The Story of the Trapp Family Singers,* written by Maria von Trapp, tells the true story behind the musical phenomenon. Stefan Zweig's *World of Yesterday* looks at how he became a successful writer in the "lost world" of pre-war Vienna.

Fiction

Much fiction set in Vienna concerns the imagined lives of famous artists. *The Painted Kiss* (Hickey) reflects the lush elegance of fin-de-siecle Vienna and the relationship between painter Gustav Klimt and his pupil Emilie Flöge, who posed for Klimt's masterpiece *The Kiss*. In *The Seven-Per-Cent Solution* (Meyer), Sherlock Holmes travels to Vienna to meet with Sigmund Freud and gets involved in a case. *Henry James' Midnight Song* (Hill) is another literary mystery with a cast of famous historical characters. Mystery fans could also consider *Airs Above the Ground* (Stewart), with Lipizzaner stallions and the Austrian Alps as a backdrop, as well as *A Death in Vienna* (Tallis), which involves a cover-up by the Catholic Church.

Austrian feminist Elfriede Jelinek, known for exploring dark themes, won the 2004 Nobel Prize in Literature. Her most famous novel, *Die Klavierspielerin* (*The Piano Player,* made into a movie) is about a troubled piano teacher who messes up the lives of her students. Viennese writer Joseph Roth's classic novel *Radetzky March* follows four generations of a family during the decline and fall of the Habsburgs.

Films

The Great Waltz (1938) portrays the life of composer Johann Strauss. Orson Welles infuses *The Third Man* (1949, actually shot in a bombed-out and Soviet-occupied Vienna) with noir foreboding. In *Miracle of the White Stallions* (1963) the Lipizzaner stallions are the stars in this true story of how the horses were liberated by General Patton after World War II. The beloved musical *The Sound of Music* (1965), also partially set in World War II, helped turn Julie Andrews into a star. *Mayerling* (1968) is about the suicide of Habsburg heir Archduke Rudolf (played by Omar Sharif), which played a pivotal role in Austrian history.

Mahler (1974) describes the man behind the music, and *Amadeus* (1984) made Mozart into a flesh-and-blood man (who giggles), as did *Immortal Beloved* (1994) for Beethoven. For a list of films made about Sisi (a.k.a. Austria's Empress Elisabeth, a 19th-century Princess Diana), see page 112.

In *Before Sunrise* (1995), Ethan Hawke sightsees, talks, romances, and talks some more with Julie Delpy in Vienna. *The Illusionist* (2006) set in circa-1900 Vienna, is about a magician who uses his abilities to gain the love of a woman engaged to the crown prince.

TELEPHONES, EMAIL, AND MAIL

Telephones

Smart travelers learn the phone system and use it daily to book or reconfirm rooms, get tourist information, reserve restaurants, confirm tour times, or phone home.

Types of Phones

You'll encounter various kinds of phones in Austria:

Card-operated phones—in which you insert a locally bought phone card into a public pay phone—are common in most of Europe, but are disappearing across Austria.

Coin-operated phones are a little easier to find, but require you to have enough change to complete your call.

Hotel room phones are sometimes cheap for local calls (confirm at the front desk first), but can be a rip-off for long-distance calls ($1–2/min unless you use an international phone card—described later in this section). But incoming calls are free, making this a cheap way for friends and family to stay in touch, provided they have a good long-distance plan for calls to Europe.

American mobile phones work in Europe if they're GSM-enabled, tri-band or quad-band, and on a calling plan that includes international calls. They're convenient, but pricey. For example, with a T-Mobile phone, you'll pay $1 per minute for calls and about $0.35 for text messages.

Austrian mobile phones are affordable to buy and come without contracts. These phones are loaded with prepaid calling time that you can recharge as you use up the minutes. As long as you're not "roaming" outside the phone's home country, incoming calls are free. If you're traveling to multiple countries within Europe, make sure the phone is electronically "unlocked," so that you can swap out its SIM card (a fingernail-sized chip that holds the phone's information) for a new one in other countries. For more information on mobile phones, see www.ricksteves.com/phones.

Using Phone Cards

Get a phone card for your calls. Prepaid phone cards come in two types: international and insertable.

International Phone Cards: These offer the cheapest way

to make international calls from Austria (they also work for local calls). Some even work in multiple countries—if you'll be traveling to both Austria and Germany, try to buy a card that will work in both places.

The cards are sold at small newsstand kiosks and hole-in-the-wall long-distance shops. There are many different brands of cards, so ask the clerk which one has the best rates for calls to America. Some cards are rechargeable; you can call the number on the card, give your credit-card number, and buy more time. Because cards are occasionally duds, avoid the more expensive denominations.

You can use international phone cards from any type of phone, even your hotel-room phone (check to make sure that your phone is set on tone instead of pulse, and ask at the desk if there are any fees for toll-free calls).

To use a card, scratch off the back to reveal your PIN (Personal Identification Number). Dial the number listed on the card to reach an automated operator. When prompted, dial in the PIN code. Then dial your number (if you need help, see "How to Dial," later in this section).

Remember that you don't need the actual card to use a card account, so it's sharable. You can write down the access number and PIN code in your notebook and share it with friends. Give the number of a still lively card to another traveler if you're leaving the country.

Insertable Phone Cards: This type of card can be used only at pay phones, and are sold in denominations starting at about €5 at TIs, tobacco shops, post offices, and train stations. To use the card, you physically insert it into a slot in the pay phone. The price of the call is automatically deducted while you talk. Calling the US with an insertable phone card is reasonable (about 2–3 min per euro), but more expensive than using an international phone card. Note that insertable phone cards don't work outside of Austria.

Using Hotel Room Phones, VoIP, or US Calling Cards

The best way to call home is using an international phone card, but you have other options:

Calling from the phone in your **hotel room** is convenient...but expensive (unless you use an international phone card, described above). While incoming calls (made by folks back home) can be the cheapest way for you to keep in touch, charges for *outgoing* calls can be a very unpleasant surprise. Before you dial, get a clear explanation from the hotel staff of the charges, even for local and (supposedly) toll-free calls.

If your family has an inexpensive way to call Europe, either through a long-distance plan or prepaid calling card, have them call you in your hotel room. Give them a list of your hotels' phone

Hurdling the Language Barrier

Austrians speak German (though with a distinctly Austrian flair that differs a bit across regional dialects). Most young and/or well-educated Austrians—especially those in larger towns and the tourist trade—speak at least some English. Still, you'll get more smiles by using the German pleasantries (see the "German Survival Phrases for Austria" on page 402). In smaller, non-touristy towns, the language barrier is higher.

German—like English, Dutch, Swedish, and Norwegian—is a Germanic language, making it easier on most American ears than Romance languages (such as Italian and French). These tips will help you pronounce German words: The letter *w* is always pronounced as *v* (e.g., the word for "wonderful" is *wunderbar*, pronounced VOON-der-bar). The letter *j* is always pronounced as *y* (so *Joghurt* is pronounced the same as English "yogurt"), and the letter *v* is pronounced as *f* (so the number *vier*—four—sounds just like "fear"). There are no silent letters. The rule for pronouncing *ie* and *ei* never changes: Always say the second letter. So *ie* sounds like the letter "e" (as in *hier* and *Bier*, the German words for "here" and "beer"), while *ei* sounds like the letter "i" (as in *nein* and *Wein*, the German words for "no" and "wine"). The vowel combination *au* is pronounced "ow" (as in *Frau*). The vowel combinations *eu* and *äu* are pronounced "oy" (as in *neu*, *Deutsch*, and *Bräu*, the German words for "new," "German," and "brew"). To pronounce *ö* and *ü*, purse your lips when you say the vowel; the other vowel with an umlaut, *ä*, is pronounced the same as "e" in "men." (In typewritten German, these can be depicted as the vowel followed by an *e*—*oe*, *ue*, and *ae*, respectively.) The letter

numbers before you go. Then, as you travel, send them an email or set up a time for them to give you a ring.

If you're traveling with a laptop, consider trying **VoIP (Voice over Internet Protocol).** With VoIP, two computers act as the phones, allowing for a free Internet-based call. The major providers are Skype (www.skype.com) and Google Talk (www.google.com/talk).

US Calling Cards (such as the ones offered by AT&T, MCI, and Sprint) are the worst option. You'll nearly always save a lot of money by paying with a phone card (see page 380).

How to Dial

Calling from the US to Europe, or vice versa, is simple—once you break the code. The European calling chart on page 384 will walk you through it.

Eszett (ß) represents "ss". Written German always capitalizes all nouns.

Regional dialects aside, the language spoken by Austrians isn't all that different from the *Deutsch* spoken by Germans—but those small differences are a big deal to Austrians. The most important one is how you say "hello": Austrians will greet you (and each other) with a *Grüss Gott,* or perhaps *Servus*—but never with the German *Guten Tag,* a phrase that sounds oddly uptight to Austrians (and as foreign as being wished a "G'day" in the US). Instead, stick to *Grüss Gott* ("May God greet you"), or a simple *Grüss,* for "hello." You'll get the correct pronunciation after the first volley—listen and copy.

You're likely to run into a few other un-German German words on your trip, such as *Jänner* and *Feber* for January and February (rather than the German *Januar* and *Februar*). A lot of food names are different: In Austria, potatoes are *Erdäpfel* (not *Kartoffeln*), tomatoes are *Paradeiser* (not *Tomaten*), a bread roll is a *Semmel* (not *Brötchen*), corn is *Kukuruz* (not *Mais*), green beans are *Fisolen* (not *grüne Bohnen*), cauliflower is *Karifiol* (not *Blumenkohl*), whipped cream is *Obers* (not *Schlagsahne*), and apricot jam and ice cream will be labeled as *Marille* (not *Aprikose*). Tacking an *-l* or *-erl* on the end of a word makes it a diminutive form—like adding "-ette" or "-ie" to an English word (or *-chen* in German German).

Austrians appreciate any effort on your part to speak German—even if it's just *ein Bissl* (a little bit)—and if you already speak some German German, they'll understand you just fine. Give it your best shot.

Dialing Domestic Calls

Austria, like much of the US, uses an area-code dialing system. If you're dialing within an area code, you just dial the local number to be connected; but if you're calling outside your area code, you have to dial both the area code (which starts with a 0) and the local number. You'll find area codes listed throughout this book, or you can get them from directory assistance (tel. 16).

For example, Vienna's area code is 01 and the number of one of my recommended Vienna hotels is 534-050. To call the hotel within Vienna, you'd dial 534-050. To call it from Salzburg, you'd dial 01/534-050.

Don't be surprised if local phone numbers in Austria have different numbers of digits within the same city or even the same hotel (for example, a hotel can have a 6-digit phone number and an 8-digit fax number).

European Calling Chart

Just smile and dial, using this key:
AC = Area Code, LN = Local Number.

European Country	Calling long distance within ...	Calling from the US or Canada to ...	Calling from a European country to ...
Austria	AC + LN	011 + 43 + AC (without the initial zero) + LN	00 + 43 + AC (without the initial zero) + LN
Belgium	LN	011 + 32 + LN (without initial zero)	00 + 32 + LN (without initial zero)
Bosnia-Herzegovina	AC + LN	011 + 387 + AC (without initial zero) + LN	00 + 387 + AC (without initial zero) + LN
Britain	AC + LN	011 + 44 + AC (without initial zero) + LN	00 + 44 + AC (without initial zero) + LN
Croatia	AC + LN	011 + 385 + AC (without initial zero) + LN	00 + 385 + AC (without initial zero) + LN
Czech Republic	LN	011 + 420 + LN	00 + 420 + LN
Denmark	LN	011 + 45 + LN	00 + 45 + LN
Estonia	LN	011 + 372 + LN	00 + 372 + LN
Finland	AC + LN	011 + 358 + AC (without initial zero) + LN	999 + 358 + AC (without initial zero) + LN
France	LN	011 + 33 + LN (without initial zero)	00 + 33 + LN (without initial zero)
Germany	AC + LN	011 + 49 + AC (without initial zero) + LN	00 + 49 + AC (without initial zero) + LN
Greece	LN	011 + 30 + LN	00 + 30 + LN
Hungary	06 + AC + LN	011 + 36 + AC + LN	00 + 36 + AC + LN
Ireland	AC + LN	011 + 353 + AC (without initial zero) + LN	00 + 353 + AC (without initial zero) + LN

European Country	Calling long distance within ...	Calling from the US or Canada to ...	Calling from a European country to ...
Italy	LN	011 + 39 + LN	00 + 39 + LN
Montenegro	AC + LN	011 + 382 + AC (without initial zero) + LN	00 + 382 + AC (without initial zero) + LN
Netherlands	AC + LN	011 + 31 + AC (without initial zero) + LN	00 + 31 + AC (without initial zero) + LN
Norway	LN	011 + 47 + LN	00 + 47 + LN
Poland	LN	011 + 48 + LN (without initial zero)	00 + 48 + LN (without initial zero)
Portugal	LN	011 + 351 + LN	00 + 351 + LN
Slovakia	AC + LN	011 + 421 + AC (without initial zero) + LN	00 + 421 + AC (without initial zero) + LN
Slovenia	AC + LN	011 + 386 + AC (without initial zero) + LN	00 + 386 + AC (without initial zero) + LN
Spain	LN	011 + 34 + LN	00 + 34 + LN
Sweden	AC + LN	011 + 46 + AC (without initial zero) + LN	00 + 46 + AC (without initial zero) + LN
Switzerland	LN	011 + 41 + LN (without initial zero)	00 + 41 + LN (without initial zero)
Turkey	AC (if no initial zero is included, add one) + LN	011 + 90 + AC (without initial zero) + LN	00 + 90 + AC (without initial zero) + LN

- The instructions above apply whether you're calling a land line or mobile phone.
- The international access codes (the first numbers you dial when making an international call) are 011 if you're calling from the US or Canada, or 00 if you're calling from virtually anywhere in Europe (except Finland, where it's 999).
- To call the US or Canada from Europe, dial 00, then 1 (the country code for the US and Canada), then the area code and number. In short, 00 + 1 + AC + LN = Hi, Mom!

Dialing Internationally

If you want to make an international call, follow these steps:

Dial the international access code (00 if you're calling from Europe, 011 from the US or Canada).

Then dial the country code of the country you're calling (43 for Austria, or 1 for the US or Canada).

Then dial the area code (without its initial 0) and the local number.

For example, to call the recommended Vienna hotel from the US, dial 011 (the US international access code), 43 (Austria's country code), 1 (Vienna's area code without the initial 0), and 534-050.

To call my office in Edmonds, Washington, from Austria, I dial 00 (Europe's international access code), 1 (the US country code), 425 (Edmonds' area code), and 771-8303.

Useful Phone Numbers

Directory Assistance

National—tel. 16, International—tel. 08.

Train info

Tel. 051-717 (to get an operator, dial 2, then 2); ask for an English speaker.

US Embassy in Vienna

Boltzmanngasse 16, tel. 01/313-390, embassy@usembassy.at; consular services at Parkring 12, daily 8:00–11:30, tel. 01/313-397-535, www.usembassy.at, consulatevienna@state.gov

Email and Mail

Email: Many travelers set up a free email account with Yahoo, Microsoft (Hotmail), or Google (Gmail). Internet cafés are easy to find in big cities. Most of the small towns I cover in this book also have Internet cafés. Many libraries offer free access, but they also tend to have limited opening hours, restrict your online time to 30 minutes, and may require reservations. Look for the places listed in this book, or ask the local TI, computer store, or your hotelier.

Most hotels have a dedicated desktop computer for guests' email needs. Small places with no guest computer or Wi-Fi sometimes let clients (who've asked politely) sit at their desk for a few minutes just to check their email; remember it's their business computer and get off quickly.

Internet access for laptop users is becoming commonplace at most hotels and even smaller *Pensions*. Many hotels that offer this do so for free, but some charge (about €8/hr, up to €18–25/day at fancier places). You'll either access the hotel's wireless Internet (Wi-Fi, also called "WLAN"—VAY-lahn—in German-speaking Europe), sometimes using a password provided by the hotelier; or you'll plug your computer directly into an Internet wall socket (they can usually loan you a cable). These days, I can get online at most hotels in this book, and I've noted this in each listing. If I say "Internet access," there's a public terminal in the lobby for guests to use. If I say "Wi-Fi" or "cable Internet," you can generally access it in your room, but only if you have your own laptop.

Mail: Get stamps at the neighborhood post office, newsstands within fancy hotels, and some mini-marts and card shops. Avoid standing in line at the post office by using the handy yellow stamp *(Briefmarke)* machines found just outside the building. Warning: These machines give change only in stamps, not in coins. Postcard stamps to the US or Canada cost €1.25 from Austria.

To arrange for mail delivery, reserve a few hotels along your route in advance and give their addresses to friends. Allow 10 days for a letter to arrive. Phoning and emailing are so easy that I've dispensed with mail stops altogether.

TRANSPORTATION

By Car or Train?

Cars are best for three or more traveling together (especially families with small kids), those packing heavy, and those scouring the countryside. Trains and buses are best for solo travelers, blitz tourists, and city-to-city travelers. While a car gives you the ultimate in mobility and freedom, enables you to search for hotels more easily, and carries your bags for you, the train zips you effortlessly from city to city, usually dropping you in the center and near the tourist office. A car is a worthless headache in cities such as Vienna and Salzburg.

Trains

Trains are generally slick, speedy, and punctual, with synchronized connections. They cover cities well, but some frustrating schedules make a few out-of-the-way recommendations (such as the Mauthausen concentration camp memorial, and Bavaria's Wieskirche) not worth the time and trouble for the less determined. Note that it's illegal to smoke on Austria's trains and most of its buses.

Types of Trains

The Austrian Railways (a.k.a. Österreichische Bundesbahn, or ÖBB) operates several classes of trains, which differ substantially in price, speed, and comfort.

Austria's newest, fastest, and reddest train, the Railjet, streaks between Budapest, Vienna, and either Munich or Innsbruck (and on to Zürich). ICE trains (white with red trim and streamlined noses) also cover those same main routes in air-conditioned comfort. Both of these high-speed trains cost proportionately more than other Austrian trains.

Red regional trains (labeled R and REX on schedules) are the slowest—the milk-run R trains stop at every small station—but cost much less. Mid-level IC and EC trains are air-conditioned, but look older than the Railjets and ICEs (and many lack electrical outlets).

If you have a railpass, take the fastest train available—railpass holders don't pay a supplement for the fast ICE trains (but first-class railpasses don't cover the supplement for the ritzy business compartments on high-speed and mid-range trains). If you're buying point-to-point tickets, taking a slower train can save a lot of money.

Schedules

Schedules change by season, and vary between weekdays and

weekends. To verify train times shown in this book, visit http://bahn.hafas.de/bin/query.exe/en or www.oebb.at (Austrian Rail). At staffed train stations, attendants will print out a step-by-step itinerary for you, free of charge. You can also produce an itinerary yourself by using the computerized trackside machines marked *Fahrkarten*. The touch-screen display gives you an English option; choose "Timetable Information," indicate your point of departure and destination, and then hit "Print" for a personalized schedule, including transfers and track numbers. You can also buy tickets from these machines—cash only, since they don't accept non-European bankcards (for more information, see "Tickets," page 391).

You can call Austria's train information number from anywhere in the country: tel. 051-717 (€0.60/min—to get an operator, dial 2, then 2). Ask for an English speaker.

Railpasses

The Austria Pass is a great value for rail travel within Austria. If you're traveling in a neighboring country as well, consider a

Railpasses

Prices listed are for 2010 and are subject to change. For the latest prices, details, train schedules, and easy online ordering, see my comprehensive *Guide to Eurail Passes* at www.ricksteves.com/rail.

"Saver" prices are per person for two or more people traveling together. "Youth" means under age 26. The fare for children 4–11 is half the adult individual fare or Saver fare. Kids under age 4 travel free.

AUSTRIA PASS

	Indiv. 1st Cl.	Indiv. 2nd Cl.	Saver 1st Cl.	Saver 2nd Cl.	Youth 2nd Cl.
3 days in 1 month	$244	$170	$207	$145	$111
Extra rail days (max. 5)	28	20	24	16	13

AUSTRIA–GERMANY PASS

	Indiv. 1st Cl.	Indiv. 2nd Cl.	Saver 1st Cl.	Saver 2nd Cl.	Youth 2nd Cl.
5 days in 2 months	$439	$374	$374	$321	$321
6 days in 2 months	483	411	411	355	355
8 days in 2 months	575	488	488	420	420
10 days in 2 months	668	568	568	488	488

AUSTRIA–SWITZERLAND PASS

	Individual 1st Class	Saver 1st Class	Youth 2nd Class
4 days in 2 months	$413	$351	$289
Extra rail days (max. 6)	47	39	32

AUSTRIA–CZECH or AUSTRIA–HUNGARY PASS

	Individual 1st Class	Saver 1st Class	Youth 2nd Class
4 days in 2 months	$274	$233	$178
Extra rail days (max. 6)	38	31	24

AUSTRIA–CROATIA–SLOVENIA PASS

	Individual 1st Class	Saver 1st Class	Youth 2nd Class
4 days in 2 months	$289	$252	$208
Extra rail days (max. 6)	43	37	32

EUROPEAN EAST PASS

	1st Class	2nd Class
5 days in 1 month	$324	$226
Extra rail days (max. 5)	38	31

Covers Austria, Czech Republic, Slovakia, Hungary and Poland. This is the only pass that covers Slovakia.

Map key:

Approximate point-to-point one-way second-class rail fares in US dollars. First class costs 50 percent more. Add up the approximate ticket costs for your trip to see if a railpass will save you money.

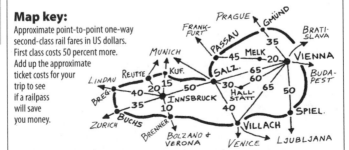

two-country Eurailpass, which allows you to pair Austria with Germany, Switzerland, the Czech Republic, or Hungary. The Austria-Croatia-Slovenia Pass covers travel in those three countries, and the European East Pass covers Austria and the Czech Republic, Slovakia, Hungary, and Poland. Another option is the Eurail Selectpass, which gives you up to 15 travel days (within a two-month period) in three, four, or five adjacent countries—you could choose Austria, Germany, and another bordering country. If you're planning a whirlwind tour of Europe, another possibility is the 21-country Eurail Global Pass. These passes are available in a Saverpass version, which gives a 15 percent discount on railpasses for two or more companions traveling together. For specifics, check the railpass chart on page 390 and visit www.ricksteves.com/rail.

Railpass travelers should know what extras are covered by their pass, such as discounts on Danube boats. Flexipass holders should note that discounted trips don't use up a flexi-day, but fully covered ("free") trips do. The "used" flexipass day can also cover your train travel on that day (but if you're not planning to travel more that day, it makes sense to pay for, say, a short boat ride rather than use up a day of your pass for it).

Tickets

People of any age buying individual tickets should remember that traveling in second class instead of first class provides the same transportation for 33 percent less. Bikes cost €4–7 extra on EC and IC trains, and €3 extra for a day of travel on local trains. Ticket fares are shown on the map on page 390 and at www.oebb.at.

Deals: If you're not using a railpass, it's worth knowing about ticket specials in Austria.

Austrian Railways' Einfach-Raus-Ticket ("Just Get Outta Here" ticket) is a cheap way for couples and small groups to travel on regional trains (€28, covers 2–5 people for a whole day of travel on R, REX, S-Bahn, RSB, ER, and EZ trains, not available Mon–Fri before 9:00). They also offer €29 advance-purchase

DRIVING IN AUSTRIA: DISTANCE AND TIME

Note: Your times may vary based on traffic, construction, and road conditions.

"SparSchiene" deals to major cities around Europe (limited availability; see www.oebb.at).

Kids and seniors can get deals, too. Up to two kids under six years old travel for free, though they aren't guaranteed a seat. Youths and seniors receive discounts only with a Vorteils card, which requires some effort to get, but pays for itself fairly quickly (€20, gives 50 percent discount for one year, photo required, see www.oebb.at or ask at station).

For travel on local trains in Bavaria, consider the Bayern-Ticket (€27 for up to 5 people after 9:00 on weekdays on local trains within Bavaria).

Buying Tickets: Major Austrian stations have a handy *Reisezentrum* (Travel Center) where you can ask questions and buy tickets. Many smaller stations, though, are unstaffed, with tickets sold only from machines (marked *Fahrkarten*, which means "tickets"). You can pay with bills, coins, or credit cards that have a PIN code; these machines also print schedules for free. You can buy tickets on board ICE, EN, and EC trains for a

€3 fee. Boarding a local train without a ticket, however, can earn you a hefty fine.

Car Rental

Car rental is cheapest if arranged from home. Call several companies, look online, or arrange a rental through your hometown travel agent, who can help you out if anything goes wrong during your trip. Two reputable companies among many are Auto Europe (www.autoeurope.com) and Europe by Car (www.europebycar.com). For the best deal, rent by the week with unlimited mileage (but for long trips, consider leasing).

Expect to pay about $350 per person (based on two people sharing the car) for a small economy car for 10 days with unlimited mileage, including gas, parking, and insurance. I normally rent a small, inexpensive model like a Ford Fiesta. For a bigger, roomier, more powerful but inexpensive car, move up to a Ford Focus or VW Polo. Minibuses are a great budget way to go for 5–9 people.

Car-rental companies have age restrictions (confirm age

requirements when you book). Most Austrian companies will not rent to someone under 19, and restrictions and "underage fees" can apply if you're under 24. There's generally not a maximum age limit, but if you are 70 or older, it's smart to ask. If you're considered too young or old, look into leasing, which has less-stringent age restrictions (see "Leasing," later in this section).

If you want an automatic, reserve the car at least a month in advance and specifically request an automatic. You'll pay about 40 percent more to rent a car with an automatic instead of a manual transmission.

When you pick up the car, check it thoroughly and make sure any damage is noted on your rental agreement. Find out how your car's headlights, turn signals, wipers, and gas cap function.

Returning a car at a big-city train station can be tricky; get precise details on the car drop-off location and hours. When you return the car, make sure the agent verifies its condition with you.

If you drop your car off early or keep it longer, you'll be credited or charged at a fair, prorated price. But keep your receipts in case any questions arise about your billing.

Car Insurance Options

When you rent a car, you are liable for a very high deductible, sometimes equal to the entire value of the car. You can limit your financial risk in case of an accident by choosing one of these three options: buy Collision Damage Waiver (CDW) coverage from the car-rental company, get coverage through your credit card (free, if your card automatically includes zero-deductible coverage), or buy coverage through Travel Guard.

CDW includes a very high deductible (typically $1,000–1,500). When you pick up the car, you'll be offered the chance to "buy down" the deductible to zero (for $10–30/day; this is often called "super CDW").

If you opt instead for credit-card coverage, there's a catch. You'll technically have to decline all coverage offered by the car-rental company, which means they can place a hold on your card for the full deductible amount. In case of damage, it can be time-consuming to resolve the charges with your credit-card company. Before you decide on this option, quiz your credit-card company about how it works and ask them to explain the worst-case scenario.

Buying CDW insurance (plus "super CDW") is the easier but pricier option. Using the coverage that comes with your credit card saves money, but can involve more hassle.

Finally, you can buy CDW insurance from Travel Guard ($9/day plus a one-time $3 service fee covers you up to $35,000, $250 deductible, tel. 800-826-4919, www.travelguard.com). It's valid throughout Europe, but some car-rental companies refuse to honor it (especially in the Republic of Ireland and in Italy). Oddly, residents of Washington State aren't allowed to buy this coverage.

For more fine print about car-rental insurance, see www.rick steves.com/cdw.

Leasing

For trips of two and a half weeks or more, leasing (which automatically includes CDW-type insurance with no deductible) is the best way to go. By technically buying and then selling back the car, you save lots of money on tax and insurance. Leasing provides you a new car with unlimited mileage and a 24-hour emergency assistance program. You can lease for as little as 17 days to as long as six months. Car leases must be arranged from the US. A reliable company offering 17-day lease packages for about $1,100 is Europe by Car (US tel. 800-223-1516, www.europebycar.com).

Driving

If you plan to drive in Austria, you are required to have an International Driving Permit (get through your local AAA office before you go; $15 plus the cost of two passport-type photos; www .aaa.com). Bring along your US driver's license as well.

Austria charges drivers who use their major roads. You'll need to have a *Vignette* sticker stuck to the inside of your rental car's windshield (buy at the border crossing, big gas stations near borders, or a rental-car agency). The cost is €8 for 10 days, or €22 for two months. Not having one earns you a stiff fine.

STOP AND LEARN THESE ROAD SIGNS

Speed Limit (km/hr) — Yield — No Passing — End of No Passing Zone

One Way — Intersection — Main Road — Freeway

Danger — No Entry — No Entry for cars — All Vehicles Prohibited

Parking — No Parking — Customs — Peace

Learn the universal road signs (explained in charts in most road atlases and at service stations). Seat belts are required, and two beers under those belts are enough to land you in jail. You're required to use low-beam headlights when driving in urban areas.

Use good local maps and study them before each drive. Learn which exits you need to look out for, which major cities you'll travel toward, where the ruined castles lurk, and so on.

To get to the center of a city, follow signs for *Zentrum* or *Stadtmitte*. Ring roads go around a city. For parking, you can pick up a cardboard clock (*Parkscheibe,* available free at gas stations, police stations, and *Tabak* shops). Display your arrival time on the clock and put it on the dashboard, so parking attendants can see you've been there less than the posted maximum stay (blue lines indicate 90-min zones on Austrian streets).

Every long drive between my recommended destinations is via the autobahn (super-freeway) and *Schnellstrassen* (expressway) system, and nearly every scenic backcountry drive is paved and comfortable.

The shortest distance between any two points is the autobahn. Blue signs direct you to the autobahn, and in Austria, unlike in Germany, the autobahn has a speed limit (130 km/hr, unless otherwise signed). Learn the signs: *Dreieck* ("three corners") means a Y in the road; *Autobahnkreuz* is an intersection. While all roads seem to lead to the little town of Ausfahrt, that's the German word for exit. Exits are spaced about every 20 miles and often have a gas station (*bleifrei* means "unleaded"), a restaurant, a mini-market, and sometimes a tourist information desk. Exits and intersections refer to the next major city or the nearest small town. Peruse the map and anticipate which town names to look out for. Know what you're looking for—miss it, and you're long autobahn-gone. When navigating, you'll see *nord, süd, ost,* and *west.*

Cheap Flights

If you're visiting one or more cities on a longer European trip, consider intra-European airlines. While trains are usually the best way to connect places that are close together, a flight can save both time and money on longer journeys.

One of the best websites for comparing inexpensive flights is www.skyscanner.net. Other comparison search engines include www.kayak.com, www.mobissimo.com, www.sidestep.com, and www.wegolo.com.

Well-known cheapo airlines in Europe include easyJet (www.easyjet.com), Ryanair (www.ryanair.com), SkyEurope Airlines (www.skyeurope.com), and Austria's own Niki (www.flyniki.com).

Be aware of the potential drawbacks of flying on the cheap: nonrefundable and nonchangeable tickets, rigid baggage restrictions (and fees if you have more than what's officially allowed), use of airports far outside town, tight schedules that can mean more delays, little in the way of customer assistance if problems arise, and, of course, no frills. Read the small print—especially baggage policies—before you book.

HOLIDAYS AND FESTIVALS

This is a partial list of holidays and festivals. For more information, contact the tourist information office listed on page 375. Vienna and Salzburg have music festivals nearly every month.

Jan	Perchtenlaufen (winter festival, parades), Salzburg
Jan–Feb	Fasnacht (carnival season, balls, parades), western Austria
Good Friday	Karfreitag, April 2 in 2010
Easter	Ostern, April 4 in 2010; Easter Festival, Salzburg
May	Vienna Festival of Arts and Music (www.festwochen.or.at)
May 1	May Day with maypole dances, throughout Austria
Pentecost Monday	Pfingstmontag, May 24 in 2010
Corpus Christi	Fronleichnam, June 3 in 2010
Late June	Midsummer Eve Celebrations, throughout Austria
Late July–Aug	Salzburg Summer Festival (www.salzburgfestival.at)
Aug 15	Assumption (Mariä Himmelfahrt), parts of Austria
Late Sept	Ruperti-Kirtag (St. Rupert's Day), Salzburg
Mid-Sept–early Oct	Fall beer festivals, throughout Bavaria
Oct 26	Austrian National Day (Nationalfeiertag)
Nov 1	All Saints' Day (Allerheiligen)
Nov 11	St. Martin's Day Celebrations (feasts), Austria and Bavaria
Dec	St. Nicholas Day parades and Christmas Markets, throughout Austria
Dec 6	St. Nicholas Day (Nikolaustag, parades), throughout Austria
Dec 24	Christmas Eve (Heilige Abend), when Austrians celebrate Christmas
Dec 25	Christmas
Dec 31	New Year's Eve (Silvester, a.k.a. Altjahrstag; fireworks), throughout Austria, particularly Vienna

CONVERSIONS AND CLIMATE

Numbers and Stumblers

- Europeans write a few of their numbers differently than we do. 1 = 1, 4 = 4, 7 = 7.
- In Europe, dates appear as day/month/year, so Christmas is 25/12/09.
- Commas are decimal points and decimals commas. A dollar and a half is 1,50, and there are 5.280 feet in a mile.
- When counting with fingers, start with your thumb. If you hold up your first finger to request one item, you'll probably get two.
- What Americans call the second floor of a building is the first floor in Europe.
- On escalators and moving sidewalks, Europeans keep the left "lane" open for passing. Keep to the right.

Metric Conversions (approximate)

1 foot = 0.3 meter	1 square yard = 0.8 square meter
1 yard = 0.9 meter	1 square mile = 2.6 square kilometers
1 mile = 1.6 kilometers	1 ounce = 28 grams
1 centimeter = 0.4 inch	1 quart = 0.95 liter
1 meter = 39.4 inches	1 kilogram = 2.2 pounds
1 kilometer = 0.62 mile	32°F = 0°C

Climate

The first line is the average daily high; the second line, the average daily low. The third line shows the average number of days without rain. For more detailed weather statistics for destinations throughout Austria (as well as the rest of the world), check www.worldclimate.com.

J	F	M	A	M	J	J	A	S	O	N	D
Vienna											
34°	38°	47°	58°	67°	73°	76°	75°	68°	56°	45°	37°
25°	28°	30°	42°	50°	56°	60°	59°	53°	44°	37°	30°
16	17	18	17	18	16	18	18	20	18	16	16

Temperature Conversion: Fahrenheit and Celsius

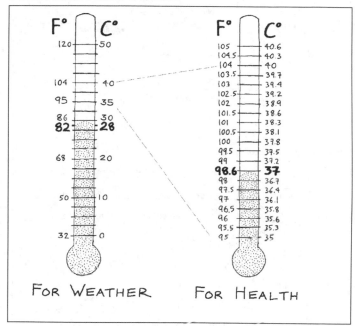

FOR WEATHER   FOR HEALTH

Europe takes its temperature using the Celsius scale, while we opt for Fahrenheit. For a rough conversion from Celsius to Fahrenheit, double the number and add 30. For weather, remember that 28°C is 82°F—perfect. For health, 37°C is just right.

Hotel Reservation

To: _____   _____
            hotel   *email or fax*

From: _____   _____
            name   *email or fax*

Today's date: _____ /_____ /_____
                      day   *month*   *year*

Dear Hotel _____ ,
Please make this reservation for me:

Name: _____

Total # of people: _____   # of rooms: _____   # of nights: _____

Arriving: _____ /_____ /_____   My time of arrival (24-hr clock): _____
                day *month* *year*   (I will telephone if I will be late)

Departing: _____ /_____ /_____
                 day   *month*   *year*

Room(s): Single____   Double ____   Twin____   Triple ____   Quad____

With: Toilet ____   Shower____   Bath____   Sink only____

Special needs: View___   Quiet___   Cheapest ___   Ground Floor___

Please email or fax confirmation of my reservation, along with the type of room reserved and the price. Please also inform me of your cancellation policy. After I hear from you, I will quickly send my credit-card information as a deposit to hold the room. Thank you.

_____
Name

_____
Address

_____
City   *State*   *Zip Code*   *Country*

Before hoteliers can make your reservation, they want to know the information listed above. You can use this form as the basis for your email, or you can photocopy this page, fill in the information, and send it as a fax (also available online at www.ricksteves.com/reservation).

Essential Packing Checklist

Whether you're traveling for five days or five weeks, here's what you'll need to bring. Remember to pack light to enjoy the sweet freedom of true mobility. Happy travels!

- ❑ 5 shirts
- ❑ 1 sweater or lightweight fleece jacket
- ❑ 2 pairs pants
- ❑ 1 pair shorts
- ❑ 1 swimsuit (women only—men can use shorts)
- ❑ 5 pairs underwear and socks
- ❑ 1 pair shoes
- ❑ 1 rainproof jacket
- ❑ Tie or scarf
- ❑ Money belt
- ❑ Money—your mix of:
  - ❑ Debit card for ATM withdrawals
  - ❑ Credit card
  - ❑ Hard cash in US dollars
- ❑ Documents (and back-up photocopies)
- ❑ Passport
- ❑ Airplane ticket
- ❑ Driver's license
- ❑ Student ID and hostel card
- ❑ Railpass/car rental voucher
- ❑ Insurance details
- ❑ Daypack
- ❑ Sealable plastic baggies
- ❑ Camera and related gear
- ❑ Empty water bottle
- ❑ Wristwatch and alarm clock
- ❑ Earplugs
- ❑ First-aid kit
- ❑ Medicine (labeled)
- ❑ Extra glasses/contacts and prescriptions
- ❑ Sunscreen and sunglasses
- ❑ Toiletries kit
- ❑ Soap
- ❑ Laundry soap (if liquid and carry-on, limit to 3 oz.)
- ❑ Clothesline
- ❑ Small towel
- ❑ Sewing kit
- ❑ Travel information
- ❑ Necessary map(s)
- ❑ Address list (email and mailing addresses)
- ❑ Postcards and photos from home
- ❑ Notepad and pen
- ❑ Journal

German Survival Phrases for Austria

When using the phonetics, pronounce ī as the long I sound in "light."

English	German	Phonetics
Good day.	Grüss Gott.	**grews** gote
Do you speak English?	Sprechen Sie Englisch?	**shprehkh**-ehn zee **ehng**-lish
Yes. / No.	Ja. / Nein.	yah / nīn
I (don't) understand.	Ich verstehe (nicht).	ikh fehr-**shtay**-heh (nikht)
Please.	Bitte.	**bit**-teh
Thank you.	Danke.	**dahng**-keh
I'm sorry.	Es tut mir leid.	ehs toot meer līt
Excuse me.	Entschuldigung.	ehnt-**shool**-dig-oong
(No) problem.	(Kein) Problem.	(kīn) proh-**blaym**
(Very) good.	(Sehr) gut.	(zehr) goot
Goodbye.	Auf Wiedersehen.	owf **vee**-der-zayn
one / two	eins / zwei	īns / tsvī
three / four	drei / vier	drī / feer
five / six	fünf / sechs	fewnf / zehkhs
seven / eight	sieben / acht	**zee**-behn / ahkht
nine / ten	neun / zehn	noyn / tsayn
How much is it?	Wieviel kostet das?	**vee**-feel **kohs**-teht dahs
Write it?	Schreiben?	**shrī**-behn
Is it free?	Ist es umsonst?	ist ehs oom-**zohnst**
Included?	Inklusive?	in-kloo-**zee**-veh
Where can I buy / find...?	Wo kann ich kaufen / finden...?	voh kahn ikh **kow**-fehn / **fin**-dehn
I'd like / We'd like...	Ich hätte gern / Wir hätten gern...	ikh **heh**-teh gehrn / veer **heh**-tehn gehrn
...a room.	...ein Zimmer.	īn **tsim**-mer
...a ticket to ___.	...eine Fahrkarte nach ___.	ī-neh **far**-kar-teh nahkh
Is it possible?	Ist es möglich?	ist ehs **mur**-glikh
Where is...?	Wo ist...?	voh ist
...the train station	...der Bahnhof	dehr **bahn**-hohf
...the bus station	...der Busbahnhof	dehr **boos**-bahn-hohf
...tourist information	...das Touristen- informationsbüro	dahs too-**ris**-tehn- in-for-maht-see-**ohns-bew**-roh
...toilet	...die Toilette	dee toh-**leh**-teh
men	Herren	**hehr**-rehn
women	Damen	**dah**-mehn
left / right	links / rechts	links / **rehkhts**
straight	geradeaus	geh-**rah**-deh-**ows**
When is this open / closed?	Um wieviel Uhr ist hier geöffnet / geschlossen?	oom **vee**-feel oor ist heer geh-**urf**-neht / geh-**shloh**-sehn
At what time?	Um wieviel Uhr?	oom **vee**-feel oor
Just a moment.	Moment.	moh-**mehnt**
now / soon / later	jetzt / bald / später	yehtst / bahld / **shpay**-ter
today / tomorrow	heute / morgen	**hoy**-teh / **mor**-gehn

In the Restaurant

I'd like / We'd like...	Ich hätte gern / Wir hätten gern...	ikh **heh**-teh gehrn / veer **heh**-tehn gehrn
...a reservation for...	...eine Reservierung für...	ī-neh reh-zer-**feer**-oong fewr
...a table for one / two.	...einen Tisch für ein / zwei.	ī-nehn tish fewr īn / tsvī
Non-smoking.	Nichtraucher.	**nikht**-rowkh-er
Is this seat free?	Ist hier frei?	ist heer frī
Menu (in English), please.	Speisekarte (in Englisch), bitte.	**shpī**-zeh-kar-teh (in **ehng**-lish) **bit**-teh
service (not) included	Trinkgeld (nicht) inklusive	**trink**-gehlt (nikht) in-kloo-**zee**-veh
cover charge	Eintritt	**īn**-trit
to go	zum Mitnehmen	tsoom **mit**-nay-mehn
with / without	mit / ohne	mit / **oh**-neh
and / or	und / oder	oont / **oh**-der
menu (of the day)	(Tages-) Karte	(**tah**-gehs-) **kar**-teh
set meal for tourists	Touristenmenü	too-**ris**-tehn-meh-**new**
specialty of the house	Spezialität des Hauses	shpayt-see-ah-lee-**tayt** dehs **how**-zehs
appetizers	Vorspeise	**for**-shpī-zeh
bread	Brot	broht
cheese	Käse	**kay**-zeh
sandwich	Sandwich	**zahnd**-vich
soup	Suppe	**zup**-peh
salad	Salat	zah-**laht**
meat	Fleisch	flīsh
poultry	Geflügel	geh-**flew**-gehl
fish	Fisch	fish
seafood	Meeresfrüchte	**meh**-rehs-**frewkh**-teh
fruit	Obst	ohpst
vegetables	Gemüse	geh-**mew**-zeh
dessert	Nachspeise	**nahkh**-shpī-zeh
mineral water	Mineralwasser	min-eh-**rahl**-vah-ser
tap water	Leitungswasser	**lī**-toongs-vah-ser
milk	Milch	milkh
(orange) juice	(Orangen-) Saft	(oh-**rahn**-zhehn-) zahft
coffee	Kaffee	kah-**fay**
tea	Tee	tay
wine	Wein	vīn
red / white	rot / weiß	roht / vīs
glass / bottle	Glas / Flasche	glahs / **flah**-sheh
beer	Bier	beer
Cheers!	Prost!	prohst
More. / Another.	Mehr. / Noch ein.	mehr / nohkh īn
The same.	Das gleiche.	dahs **glīkh**-eh
Bill, please.	Rechnung, bitte.	**rehkh**-noong **bit**-teh
tip	Trinkgeld	**trink**-gehlt
Delicious!	Lecker!	**lehk**-er

For more user-friendly German phrases, check out *Rick Steves' German Phrase Book and Dictionary* or *Rick Steves' French, Italian & German Phrase Book.*

INDEX

Audio Europe

RICK STEVES AUDIO EUROPE

Free mobile app (and podcast)

With the **Rick Steves Audio Europe** app, your iPhone or smartphone becomes a powerful travel tool.

This exciting app organizes Rick's entire audio library by country—giving you a playlist of all his audio walking tours, radio interviews, and travel tips for wherever you're going in Europe.

Let the experts Rick interviews enrich your understanding. Let Rick's self-guided tours amplify your guidebook. With Rick in your ear, Europe gets even better.

Thanks Facebook fans for submitting photos while on location! From top: John Kuijper in Florence, Brenda Mamer with her mother in Rome, Angel Capobianco in London, and Alyssa Passey with her friend in Paris.

Find out more at ricksteves.com/audioeurope

Join a Rick Steves tour

Enjoy Europe's warmest welcome...

with the flexibility and friendship of a small group

getting to know Rick's favorite places and people.

It all starts with our free tour catalog and DVD.

Great guides, small groups, no grumps.

Start your trip at

Free information and great gear to

▶ Plan Your Trip

Browse thousands of articles and a wealth of money-saving tips for planning your dream trip. You'll find up-to-date information on Europe's best destinations, packing smart, getting around, finding rooms, staying healthy, avoiding scams and more.

▶ Eurail Passes

Find out, step-by-step, if a railpass makes sense for your trip—and how to avoid buying more than you need. Get a bunch of free extras!

▶ Graffiti Wall & Travelers' Helpline

Learn, ask, share—our online community of savvy travelers is a great resource for first-time travelers to Europe, as well as seasoned pros.

Rick Steves' Europe Through the Back Door, Inc.

NOW AVAILABLE: eBOOKS, APPS, DVDs, & BLU-RAY

eBOOKS

Most guides available as eBooks
from Amazon, Barnes & Noble,
Apple iBook and Sony eReader,
beginning January 2011

RICK STEVES' EUROPE DVDs

Austria & the Alps
Eastern Europe, Israel & Egypt
England & Wales
European Travel Skills & Specials
France
Germany, Benelux & More
Greece & Turkey
Iran
Ireland & Scotland
Italy's Cities
Italy's Countryside
Rick Steves' European Christmas
Scandinavia
Spain & Portugal

BLU-RAY

Celtic Charms
Eastern Europe Favorites
European Christmas
Italy Through the Back Door
Surprising Cities of Europe

PHRASE BOOKS & DICTIONARIES

French
French, Italian & German
German
Italian
Portuguese
Spanish

JOURNALS

Rick Steves' Pocket Travel Journal
Rick Steves' Travel Journal

APPS

Rick Steves' Ancient Rome Tour
Rick Steves' Historic Paris Walk
Rick Steves' Louvre Tour
Rick Steves' Orsay Museum Tour
Rick Steves' St. Peter's Basilica Tour
Rick Steves' Versailles

PLANNING MAPS

Britain, Ireland & London
Europe
France & Paris
Germany, Austria & Switzerland
Ireland
Italy
Spain & Portugal

Rick Steves books and DVDs are available at bookstores
and through online booksellers.

CREDITS

Researchers

To help update this book, Rick relied on...

Gretchen Strauch

Gretchen lived in Konstanz, Germany for three years, where she taught English, and made frequent strudel-fueled trips around Austria. Raised in rural California, she now lives in Seattle and edits the Rick Steves guidebooks. She still does not like sauerkraut.

Gene Openshaw

Gene is the co-author of seven Rick Steves books. For this book, he wrote material on art, history, and contemporary culture. When he's not traveling, Gene enjoys composing music, recovering from his 1973 trip to Europe with Rick, and living everyday life with his daughter.

Cameron Hewitt

Cameron writes and edits guidebooks for Rick Steves, specializing in Eastern Europe (where he has co-authored three guidebooks). For this book, Cameron wrote the chapter on Bratislava, Slovakia. When he's not traveling, Cameron lives in Seattle with his wife Shawna.

Local Experts

Rick and his staff extend sincere thanks to tour guides Ursula Klaus, Wolfgang Höfler, and Lisa Zeiler for their help with the first edition of this book.

IMAGES

Location	Photographer
Vienna (full-page): St. Peter's Church	Cameron Hewitt
Salzburg (full-page): Mirabell Gardens	Gretchen Strauch
Tirol (full-page): Main Square, Hall	Gretchen Strauch

Avalon Travel
a member of the Perseus Books Group
1700 Fourth Street
Berkeley, CA 94710

Printed in the USA by Worzalla. Third printing July 2010.

ISBN (13) 978-1-59880-216-0
ISSN 1946-617X

For the latest on Rick's lectures, guidebooks, tours, public radio show, and public television series, contact Europe Through the Back Door, Box 2009, Edmonds, WA 98020, tel. 425/771-8303, fax 425/771-0833, www.ricksteves.com, rick@ricksteves.com.

Thanks to my wife, Anne, for her support.

Europe Through the Back Door Senior Editor: Jennifer Madison Davis
ETBD Editors: Gretchen Strauch, Cathy McDonald, Tom Griffin, Sarah McCormic
ETBD Managing Editor: Risa Laib
Avalon Travel Senior Editor and Series Manager: Madhu Prasher
Avalon Travel Project Editor: Kelly Lydick
Research Assistance: Gretchen Strauch, Gene Openshaw, Cameron Hewitt, Lee Evans
Copy Editor: Ellie Behrstock
Proofreader: Janet Walden
Indexer: Carl Wikander
Production & Typesetting: McGuire Barber Design
Cover Design: Kimberly Glyder Design
Graphic Content Director: Laura VanDeventer
Maps & Graphics: David C. Hoerlein, Laura VanDeventer, Lauren Mills, Brice Ticen, Barb Geisler, Mike Morgenfeld
Photography: Rick Steves, Gene Openshaw, Gretchen Strauch, Cameron Hewitt, David C. Hoerlein, Dominic Bonuccelli, Debi Jo Michael, Karoline Vass, K&T Boarding House
Front Matter Color Photo: p. i, National Theater at Night © Rick Steves
Cover Photo: Schönbrunn Palace © Dominic Bonuccelli

Rick Steves' Guidebook Series

Country Guides

Rick Steves' Best of Europe
Rick Steves' Croatia & Slovenia
Rick Steves' Eastern Europe
Rick Steves' England
Rick Steves' France
Rick Steves' Germany
Rick Steves' Great Britain
Rick Steves' Ireland
Rick Steves' Italy
Rick Steves' Portugal
Rick Steves' Scandinavia
Rick Steves' Spain
Rick Steves' Switzerland

City and Regional Guides

Rick Steves' Amsterdam, Bruges & Brussels
Rick Steves' Athens & the Peloponnese
Rick Steves' Budapest
Rick Steves' Florence & Tuscany
Rick Steves' Istanbul
Rick Steves' London
Rick Steves' Paris
Rick Steves' Prague & the Czech Republic
Rick Steves' Provence & the French Riviera
Rick Steves' Rome
Rick Steves' Venice
Rick Steves' Vienna, Salzburg & Tirol

Rick Steves' Phrase Books

French
French/Italian/German
German
Italian
Portuguese
Spanish

Other Books

Rick Steves' Europe 101: History and Art for the Traveler
Rick Steves' Europe Through the Back Door
Rick Steves' European Christmas
Rick Steves' Postcards from Europe

(Avalon Travel)